Beyond Reductionism

This is a book about the work of scientists in the era of the Anthropocene, where human beings appear to have become a driving force in the evolution of the planet. It is a diverse collection of empirical, methodological and theoretical chapters concerned with the practice of interdisciplinary social-ecological systems research. The aim of the contributors is to give the reader an appreciation of the range and complexity of the challenges faced by researchers, research institutions and wider communities trying to make sense of the causes and consequences of this new era of global environmental change.

The tragedy of the Anthropocene, of the large-scale anthropogenic habitat destruction and planet-wide impacts of anthropogenic climate change, is not that science has failed humanity but rather that it has served humanity all too well, making possible in just a few hundred years, volumes and scales of human activity far exceeding anything ever seen before. Coming to terms with that success was the aim of the 1969 Alpbach Symposium, from which this book draws its name, where contributors including Friedrich Hayek and Ludwig von Bertalanffy asked themselves: what theory, practices and standards are required to move beyond reductionism? Like those from 1969, the answers presented in this collection are hugely diverse, ranging from the work of PhD students concerned with research methods and institutional obstacles, to mid-career scholars presenting their innovative 'beyond reductionism' research methods, to emeritus professors looking back over what has been achieved in the past thirty years and suggesting where things might go from here.

This text aims to help a growing community of passionate thinkers and actors better understand themselves and their work.

Katharine N. Farrell is an Associated Researcher at the Institute of Environmental Science and Technology at the Autonomous University of Barcelona, Spain, and Lecturer at the Division of Resource Economics at the Humboldt-University of Berlin, Germany.

Tommaso Luzzati is Professor of Economics in the Department of Economics and Management at the University of Pisa, Italy.

Sybille van den Hove is Director and Partner of MEDIAN S.C.P. and Visiting Professor at the Institute for Environmental Science and Technology at the Autonomous University of Barcelona, Spain.

Routledge studies in ecological economics

1 **Sustainability Networks**
Cognitive tools for expert collaboration in social-ecological systems
Janne Hukkinen

2 **Drivers of Environmental Change in Uplands**
Aletta Bonn, Tim Allot, Klaus Hubaceck and Jon Stewart

3 **Resilience, Reciprocity and Ecological Economics**
Northwest coast sustainability
Ronald L. Trosper

4 **Environment and Employment**
A reconciliation
Philip Lawn

5 **Philosophical Basics of Ecology and Economy**
Malte Faber and Reiner Manstetten

6 **Carbon Responsibility and Embodied Emissions**
Theory and measurement
João F.D. Rodrigues, Alexandra P.S. Marques and Tiago M.D. Domingos

7 **Environmental Social Accounting Matrices**
Theory and applications
Pablo Martínez de Anguita and John E. Wagner

8 **Greening the Economy**
Integrating economics and ecology to make effective change
Bob Williams

9 **Sustainable Development**
Capabilities, needs, and well-being
Edited by Felix Rauschmayer, Ines Omann and Johannes Frühmann

10 **The Planet in 2050**
The Lund discourse of the future
Edited by Jill Jäger and Sarah Cornell

11 **Bioeconomics**
Edited by Mauro Bonaiuti

12 **Socioeconomic and Environmental Impacts on Agriculture in the New Europe**
Post-communist transition and accession to the European Union
S. Şerban Scrieciu

14 **Global Ecology and Unequal Exchange**
Fetishism in a zero-sum world
Alf Hornborg

15 **The Metabolic Pattern of Societies**
Where economists fall short
Mario Giampietro, Kozo Mayumi and Alevgül H. Sorman

16 **Energy Security for the EU in the 21st Century**
Markets, geopolitics and corridors
Edited by José María Marín-Quemada, Javier García-Verdugo and Gonzalo Escribano

17 **Hybrid Economic-Environmental Accounts**
Edited by Valeria Costantini, Massimiliano Mazzanti and Anna Montini

18 **Ecology and Power**
Struggles over land and material resources in the past, present and future
Edited by Alf Hornborg, Brett Clark and Kenneth Hermele

19 **Economic Theory and Sustainable Development**
What can we preserve for future generations?
Vincent Martinet

20 **Paving the Road to Sustainable Transport**
Governance and innovation in low-carbon vehicles
Edited by Måns Nilsson, Karl Hillman, Annika Rickne and Thomas Magnusson

21 **Creating a Sustainable Economy**
An institutional and evolutionary approach to environmental policy
Edited by Gerardo Marletto

Beyond Reductionism

A passion for interdisciplinarity

Edited by Katharine N. Farrell, Tommaso Luzzati and Sybille van den Hove

Routledge
Taylor & Francis Group
LONDON AND NEW YORK

First published 2013
by Routledge
2 Park Square, Milton Park, Abingdon, Oxon OX14 4RN

Simultaneously published in the USA and Canada
by Routledge
711 Third Avenue, New York, NY 10017

Routledge is an imprint of the Taylor & Francis Group, an informa business

British Library Cataloguing in Publication Data
A catalogue record for this book is available from the British Library

Library of Congress Cataloging in Publication Data
Beyond reductionism: a passion for interdisciplinarity/edited by Katharine Farrell, Tommaso Luzzati and Sybille van den Hove.
p. cm.
1. Ecology–Economic aspects. 2. Environmental economics. 3. Environmental policy. 4. Interdisciplinary research. 5. Reductionism. I. Farrell, Katharine, 1969– II. Luzzati, Tommaso. III. Hove, Sybille van den.
QH541.15.E25B49 2012
577–dc23

2011052102

ISBN: 978-0-415-47014-8 (hbk)
ISBN: 978-0-203-11228-1 (ebk)

Typeset in Times New Roman
by Wearset Ltd, Boldon, Tyne and Wear

This book is dedicated to the memory of Paul Cilliers (1956–2011), who was Professor of Complexity and Philosophy at the University of Stellenbosch in South Africa and founder of its Centre for Studies in Complexity and Elinor Ostrom (1933–2012), Nobel Laureate in Economics and founder of the Vincent and Elinor Ostrom Workshop in Political Theory and Policy Analysis. Without Lin's vision and tenacity, the doors through which we walk in the following pages would not have been opened. Without Paul's courage and conviction to think differently about life and his willingness to share this with those around him, this book would never have come to fruition.

Contents

Contributors

John Barry is Reader in Politics in the School of Politics, International Studies and Philosophy and Assistant Director of the Institute for a Sustainable World, both at Queen's University Belfast. He has been directly involved in politics in Ireland, where he has helped to build the all-Ireland Green Party. His research interests include the relationship between moral/political theory and the environment, with particular focus on ecofeminism, the implications of green theory for thinking about justice, and theories of political economy in relation to the environment.

Mary E. Clark was originally trained as a biologist and in the course of her academic career has taught at university level on topics ranging from biology to interdisciplinary studies to conflict resolution. Now retired, Professor Clark was formerly Drucie French Crumbie Chair in Conflict Resolution at George Mason University. Her books include *Contemporary Biology*, *Ariadne's Thread: The Search for New Modes of Thinking* and *In Search of Human Nature*.

Katharine N. Farrell is an Associated Researcher with the Institute of Environmental Science and Technology at the Autonomous University of Barcelona and a Lecturer with the Division of Resource Economics at the Humboldt-University of Berlin. Her main topics of research are the political economy of knowledge in local and international environmental governance, ecological political economy, green constitutional theory, institutional aspects of ecosystems services valuation, and the legitimacy of environmental policies; the role of science (and scientists) in sustainable development; and the role of time and tradition in processes and principles of ecological economic production. She is the author of *Making Good Decisions Well: A Theory of Collective Ecological Management.*

Mario Giampietro holds an ICREA Research Professorship at the Autonomous University of Barcelona (UAB), where he is affiliated with the Institute of Environmental Science and Technology (ICTA) and is one of the founders of the Liphe4 research network. He works on integrated assessment of sustainability. Using concepts derived from complex systems theory (multi-purpose grammars, impredicative loop analysis, Sudoku effects), he developed an innovative scientific approach to the study of ecological economics – Multi-Scale Integrated Analysis of Societal and Ecosystem Metabolism (MuSIASEM) – that can be used to integrate different, incommensurable narratives, used in different quantitative analyses. His books include *The Metabolic Pattern of Societies: Where economists fall short* and *Energy Analysis for a Sustainable Future: Multi-Scale Integrated Analysis of Societal and Ecosystem Metabolism*, both co-authored with Kozo Mayumi and Alevgul Sorman and published by Routledge.

C.S. Holling is an ecologist by training and creator of the ecology-based discourse on resilience, which first led to a revolution within systems ecology in the 1970s and eventually formed the basis for the current discourse on resilience of social-ecological systems. He is Emeritus Professor of Zoology at the University of Florida and the founding editor of the journal *Ecology and Society*, and has served as director of the Institute for Animal Resource Ecology in Vancouver, British Columbia, which he helped to establish, and of the International Institute of Applied Systems Analysis (IIASA) in Vienna. He is the author of several classic systems ecology papers, including 'Functional response of predators to prey density and its role in mimicry and population regulation' and 'Resilience and stability of ecological systems'. His books include the edited collections *Adaptive Environmental Assessment and Management* and *Panarchy*, edited with Lance Gunderson.

Catherine Jolibert holds a Master's degree in Biology of Evolution and Ecology and has worked as a coordinator and writer at the French Institute for the Environment, as project manager on the study of the impact of the December 1999 storms at the French Ministry of Environment and as teacher of ecology in Management and Protection of Nature. She is involved as Research Fellow at the Institute of Environmental Science and Technology (ICTA), Autonomous University of Barcelona (UAB), where she is currently completing her PhD on the contribution that stakeholder engagement in EU-funded biodiversity research makes to the biodiversity governance. She is particularly interested in the design of stakeholder engagement processes in research projects and in stakeholders' needs, and is using the Human scale Development (HsD) approach in her investigations.

Tommaso Luzzati is Professor of Economics in the Department of Economics and Management at the University of Pisa. His research focuses in the area of ecological economics, with topics of concern being links between growth and the environment, energy issues, the causes of environmental degradation, environmental policy concerning the adoption and diffusion of good environmental practices, the economic consequences of endogenous preferences (conformism), social norms, behaviour and rationality, and the work and ideas of K.W. Kapp. He recently completed a textbook on ecological economics with Jordi Roca and Joan Martinez-Alier, and participates, as the coordinator, in several research groups on the local sustainable development of Tuscany, including working directly with research institutions and the regional government of Tuscany.

Joan Martinez-Alier is Emeritus Professor of Economics and Economic History at the Autonomous University of Barcelona. He is among the founders of, and is a former president of, the International Society for Ecological Economics. His current research focuses on ecological economics and languages of valuation, political ecology, environmental justice and the environmentalism of the poor. His books include *Ecological Economics: Energy, Environment and Society*, *Varieties of Environmentalism: Essays North and South*, written with Ramachandra Guha, *The Environmentalism of the Poor* and *Getting down to Earth: Practical Applications of Ecological Economics*, which he co-edited with Robert Costanza and Olman Segura.

Kozo Mayumi is Professor at the University of Tokushima, Japan, where he is affiliated with the Institute of Socio-Arts and Sciences, the Faculty of Integrated Arts and Sciences and the Graduate School of Integrated Arts and Sciences. His research areas include energy analysis, resources and environmental economics. His books include *The Origins of Ecological Economics: The Bioeconomics of Georgescu-Roegen*, *Bioeconomics and Sustainability: Essays in Honor of Nicholas Georgescu-Roegen*, which he co-edited with John Gowdy, and *The Biofuel Delusion*, written with Mario Giampietro.

Mary Mellor is Emeritus Professor in the Department of Social Science at Northumbria University, Newcastle upon Tyne. She has published widely on ecofeminism and alternative economics. Her books include *The Future of Money: From Financial Crisis to Public Resource*, *The Politics of Money: Towards Sustainability and Economic Democracy*, written with Frances Hutchinson and Wendy Olsen, and *Feminism and Ecology*.

Cordula Mertens holds a Diploma degree in Biology from the University of Regensburg and is currently completing her PhD on the role of NGOs in biodiversity governance in Hungary at the Environmental Science Doctoral School of Szent István, at the Gödöllő University in Hungary. Her research interests lie in biodiversity governance, challenges and conflicts in nature conservation, and conservation of agro-biodiversity. She worked as an Early Stage Researcher in the EU Marie Curie Research Training Network GoverNat. In 2006 she was a volunteer for the GIAHS initiative at the Sustainable Development Department of the Food and Agriculture Organization in Rome.

Jesus Ramos-Martin is Assistant Professor in the Department of Economics and Economic History of the Autonomous University of Barcelona and a close collaborator with the Institute of Environmental Science and Technology of the same university. His research focuses on societal metabolism, with emphasis on household metabolism, mainly for energy consumption. He has published numerous internationally peer-reviewed journal articles within his subject area, has worked as a researcher and lecturer on ecological economics in Austria, Italy and Ecuador, and is a founding member of the consultancy ENT Environment and Management and the Scientific Society LIPHE4.

Jerome R. Ravetz is author of the classic study *Scientific Knowledge and Its Social Problems*, was formerly Reader in History and Philosophy of Science at the University of Leeds and is a pioneer in the area of science and safety. His selected essays were published in *The Merger of Science with Power*, and with Silvio Funtowicz he co-authored *Uncertainty and Quality in Science for Policy*. He is currently Associate Fellow with the Institute for Science, Innovation and Society, Saïd Business School, Oxford University, and an independent scholar and self-employed consultant working mainly on the problems of management of uncertainty in risk and environmental issues.

Ariel Salleh is a sociologist and Honorary Associate Professor in Political Economy at the University of Sydney, Australia. She has taught at New York University; the Institute of Women's Studies, Manila; and in Social Ecology at the University of Western Sydney for a number of years. She has served as a governor of the International Sociological Association Research Committee for Environment and Society; as a member of the Australian Government's Gene Technology Ethics Committee; and as a senior editor of the journal *Capitalism Nature Socialism*. Her publications include *Ecofeminism as Politics; the anthology Eco-Sufficiency and Global Justice*; and some 150 chapters and articles on eco-political thought.

Minna Santaoja has studied environmental policy and completed her PhD on amateur naturalists and affective biodiversity science at the University of Tampere, Finland. Her research interests focus on citizen science, participation, environmental citizenship and knowledge practices. She has a background in environmental engineering and has been active in local environmental NGOs in Finland for many years. In 2007–2010 she worked at the University of Stuttgart in Germany as an Early Stage Researcher as part of the EU Marie Curie Research Training Network 'GoverNat'. She is also the proud mother of a 4-year-old and an early-stage gardener.

Vandana Shiva is a Director of the Research Foundation on Science, Technology, and Ecology and founder of Navdanya, a seed sanctuary set up to preserve ancient Indian agricultural knowledge placed in jeopardy by the rapid industrialization of the country and its agricultural systems. In 1993 she won the Alternative Nobel Peace Prize (the Right Livelihood Award). Before becoming an activist, Shiva was one of India's leading physicists. She holds a Master's degree in the philosophy of science and a PhD in particle physics. Her books include *Ecofeminism*, written with Maria Mies. *Staying Alive: Women, Ecology, and Development*, *Earth Democracy: Justice, Sustainability, and Peace* and *Water Wars: Privatization, Pollution, and Profit*.

Raphael Treffny completed his PhD on the implementation of the Water Framework Directive in the United Kingdom at Lancaster University in 2011.

He has studied and worked in Germany, the Netherlands, Australia, New Zealand and the United Kingdom, and his research interests range from theoretical debates on legitimacy in environmental policy-making to the practical application of Global Navigation Satellite and Geographic Information Systems for navigation and management. Raphael has a background in geography and sustainable resource management and is currently working as a GIS Specialist for a satellite navigation systems developer, Forsberg Services Ltd, in Lancaster, England.

Sybille van den Hove is Director and Partner of MEDIAN S.C.P. and Visiting Professor at the Institute for Environmental Science and Technology of the Autonomous University of Barcelona. Her core expertise is in sustainability governance, science–policy interfaces, decision-making and policy formation under conditions of complexity, integration of natural and social sciences research, environmental research strategies and corporate environmental responsibility. She is a member of the Scientific Committee of the European Environment Agency and has served as Chair of the Scientific Advisory Council of the European Distributed Institute of Taxonomy (EDIT) and as Vice-Chair of the Steering Committee of the European Platform for Biodiversity Research Strategy (EPBRS).

Arild Vatn is Thor Heyerdahl Professor in the Department of International Environment and Development Studies at the Norwegian University of Life Sciences. His research is concerned with the links between institutional and ecological economics. He has served as head of the board for the Norwegian Research Council research programme 'Miljø 2015' as well as in various other offices supporting the development of environmental policies in Norway. He was President of the European Society for Ecological Economics (ESEE) from 2006 to 2009. He is the author of the widely acclaimed institutional economics text *Institutions and the Environment* and co-authored, with Daniel Bromley, the classic environmental economics paper 'Choices without prices without apologies'.

Brian H. Walker is retired Chief of Australia's CSIRO Wildlife and Ecology department. He is now a Research Fellow in CSIRO with its Sustainable Ecosystems group, has a part-time appointment in the Stockholm Resilience Centre and is Chair of the Resilience Alliance (www.resalliance.org). He was born in Zimbabwe, had his tertiary education in South Africa and Canada, was a Charles Bullard Fellow at Harvard, lectured at the University of Zimbabwe and was Professor of Botany and Director of the Centre for Resource Ecology at the University of Witwatersrand in Johannesburg before moving to Australia in 1985.

Preface 1

Beyond the argument culture

Robert Costanza

We are experiencing today an explosion of new scientific information about the environment and humanity's past, present and future relationships to it (Diamond 2005; Costanza *et al.* 2007). And yet the linkages between science and environmental policy continue to be poor. What are the root causes of this lack of connection on an issue that is so central to humanity's current and future health, and how can we rectify the problem?

One of the root causes is that we live today in an 'argument culture' (Tannen 1998) in which even the most complex problems are cast as polar opposites. Most discussion is cast as a debate between two extremes in which one side is presumed to be right while the other is wrong. The media, the law, politics and especially academia are all caught up in this argument culture, and its influence and control over our lives is increasing. For example, the current structure of academic disciplines highly reinforces the argument culture. There is an almost obsessive desire in academia to stake out intellectual turf and defend it against outsiders, because that is the kind of behaviour that is most highly rewarded. As Tannen notes:

> Throughout our educational system the most pervasive inheritance is the conviction that issues have two sides, that knowledge is best gained through debate, that ideas should be presented orally to an audience that does its best to poke holes and find weaknesses, and that to get recognition, one has to 'stake out a position' in opposition to another.
>
> (1998: 261)

The argument culture encourages the defining and protecting of personal and disciplinary territories on the intellectual landscape. Sharp boundaries between disciplines, unique languages and cultures within disciplines, and lack of any overarching view makes problems that cross disciplinary boundaries (including most environmental problems) very difficult, if not impossible, for traditional academics (both faculty and students) to deal with. There are also large gaps in the intellectual landscape that are not covered by any discipline.

The situation is analogous in the media, politics, law and other areas that influence science and environmental policy. In the media, conflict and controversy sell, while consensus does not. The law is at its core an adversarial system and the modern, confrontational courtroom is taken as a model for how to resolve all issues. Politics is becoming more fractious and polarized by the day.

The problem is that, while there is nothing inherently wrong with debate and direct confrontation on some issues, it does not work for all issues. Certainly the complex environmental issues that we face today require a more multifaceted, complex approach – one that encourages real dialogue and does not cast every discussion as a zero-sum, win–lose, either–or dichotomy (Costanza *et al.* 2000).

The argument culture is so pervasive in the world today that it is difficult to break from its grasp. Even within the ecological economics community, some continue to argue that what we should be doing is differentiating ourselves from other disciplines. For example, some argue that there is 'too much of this discipline' or 'too much of that conventional approach' appearing in the journal. They imply that if an article overlaps substantially with some existing discipline, it cannot also be ecological economics. This only reinforces the argument culture and misses what truly differentiates ecological economics – that it is a transdiscipline.

Tannen concludes her book with a summary of what's fundamentally wrong with the argument culture. She notes:

> What's wrong is that it obscures the complexity of research. Fitting ideas into a particular camp requires you to oversimplify them. Again, disinformation and distortion can result. Less knowledge is gained, not more. And time spent attacking an opponent or defending against attacks is not spent doing something else – like original research.
>
> (1998: 289)

She goes on to challenge us to find ways to go beyond the argument culture: 'It will take creativity to find ways to blunt the most dangerous blades of the argument culture. It's a challenge we must undertake, because our public and private lives are at stake' (ibid.: 290).

The argument culture has also been described (in more academic terms) by Jürgen Habermas (1979, 1996) as the 'culture of technical control'. According to Habermas, information in the modern world is compartmentalized and controlled by various technical elites who do not communicate with each other. The result is that experts from various fields often hold contradictory opinions and the public cannot resolve these conflicts. The public therefore develops inconsistent and volatile opinions and policies. One implication of this compartmentalization is that each group involved in science and environmental policy (different disciplines, different policy communities, different affected stakeholder groups) has in the past determined which problems are important without adequate reference to the other groups and to society's basic needs. For example, scientists determine their research priorities too often with reference only to their own discipline (or subdiscipline), which frequently covers only one time and space scale and one piece of the system. Policy-makers and implementers see only their own short-term needs for information of a particular kind in order to make a specific decision, without adequate reference to the broader scientific and policy enterprise and longer-term policy questions. The result is a lack of effective communication of scientific work, both across scientific disciplines and between science and policy. Disciplinary isolation has hindered understanding of the interconnections between different parts of the environment and between the environment and human systems.

Effectively linking science and environmental policy also faces several other difficulties, including:

- the inherent complexity of environmental systems and the inherent uncertainties in understanding and modelling their behaviour and their impacts;
- the inadequacy of baseline data coupled with the difficulty in obtaining and interpreting reliable observations of the environment's behaviour and in synthesizing data and information into an effective knowledge base;
- the uncertainties in the way in which humans affect the environment and the inherent uncertainties in understanding human responses to environmental change.

Major problems also arise because of the multiplicity of scales at which different decision-makers have to operate, from the global to the regional, national, state, local, individual business and to the individual human being. The environmental significance of change often varies enormously between these scales. Regulatory frameworks also vary with scale and context. Thus, state, national and international regulations and agreements can often be in conflict, hindering rational decision-making.

Effective environmental policy-making demands that we synthesize understanding between the natural and social sciences. For example, understanding of fundamental concepts such as 'risk', 'uncertainty' and 'value' has to be integrated with an understanding of changing societal values. But integrated work between these groups is often missing, and few research institutions have mechanisms to encourage such collaborations.

Ecological economics, as described in this collection, is an ongoing effort to get beyond the argument culture and move towards real, sustainable solutions to integrated environmental and social issues. These solutions will come from building a shared transdisciplinary understanding of complex living systems at all scales, from cells to the entire planet. The solutions will come from building an extended peer community that can effectively communicate and overcome the 'culture of technical control'. The solutions will come only with a concerted and sustained effort directed towards a shared goal: creating a sustainable and desirable future.

References

Costanza, R., H. Daly, C. Folke, P. Hawken, C.S. Holling, A.J. McMichael, D. Pimentel and D. Rapport. 2000. 'Managing our environmental portfolio.' *BioScience* 50(2): 149–155.

Costanza, R., L. Graumlich, W. Steffen, C. Crumley, J. Dearing, K. Hibbard, R. Leemans, C. Redman and D. Schimel. 2007. 'Sustainability or collapse: what can we learn from integrating the history of humans and the rest of nature?' *Ambio* 36(7): 522–552.

Diamond, J. 2005. *Collapse: How Societies Choose to Fail or Succeed.* New York: Viking.

Habermas, J. 1979. *Communication and the Evolution of Society.* Boston: Beacon Press.

Habermas, J. 1996. *Between Facts and Norms: Contributions to a Discourse Theory of Law and Democracy.* Cambridge, MA: MIT Press.

Tannen, D. 1998. *The Argument Culture: Moving from Debate to Dialogue.* New York: Random House.

Preface 2

Embracing fewer answers

Richard Norgaard

The transdiscipline of ecological economics came of age two decades ago, at the turn from the 1980s into the 1990s, when the world was seeking answers to two questions: how to sustain ecological systems and how to create just societies. While the global economy is in free fall as I write, in early 2009, continuing human population growth, rampant materialism and market expansion have further exacerbated ecosystem decay and social injustice during the transdiscipline's short history. The chaos of climate change has arrived sooner than expected. Decisions must be made to reduce and reverse the accumulation of greenhouse gases, not because we have clear scientific answers, or even rough predictions as to how the future will unfold if we do not act, but because of the immensity of the uncertainty that is overtaking nature and humanity.

Nearly a century and a half ago, a keen observer of history described this dilemma between the slow pace at which science provides answers and the pressing need for public decisions. For the two closing paragraphs of chapter 1 of *Man and Nature*, George Perkins Marsh wrote:

> But we are, even now, breaking up the floor and wainscoting and doors and window frames of our dwelling, for fuel to warm our bodies and seethe our pottage, and the world cannot afford to wait till the slow and sure progress of exact science has taught it a better economy. Many practical lessons have been learned by the common observation of unschooled men; and the teachings of simple experience, on topics where natural philosophy has scarcely yet spoken, are not to be despised.
>
> In these humble pages, which do not in the least aspire to rank among scientific expositions of the laws of nature, I shall attempt to give the most important practical conclusions suggested by the history of man's efforts to replenish the earth and subdue it; and I shall aim to support those conclusions by such facts and illustrations only, as address themselves to the understanding of every intelligent reader, and as are to be found recorded in works capable of profitable perusal, or at least consultation, by persons who have not enjoyed a special scientific education.
>
> (1965 [1864]: 52)

Ecological economists are well aware that the central idea of the European Enlightenment – the idea that people could make superior, indeed ever better, decisions by opening their minds to reason and facts, leading (ever more so over time) to their material progress and overall betterment – for all that it has brought into the world, has not turned out nearly so well as was expected. In retrospect, the reasons are clear. Reductionist science produced partially correct answers that proved extremely powerful, giving humankind the ability to deflect and direct the forces of nature in entirely new ways – for example, with the internal combustion engine, electricity and industrial chemical manufacture – but these partial answers never cohered into an understanding of the whole. They were, in effect, partly correct but wholly wrong.

This purely epistemological definition of the problem of reductionism is, however, terribly incomplete. The broader problem is that a whole global economic system, complete with a supporting governance system, co-evolved around these partly correct but wholly wrong answers, and mainly around those that could be captured in the invention of new technologies, economically produced and exchanged in markets. Science and its supporting institutions also co-evolved around this 'thinking only in parts' economy, now somehow being driven also from the outside by the reductive forces of its own incomplete understanding. Indeed, had our understanding of the Industrial Revolution been complete, it is very difficult to imagine how human history might have unfolded, what sort of a global economy and complementary global governance we would now have. In the past two centuries we have blindly embraced far too many partly correct but wholly wrong answers, and now we live in a world of material things and technological processes, with a global economy and governance institutions that encourage us towards ever tighter embrace of the partly correct. Meanwhile, with our narrow focus on technological solutions and human aspirations, we continue to stab our now badly injured antagonist, nature, again and again, creating in the process new and deeper problems, for which we duly prepare new partly correct but wholly wrong answers. Nor have we created the social utopia that the thinkers of the European Enlightenment once anticipated, not even an ephemeral one, in the process.

As this book well attests, ecological economists are somewhat humbled by the difficulties of finding a common method across ecology and economics, of appropriately matching different combinations of methods to particular socio-ecological situations and institutional contexts, or imagining the social conditions under which the complementary and contradictory insights of multiple methods might be constructively used. Even as the earth's social-ecological systems are crashing down around us, our academic communities, the global economy and global governance remain trapped in the hopes of the Enlightenment, in the belief that the search for and embracing of better answers, based in ever higher reasoning and superior evidence, will eventually lead humanity out of misery and into a life of freedom and plenty. But these hopes brought us to the disaster that many ecological economists now feel we were somehow meant to solve.

George Perkins Marsh was right, but now the practical lessons learned by the common observation of unschooled men, and the teachings of simple experience, are also highly compartmentalized and differentiated through specializations intended to serve the global market. Still, many people may well understand that the rapid change we are now experiencing stems from our ignorance of the larger system that we are within, yet also changing. Will the community of scientists, perhaps with ecological economists in the lead, have the courage to admit that we never understood the whole social-ecological system of the planet, or even any of the smaller but also complex local social-ecological systems? Will we have the courage to admit that the current level of human activity is driving systemic change so fast that even if we could understand the whole, even for a short time, we would never be able to monitor emergent phenomena and shift our understanding fast enough to keep track of our impacts?

Enlightenment hopes facilitated both the process of social-ecological change and the ability of scientists to better see the dangers of change. Scientists in the nineteenth century decried the devastation of nature that accompanied the first stages of the Industrial Revolution, and they were instrumental in the social movements that led to the preservation of parklands, the creation of wildlife preserves, and the establishment of land conservation principles and progressive practices of resource management. These decisions were made with rudimentary ecological knowledge and without cost–benefit analyses. Action was taken because a conscious choice was made: that it was better to act on partial understanding that suggested potential disaster than to wait for confirmation that disaster had come and gone. But these conscious decisions were exceptions to the rule, focused mainly around special cases with exceptional scenic beauty, majestic landscapes and sensitive natural resources, and scientists did not, in general, advocate that we release our embrace of partially correct and wholly wrong answers.

Later, scientists across the world were instrumental in the environmental revolution of the 1960s and 1970s, helping to expand public understanding of pollution, finding new technological solutions to environmental problems, and helping to set up regulatory systems for environmental protection, usually with the hope of optimizing total benefits and total costs. But only a few advocated capping energy and material flows, and practically no one tied the problem back to the nature of our technology-obsessed global society driven by the principles of reductionist science.

As the forces of change continued, scientists helped point out in the 1980s that we had to look ahead, to guide the driving forces of the global economy in sustainable ways. Yet a quarter-century search for guidance criteria, never mind their implementation, has pretty much come to naught. It seems that somehow all that has been accomplished is that more and more people have joined the embrace of partially correct and wholly wrong answers. Now the living planet that was exposed to potential damage in the nineteenth century and first threatened with nuclear destruction in the twentieth is covered with the festering boils of contamination and desertification and weighed down with a nasty set of respiratory problems. The idea that the main task now is to get the ecology and values right before picking the best path forward is at best pure hubris and at worst a form of folly.

Yet for all that I have said here, I am not an Enlightenment anarchist: the need to rely on reason and evidence is reiterated, not rebuked, in the chapters that follow here. Reasoning and evidence brought me to the interpretation I have outlined here and may, I hope, bring more people to this understanding in time. If sufficient proportions of humanity and nature make it through this century, reason and evidence will still be two of our best tools for designing a social system that makes use of the actual abilities that we humans have, as opposed to presumptions of omniscience based on an overestimation of our capacities to understand the world around us. Progressive hopes, to reason and to gather and process evidence, might, at that time, work better than ever before. I do not advocate abandoning reason and evidence. On the contrary, it is precisely reason and evidence, as discussed in the following pages of this book and through the broad community of ecological economics research, that allow us to see how the hope of the Enlightenment has blinded us: how the belief that steady progress in science and society would always be more than sufficient to counter the follies of prior actions has kept us from assessing the cumulative, global evidence to the contrary in an empirically informed and reasonable way.

Going beyond reductionism does not entail accepting responsibility for solving the problems that reductionism has wrought. Instead, it entails accepting, humbly, that the finding of ways to scale back unrealistic expectations about our human abilities to solve complex problems may itself be one of the greatest problems facing humanity. Going beyond reductionism certainly requires new approaches to discovery and perhaps even new academic and social institutions, ones that can complement and even replace those that have consistently facilitated scientific reductionism and the associated cascading onslaught of inappropriate technological fixes that often simply create further demand for technological corrections. I imagine that operating beyond reductionism may only be possible, in the end, from a conceptual basis entirely different from the one that has guided humanity through the post-Enlightenment eras of Industrialization and Globalization: from a starting point that draws not only on its lessons but also from its failures. Getting to that point is probably not going to be possible solely through reliance on Enlightenment ideals. Within the transdisciplinary field of ecological economics, over the past twenty years we have begun to explore and to build pieces of this new basis for understanding social-ecological systems, but, as the chapters in this book each point out in various ways, there is still much work to be done. If and when we do eventually we get there and can set out again in a new direction of ecologically and socially sustainable human development, one thing I am pretty sure about is that getting beyond reductionism will entail embracing fewer answers.

Reference

Marsh, G.P. 1965 [1864]. *Man and Nature*. Reprint. Cambridge, MA: Harvard University Press.

Abbreviations

ADHD	attention deficit hyperactivity disorder
BPD	borderline personality disorder
CBA	cost–benefit analysis
CDM	clean development mechanism
CEM	collective ecological management
CPR	common property resource
CSIRO	Commonwealth Scientific and Industrial Research Organisation (Australia)
DE	domestic extraction
DSM-V	*Diagnostic and Statistical Manual of Mental Disorders*, Fifth Edition
EFA	energy flow accounting
EPE	ecological political economy
EROI	energy return on energy input
FAO	Food and Agriculture Organization
GDP	gross domestic product
GDR	(former) German Democratic Republic
GIAHS	Globally Important Agriculture Heritage Systems
GM	genetically modified
GMO	genetically modified organism
GRAINN	genomics, robotics, artificial intelligence, nanotechnology and neuroscience
HANPP	human appropriation of net primary production
HDI	Human Development Index
IIASA	International Institute of Applied Systems Analysis
IARE	Institute of Animal Resource Ecology
ICTA	Institut de Ciència i Tecnologia Ambientals (Barcelona)
ILA	impredicative loop analysis
ILO	International Labour Organization
IPCC	Intergovernmental Panel on Climate Change
IRC	institutions-as-rationality-context
ISEE	International Society for Ecological Economics
IT	information technology

IUCN	International Union for Conservation of Nature
LH	left hemisphere (of the brain)
MA	Millennium Ecosystem Assessment
MCE	multi-criteria evaluation
MDGs	Millennium Development Goals
MEFA	material and energy flow accounting
MFA	material flow accounting
MuSIASEM	Multi-Scale Integrated Analysis of Societal and Ecosystem Metabolism
NGO	non-governmental organization
NIA	national income account
NPP	net primary production
OECD	Organisation for Economic Co-operation and Development
PPP	purchasing power parity
PTB	physical trade balance
PTSD	post-traumatic stress disorder
RA	Resilience Alliance
RH	right hemisphere (of the brain)
RMIU	rationality as maximizing individual utility
SES	social-ecological system(s)
SHEE	safety, health, environment, ethics
SRC	Stockholm Resilience Centre
TCE	tonnes of coal equivalent
TOE	tonnes of oil equivalent
WMD	weapon of mass destruction
WTO	World Trade Organization
WWF	World Wildlife Fund/World Wide Fund for Nature

1 Introduction

Katharine N. Farrell, Tommaso Luzzati and Sybille van den Hove

Introduction

This diverse collection of empirical, methodological and theoretical chapters concerning the practice of interdisciplinary research is intended to give the reader a glimpse at the state of the art and the main challenges facing researchers, research institutions and communities that aspire to carry out and develop non-reductive, interdisciplinary investigations of social ecological systems. The topics addressed within its pages may be assigned labels such as social-ecological systems research, sustainability science or ecological economics – all of which, of course, somehow describe what the contributing authors aim to address, both here and elsewhere in their work. However, as the name of this collection, which we borrow from Koestler and Smythies (1969), would suggest, we prefer to think of this text and its contributions in a broader context, as part of the more general work of discovering what it means to be doing science well in the twenty-first century.

The human innovation 'methodological reductionism', which may be said to have seen its first comprehensive explication in René Descartes' *Discourse on Method* (1978 [1641]) and its early practical application in the factories of eighteenth-century England, has produced great changes in the economic productivity and the ecological impact of human societies across the planet over the past 300 years. When taken in historical context, the speed of these transformations is impressive: the Palaeolithic period (Early Stone Age) lasted around 1 million years; the Late Stone Age (comprising the Mesolithic and Neolithic periods) lasted several thousand years; while the era of industrialization, which Crutzen and Stoermer (2000) have dubbed the Anthropocene, has so far lasted a few hundred (Gowdy 1994). The magnificent speed of modern technical innovation can be understood as a testament to the powers of methodological reductionism – to the systematic and, to a large extent, successful endeavour to interrogate the physical world, piece by piece, disclosing the secrets of nature (Bacon 1875 [1623]). Ironically, the tragedy of the Anthropocene era is not the failure but rather the success of this reductionism.

Coming to terms with that success was the topic of the Alpbach Symposium, held in 1968, which brought together leading life sciences experts from a range of different disciplines, including Arthur Koestler, Friedrich Hayek, Victor Frankel, Ludwig von Bertalanffy and many others (Koestler and Smythies 1969). What these men (and they were all men) argued in 1968 was (1) that moving beyond reductionism was necessary in order to describe the special characteristics of complex life related phenomena, and (2) that there were points of connection and overlap between the various life sciences disciplines, which could help to provide a map for how knowledge from these various disciplines could be combined without being reduced. Koestler and Smythies described their objective as 'the emancipation of the life sciences from the mechanistic concepts of nineteenth-century physics, and the resulting crudely reductionist philosophy' (ibid.: 2).

Forty years on, although there remains little argument regarding its merits, moving beyond reductionism still presents great challenges for the scientists, citizens, bureaucrats, technocrats and politicians of the twenty-first century. While we do not imagine that the contributions to this collection should or will single-handedly enable its readers to surmount these in a single leap, it is our hope that they may encourage those who may have become discouraged and inspire those who are wondering what might be waiting to happen.

The field of ecological economics, which can be understood as one of the homes for this collection, now just over twenty years old, has explicitly taken up the challenge of moving beyond reductionism as one of its core methodological tasks, as has been pointed out by in the prefaces by both Robert Costanza and Richard Norgaard, two of its founders, who have kindly offered their reflections on this topic as an overture to the chapters that follow. Operating, as it does, at the interface between the life sciences of ecology and economics, ecological economics is, by definition, concerned with the interplay between complex living systems. It is, by definition, oriented at a point of study that lies beyond reductionism. In this respect, the story of how ecological economic methods have developed over the past twenty years is a central part of the story of how new interdisciplinary scientific methods, ones that lie beyond reductionism, have developed over this period. Telling a part of that story is the basic aim of this book, and in order to do so we have invited contributions from a diverse selection of scholars, ranging from PhD students working to find their footing in the amorphous field of social-ecological/ecological economics research (Barry and Farrell; Santaoja *et al.*), to scholars in the middle of their careers, actively producing these new tools and approaches (Farrell *et al.*; Giampietro *et al.*; Salleh *et al.*; Vatn), to those most senior, who have helped to give this fields it features, who here look back over what has been achieved but also, perhaps more importantly, point out for us their visions of where things might or should go from here (Martinez-Alier; Ravetz; Clark; Walker and Holling).

Structure of the text

The collection is divided into three parts that delimit the main themes of the book: Part I, concerned with the idea of ecological economics; Part II, on life after reductionism; and Part III, titled 'Into the woods'.

Part I, 'The idea of "ecological economics": interdisciplinarity in theory, method and practice', is intended to give the reader a feeling for the general subject of interdisciplinary research concerning social-ecological systems and relationships, and to highlight the challenges that its practitioners can expect to face, and do face, on a daily basis in their work. It begins with a history text by Martinez-Alier that documents a variety of approaches to the study of social metabolism that have been employed by scholars since the start of the industrial era up until today. The editors themselves then continue with the work of documenting the shape of this field or research, but with the explicit aim of developing a tentative ontology of social-ecological systems research, which they then use to explore ways in which it may be possible to standardize the design of interdisciplinary methodologies without reverting to reductionism. Next, Ravetz, again with a historical approach that walks up into the present, considers the predicament of controlling the quality of this type of interdisciplinary research, on the one hand reminds the reader precisely how and why such control is so important and on the other discusses the empirical grounds for imagining that it may be almost impossible to achieve, at least if the social practices of science are not changed substantially. Closing out Part I are the reflections of Clark on the challenges and promise of interdisciplinary studies. Clark wrote her first major work on the topic of developing interdisciplinary research methodologies (1989) in the 1980s, as she was expanding her studies of biology and environment to incorporate the social complexity of human biology.

Part II, 'Life after reductionism: exemplary ecological economics beyond reductionism, in practice', is intended to provide the reader with a look into the world of applied interdisciplinary ecological economics investigations and analysis. Perhaps the most diverse part of the book, here the authors present concrete examples of how they are reaching beyond reductionism in their works. Starting Part II with a discussion of the practical challenges they encountered when beginning their collaborative work as supervisor and student, Barry and Farrell bring us from the close-up vantage of their personal experiences up and out to a formal political theory discussion concerning how the typical constitution of the modern university serves to inhibit and constrain the development of interdisciplinary work. Next, Salleh *et al.* illustrate, through reference to the development and ongoing contributions of the discourse on ecofeminism, how it is nonetheless possible to establish and conduct a discourse beyond reductionism. As they describe the discourse of ecological feminism, it offers a transdisciplinary analysis of how the dominant system of economic globalization is destroying the environment, people's sustenance, and democracy. Ecofeminists, they argue, examine class, ethnic, and gender power relations, and draw on this social complexity to explain the embodied and ecologically embedded character of production and reproduction. In so doing, they provide a critique that challenges the instrumentalism of science and many methodological assumptions within ecological economics. Closing out Part II, Giampietro *et al.* provide us with an elaboration and justification for a new analytical tool called MuSIASEM (Multi-Scale Integrated Analysis of Societal and Ecosystem Metabolism) that provides non-reductionist sets of indicators for measuring the combined social and environmental well-being of a community, which they have developed building on the work of Nicholas Georgescu-Roegen (1971) and on principles from biology, chemistry and physics.

Part III, 'Into the woods: mapping the challenges and the possibilities for continuing the development of methods that extend beyond reductionism', is intended to give a hint as to how this field of research might be successfully developed in future. Here Santaoja *et al.*, a group of PhD students who have conducted their doctoral studies as part of the social ecological research project GoverNat, document how they overcame the challenges they faced in concretizing their research within an international, interdisciplinary context and provide suggestions and advice to other students who may set out to follow this path. Moving on from the vantage point of the early stage researcher to that of the experienced scholar, Walker and Holling, in an elaborated version of the keynote lectures that they gave at the Stockholm Resilience Conference in 2008, draw upon their decades of experience to provide a reflection on what has been accomplished so far and to suggest: (1) research agenda items and key topics that they believe now need to be studied, and (2) strategies for effectively organizing social-ecological systems research teams. Finally, taking up the task of organizing social-ecological systems research teams as an empirical object of study, Vatn closes the collection with an analysis of the institutional context within which this kind of research is carried out today and a series of recommendations, based on institutional theory, regarding how the applied work of interdisciplinary ecological economics could be made more effective.

This text draws together contributions from a huge range of scholars, working in fields stretching from resilience studies to ecofeminism, who are all engaging with the same theme but often coming from quite different directions. This gives the text a distinct voice and perhaps a sometimes jumbled feel. We hope that readers will find the sometimes bumpy ride stimulating and that they will be patient with the authors whose positions seem odd or unfamiliar, looking for the links between the chapters rather than their differences. Reaching back to the general system theory origins, which underlie many of the current ecological economics methods that lie beyond reductionism, this text aims to provide a scholarly, robust but fresh and innovative perspective on this important methodological problem. Theoretical insights and methodological challenges associated with the need to move beyond reductionism are central to ecological economics. However, they are often assumed, as opposed to argued and systematically discussed. By putting these critical issues squarely on the table for discussion, we aim to fill a pressing gap in the literature and to help a growing community of passionate thinkers and actors to better understand themselves and their work.

References

Bacon, F. 1875 [1623]. 'De Dignitate et Augmentis Scientiarum.' In *Works*, ed. J. Spedding, R.L. Ellis and D.D. Heath. London : Longmans Green.

Clark, M.E. 1989. *Ariadne's Thread: The Search for New Modes of Thinking*. London: Macmillan.

Crutzen, P.J. and E.F. Stoermer. 2000. 'The Anthropocene.' *IGBP [International Geosphere-Biosphere Programme] Newsletter* 41.

Descartes, R. 1978 [1641]. *Discourse on Method, with Meditations on First Philosophy, Objections against Meditations and Replies*. London: William Benton.

Georgescu-Roegen, N. 1971. *The Entropy Law and the Economic Process*. Cambridge, MA: Harvard University Press.

Gowdy, J. 1994. *Co-evolutionary Economics*. Dordrecht, the Netherlands: Kluwer Academic.

Koestler, A. and J.R. Smythies eds. 1969. *The Alpbach Symposium 1968: Beyond Reductionism: New Perspectives in the Life Sciences*. London: Hutchinson.

Part I

The idea of ‘ecological economics’

Interdisciplinarity in theory, method and practice

2 Social metabolism, ecological distribution conflicts and languages of valuation[1]

Joan Martinez-Alier

Introduction

There is common ground between social history, economic history and environmental history, between ecological economics and political ecology, between sustainability science and environmental sociology. It lies in the three-tier relation between the increasing social metabolism of human economies pushed by population and economic growth, the ecological distribution conflicts among human groups, and the different languages of valuation deployed by such groups when they reaffirm their rights to use the environmental services and products in dispute. Authors working on 'industrial metabolism' or in 'social metabolism' look at the economy in terms of flows of energy and materials (Ayres 1989; Fischer-Kowalski 1998; Fischer-Kowalski and Huettler 1998; Haberl 2001; Martinez-Alier 2007a, b). The economy is a system embedded in the environment, open to the entry of energy and materials, and to the exit of waste. In this chapter we will walk together through social metabolism, ecological distribution conflicts, languages of valuation, and their links.

Social metabolism

The economy is described in terms of economic indicators such as GDP (gross domestic product) growth, savings ratio and current account balance in the external sector. Economic historians even reconstruct the GDPs of centuries ago (Maddison 2001). Social factors are taken into account in demographic and public health statistics, and in the Human Development Index. The economy may also be described in terms of physical indicators. Economic, social and physical indicators are non-equivalent descriptions but there is a certain degree of congruence among them. It is clear that there is no one correct way to conceptualize or investigate this common ground, but that does not mean that anything goes. This leads us then to the question of what kinds of conceptualizations may be more or less helpful for understanding a particular question, which may be more or less appropriate for reflecting the ecological economics of an issue, which may be more or less respectful or empowering of the people who inevitably make up the subjects of such work. In the following pages we will examine examples of several key approaches that have been adopted to explore ecological economics topics and we will consider whence they have come – not because at the end one can be dubbed best or most correct, but because a richer understanding of where these approaches come from and what they can and cannot provide will hopefully improve our collective ability to use them well.

The idea of talking about the metabolism of societies

Looking at the economy in terms of flows of energy and materials is the cornerstone of 'social metabolism' or 'industrial metabolism' approaches (Ayres 1989; Fischer-Kowalski 1998; Fischer-Kowalski and Huettler 1998; Haberl 2001). The term 'metabolism' is used in analogy with the metabolism of living beings: energy and materials enter the system to sustain it and are discarded outside as waste. Thus, a profile for an economy might be as follows. Income per capita is US$22,000 (at 2000 PPP); it occupies place 10 in the Human Development Index (HDI); it provides 290 GJ (gigajoules) of energy per person per year; its human appropriation of net primary production (HANPP) is 35 per cent; material flows amounts to 16 tonnes per person per year, of which fossil fuels account for 5 tonnes; material flows imports amount to 6 tonnes while 1 tonne is exported; different social classes have very different metabolic profiles; and so on.

A major advantage of such an approach is that it highlights the differences among communities and practices of social organization and, consequently, their different impacts on the environment and on the world. For example, Marina Fischer-Kowalski and Helmut Haberl of the Faculty for Interdisciplinary Studies in Vienna recently edited a book (2007) on socio-ecological transitions which is much influenced by the environmental historian Rolf Peter Sieferle and by ecological anthropologists, ecological economists and industrial ecologists.[2] From hunter-gatherer societies to agricultural societies to industrial societies, the authors of this book find quantifiable patterns of use of energy and materials, population densities, land use and working time. They try also to distinguish possible from impossible futures. For instance, is it plausible to think of a world of 9 billion people with an energy expenditure of 300 GJ and a material use of 16 tons per capita per year (the present European average)?

To illustrate this, let us take the case of energy use. One basic notion of human ecology is the distinction, attributable to Lotka (1925), between the endosomatic use of energy (as food) and the exosomatic use of energy as fuel for cooking and heating, and as power for the artefacts and machines produced by human culture. Thus, one person per day must eat the equivalent of 1,500, 2,000 or 2,500 kcal. Since 1 calorie is equal to 4.18 joules, a daily food intake of 2,400 kcal is equal to 10 MJ (megajoules), a convenient round number. Clearly, a person who is five or ten times richer than the average for his or her society is not going to consume five or ten times the average food energy. In affluent societies almost nobody starves, and poor people (as in the United States) are fatter on average than rich people – probably the first time in human history that this has happened. As regards the exosomatic use of energy, humans have in the course of history developed many artefacts and machines that use energy for production or amusement. While the endosomatic energy consumption of one well-fed person per day is *c.*10 MJ and therefore per year is *c.*3.65 GJ, the exosomatic use of energy varies a great deal. Poor people use some energy for cooking (sometimes even more than they do for eating, if they cook on open fires), and also some energy for feeding small domestic animals, and for making some clothes and repairing their houses. They might have a pump for the well, if they are better off; if not, they will use human work to get water, such work being a transformation of the food energy intake. They will also do some travelling in overcrowded buses or trains. Altogether, perhaps another 10 GJ per person per year will be used exosomatically, roughly three times more than for food energy. (We are not counting here the warmth provided directly by the sun and indeed the other environmental services such as rain, wind and the carbon cycle, driven by solar energy.) Consider now a citizen of a rich suburb, every day driving 50 kilometres (25 kilometres each way) to work, consuming therefore at least 3 litres of petrol (30,000 kcal). This single exosomatic energy expenditure of *c.*28 GJ just for moving the automobile to and from the office (calculated using 233 working days as a basis) is *c.*28 GJ, nearly eight times more than the direct food energy intake of a well-fed person.

In poor countries, food energy is a substantial part of the total use of energy, which involves an exo/endo energy use ratio of 2 or 3. In the countries of the European Union, the energy use per person per year is of the order of 200 to 300 GJ; in the United States it is even more than this, so that the exo/endo ratio can reach 100 (Giampietro 2003).

Material and energy flow accounting

Material and energy flow accounting (MEFA) is a set of methods for describing and analysing socio-economic metabolism. It examines economies as systems that reproduce themselves not only socially and culturally, but also physically through a continuous exchange of energy and matter with their natural environments and with other socio-economic systems. Eurostat now publishes material flow accounts (MFA), and the OECD will publish them soon (Weisz *et al.* 2006; Moriguchi 2007). The main MFA indicator from the input side is domestic extraction (DE), which covers the annual amount of raw materials (except water and air) extracted to be used as material factor inputs to economic processing. These materials are classified as biomass, construction and industrial minerals, and fossil fuels (Figure 2.1).

Physical imports and physical exports measures all imported or exported commodities in tonnes. Traded commodities comprise goods at all stages of processing from raw materials to finals products. *Physical trade balance* (PTB) equals physical imports minus physical exports. Such accounts are relevant for historical and current debates on ecologically unequal exchange and the ecological debt.

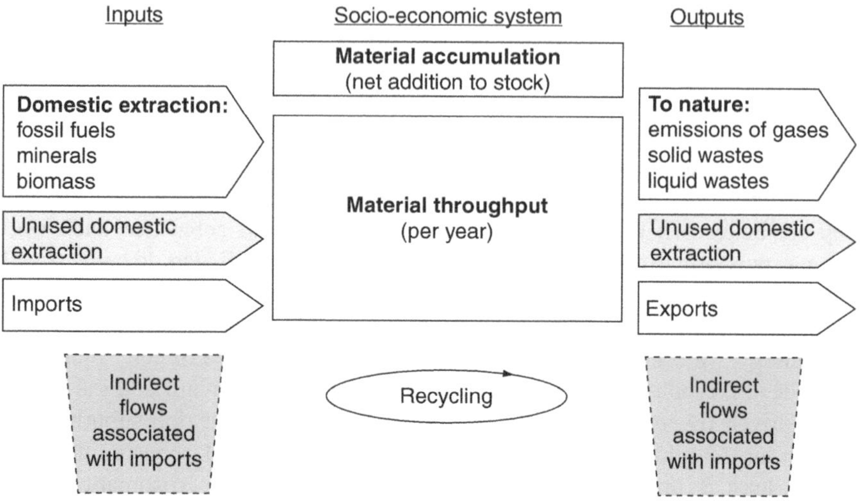

Figure 2.1 Economy-wide material balances (excluding air and water) (source: Eurostat 2001).

Energy flow accounting (EFA) is also an integral part of the analysis of social metabolism. Primary and final energy delivered are usually classified in the statistics according to source. The idea of linking economic history to the use of energy goes back to Wilhelm Ostwald, and later to Leslie White (1943, 1959) and other authors, but it was only in the 1980s that several histories of the use of energy in the economy were published. The most interesting EFA indicator is that of energy return on energy input (EROI). EROI is an indicator of energy efficiency, a useful statistic for assessing the increasing costs of obtaining energy (Hall *et al.* 1986). It is relevant in connection with the developing of oil sands or heavy oil in Alberta or the Orinoco Delta in Venezuela, or for agro-fuels (with very low EROI) (Martinez-Alier with Schlüpmann 1987; Sieferle 2001 [1982]; Hall *et al.* 1986; Debeir *et al.* 1986; Cleveland 1987; Rappaport 1967; Odum 1971; Pimentel *et al.* 1973; Pimentel and Pimentel 1979; Leach 1975).[3]

The HANPP

Land use fundamentally alters the production ecology of terrestrial ecosystems. The notion of 'human appropriation of net primary production' is defined as the difference between what net primary production (NPP) would be in the absence of human activities and the amount of NPP which actually remains in the ecosystems. HANNP, therefore, takes into account not only what is directly harvested or used by society, but also what is normally lost as a result of human-induced changes in ecosystem productivity (e.g. ecosystem degradation mainly because of agricultural simplification and soil sealing). On a global level, HANPP amounts to 20–40 per cent of the potential NPP. Global population growth (if it takes place) and increased demand for wood and agro-fuels will lead to further increases in HANPP (Haberl *et al.* 2007).[4]

In contrast to material and energy flows, HANPP is not yet an official statistic. HANPP is meant to be an index of loss of biodiversity and as such it is of great interest for the history of wildlife conservation. One can also do research historically and at present on the different social groups (pastoralists, agriculturalists, industrial commercial plantations) that have claims on the HANPP. The HANPP has decreased slightly in Europe since the 1950s but it is growing in many regions of the world, signalling loss of biodiversity, and also increasing social conflicts, as different forms of appropriation compete with each other. Thus, in the struggles for the net primary production of biomass and against the privatization of common property lands, the eucalyptus or other plantation trees are pulled out and locally useful trees are put in (Gerber 2008).[5]

Virtual water

Water use should also be included in metabolic profiles. There are historical and present conflicts on dams such as, in India, the Narmada Bachao Andolan, and also new conflicts in the North-East, and complaints against the 'interlinking of the rivers'. There are conflicts over the use and pollution of aquifers (of which the Plachimada conflict in Kerala between farmers and the Coca-Cola company became world-famous in the early 2000s) and water transfers from rivers; for example, in Brazil there is an organized movement of *atingidos por barragens* (dam-affected people), where, in 2005, a successful civic resistance movement led by Bishop Luiz Carpio momentarily stopped water transfer from the São Francisco River. There are also conflicts on the dumping of waste into water, and debates on the energy and environmental impacts of new desalination projects.

There is a new debate on 'virtual water' – that is, the volume of water 'hidden' or 'embodied' (actually, not embodied but used or evaporated) in products. For example, it is estimated that to produce 1 kilogram of grain, grown under rain-fed and favourable climatic conditions, we need about 1 to 2 cubic metres of water. In principle, a water-scarce country can aim at importing water-intensive products and exporting products or services that require less water (water-extensive products). In practice, it might be the case that water-scarce regions are exporting virtual water. For example, in Argentina the soya bean frontier has reached the relatively dry region of Chaco. Seen from Europe, importing soya beans involves importing virtual water (as opposed to the importing of real water, which is generally too expensive), which relieves pressure on Europe's own water resources and shifts this demand to other countries, triggering eco-social distributional effects (Hoekstra and Hung 2005).

Early debates on social metabolism and neo-Malthusianism

Until John McNeill's *Something New under the Sun* (2001; see also McNeill 2003) systematically analysed energy use and the changes in the main biochemical cycles, the subject of environmental history had little ambition to look at the economy in terms of energy and material flows (Radkau 2008).[6] Now, books and articles published in the past on the history of land use, historical geography, agricultural history, climate history, biogeography, urban pollution, sanitation and health are coherently classified into the field of environmental history.

Before this, there were influential attempts to trace the modifications to the face of the earth arising from human action (Thomas *et al.* 1956). What was lacking was a systems ecology approach counting the human impacts in the great biochemical cycles and the changes in material and energy flows. In fact, since the 1860s there have been proposals to see the economy in terms of energy and material flows. Marx (inspired by Moleschott and Liebig) used the word 'metabolism' to describe the relations between nature and human society. I would recall here the agricultural energetics of S.A. Podolinsky, received negatively by Engels in 1882 and positively by Vernadsky in 1924. Several authors (Felix Auerbach with his notion of *Ektropismus*; John Joly) had explained life as a process that reversed or slowed down the dissipation of energy. Vernadsky then gave a short biography of S.A. Podolinsky (1850–1891), and added a memorable phrase: Podolinsky had studied the energetics of life and tried to apply his findings to the study of the economy (Vernadsky 1924: 334–335).[7] This view of the economy has an intellectual foundation in the works of some nineteenth-century scientists. Economists, on the contrary, did not adopt a socio-metabolic view, but economic historians need not be the intellectual servants of economists. In any case, there was no economic-environmental historiography counting the flows of energy and materials (Weisz *et al.* 2006; Moriguchi 2007). Only much later, in the 1960s, did some natural scientists and also this time some dissident economists (Nicholas Georgescu-Roegen, Kenneth Boulding, K.W. Kapp, Herman Daly, Robert Ayres – who is actually a physicist) start to see the economy as a subsystem embedded in a physical system described in terms of flows of materials and energy. Some years later still, in the 1980s, there arose schools of ecological economics and industrial ecology that today look at the economy in terms of social metabolism. Marx and Engels had a profound interest in the metabolism shared between the economy and the natural environment, particularly as regards capitalist agriculture. Marx's use of 'metabolism' became widely known with Alfred Schmidt's work. He noted Moleschott's and Liebig's influences, and also Marx's substantive use of the term in his discussion of the cycling of plant nutrients (Schmidt 1978: 86–89; Martinez-Alier with Schlüpmann 1987: 220–226). However, there has been no school of Marxist economic and social history working on the accounts of material and energy flows.[8]

Marx and Engels were one generation younger than the agricultural chemists (Justus von Liebig, 1803–1873; Jean-Baptiste Boussingault 1802–1887) who from 1840 onwards published their research on the cycles of plant nutrients (phosphorus, nitrogen, potassium). Their work was influenced by the debates on the threat of decreasing agricultural yields and by the wholesale imports from Peru of guano, an essential bulk commodity for agriculture in that period. Their analyses of the composition of imported guano, and also of other manures and fertilizers (bones, for instance), laid the foundations for agricultural chemistry. Liebig's name was associated by his own wish with a new leading sector of the economy, the fertilizer industry. Liebig may also be seen as one of the founders of ecology, before the name itself was invented (Kormondy 1965). Politically, he developed an argument against latifundist agriculture (large-scale agriculture intended for export) and agricultural exports because the plant nutrients would not return to the soil. He was in favour of small-scale agriculture and dispersed settlements. Marx quoted this opinion favourably on several occasions. Foster, who rediscovered Marx's 'metabolism', analysed in great depth Marx's debt to Liebig – though not to Moleschott (Bellamy Foster 2000).

Marx found Liebig supremely relevant because he discussed the natural conditions of agricultural fertility and promoted the development of the productive forces by the fertilizer industry. This was useful for the polemics against Malthus. Marx wrote to Engels on 13 February 1866 that Liebig's agricultural chemistry was more important for the discussion on decreasing returns than all the economists put together. Marx dismissed the notion of decreasing returns in agriculture in the context of his praise for Liebig's chemistry and its promise of industrial fertilizers.

Marx was not worried about crises of subsistence. He attacked Malthus not only because Malthus believed in decreasing returns in agriculture but also because Malthus said that improving the situation of the poor was counterproductive since they would have more children. Later, there were many debates around 1900 on how many people could be fed, and the immediate importance of population growth for increased social metabolism is obvious. Paul Ehrlich's equation $I=PAT$ (meaning that environmental impact, I, is the product of population, P, affluence, A, and technology, T) could be applied historically: if there was an adequate indicator for T, it could be expected to show that appropriation has gone up, not only as a result of technological advances but also because of increasing human population. A trend towards a decrease in the world population which might appear soon (Lutz *et al.* 2004) could bring a welcome reduction in this pressure.

What is significant about Malthusian arguments, and critiques of them, is that they engage with the question of how and when the ecological impacts of human societies may exceed the abilities of the affected ecosystems to continuing producing. Here we have a set of questions that are neither purely economic nor purely ecological but fundamentally ecological-economic. For example, it is likely that the social perception of environmental pressures has an influence on demographic behaviour. Work by Francis Ronsin on French neo-Malthusianism with the title *La Grève des ventres* and by Eduard Masjuan on Spanish, Portuguese, Latin American and Italian neo-Malthusianism has documented the radical feminist movement in favour of limiting births that arose in Great Britain after 1880. The neo-Malthusians of 1900 were political radicals (Paul Robin, Emma Goldman). There is a difference between the T.R. Malthus of 1798 and the neo-Malthusianism of 1900, which allows me to present the following definitions:

- *Malthusianism*: Population undergoes exponential growth unless checked by war and pestilence, or by chastity and late marriages. Food grows less than proportionately to the labour input, because of decreasing returns – hence subsistence crises.
- The *neo-Malthusianism of 1900*: Human populations could regulate their own growth through contraception. Women's freedom was required for this, and desirable for its own sake. Poverty was explained by social inequality. 'Conscious procreation' was needed to prevent low wages, and pressure on natural resources. This was a successful bottom-up movement in Europe and America against states (which wanted more soldiers) and churches (Gordon 1976; Ronsin 1980; Masjuan 2000).[9]
- *Neo-Malthusianism after 1970*: A doctrine and practice sponsored by international organizations and some governments. Population growth is seen as a main cause of poverty and environmental degradation. Therefore, states must introduce contraceptive methods, even without women's prior consent.
- *Anti-Malthusianism*: The view that assumes that human population growth is no major threat to the natural environment, and that it is even conducive to economic growth, as Esther Boserup and other economists argued.

Otto Neurath's *Naturalrechnung* and Max Weber's misguided critique of Wilhelm Ostwald

One reason for the difficulty of introducing environmental history as a subject that would account for the changes in the social metabolism of human economies was the resistance in the first half of the twentieth century from prominent sociologists and economists (Max Weber, F.A. von Hayek) against authors who emphasized the importance of the flow of energy in the economy, as Otto Neurath did in the Socialist Calculation Debate of the 1920s. In this debate he defended a democratically planned economy based on physical accounting in energy and material terms (*Naturalrechnung*) influenced by Popper-Lynkeus's and Ballod-Atlanticus's quantitative, realistic 'utopias'.

Neurath also introduced the idea of incommensurable values in the economy (Martinez-Alier with Schlüpmann 1987; Martinez-Alier *et al.* 1998; O'Neill 2002, 2004; Uebel 2005), which was to have an influence on both Karl Polanyi and K.W. Kapp.[10] Otto Neurath (1882–1945) was a famous logical empiricist philosopher of the Vienna Circle and had a very clear view of how knowledge from various fields should be combined to allow the understanding of complex problems.

Hayek rudely dismissed Patrick Geddes, Wilhelm Ostwald, Lancelot Hogben, Frederick Soddy and Lewis Mumford because they viewed the economy in socio-metabolic terms, and took Neurath's *Naturalrechnung* and democratic planning as his main targets (Hayek 1952; O'Neill 2004).

One is also reminded of Max Weber's (1978) comments against Neurath in *Economy and Society*, and even more of his critique of Wilhelm Ostwald in 1909 (Weber 1909; cf. Martinez-Alier with Shlüpmann 1987: ch. 12). Ostwald (a well-known chemist) interpreted human history in terms of the use of energy, influencing Henry Adams (1838–1918), who believed there was a 'law of acceleration' of the use of (final) energy: '[T]he coal output of the world, speaking roughly, doubled every ten years between 1840 and 1900, in the form of utilized power, for the ton of coal yielded three or four times as much power in 1900 as in 1840' (Adams 1906: ch. 34). One hundred years later, research shows the close relation between economic growth and the use of energy in the economy, measured as 'physical work output as distinguished from energy (exergy)' (Ayres and Warr 2003). Ostwald had proposed two simple laws which might act or not in opposite directions (depending on the strength of what is now called the Jevons paradox or rebound effect): first, that the growth of an economy implies the use of more energy and the substitution of human energy by other forms of energy; and second, that this comes together with a trend towards higher efficiency in the transformation of energy in particular technologies and processes.

Max Weber wrote a famous ironic review of Ostwald's views, in which he insisted on the separation between the sciences. Chemists should not write on the economy. This review was praised by Hayek in *The Counter-revolution of Science*. Weber's basic point was that economic decisions by entrepreneurs on new technologies or new products were based on costs and prices. It could so happen that a production process was less efficient in energy terms but nevertheless it would be adopted because it was cheaper. Energy accounting was irrelevant for the economy. Max Weber did not question energy prices as we do now when taking into account the enhanced greenhouse effect and the intergenerational allocation of exhaustible resources.

Understanding ecological distribution conflicts

The statistics on energy use are relevant for explaining some conflicts among humans. For instance, the need for poor people to gain access to forests is explained by their need for fuel. There are historical and current conflicts over coal extraction (miners' health, land subsidence, evictions, production of sulphur dioxide) and oil extraction (gas flaring, biodiversity loss). At the global level, more fossil fuel extraction and use means more carbon dioxide production, and a conflict on the distribution of responsibilities and damage from climate change. Increased use of energy also leads to conflicts over transport, such as those created by oil spills. Even wind energy is provoking new conflicts in Europe because of the ('post-materialist'?) valuation of landscapes (Zografos and Martínez-Alier 2009; Gamboa and Munda 2007). Other sources of energy give rise to more robust conflicts, as with nuclear energy (uncertain risks of accident, disposal of nuclear waste, military proliferation), while agro-fuels are criticized because of their low EROI, because they increase HANPP to the detriment of other species, and because of their 'virtual' water content. Material flows are equally relevant for understanding many conflicts. Such local and global conflicts have different actors with different interests and values. Neo-classical economists attribute 'externalities' to so-called market failure, but from a socio-historic point of view externalities can be seen as 'cost-shifting successes' that are not always accepted quietly.

In the nineteenth and early twentieth centuries the countries of today's European Union depended on their own coal and biomass as energy sources. Now they have become large net importers of oil and gas. Taking all materials together (energy carriers, minerals, metals, biomass), the European Union was importing in 2000 about four times more tonnes than it was exporting. Meanwhile, Latin America appears to be exporting six times more tonnes than it imports. Moreover, Southern exports carry heavier 'ecological rucksacks' than the imports; for example, if we compare the energy dissipated and the carbon dioxide produced by each dollar of exports and of imports (Giljum and Eisenmenger 2004; Machado *et al.* 2001; Muradian *et al.* 2002; Pérez-Rincón 2006). Walter Pengue (2005) computed the hidden flows in the soya bean trade of Argentina in the form of loss of nutrients (doing so would have pleased Liebig and Marx) and 'virtual water', and soil erosion. Pengue also mentions the new resistance against pesticides (glyphosate) acquired by some weeds, which then become invaders.

In an ecological-economic theory of unequal exchange, attention is drawn to physical measurements, focusing on the unequal amounts of energy (or exergy, i.e. available energy), or materials (in tonnes), or land used up. Market prices, which do not necessarily reflect exergy and materials dissipated in producing the exchanged goods, are, as Hornborg wrote, 'the means by which world system centres extract exergy from the peripheries' (1998; see also Naredo 2001).

However, not all poor countries are net physical exporters. India and China, for example, are net importers (because of their imports of oil and other materials). Internally, some regions in India and China provide coal and other minerals, and become the site of famous ecological distribution conflicts.[11] Meanwhile, some rich countries with low populations (and high material and energy use per capita) are still net resource exporters (Canada, Australia) following the path of Harold Innis's 'staple theory of growth'. Whatever the historically changing positions of different countries or regions, it is clear that the metabolic processes that maintain the world system centres are guaranteed, in part, by ecologically unequal exchange, deteriorating terms of trade for natural resources, cheap labour and cheap human lives in the peripheries, and, when needed to secure these, by military power. When resource exports are produced by transnational corporations, demands for *corporate accountability* arise, with affected people claiming compensation for damages caused in poor countries (Uttig and Clapp 2008).

The environmentalism of the poor

Thirty-five years after the start of the Chipko movement in 1973, twenty years after the death of Chico Mendes in December 1988 in Brazil as the victim of a 'tragedy of enclosures', thirteen years after the death of Ken Saro-Wiwa and his companions for defending the Niger Delta and its populations against the Shell company and the government of Nigeria, the debate on the 'environmentalism of the poor' is growing.[12]

The environmental sociologist Riley Dunlap disputes the long-held assumption that the citizens of poor nations will not support efforts to protect the environment since they are too preoccupied with meeting basic needs such as food and housing. An article by Dunlap and York (2008) compared results from four large cross-national surveys conducted in many nations with differing levels of average income. Results showed that citizens of poorer nations were just as concerned about the environment as citizens in wealthier countries, if not more so. Coinciding with the thesis on the 'environmentalism of the poor', Dunlap and York (ibid.) argue that Inglehart's explanation of the growth of environmentalism because of a change towards 'post-materialist' values failed to recognize that environmental problems are often a threat to material welfare. For example, deforestation may threaten the livelihoods of people who depend on forests for firewood, food sources and medicinal products.

Of course, this does not mean that poor people are always on the side of conservation, which would be patently untrue. What has to be acknowledged is that in many conflicts of resource extraction or pollution, the local poor people (indigenous or not) are often on the side of conservation and that this occurs not so much because they are self-conscious environmentalists but because of their livelihood needs and their cultural values, which place their social and their physical conditions within a single frame.

Sociologists, political scientists and economists ignored 'the environmentalism of the poor'. It was also forgotten by the two main currents of environmentalism: the 'cult of wilderness' and the 'gospel of eco-efficiency'. Adams and Jeanrenaud in the International Union for Conservation of Nature (IUCN) booklet for the World Conservation Congress in Barcelona of October 2008 notice that the 'global environment and conservation movement' (epitomized by the membership of the IUCN) excludes many organizations dedicated to environmental justice, including the US environmental justice movement, and many others across the world: OilWatch, Mines and Communities, the International Rivers Network, the Mangrove Action Project (MAP), and the World Rainforest Movement (wrm.org.uy) that uses the slogan 'Tree plantations are not forests'. In India, Toxics Link denounces the exports of ships for dismantling to Alang on the coast of Gujarat, and the export of electronic waste from rich to poor countries. The Via Campesina is a world network of peasant organizations which realize that modern agriculture is less energy-efficient than traditional peasant agriculture, uses more chemical pollutants, and simplifies biodiversity by placing little value on the many varieties of seeds that have co-evolved over thousands of years through peasant farming. Also, some organizations ask for Climate Justice and the repayment of the so-called ecological debt from North to South, bringing together the 'carbon debt' – that is, damages from rich countries on account of excessive per capita emissions of carbon dioxide (the main effluent of affluence) – with claims also because of biopiracy, ecologically unequal exchange, and environmental liabilities by private or public companies.

These movements combine livelihood, social, economic and environmental issues with emphasis on issues of extraction and pollution. They set their 'moral economy' in opposition to the logic of extraction of oil, minerals, wood or agro fuels at the 'commodity frontiers', defending biodiversity and their own livelihood. In many instances they draw on a sense of local identity (indigenous rights and values such as the sacredness of the land), but they also connect easily with the politics of the left. However, the traditional left in Southern countries still tends to see environmentalism as a 'luxury of the rich', although such movements position themselves in opposition to corporate power and to the coercive forces of the state – indeed, as Bill Adams remarks, these organizations have often been formed explicitly to oppose annexation of land, forests, mineral resources and water by governments and business corporations.

In the magazine *Down to Earth* (15 August 2008), Sunita Narain gave current examples from India:

> In Sikkim, bowing to local protests, the government has cancelled 11 hydroelectric projects. In Arunachal Pradesh, dam projects are being cleared at breakneck speed and resistance is growing. In Uttarakhand last month 2 projects on the Ganga were put on hold and there is growing concern about the rest. In Himachal Pradesh, dams are so controversial that elections were won where candidates said they would not allow these to be built. Many other projects, from thermal power stations to 'greenfield' mining, are being resisted. The South Korean giant Posco's iron ore mine, steel plant and port are under fire. The prime minister has promised the South Korean premier the project will go ahead by August. But local people are not listening. They don't want to lose their land and livelihood and do not believe in promises of compensation. In Maharashtra, mango growers are up in arms against the proposed thermal power station in Ratnagiri. In every nook and corner of the country where land is acquired, or water sourced, for industry, people are fighting even to death. There are wounds. There is violence. There is also desperation. Like it or not, there are a million mutinies today.... After I visited Kalinganagar, where villagers died protesting against Tata's project, I wrote this was not about competition or Naxalism. These were poor villagers who knew they did not have the skills to survive in the modern world. They had seen their neighbours displaced, promised jobs and money that never came. They knew they were poor. But they also knew modern development would make them poorer. It was the same in prosperous Goa, where I found village after village fighting against the powerful mining lobby.

The poor, because of their direct reliance on natural resources outside the market, are often careful environmental managers. The environment provides commodities and amenities, but it also provides the very conditions of livelihood and existence. In India there is well-intentioned economic research showing that common property resources (CPRs) contribute a larger amount of money per year than foreign assistance. Actually, economic valuation is irrelevant in assessing the livelihood values of water, firewood, soil fertility and pastures that are essential for Adivasi and other poor people who have no money to buy substitutes for them. A part of income growth goes simply to compensate for the loss of free resources no longer available because of environmental degradation and population growth, and sometimes to cope with the displacement of poor people because of new dams or mining projects.

Hence the idea of 'the GDP of the poor' proposed by Gundimedia and Sukhdev (Sukhdev 2008: ch. 3). In national income accounts (NIAs) one could introduce valuations of ecosystem and biodiversity losses either in satellite accounts (physical and monetary) or in adjusted GDP accounts ('green accounts'), but neither method guarantees an adequate representation. The valuation of losses might still be low compared to the economic gains from projects that destroy biodiversity. However, which groups of people suffer most by such losses? In the project 'Green Accounting for India' the authors found that the most significant beneficiaries of forest biodiversity and ecosystem services are the poor, and the predominant impact of a loss or denial of these inputs is on the well-being of the poor. The poverty of the beneficiaries makes these losses even more acute, as they constitute a greater proportion of the livelihood incomes for the poor than is the case for the people of India at large.

The question of who the 'poor' are arises, and so does the question of whether the definition of 'agency' in such conflicts may rest on such a vague description. In ecological distribution conflicts the leaders are often women but also men, peasants, mine or plantation workers, urban dwellers, indigenous representatives, civil rights leaders – the list goes on. Women indeed often play a crucial role in such conflicts, because of the common division of work, power and access rights to environmental resources according to gender.

But what is meant by the 'poor'? I see two answers to this. First, in any society we could resort to studies on poverty to classify those below a certain poverty line and then look to see whether the main actors in certain types of ecological distribution conflicts belong to this category. We know, however, that some indigenous groups are not poor; they simply adapt to their surrounding natural wealth with production systems that are not labour-intensive. A second answer is to realize that in some societies, some people see themselves as 'we the poor'. This was obvious in the mid-1960s in rural Andalusia, where *nosotros los pobres* (we the poor) was a common phrase that helped to explain power relations, food consumption patterns, migration and the conditions of a life of manual labour. Economic growth, social mobility, and immigration from outside Spain mean that this phrase is (I believe) no longer used in Spain. But it is used elsewhere. In Thailand, opposition to some dams was organized by the aptly named (in English) Assembly of the Poor. In South Africa, Ashwin Desai wrote a book on social and environmental community struggles after apartheid, particularly in Durban, with the title *We Are the Poors* [*sic*].

In their text for the 2008 World Conservation Congress, Adams and Jeanrenaud conclude that to make a transition to sustainability, the environmental movements of the poor must get into the sustainability mainstream, beyond their participation in 'community-based conservation' or co-management of natural parks. An alliance of conservation environmentalism with social justice organizations, feminist groups and indigenous groups is needed. Both academics and policy-makers have assumed that residents of poor nations were too preoccupied with satisfying their 'material' needs to be able to support the 'post-materialist' values of environmental protection. However, the actual struggles for the environment by poor communities and historical and contemporary research on ecological distribution conflicts have given much support to the thesis of 'the environmentalism of the poor', an environmentalism that begins from the presumption that the social and physical conditions of humanity are fundamentally related to each other.

Sunita Narain explains why the environmentalism of the poor may become a strong force for sustainability:

> The fact is in India vast numbers depend on the land, the forests and the water they have in their vicinity for their livelihood. They know once these resources are gone or degraded, they have no way ahead. This is the environmental movement of the very poor. Here, there are no quick-fix techno solutions in which the real problems can be fobbed off for later. In this environmentalism, there is only one answer: changing the way we do business, with them and with their environment.... If we can listen and learn, maybe this environmentalism of the poor may teach not just us but the entire world how to walk lightly on earth.

Meanwhile, Vedanta is about to destroy the Niyamgiri hill in Orissa, India, damaging the Dongria Kondh tribe in its search for bauxite.

Some conflicts on material flows and the HANPP

I shall here summarize one case in India and one in Africa where social conflicts over access to the HANPP have arisen. This will help also to show that the multiplicity of evaluation languages imposes on us, as scholars, and the need to begin our work by making an effort to understand these languages. If we are to work with these people, to understand and address their grievances, then our work needs to be able to honour this intertwining, which means it must combine social and physical, as well as quantitative and qualitative, assessments.

Fishermen protected by the turtles in Kerala

In northern Kerala, India, the Theeram Pakriti Samrakshana Samiti (Coastal Ecosystem Protection Committee) was formed in 1992 in Kolavipalam when a group of young common fishermen read an article in a national newspaper about the threats to the olive ridley turtles (*Lepidochelys olivacea*) from the extraction of sand. They realized these were the turtles that nested on their beach, and whose eggs were consumed locally. With their own meagre resources they paid for some members to keep watch over the beach during the nesting season from October to March. The eggs of all nests that are encountered are relocated to a fenced hatchery on the beach to protect them from stray dogs and jackals. Media publicity about this project has helped to spread awareness to neighbouring coastal villages.

The protection of turtles is often done by conservationist groups motivated by 'post-materialist' values, but in this case the struggle for the livelihood of poor fishermen was successfully combined with the conservation of turtles because there was a common enemy. The 'cult of wilderness' and the 'environmentalism of the poor' here become allies. Similarly, conservationist groups sometimes support the struggles of indigenous or peasant communities against the dams or the mining projects built to assuage the growing thirst of the economy for more and more energy and materials.

What was the reason for the interest of the young local fishermen in the protection of turtles? Not only were the eggs locally consumed but local fishing is known to threaten turtles. However, in this case the beach had become open to sand mining. The local fishermen complained about sand mining on the beach and also along the rivers, which aggravates coastal erosion. They obtained some support from the Kerala High Court. The fishermen realized also the importance of mangroves in protecting against erosion, and there is a local programme for planting mangrove seedlings. A film, *Aaamakaar: The Turtle People* (see http://www.peopleandplanet.net/?lid=27679&section=35&topic=25), documents their history and efforts (Shanker 2007).

Here, the increased social metabolism of the Indian economy, whose building industry requires sand (a material that in itself is not particularly noxious), has damaged the coast and rivers. Sand mining, as it is called, is often done outside the law. There are sand 'mafias' in southern India, and their activities appear in newspapers when they fight against the environmental authorities and the police: 'Special squad needs more men to stop illegal sand mining.... Revenue officials said that illegal mining of three metric tonne of sand would fetch a lorry owner around Rs. 3,000. They usually make a total of three trips every day' (*The Hindu* (Tamil Nadu), 26 February 2008).

The Tana Delta: who gets the HANPP? The threat of sugar cane plantations 2008[13]

Some land conflicts in Kenya conform to the pattern seen the world over: poor people are confronted by new claims made by agricultural, energy or mining enterprises. Poor people then reaffirm a prior claim on the land based on legally valid title deeds, or on their livelihood needs or the sacredness of the land in question or its ecological values. Such claims could be expressed also by exercising the right of previous consultation against resource extraction as recognized by Convention 169 of the International Labour Organization (ILO) for tribal peoples, but Kenya (like India) has not ratified it.

In the Tana Delta, near the Somali border, the land is used by Orma pastoralists and Pokomo agriculturalists, while Luo fishermen make use of aquatic resources. The mangroves at the mouth of the river are still intact. No shrimp farming has yet ruined them, as nearly happened in the Rufiji Delta in Tanzania. But there is pressure on the land from the thousands of cattle that the Orma have brought there and now keep there on a permanent rather than a seasonal basis. A couple of kilometres from the mouth of the river the mangroves have been cut to leave space for agriculture. Further up the river the banks are deprived of any trees, and pastures, eroded by cattle, reach all the way to the river. Crocodiles and hippopotamuses still abound in the river and in the lakes of the Delta, and some Pokomo communities are trying to develop eco-tourism in this beautiful environment.

The old conflict between pastoralists and the agriculturalists is still very much alive elsewhere in Kenya, as is the conflict between pastoralists and cattle rustlers. The most famous Kenyan pastoralists are in the highlands, the confederation of tribes called the Maasai with their colourful red clothing. While the Luo (to which Prime Minister Raila Odinga belongs) are a fishing and agricultural tribe of Nilotic origin, the Maasai, like the Kikuyu (to which Jomo Kenyatta belonged, as does President Mwai Kibaki), came hundreds of years ago from Western Africa and are mostly of Bantu heritage. The pastoralist Orma of the Tana Delta arrived much earlier from Ethiopia and Somalia, reaching what is now Kenyan territory perhaps 3,000 years ago. In the Tana Delta the agriculturalist Pokomo see the Orma as nomad invaders without real roots, although as a matter of fact, in many schools of the area Orma children are in the majority and their elders have built permanent settlements.

Increasing population pressure on the land and its resources has added to the old enmities. Moreover, new actors are now appearing. Africa is still remembered by many as a source of precious commodities such as ivory, rhino horns, gold and precious stones, and as a source of slaves, but it is today more and more a source for raw materials essential for the metabolism of the importing countries' economies. One example is oil, found in Angola, Chad, Nigeria and Sudan. Another is uranium, mined in Niger for export to France, causing a socio-environmental conflict with the Tuareg tribes (Chamaret and Sunde 2008). Another case is titanium mining in Kwale, on the southern coast of Kenya, which has displaced 400 farming families. The ore concentrate will be exported to the tune of one big lorry every half-hour for twenty-four hours each day, and a big tailings dam will be left behind. This is certainly not a 'precious commodity'.

In ancient times the Swahili coast was a centre of trade with Arabia and India. As described in the panels of the museum at the Gede ruins, from the eighth century onwards porcelain and other luxury goods were imported from China. The trade in precious commodities continues. Vigorous campaigns were directed against the ivory trade in Kenya in the early 1970s, in the last years of Jomo Kenyatta's presidency. The National Museum in Nairobi houses the skeleton of the body of the elephant Ahmed as one of its main exhibits, together with remains of the early hominids in the Rift Valley. Ahmed received police protection around the clock by the direct order of Jomo Kenyatta and he died a natural death with his tusks intact, a victory against poachers.

The export of bulk commodities from South to North (which now includes parts of China and India) is increasing. The Tana Delta might soon also become an exporter of gas. For the moment it is threatened by the development of new, very large industrial sugar cane plantations (belonging to private or state enterprises). The Mumia Sugar Corporation is trying to acquire title to about 20,000 hectares in order to grow sugar cane for the production of sugar for domestic demand and also to make ethanol for export, while burning part of the bagasse to produce electricity which can be sold. These are mature technologies easy to put in place. The cane will have to be irrigated during some months of the year and there are concerns about the social and environmental opportunity costs of using this water for such a purpose. In the Tana Delta, many of the Pokomo are not averse to the sugar cane plantations, seeing themselves optimistically as potential small-scale outgrowers of cane for the sugar factories. But the pastoralists (and also the fishermen) are adamant in their opposition.

The conservationists of the East African Wildlife Society and other groups dedicated to the preservation of wetlands have taken an active role in the growing conflict of the Tana Delta. On 11 July 2008 they obtained an injunction stopping the sugar cane farming projects. There are technical ecological-economic arguments against the projects: the low EROI of sugar cane ethanol, factoring into the accounts the energy value of the naturally produced pastures, which would be destroyed, the 'virtual water' expenditure for growing the sugar cane, the increased HANPP at the expense of the biomass needs of other species. The judicial case was argued in the High Court of Malindi, a city and tourist resort between Mombasa and the Tana Delta, famous for being the point from where Vasco de Gama sailed to India looking for pepper. The conservationists emphasize the values of the environmental services of the wetlands: they want most of the Tana Delta to be designated as a Ramsar site, thus putting it under the protection of this international environmental agreement for the defence of wetlands. At the same time, the conservationists support the Orma pastoralists whose representatives went to court together with them against the sugar cane plantations. Here again the global 'cult of wilderness' enters into a marriage of convenience with the local 'environmentalism of the poor'. Some people in Kenya regard the plans for ethanol exports as especially irritating in a country where many people are living barely above the hunger line. In interviews in the Tana Delta in 2008 we found that land access, including the threat of dispossession by private or state agro-business companies, was the major concern of the poor.

Cost–benefit analysis or the language of environmental justice: the loss of NPP by the destruction of mangroves

Mangroves have been destroyed by urban reclamation and pollution; by lack of fresh water because of dams (as in the Indus); by excessive wood cutting for the purposes of building, charcoal-making, or using tannin for dyes; by cattle grazing; and even, as in Vietnam, by military bombing and herbicide spraying (Vanucci 2004). Another main cause of destruction is the itinerant export shrimp industry, as in Honduras, Ecuador, Brazil, Thailand, the Philippines, Bangladesh, Vietnam, etc. The NPP declines to zero when shrimp aquaculture is substituted for mangroves that would provide many environmental services, some of which immediately relate to human livelihood.

As for any other investment project, a tree plantation or a mining project or a dam, or historically an *assèchement des marais* or *bonifica* (the swamp drainage techniques used in Renaissance France and ancient Rome, respectively), one could perform an extended cost-benefit analysis. If a mangrove is destroyed in order to have a shrimp pond instead, where are the benefits and where are the costs?[14] Assuming a shrimp farm produces, per hectare per year, about 4,000kg of shrimp, selling at a farm price of US$5 per kilogram, the gross revenue is *c*. US$20,000 per hectare per year. This is difficult to match with the (market and non-market) economic values provided by 1 hectare of mangroves. However, the shrimp pond lasts perhaps only five years, while the mangrove destruction will last for a few years after the end of shrimp farming, when the soil becomes less acidic and allows replanting, and may last for ever if there is no one there to take care of the replanting. So, we have five years of shrimp revenue to compare, say, to fifteen years (five years for soil regeneration plus ten years for regrowth) of loss of mangrove revenue.

Certainly we should deduct from the gross revenue the monetary costs of producing the shrimp. Assuming that labour has other work opportunities, we would therefore deduct labour costs (which are low), and also deduct the costs of the inputs (nutrients, antibiotics). Moreover, we would deduct the amortization of the investment costs, which are of the order of US$10,000 per hectare, spread over five years, i.e. US$2,000 per hectare per year. We could then deduct the costs of water pollution, according to one of two methods: the economic value attributed to the damage produced, or the economic cost of the abatement of pollution down to the desired level. We could also deduct the economic values of other negative externalities (illnesses suffered by women and children collecting seedlings, and costs of illnesses associated with new resistance to antibiotics). Moreover, an obligation could be imposed requiring replanting of mangroves once a shrimp farm is abandoned, after the five years during which it is productive. Assuming all this to be technically possible, costs may still vary considerably (Lewis 2001). They could amount to anywhere from US$300 to US$8,000 per hectare, spread out over the five years of operation. Depending, then, on various assumptions, we could come up with a figure for benefits (net of market and non-market costs) equivalent to US$10,000 per hectare per year, or also plausibly also a figure much lower than this, even a negative one.

If instead we keep the mangroves, what are the market and non-market revenues produced per hectare? Here we distinguish between direct and indirect economic values. The direct values are the collected products from the mangroves (shells, crabs, fish, honey, etc.), whether for self-consumption or for marketing. The collected products are only a small part of the production of biomass. A mangrove forest will produce over 10 tonnes of biomass per year, mostly as detritus from fallen leaves. A small part of the biomass (as wood, crabs, etc.) would be collected by humans who depend on the mangrove forest for their livelihood. This biomass is essential for their life. However, in money terms (and once we factor in the costs of collection, at a local wage rate) this biomass in the form of fish, crabs, shellfish, wood and honey is not worth much (say US$100 or US$200 per hectare per year) because the prices it fetches or would fetch in the market are low. If relevant, we would add here the eco-tourism revenues that would make a significant difference for a few locations in the world.

Indirectly, the mangroves provide other current or future (optional) benefits that must be valued in money terms in order to complete the cost–benefit analysis (CBA). These range from being a nursery for offshore fisheries to serving as a coastline defence against erosion, including also carbon uptake, serving as a repository of salinity-resistant genetic resources, and other forms of unused biodiversity. Here methods of monetary valuation will be very different. Thus, the coastal defence service is valued at the 'replacement cost', assuming that a wall would be built instead. Then this money value easily reaches thousands of dollars per hectare of mangrove, overshadowing the direct money values of collected biomass. For biodiversity, there is no 'replacement cost' since there are no technologies available to reproduce (as in a 'Jurassic Park') the disappearing species. Then we would resort to extrapolations from payments in bioprospection contracts, or to 'willingness-to-pay' valuations, which usually give relatively low monetary values. Carbon uptake may be given very different values according to which concrete clean development mechanism (CDM) case we take as our reference value. Typically it will not change the general picture because the 'price' is at most two or three dollars per tonne of carbon. This 'price' does not reflect in any way the usefulness of the carbon uptake service for humankind and nature but depends instead simply on the strength of the Kyoto and post-Kyoto commitments and the carbon permit trading market. Assuming the reduction commitments to be stronger in future, we could argue that the right price to use is $US100 per tonne of carbon, but this is not the present situation.

Bringing it all together, one could argue that the economic value of the standing mangroves amounts, per hectare per year, to anywhere from a few hundred dollars up to US$10,000 or more (Costanza *et al.* 1998). Given that the benefits from shrimp farming accrue in only the first few years, while the benefits from the mangroves are forgone for ever, or at least until successful replanting is completed, after fifteen or twenty years, it is easy to conclude that the mangroves may be defended through reference to CBA. However, much will depend on the rate of discount, the assumptions behind the figures and the methods of economic valuation that are used. It would not be difficult for a pro-shrimp economist to argue in favour of shrimp farming by using CBA. He or she would use a high discount rate, would lower the replanting costs and would give a relatively low value to the coastal defence function.

However, another type of comparison between mangrove conservation and shrimp farming development could be carried out, according to multi-criteria evaluation (MCE) that takes into account a variety of relevant incommensurable dimensions, all of them expressed in their own quantitative units or qualitative descriptions (economic profitability, employment, biodiversity, coastal defence, carbon uptake, landscape, genetic resources, human livelihood, local culture (possibly including sacredness), etc.). Here, the word 'valuation' does not only mean monetary valuation.

Mangroves, being in the tidal zone, are usually public property. They belong to the state. In practice, they have been used by local communities according to customary rules and specialized trades (e.g. women shell-collectors, male charcoal-makers). The required investment for a large commercially viable shrimp farm is of the order of US$1 million, which is within the reach of local entrepreneurs in most of the affected countries. But they must have the local political clout to gain concessions to the mangrove areas, or to invade them illegally. This must not be described as an 'open access' situation but rather as an 'enclosure' movement. Resources in open access are often mismanaged, but that does not mean that resources in private property will be well managed. The pressure of the interest (or discount) rate will make entrepreneurs forget about the future, and the logic of the market will make them forget about the multifunctionality of the ecosystem. So, under private property, rapid-growth tree plantations are substituted for forests, while mangroves are sacrificed to the monoculture of shrimp farming.

In July 1998 I took part as a sympathetic observer in an action by Greenpeace together with Fundecol (a local grassroots group of about 300 people in Muisne, Ecuador) in destroying at sunrise one crop of shrimps from an illegal pond, by opening a hole in one wall, letting the water flow out and replanting mangrove seedlings. I shall quote (in my own translation) a call from a woman of Muisne, Ecuador, a few months after the visit by Greenpeace, distributed to international networks by Fundecol on 11 March 1999. She used a different language of valuation to that of CBA. She said nothing about the money value of environmental services. She argued in terms of what in the United States would be called 'environmental justice' against 'environmental racism':

> We have always been ready to cope with everything, and now more than ever, but they want to humiliate us because we are black, because we are poor, but one does not choose the race into which one is born, nor does one choose not to have anything to eat, not to be ill. But I am proud of my race and of being *Conchera* because it is my race that gives me strength to do battle in defence of what my parent were, and my children will inherit; proud of being *Conchera* because I have never stolen anything from anyone, I have never taken anybody's bread from his mouth to fill mine, because I

> have never crawled on my knees asking anybody for money, and I have always lived standing up. Now we are struggling for something which is ours, our ecosystem, but not because we are professional ecologists but because we must remain alive, because if the mangroves disappear, a whole people disappears, we all disappear, we shall no longer be part of the history of Muisne, we shall ourselves exist no longer.... I do not know what will happen to us if the mangroves disappear, we shall eat garbage in the outskirts of the city of Esmeraldas or in Guayaquil, we shall become prostitutes, I do not know what will happen to us if the mangroves disappear.... We think, if the *camaroneros* who are not the rightful owners nevertheless now prevent us and the *carboneros* from getting through the lands they have taken, not allowing us to get across the *esteros*, shouting and shooting at us, what will happen next, when the government gives them the lands, will they put up big 'Private Property' signs, will they even kill us with the blessing of the President?[15]
>
> (a call from a woman of Muisne, Ecuador, distributed to international networks by Fundecol on 11 March 1999)

Conclusion

The metabolism of industrial societies requires increasing amounts of energy and materials, and also increased appropriation of the production of biomass. Hence, new extractions arise at the commodity frontiers. These are often 'bulk commodities' but they can also be 'precious commodities' (gold, diamonds, mahogany or shrimp). One may study the material flows to test historical trends towards dematerialization, or to follow the ups and downs of the building industry. One may study the use of energy from the different fossil fuels to see the trend in the world aggregate production of carbon dioxide. One may study the HANPP in a given territory and see whether it really indicates historical trends towards loss of biodiversity. Another approach consists of studying the MEFA and HANPP indicators, and their links to historical or contemporary environmental conflicts among groups of humans. Such conflicts are expressed as conflicts over valuation, either inside a single standard of value or across plural values. They tell us about the complexity of the social and physical relationships between humans and nature and among humans, that lie at the heart of our current environmental crisis. It might be that an agreement is sought among diverse interests by appealing to the common language of economic valuation, trying to ascertain through extended CBA whether the benefits from a project are large enough to compensate for the losses, with a net gain on top. But the requirement for such an exercise is commensurability of values and a single language of valuation. Social, cultural, economic and environmental aspects are all measured in money. Such measurements are technically difficult to achieve, as we have seen, but not impossible. More importantly, the money-reductionism of CBA disregards the social legitimacy of values such as human rights, collective territorial rights, sacredness, ecological and aesthetic values, and the biological requirements of the ecosystems and sometimes also the people involved. Some languages of valuation (livelihood, indigenous rights, sacredness) that were powerful in the past are slowly becoming worthless in this era of the generalized market system, where even 'the fetishism of fictitious commodities' is in the ascendant, with schemes for payment of environmental services. However, other languages (human rights, environmental justice against 'environmental racism') are gaining in strength.

To conclude, we may write, 'shrimp exports [or copper or bauxite mining] are a valuable item of world trade', and also, 'valuable ecosystems and valuable local cultures are destroyed by shrimp farming [or copper or bauxite mining]'. The reduction of all goods and services to actual or fictitious commodities, as in CBA, can be recognized as one perspective among several, legitimate, as a reflection of real power structures but not necessarily the most sustainable or indeed the most desirable (Funtowicz and Ravetz 1994). So, we continue to face the question of who has then the power to simplify complexity, imposing a particular standard and procedure of valuation. As in other environmental conflicts, political power appears at two levels: first, as the ability to impose a decision; second, as the power to impose one particular decision procedure and standard of valuation. How this power is exercised in different societies in different moments of history is indeed a worthwhile topic of study for sociologists, political scientists and social historians.

The present chapter is in line with the paper by Armiero and Peluso (2008). A different approach is the study of social adaptations to environmental constraints and changes, and also the study of human impacts on the environment, not focusing so much on social conflicts. Each approach, like the social metabolism approaches discussed above, has its merits. Whichever approach we choose, understanding how current power structures inhibit and undermine the kinds of complex social physical standards that are reflected in the language of the environmentalism of the poor may also be, increasingly, a challenge not only for environmental historians but for anyone working to understand and address the environmental challenges of the twenty-first century.

Notes

1 This chapter is a revised version of a paper originally presented as the Opening Lecture for the conference 'Common Ground, Converging Gazes: Integrating the Social and Environmental in History', le Centre de Recherches Historiques, École des Hautes Études en Sciences Sociales (EHESS), Paris, 11–13 September 2008.

2 Fischer-Kowalski is a sociologist and, at the same time, president of the International Society of Industrial Ecology.

3 One excellent early book on this topic is Fred Cottrell's *Energy and Society* (1955), while Carlo Cipolla cited the debates on energy and history of the early twentieth century in his absurdly anti-Malthusian text *The Economic History of World Population* (1974 [1962]). Anthropologists were familiar with these debates through White (1943, 1959). Finally, a general survey can be found in Smil (1991).

4 The first estimates of the HANPP were by Vitousek *et al.* in 1986.

5 See also Guha and Martinez-Alier (1997: ch. 1), with a study on claiming the commons in Karnataka against industrial plantations of eucalyptus.

6 This is in contrast to Mosley (2006). My own approach is similar to Mosley's. Two excellent though quite different surveys of the field of environmental history are those by McNeill (2003), whose approach I share, and Grove and Damodaran (2006).

7 I have discussed the negative reception of Podolinsky's energy accounts by Engels in Martinez-Alier with Schlüpmann (1987) and again more recently in Martinez-Alier (2007a).

8 However, Susiluoto analysed the writings on energy and history by Bogdanov and Bukharin in *The Origins and Development of Systems Thinking in the Soviet Union* (1982). This was discussed in Martinez-Alier with Schlüpmann (1987).

9 The French neo-Malthusians Gabriel Giroud and Sébastien Faure published books and pamphlets on population and resources; cf. Cohen (1995). At the time, the discussion did not take into account the biomass needed for wildlife, i.e. how large the HANPP should be.

10 In a book review in the *American Economic Review*, K.W. Kapp (1955) complained that 'the controversy initiated by O. Neurath, von Mises and Max Weber got sidetracked in various attempts to calculate the prices of productive factors ... and O. Lange's later elaboration of a theoretical model of "competitive socialism"'.

11 See Temper and Martinez-Alier 2007, particularly Sunita Narain's list of conflicts in the first section of this chapter.

12 See Guha's *The Unquiet Woods* (1989). There are many differences between the colonial experiences of Latin America and India, not least in the demographic consequences of the conquest of the indigenous peoples of the Americas (Mallon 1983; Melville 1994; Crosby 1986; Peluso 1992; Ortega Santos 2002).

13 I spent the week from 30 July to 4 August 2008 doing interviews in the Tana Delta and in Kwale with Leah Temper and Beatriz Rodriguez-Labajos.

14 The accounts below owe much to the study by Sathirathai and Barbier (2003).

15 *Concheras* are women who collect shellfish, mostly for selling but also for subsistence. *Camaroneros* are the owners of the shrimp farms ('*camarón*' means shrimp). *Carboneros* are charcoal-makers. *Concheras* get across *esteros* (the swamps) by boat to get to the mangroves and collect the shells at low tide. The coastal population of the province of Esmeraldas in Ecuador (and also across the border in Colombia) is, in its majority, of African descent.

References

Adams, H. 1906. *The Education of Henry Adams: An Autobiography*. Privately printed.

Adams, W.M. and Jeanrenaud, S.J. (2008). *Transition to Sustainability: Towards a Humane and Diverse World*. Gland, Switzerland: IUCN.

Armiero, M. and N.L. Peluso. 2008. 'Conflict: the potential contributions of a conflict-centred approach to blending social and environmental history.' In *Common Ground, Converging Gazes: Integrating the Social and Environmental in History*, ed. UMR 8558 (CNRS/EHESS), le Centre de Recherches Historiques. Paris: École des Hautes Études en Sciences Sociales (EHESS).

Ayres, R.U. 1989. 'Industrial metabolism.' In *Technology and Environment*, ed. J. Ausubel. Washington, DC: National Academy Press.

Ayres, R.U. and B. Warr. 2003. 'Accounting for growth: the role of physical work.' In *Advances in Energy Studies*, ed. S. Ulgiati. Padua: SG Editoriali.

Bellamy Foster, J. 2000. *Marx's Ecology: Materialism and Culture*. New York: Monthly Review Press.

Chamaret, A. and C. Sunde. 2008. 'Cross-cultural dialogue: a proposition for dealing with conflicts between mining companies and local populations: the case of uranium mining and the Tuareg nomads in Niger.' Paper given at Tenth Biennial Conference, International Society for Ecological Economics, Nairobi, 7–11 August.

Cipolla, C. 1974 [1962]. *The Economic History of World Population*, 6th ed. London: Penguin.

Cleveland, C.J. 1987. 'Biophysical economics: historical perspectives and current recent trends.' *Ecological Modelling* 38(1–2): 47–73.

Cohen, J.E. 1995. *How Many People Can the Earth Support?* New York: W.W. Norton.

Costanza, R., R. D'Arge, R. De Groot, S. Farber, M. Grasso, B. Hannon, K. Limburg, S. Naeem, R.V. O'Neill, J. Paruelo, R.G. Raskin, P. Sutton and M. Van den Belt. 1998. 'The value of the world's ecosystem services and natural capital.' *Ecological Economics* 25(1): 3–15.

Cottrell, F. 1955. *Energy and Society: The Relation between Energy, Social Change and Economic Development*. New York: McGraw-Hill.

Crosby, A.W. 1986. *Ecological Imperialism: The Biological Expansion of Europe, 900–1900*. Cambridge: Cambridge University Press.

Debeir, J.C., J.P. Deléage and D. Hémery. 1986. *Les servitudes de la puissance: une histoire de l'energie*. Paris: Flammarion.

Dunlap, R.E. and R. York. 2008. 'The globalization of environmental concern and the limits of the post-materialist explanation: evidence from four cross-national surveys.' *Sociological Quarterly* 49(3): 529–563.

Eurostat. 2001. *Economy-Wide Material Flow Accounts and Derived Indicators: A Methodological Guide*. Luxembourg: Office for Official Publications of the European Communities.

Fischer-Kowalski, M. 1998. 'Society's metabolism: the intellectual history of material flow analysis, part I, 1860–1970.' *Journal of Industrial Ecology* 2(1): 61–78.

Fischer-Kowalski, M. and H. Haberl eds. 2007. *Socioecological Transitions and Global Change: Trajectories of Social Metabolism and Land Use*. Cheltenham, UK: Edward Elgar.

Fischer-Kowalski, M. and W. Huettler. 1998. 'Society's metabolism: the intellectual history of material flow analysis, part II, 1970–1998.' *Journal of Industrial Ecology* 2(4): 107–136.

Funtowicz, S. and J.R. Ravetz. 1994. 'The worth of a songbird: ecological economics as a post-normal science.' *Ecological Economics* 10(3): 197–207.

Gamboa, G. and G. Munda. 2007. 'The problem of wind-park location: a social multi-criteria evaluation framework.' *Energy Policy* 35(3): 1564–1583.

Gerber, J.F. 2008. 'Conflicts over tree plantations: a preliminary comparison between a Cameroonian and an Ecuadorian case study.' Paper given at Tenth Biennial Conference, International Society for Ecological Economics, Nairobi, 7–11 August.

Giampietro, M. 2003. *Multi-scale Integrated Analysis of Agroecosystems*. Boca Raton, FL: CRC Press.

Giljum, S. and N. Eisenmenger. 2004. 'North–South trade and the distribution of environmental goods and burdens.' *Journal of Environment and Development* 13(1): 73–100.

Gordon, L. 1976. *Woman's Body, Woman's Right: A Social History of Birth Control in America*. New York: Grossman.

Grove, R. and V. Damodaran. 2006. 'Imperialism, intellectual networks, and environmental change: origins and evolution of global environmental history 1676–2000' (in two parts). *Economic and Political Weekly* 41(41): 4345–4354; 41(42): 4497–4505.

Guha, R. 1989. *The Unquiet Woods: Ecological Change and Peasant Resistance in the Himalaya*. New Delhi: Oxford University Press.

Guha, R. and J. Martinez-Alier. 1997. *Varieties of Environmentalism: Essays North and South*. London: Earthscan.

Haberl, H. 2001. 'The energetic metabolism of societies. Part I: Accounting concepts, the energetic metabolism of societies, Part II: Empirical examples.' *Journal of Industrial Ecology* 5(2): 71–88.

Haberl, H., K.H. Erb, F. Krausmann, V. Gaube, A. Bondeau, C. Plutzar, S. Gingrich, W. Lucht and M. Fischer-Kowalski. 2007. 'Quantifying and mapping the human appropriation of net primary production in the Earth's terrestrial ecosystems.' *Proceedings of the National Academy of Sciences* 104(31): 12942–12947.

Hall, C., C.J. Cleveland and R. Kaufman. 1986. *The Ecology of the Economic Process: Energy and Resources Quality*. Chichester, UK: John Wiley.

Hayek, F.A. von. 1952. *The Counter-revolution of Science*. Glencoe, IL: Free Press.

Hoekstra, A.Y. and P.Q. Hung. 2005. 'Globalisation of water resources: international virtual water flows in relation to crop trade.' *Global Environmental Change* 15(1): 45–56.

Hornborg, A. 1998. 'Towards an ecological theory of unequal exchange: articulating world system theory and ecological economics.' *Ecological Economics* 25(1): 127–136.

Kapp, K.W. 1955. Book review: *Einführung in die Theorie der Zentralverwaltungswirtschaft* by K. Paul Hensel. *American Economic Review* 45(4): 682–685.

Kormondy, E.J. ed. 1965. *Readings in Ecology*. Englewoods Cliffs, NJ: Prentice Hall.

Leach, G. 1975. *Energy and Food Production*. Guildford, UK: IPC Science and Technology Press.

Lewis, R.R. 2001. 'Mangrove restoration: costs and benefits of successful ecological restoration.' In *Proceedings of Mangrove Valuation Workshop, Universiti Sains Malaysia, Penang, 4–8 April*. Stockholm: Beijer International Institute of Ecological Economics.

Lotka, A.J. 1925. *Elements of Physical Biology*. Baltimore: Williams and Wilkins.

Lutz, W., W.C. Sanderson and S. Scherbov. 2004. *The End of World Population Growth in the 21st Century: New Challenges for Human Capital Formation and Sustainable Development*. London: Earthscan.

Machado, G., R. Schaeffer and E. Worrell. 2001. 'Energy and carbon embodied in the international trade of Brazil: an input–output approach.' *Ecological Economics* 39(3): 409–424.

McNeill, J. 2001. *Something New under the Sun: An Environmental History of the Twentieth-Century World*. New York: W. W. Norton.

McNeill, J. 2003. 'Observations on the nature and culture of environmental history.' *History and Theory* 42(4): 5–43.

Maddison, A. 2001. *The World Economy: A Millennial Perspective*. Paris: Development Centre, OECD.

Mallon, F.E. 1983. *The Defense of Community in Peru's Central Highlands: Peasant Struggle and Capitalist Transition, 1860–1940*. Princeton, NJ: Princeton University Press.

Martinez-Alier, J. 2007a. 'Social metabolism and environmental conflicts.' *Socialist Register* 43.

Martinez-Alier, J. 2007b. 'Marxism, social metabolism and international trade.' In *Rethinking Environmental History: World-System History and Global Environmental Change*, ed. A. Hornborg, J. McNeill and J. Martinez-Alier. Lanham, MD: AltaMira Press.

Martinez-Alier, J. with K. Schlüpmann. 1987. *Ecological Economics: Energy, Environment and Society*. Oxford: Blackwell.

Martinez-Alier, J., G. Munda and J. O'Neill. 1998. 'Weak comparability of values as a foundation for ecological economics.' *Ecological Economics* 26(3): 277–286.

Masjuan, E. 2000. *La ecología humana y el anarquismo ibérico: el urbanismo 'orgánico' o ecológico, el neo-malthusianismo y el naturismo social*. Barcelona: Icaria.

Melville, E. 1994. *A Plague of Sheep: Environmental Consequences of the Conquest of Mexico*. Cambridge: Cambridge University Press.

Moriguchi, Y. 2007. 'Material flow indicators to measure progress toward a sound material-cycle society.' *Journal of Material Cycles and Waste Management* 9(2): 112–120.

Mosley, S. 2006. 'Common ground: integrating social and environmental history.' *Journal of Social History* 39(3): 915–933.

Muradian, R., M. O'Connor and J. Martinez-Alier. 2002. 'Embodied pollution in trade: estimating the "environmental load displacement" of industrialized countries.' *Ecological Economics* 41(1): 51–67.

Naredo, J.M. 2001. 'Quantifying natural capital: beyond monetary value.' In *The Sustainability of Long-Term Growth: Socioeconomic and Ecological Perspectives*, ed. M. Munasinghe, O. Sunkel and C. de Miguel. Cheltenham, UK: Edward Elgar.

Odum, H.T. 1971. *Environment, Power, and Society*. New York: John Wiley.

O'Neill, J. 2002. 'Socialist calculation and environmental valuation: money, markets and ecology.' *Science and Society* 66(1): 137–151.

O'Neill, J. 2004. 'Ecological economics and the politics of knowledge: the debate between Hayek and Neurath.' *Cambridge Journal of Economics* 28(3): 431–447.

Ortega Santos, A. 2002. *La tragedia de los cerramientos: desarticulación de la comunidad en la provincia de Granada*. Alzira, Valencia: Instituto de Historia Social.

Peluso, N.L. 1992. *Rich Forests, Poor People: Resource Control and Resistance in Java*. Berkeley: University of California Press.

Pengue, W.A. 2005. 'Transgenic crops in Argentina: the ecological and social debt.' *Bulletin of Science, Technology and Society* 25(4): 314–322.

Pérez-Rincón, M.A. 2006. 'Colombian international trade from a physical perspective: towards an ecological "Prebisch thesis".' *Ecological Economics* 59(4): 519–529.

Pimentel, D., L.E. Hurd, A.C. Bellotti, M.J. Forster, I.N. Oka, O.D. Sholes and R.J. Whitman. 1973. 'Food production and the energy crisis.' *Science* 182(4111): 443–449.

Pimentel, D. and M. Pimentel. 1979. *Food, Energy and Society*. London: Arnold.

Radkau, J. 2008. *Nature and Power: A Global History of the Environment*. Cambridge: Cambridge University Press.

Rappaport, R. 1967. *Pigs for the Ancestors: Ritual in the Ecology of a New Guinea People*. New Haven, CT: Yale University Press.

Ronsin, F. 1980. *La Grève des ventres: propagande néo-malthusienne et baisse de la natalité en France, 19e–20e siècles*. Paris: Aubier-Montaigne.

Sathirathai, S. and E. Barbier. 2003. 'Comparative returns of mangroves for shrimp farming and local direct and indirect uses in Surat Thani Province.' In *Shrimp Farming and Mangrove Loss in Thailand*, ed. E. Barbier and S. Sathirathai. Cheltenham, UK: Edward Elgar.

Schmidt, A. 1978. *Der Begriff der Natur in der Lehre von Marx*, 3rd ed. Frankfurt am Main: EVA.

Shanker, K. 2007. 'Deconstructing sea turtle conservation in India.' In *Making Conservation Work: Securing Biodiversity in this New Century*, ed. G. Shahabuddin and M. Rangajaran. Delhi: Permanent Black.

Sieferle, R.P. 2001. *The Subterranean Forest: Energy Systems and the Industrial Revolution.*

Cambridge: White Horse Press. Originally published as *Der unterirdische Wald. Energiekrise und industrielle Revolution*. Munich: C.H. Beck, 1982.

Smil, V. 1991. *General Energetics: Energy in the Biosphere and Civilization*. New York: John Wiley.

Sukhdev, P. ed. 2008. *The Economics of Ecosystems and Biodiversity (TEEB)*. Cambridge: Banson.

Susiluoto, I. 1982. *The Origins and Development of Systems Thinking in the Soviet Union: Political and Philosophical Controversies from Bogdanov and Bukharin to Present-Day Reevaluations*. Helsinki: Suomalainen Tiedeakatemia.

Temper, L. and J. Martinez-Alier. 2007. 'Is India too poor to be green?' *Economic and Political Weekly* 42(17): 1489–1492.

Thomas, W.L., C.O. Sauer, M. Bates and L. Mumford eds. 1956. *Man's Role in Changing the Face of the Earth*. Chicago: University of Chicago Press.

Uebel, T.E. 2005. 'Incommensurability, ecology and planning: Neurath in the socialist calculation debate, 1919–1928.' *History of Political Economy* 37(2): 309–342.

Uttig, P. and J. Clapp eds. 2008. *Corporate Accountability and Sustainable Development*. New Delhi: Oxford University Press.

Vanucci, M. ed. 2004. *Mangrove Management and Conservation: Present and Future*. Paris: United Nations University Press.

Vernadsky, V. 1924. *La Géochimie*. Paris: Alcan.

Vitousek, P.M., P.R. Ehrlich, A.H. Ehrlich and P.A. Matson. 1986. 'Human appropriation of the products of photosynthesis.' *BioScience* 36(6): 363–373.

Weber, M. 1909. 'Energetische Kulturtheorien: Besprechung von Wilhelm Ostwalds "Energetische Grundlagen der Kulturwissenschaft".' *Archiv für Sozialwissenschaft und Sozialpolitik* 29(2): 575–598.

Weber, M. 1978. *Economy and Society: An Outline of Interpretive Sociology*, 2 vols. Berkeley: University of California Press.

Weisz, H., F. Krausmann, C. Amann, N. Eisenmenger, K.H. Erb, K. Hubacek and M. Fischer-Kowalski. 2006. 'The physical economy of the European Union: cross-country comparison and determinants of material consumption.' *Ecological Economics* 58(4): 676–698.

White, L.A. 1943. 'Energy and the evolution of culture.' *American Anthropologist* 45(3): 335–356.

White, L.A. 1959. 'The energy theory of cultural development.' In *Readings in Anthropology*, vol. 2, ed. M.H. Fried. New York: Thomas Y. Cromwell.

Zografos, C. and J. Martínez-Alier. 2009. 'The politics of landscape value: a case study of wind farm conflict in rural Catalonia.' *Environment and Planning A* 41(7): 1726–1744.

3 What lies beyond reductionism?

Taking stock of interdisciplinary research in ecological economics

Katharine N. Farrell, Tommaso Luzzati and Sybille van den Hove

Introduction

Although it is now commonplace to call for interdisciplinary study of social-ecological systems, the question of how one is to carry out such study remains largely open. Our aim in this chapter is to shed some light on that question, based on a small but growing discourse concerning inter- and transdisciplinary research methodology. We begin by reviewing two areas of interdisciplinary social-ecological systems (SES) research with which we have experience as researchers and evaluators: biodiversity loss and mega-contaminated site remediation. On the basis of this review we propose an ontology of SES research and develop some suggestions regarding how effective SES research methodologies can be developed. We then conclude the chapter with a series of concrete suggestions regarding how it may be possible to develop and evaluate the quality of integrative interdisciplinary SES research methods.

A first notable characteristic, common to all SES research projects, which we take as given in the following pages, is that they are at least multi-, generally inter- and often transdisciplinary. That is to say, the pool of knowledge required to investigate an SES research problematique must, by definition (since it is concerned with social-ecological relationships), span at least two and often several disciplines and is likely to have at least a policy relevance, if not a direct policy advice or even policy design orientation (Costanza 1989; Norgaard 1989; Max-Neef 2005).[1]

In recent years a great number of subtly different definitions have been proposed for distinguishing between the three categories of multi-, inter- and transdisciplinarity. Distilling them to a few common denominators, we can say that multidisciplinary research collates completed pieces of disciplinary work; that interdisciplinary research integrates various discipline-based contributions in the course of problem formulation, method development and application, and analysis of results: while transdisciplinary work moves beyond the domain of disciplinarity, generating new approaches to scientific knowledge production that either transcend the formalism of a discipline altogether and/or operationalize integrative collaborations between academics and non-academics, such as local communities and/or policy-makers, as a core part of the scientific work.

While it has been our experience that SES research projects tend to have elements of all three, we focus in this chapter only on interdisciplinarity, for two reasons. First, we believe that interdisciplinarity, as opposed to multidisciplinarity, is necessary for SES research; and second, we see it as a precondition for and logical antecedent to transdisciplinarity, which should therefore also serve as the foundation for developing transdisciplinary methodology.[2]

From our experience in the field, effective interdisciplinary collaboration is not something that just happens automatically when scientists from various disciplines sit down together but something that needs to be actively brought into being through the development of interdisciplinary research methods. For example, in HERMES, a large-scale research project concerned with deep-sea biology and sustainable exploitation of marine systems resources, biologists, oceanographers and economists involved in the project had fundamentally different concerns and research aims, all of which were independently important but which somehow needed to be combined.[3] Questions regarding the boundaries of viability of an exploited species' population are related to the biological needs of the organism in question, the dynamics of the ocean currents that provide them with oxygen and nutrients, and the dynamics of human exploitation. In order to develop coherent representations of the study objects for such research, some of the knowledge must come from species specialists conducting population surveys and studying the biological organisms within the system, some from oceanographers studying the dynamics of the system within which these organisms live and some from economists studying the ways in which humans are interacting with this environment and with the exploited species (Armstrong *et al.* 2009). While the methodological question of how to develop understanding of social-ecological systems, which must span social and physical science disciplines, is increasingly on the table for discussion (Kates *et al.* 2001; Nowotny *et al.* 2001, Max-Neef 2005, Hirsch Hadorn *et al.* 2008), this is still a very young discourse. Formal discussion of questions concerning interdisciplinary research design and quality control are still rare and tend to be quite broad in their scope (e.g. Birnbaum-More *et al.* 1990; Thompson Klein 1990; Thompson Klein *et al.* 2000; Nicolescu 1999), whereas work focused more tightly around SES research (e.g. Jasanoff and Wynne 1998; Mayumi and Giampietro 2006; Norgaard 2004; van den Hove 2007; Pielke 2007) – with notable recent exceptions such as Max-Neef (2005) and Hirsch Hadorn *et al.* (2006, 2008) – still tends to be focused on why inter- and transdisciplinary research is required, where it should be applied and what it can accomplish, rather than on how integration of interdisciplinary data and analysis can or should work in practice. An important first step in addressing this second question, and our main focus in this chapter, is to develop a clear ontological description of the characteristics of SES research and the operating contexts within which it is embedded – that is, documenting the attributes of and relationships between the aims, available tools and study objects of SES research.

We do this by drawing from our own experience and from other writings on the topic, which we use to identify a set of six key attributes that we propose are common to all SES research projects: (1) complexity, (2) ontological diversity, (3) methodological diversity, (4) dominance and gatekeeper disciplines, (5) a dual role for social science, and (6) team research. On the basis of the attributes of ontological and methodological diversity, we then distinguish between four basic types of interdisciplinary discourse – political, ontological, methodological and technical – which, we propose, require different methodological approaches. Next, we propose two overarching aspects of SES research design – discursive context and alien/ally dialectic dynamics – that can be actively managed in order to make the most of a given project's unique interdisciplinarity: discursive context is related to the ontological and methodological diversity of a given project and associated research team, and alien/ally dialectic dynamics to how the team functions as a whole (see Figure 3.1).

By identifying a set of key attributes common to all SES research projects, we are able to formalize discussion of their methodology development while still respecting the need to develop more or less unique interdisciplinary research methodologies for each individual project. Accordingly, instead of suggesting a universal methodology, our aim is to point towards the kinds of issues that it might be good to keep in mind when developing project-specific methodologies.

Finally, we consider three practical questions that are likely to arise with the implementation of our suggestions: what kinds of institutional research contexts might be more or less conducive to this kind of interdisciplinary work? What kind of educational practices might be required to prepare both junior and senior scientists for carrying out research in the ways that we propose? And how might the results of research based on these new methodologies be validated?

Two illustrations: biodiversity and Bitterfeld

When considering the characteristics of SES research we find there are some basic shared starting points common to all projects of this type. First, there is, whether implicitly or explicitly, a predisposition towards process philosophy

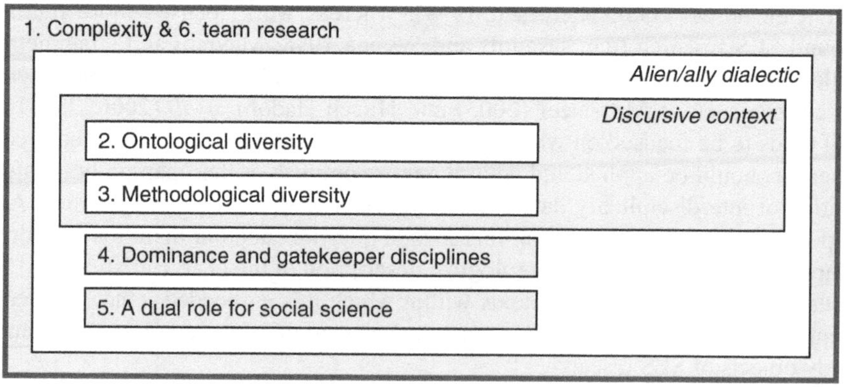

Figure 3.1 A working ontology of the typical SES research project.

(see Whitehead 1978); the idea that not only things but also processes are important is central to SES research. In addition, there is a living systems orientation, where the open systems and far-from-equilibrium thermodynamics of the processes associated with being and staying alive are seen as particularly important (see Schrödinger 1948 [1944]; Prigogine 1997). Finally, there is a complexity orientation – that is to say, a tendency to look not only at the parts but also at their relationships to each other and to their environments: presumptions of simple and deterministic cause and effect relationships are generally seen to be inadequate for SES research work, in principle if not always in practice (see Costanza 1989).

However, these are all very general points. They can guide a discourse but not a project. When concrete research begins, the question of how these and other relevant presumptions work together in practice must be addressed in greater detail by the researchers carrying out the work. In order to get a feel for what may be required to accomplish this, we begin by reviewing two concrete SES research topics that we have studied at length and in detail (van den Hove 2004; Farrell 2008c).

Illustration I: the loss of biodiversity

The loss of biodiversity has been a topic of scientific research for some time (if not always under that name), whether as an aspect of palaeoecology and related fields concerned with evolution or, more recently, in its own right. In the 1970s it came onto international political and research agendas in the form of concerns regarding (1) the possibility that large mammals, such as the blue whale, might actually become extinct as a result of human activities; and (2) large-scale die-offs of whole populations and ecosystems in agricultural environments, as first reported by Carson (1963) in her classic text *Silent Spring*.

Beginning with the 1972 revision of the Federal Insecticide, Fungicide, and Rodenticide Act of 1947 in the United States, which set new controls on the use and handling of pesticides, and the 1975 Convention on International Trade in Endangered Species of Wild Flora and Fauna (CITES), which gave full protection to several species, there now exists a set of formal international targets and objectives relating to avoiding the loss of biodiversity, culminating in the 1992 Convention on Biodiversity.

Biodiversity loss, as it is discussed today, rests at the boundary between various disciplines and between science and policy. The development of strategies for reducing and avoiding the loss of biodiversity is inevitably an inter- and transdisciplinary task that must draw insights and information from both social and physical science disciplines as well as from policy and political actors coming from local all the way through to global levels.

In a meta-study concerning the impacts of a number of European Union funded biodiversity research projects, van den Hove (2004) found that they all put a strong emphasis on interdisciplinarity. For instance, the OASIS project proposed an interdisciplinary scientific study of seamounts (offshore mountains in the sea) that integrates physical, biogeochemical, socio-economic and biological research.[4] Lessons to be learned from the OASIS approach to interdisciplinarity lie in quality of the dialogue and collaboration achieved between disciplines. This led to high-quality outputs in terms of integration. In this project the socio-economic aspects of the problem were formally identified and an institutional analysis framework was developed. However, even here the socio-economic work was mostly the task of a non-governmental organization (NGO) research partner, the World Wildlife Fund (WWF), and was not integrated with the other research. In the final analysis, several partners pointed to the need to integrate social and economic research in future marine biodiversity projects.

Van den Hove (2004) also reports interdisciplinarity as one of the major successes of the MacMan project, which effectively brought together ecologists, conservationists, laboratory geneticists, policy-makers and field ecologists in order to produce a common output concerning protection of butterfly habitats.[5] Here 'the coordinator stressed that the reviewer's comment [that MacMan is a pedagogical goldmine] during a project meeting "really was important as it has put more confidence to those interested in education; finally a working group on specifically this topic was created during the last day of the meeting"' (ibid.: 9–10). From a policy point of view the fact that the interdisciplinarity of the MacMan project went beyond science into transdisciplinarity is also important.

Finally, BioScene, which set out to investigate the implications for biodiversity conservation of agricultural system restructuring, decline and/or abandonment in Europe's mountain areas, provided an example of a project that was explicitly pursuing strong interdisciplinarity between ecological and socio-economic sciences. In each country where the project was run, there was both an ecological and a socio-economic partner, and the coordinator identified interdisciplinarity as the critical challenge for developing the project's policy-relevant research. When reflecting on the achievements of the project, he identified (i) difficulties associated with understanding the languages of different disciplines and (ii) a lack of practical real-time interaction between scientists from different disciplines, as two key barriers to successful collaboration. Interestingly, in those countries where the natural and social scientists involved in the project were physically working at the same premises, communication was found to be easier. This echoes insights from an early overview of interdisciplinary research methods presented by Birnbaum-More *et al.* (1990: 74), who note in their summary that '[i]nterteam communication is a critical factor in the process of IDR [interdisciplinary research] ... where physical proximity of team members leads to increased interaction'.

When research addresses complex, pressing and irreversible environmental change issues such as biodiversity loss, the aim of producing policy-relevant knowledge is central to the work, and the integrating of physical and social science approaches will often – if not always – be needed. This field of SES research can be understood as issue-driven, inter- and transdisciplinary (see Funtowicz and Ravetz 1994; van den Hove 2001, 2007; Lawrence and Després

2004). By this we mean, on the one hand, that the structure of the problems studied is determined by social and political (as opposed to purely scientific or private) considerations, and on the other, that the specified problem can only be understood when social and physical scientific studies are applied at the same time as and in conjunction with each other. Furthermore, since anthropogenic biodiversity loss is a consequence of collective human actions at local, regional and international levels, not only economic but also various other social science assessments (such as assessments from psychology, sociology, political studies, anthropology, history, human geography, philosophy, marketing, law, management studies and education) are relevant to understanding how and why it is happening. Although often called for, interdisciplinary research concerning the loss of biodiversity is still hindered by several barriers, many of them of a social or institutional nature.

First, there is the problem that scientists are often not rewarded by the academic system for interdisciplinary research. Investing time and energy into an interdisciplinary project can lead to difficulties in publishing in high-ranking academic journals, fewer opportunities for promotion and less recognition by 'monodisciplinary' peers (Bruce *et al.* 2004). Here it seems that significant cultural shifts are required in the academic world (its journals, performance targets, training, etc.) if scientists are to be encouraged to do interdisciplinary work.

Another difficulty is related to communication. Scientists from different disciplines may have difficulties understanding the concepts and methodologies used in other disciplines. Since a certain degree of disciplinary focus is needed if the research is to engage with its subject at depth, this is not something that can or should be overcome entirely. Nonetheless, in such situations simple communication is not enough. Where conflict leads to deadlock, and even in instances where scientists from different disciplines think they are understanding each other, an additional layer of communication about their communication (see Watzlawick *et al.* 1967) would seem to be required. In our experience we have found that with effort, goodwill, time and a good management structure (where opportunities for dialogue, debate and cross-learning exist), communication across disciplines can and does work, even when major differences of understanding remain. However, time and resources need to be set aside to support this work, and scientists from different disciplines need to be willing and able to engage in this higher-order meta-communication. At least within research concerning the loss of biodiversity, the priorities of the individual researchers and of their formal commitments within a given research project seem to have important impacts on this willingness.

Related to this is the issue of lack of training and experience. Many scientists who find themselves working within interdisciplinary projects have little or no experience with interdisciplinary approaches to research. Even among those who have worked on several projects carrying the interdisciplinarity label, the tendency for failed attempts to be discussed during the coffee beaks at conferences, rather than within the projects reports, means that there is still little experience with the methodological reflection that is our focus here.[6] We have the impression that coordinators of, and participants within, SES research projects are interested in learning how to carry out integrative interdisciplinary research but simply do not know where or how to begin.

Finally, difficulty with achieving integration also seems to arise where interdisciplinary teams of researchers begin collaborations by trying to combine abstract concepts from the various disciplines – attempting, for example, to fit together similarly structured mathematical algorithms, rather than bringing their applied insights to bear on practical, concrete issues. The result can be situations where the combination of seemingly similar approaches leaves fundamental differences in their application contexts unaddressed (e.g. Sousa and Domingos 2004).

From the examples presented in this chapter, it would seem that interdisciplinary research concerning loss of biodiversity requires more time and resources than disciplinary research. Although this may seem an obvious point, we find it to be far from trivial, since both need to be approved for inclusion in research budgets. Collaboration tools need to be developed and new methods learned. In particular, it would appear that greater resources and attention need to be invested in the following areas (adapted from van den Hove 2004: 8):

- Epistemological knowledge and methodological approaches for interdisciplinary research should be further developed and disseminated towards those who are aiming at interdisciplinary biodiversity research.
- Options for high-quality interdisciplinary training should be increased and made available not only to young researchers but also to established scientists who wish to carry out interdisciplinary work.
- Funding agencies can help induce the cultural shift needed to support interdisciplinary research in academia by providing a lead, giving out supportive messages and encouraging funding applications of this kind. To do so, they may need to allow a space for smaller-scale applied research projects, the lessons of which can then be learned more widely by subsequently bringing researchers together in larger projects and by supporting research specifically concerned with developing criteria for judging the quality of interdisciplinary work.
- Evaluation of research proposals could encourage high-quality interdisciplinary endeavours to develop issue-oriented research. It would be necessary to give clear criteria and instructions to proposers and evaluation panels, and to select panels that have the expertise required to evaluate interdisciplinary proposals.

Illustration II: management of mega-contaminated industrial sites

'Mega-contaminated site' is a term developed within the physical sciences to describe industrial sites with a large number of interconnected and potentially interacting individual sites of anthropogenic contamination covering a large area. The particular contamination site discussed here is located in the industrial city of Bitterfeld in the German state of Saxony-Anhalt. The city of Bitterfeld played a central role in the development of Germany's chemical industry before and during the two world wars and continued to be a centre for chemical manufacture during the period 1949–1989, when it was part of the German Democratic Republic (GDR) (Banzhaf and Kasperidus 1998; Banzhaf 1999; Mühlenberg and Kurt 1991). Following the fall of the Berlin Wall in 1989, the contamination in Bitterfeld, which had been accumulating since the nineteenth century, became a major environmental management issue for the reunified German government. In 1991, when efforts to deal with the contamination in Bitterfeld began in earnest, the German Green Party (*die Grünen*) was in control of the Ministry of Environment and a clear focus on cleaning up the site was established.

Researchers at the Helmholtz Centre for Environmental Research – UFZ have been studying various technical and social aspects of the situation in Bitterfeld for the past twenty years. However, that research has been overwhelmingly oriented towards physical science, looking mainly at problems of contaminant migration, toxicity, physical and chemical control of contaminate flows, and remediation of the pollution. The social science studies of Bitterfeld have focused on outmigration and economic change associated with closure of the vast majority of the city's industrial plants (Banzhaf and Kasperidus 1998; Banzhaf 1999). Social science aspects of the contamination remediation work, such as the impacts on the lifestyles of local residents, or the potential contributions they might be able to make towards remediation work, have been left largely un-investigated (for an exception, see Ring 1997).[7]

From a social science perspective, mega-contaminated sites fall into one of two basic categories: population-exposed sites and remote sites. The distinction lies in the proximity of the contamination site to centres of human habitation and potential for contaminants to migrate to these centres over time – via, for example, groundwater or wind flows. While remote sites can present major risks to non-human habitats and ecosystems, the social scientific and political issues at play are qualitatively different with human population-exposed sites.

Bitterfeld is a population-exposed site and social scientists can play an important role in helping to identify appropriate remediation strategies that minimize the current risks and long-term impacts of human exposure (Farrell *et al.* 2007; Schirmer *et al.* 2012). However, the potential contributions that any scientist can make to an interdisciplinary research project are constrained by how the project's research problem has been defined. In the case of Bitterfeld, research relating to the mega-site has been defined almost exclusively in terms of technological solutions focused on containment and site clean-up, leaving little scope for social science.

One example of the human aspects of this situation is the decision-problem of whether to reflood the Goitszche brown coal strip mine located directly next to a main contamination site in Bitterfeld. Taking this decision included a variety of physical and social implications. The reflooded lake could constitute an amenity for the citizens, following a model applied in the state of Saxony, where the Markleeberg and Cospudener recreational lakes had been developed from closed brown coal strip mines (Kabisch and Linke 2002; Hannemann *et al.* 2002; Kabisch 2003). However, the possible interplay between reflooding and contamination also needed to be taken into account. Although the mine had been closed since 1990, and several other mines had already been converted into lakes, it was not obvious whether or not the Goitzsche mine should be reflooded, and no action towards reflooding had been taken up until 2002. A general feel for the difficulties of the situation can be gathered from the following statement, made in a 1998 report on groundwater remediation strategies at the site: ' "Active" measures for groundwater remediation on a regional scale are not under consideration owing to the volumes involved and the *ad infinitum* emission of pollutants from the landfills' (Weiss *et al.* 1998: 85, italics added). In the end, nature took the decision that humans could not, when the nearby Mulde River spilled over into the Goitzsche mine in 2002.

The social and ecological consequences of that flooding would seem to be mixed. While there were immediate problems with subsidence and contamination (Kasimir and Friede 2003; Rank *et al.* 2003; Schultze *et al.* 2003), in the medium to long term it would appear that the rapid introduction of biologically active river water into the mine may be helping metabolize and fix some of the pollutants leaking from the contamination site (Hervida 2003). On the social side, attempts have been made, subsequent to the flooding, to develop Goitzsche Lake into a watersports tourist attraction. However, little progress has been made in that direction. In 2007 the city hall in Bitterfeld was closed and the administration of the city was combined with that of neighbouring Wolfen (Flämig *et al.* 2007).

Managing the contamination and associated human exposure in Bitterfeld is a complex problem. Modelling likely contaminant migration pathways, in the event of a new flood, is at best extremely difficult, if not impossible. However, this type of modelling now constitutes the main thrust of social ecological systems-oriented research concerning the mega-site (i.e. Tümpling *et al.* 2006).

Bitterfeld was one of the first industrial cities in the world, and a model city during the GDR era (Lange and Schreck 1959). The people of this city have worked with chemicals for generations and were aware, to some degree, of the contamination. Their knowledge regarding how the contamination occurred and their views regarding the level of exposure they are willing to risk could provide valuable inputs for SES research concerning environmental politics, history and sociology. However, analysis regarding the impacts and risks associated with human exposure in Bitterfeld has tended to focus on humans as the end point in the contaminant-flow pathway, treating the city's inhabitants as objects of study rather than collaborators (Heidrich *et al.* 2004; Herbarth *et al.* 2005).

An attempt in 2006 to study some of the social science issues mentioned above was abandoned, as the social and political complexity of the case made the planned research unrealistic (Farrell 2008c). In spite of these complexities, the strong (and perhaps inevitable) dominance of physical science framings of the remediation research in Bitterfeld seems also to be contributing towards the dearth of social scientific study. Coping with the physical contamination was an immediate and overwhelming task in the early 1990s, when the tone for scientific engagement with this problem was set. As a result, the vast majority of the individuals with expertise concerning the contamination in Bitterfeld are physical scientists, some of whom have now spent the better part of their careers focused mainly on this and related sites throughout eastern Germany. The result has been what we may call a hydrogeology/chemistry dominance in the character of any interdisciplinary research project concerned with the topic of mega-site remediation in Bitterfeld.

Some special attributes of interdisciplinary research

Reflecting on the two illustrations in the previous section, in this section we elaborate six key features of SES research that seem to us to be inevitable characteristics of the work: (1) complexity; (2) ontological diversity; (3) methodological diversity; (4) dominance and gatekeeper disciplines; (5) a dual role for social science; and (6) team research. Our aim in doing so is to help develop an ontology of SES research that can be used to inform the associated work of methodology design.

Complexity

It is generally agreed that it is helpful to understand the main study objects of SES research as complex systems. Following Bertalanffy (1950), we can understand complexity to be that which occurs at the level of the complex. It is those attributes and aspects, not observable when the components are separated, that make the whole greater than the sum of its parts. When conducting integrative interdisciplinary study of the complexity of SES research study objects, teams of researchers, made up of individuals and groups, each focused on their particular part of the problem, must somehow collectively characterize this complexity. For this, descriptions not only of the wholes and their parts but also of relationships between the two are required. Just as the functioning of a living organism depends upon both the purpose-specific functioning of its individual organs and their coherent cooperation towards the common purpose of maintaining the integrity of the organism, so too both individual disciplinary and collaborative interdisciplinary work play a role in structuring an interdisciplinary research project. In this respect, SES research projects can be understood as complex systems in their own right and can be expected to be as unique as any other complex system.

Ontological diversity

We have proposed in this chapter that there are some rudimentary shared starting points (ontological presumptions) common to all SES research projects, such as their focus on living systems and the presumption that both physical and social scientific inquiry, as well as some degree of cooperation with policy-makers, is required to generate meaningful research results. However, we have also argued that interdisciplinary integration of SES research requires not only broad but also deep, discipline-specific engagement with the objects of study. This means that a range of discipline-specific ontologies are simultaneously contributing to the work of an SES research team. Where ontologies are compatible – for example, between oceanography and chemistry, which have the ontological basis of physics in common – the potential for synergies and easy combination of data and analysis is high. However, where ontologies are incompatible – as, for example, between genetics and human psychology – there is potential for misunderstanding, confusion and absence of integration.

Failure to systematically consider how ontological commonalities and differences support or inhibit interdisciplinary collaboration amounts to default selection of an interdisciplinary methodology that prioritizes integration at the points of least resistance: between ontologically compatible disciplines.

Methodological diversity

Since methodology is fundamentally related to ontology, it follows that where there is ontological diversity, methodological diversity is likely to follow. In SES research projects there is also the added factor that both social and physical science are fundamental to the work. While general principles of orderly investigation and fact verification are common in both physical and social science, there are often substantial methodological differences. Here, we find it helpful to distinguish between what Norgaard (1989) calls methodological pluralism, which we see as a precondition for achieving what we may call methodological complexity, and a sort of methodological randomness, which may arise in situations where multiple methods are applied without any coherent methodology concerning how they fit together.

From our experiences and our reading of a small but growing number of formal studies on the topic (e.g. Birnbaum-More *et al.* 1990; Klein 2008; Boix-Mansilla and Gardner 2003; Boix-Mansilla *et al.* 2006), we suggest that some degree of methodological compatibility between the contributing disciplines is necessary if an SES research project is to achieve integrative results. Keeping in mind the fact that empirical research is structured by methodology, an absence of methodological compatibility within a project can be understood to carry with it an absence of what Maturana and Varela (1980 [1972]; see also Maturana 1978; Varela *et al.* 1974) call structural coupling: the process by which structural relations between a living system and its environment, including other living systems, help it to achieve coherence. Structural coupling is presented by Maturana and Varela as an operational aspect of coordination within and among living systems. Applying the concept here, we may say that where methodological structural coupling is absent, the inevitable methodological diversity of SES research projects can lead to a loss of methodological coherence. Where it is present but not taken into account, the project may take on a distorted methodological profile, favouring the development of methodological trajectories in line with methodological combinations between disciplines that have coupling opportunities, regardless of whether or not these are the combinations that best serve the overall objectives of the research project.

Dominance and gatekeeper disciplines

This last point above, concerning methodological development within an SES research project, leads us to the fourth of our six proposed attributes: dominance and gatekeeper disciplines. Because interdisciplinary research projects are typically designed to address specific, concrete problems, at least with respect to the project, not all disciplines come to the project table with the same authority and power to direct the research work. Regardless of the degree of collaborative spirit, those disciplines closest to the core of the research problem will influence the overall tone and general direction of the work.[8] Much like the dominance found in living systems, such as the tendency for humans to be right-handed, it seems to us that physical scientific approaches have a certain dominance within SES research, where even within projects combining contributions from social and physical science the orientation is often weighted towards physical science methodologies.[9]

Furthermore, if the research is genuinely interdisciplinary, meaning for us that knowledge is created at the interfaces between disciplines, then the work of all disciplines will be dependent upon data contributed by researchers working within other disciplines, and access to data associated with the dominant discipline or disciplines will be at a premium. This means that some disciplines within a project may have what we may call 'gatekeeper status', meaning that, because of their areas of expertise, they have proprietary access to core project data and analysis without which the interdisciplinary work cannot proceed. This is readily observable in both the illustrations presented earlier in this chapter: in research related to mega-site remediation in Bitterfeld it is simply not possible to begin discussing any concrete problem without the involvement of hydrogeologists and chemists; in the research related to loss of biodiversity, biologists and ecologists occupy a similar position. Although these disciplines may not be responsible for framing the general description of an SES research problem, they can nonetheless significantly influence how the research proceeds. The roles, authority, obligations and openness of these gatekeepers towards collaboration will, of course, vary from project to project. Nonetheless, we believe their place within interdisciplinary research methodology should be formally considered when developing project-specific methodologies.

The dual role of social science

Following on from this, we can see that social scientists may have, in addition to their content-related contributions, a second role to play in interdisciplinary team research (see Farrell 2004, 2008b; Farrell *et al.* 2005; Meadowcroft *et al.* 2005; Schiller *et al.* 2006; van den Hove 2007) because interdisciplinary research is a social activity. While interdisciplinary research methodology is an operational problem for all the researchers involved in an SES research project, methodological questions may also be empirical objects of analytical interest to social scientists (see Kuhn 1970 [1962]; Ravetz 1971; Latour and Woolgar 1979). If this second social science role is recognized within a project team, then social scientists may be able to help with the design and implementation of methods for supporting interdisciplinary collaboration (Farrell 2009 [2005]; Farrell *et al.* 2005; Meadowcroft *et al.* 2005; Schiller *et al.* 2006; van den Hove 2007).

Team research

Finally, while it may seem an obvious point, we think it is important to note that SES research projects are almost inevitably team research projects. While the need for good teamwork is common to many discipline-specific projects, in an interdisciplinary context it becomes indispensable, because the team cannot move forward without some kind of agreement on how to combine their different types of knowledge. Teamwork also takes on, we believe, certain special characteristics in SES research, owing to the presence of ontological and methodological diversity, which make careful attention to team dynamics particularly important. This diversity may make it easier for reseachers to work together in an interdisciplinary context, since each is, within the project, in a sense master of their discipline. However, it also opens up the door to problems of validation, since there may be no peer review checks carried out on the appropriateness or robustness of discipline-specific contributions. In addition, tensions, misunderstanding and confusion may arise. Since it is not possible to have a technical discussion across disciplines, discussions must shift either to the level of methodology, leaving important empirical contradictions between various approaches entirely unaddressed, or, if there is not even methodological common ground, they may become, in essence, purely political (Meadowcroft *et al.* 2005; Farrell 2009 [2005], 2008a). In both cases, careful, formal attention to team dynamics and to relationships between the various members of the team may mean the difference between superficial or biased discussions and integrative interdisciplinary collaboration.

Making methodologies

We have proposed in this chapter that interdisciplinary SES research methodologies will always be, to some extent, project specific. But if this is the case, how can we specify anything general about their design? Although we cannot be specific about what should be done in each case, we propose that, on the basis of the six attributes of SES research interdisciplinarity outlined above, certain types of issues can be expected to arise. Specifically, we expect: (1) that one of five basic types of discursive contexts (see Table 3.1), determined by the project's ontological and methodological diversity, will give a certain tone to interactions within the team; and (2) that a dialectic of ally and alien relations with the team will help determine its capacity to collaborate effectively. On the basis of the question of how these two dynamics are managed, we propose some general principles for approaching the project-specific work of developing an interdisciplinary research methodology suited to both the composition of team members and the research objectives of a project. Whereas the discursive context of a project – i.e. political or technical – can be understood to set the tone for interdisciplinary interactions, the heuristic of dialectical alien/ally teamwork relations (see Figure 3.2, p. 51) can be used to characterize the particular ontological and methodological diversity arising within a given interdisciplinary team. We propose that by paying attention to its unique interdisciplinary structure, as shaped by its discursive context and managed by its aliens and/or allies, an SES research team can expect a range of more or less predictable consequences for interdisciplinary methodology design and project outcomes, depending upon how the team manages (i) dominance and gatekeeper disciplines, and (ii) the dual role that social science can play in the development of SES research methodologies.

Discursive context

The specific ontological and methodological compatibilities within a given interdisciplinary team can be understood to determine what we call here its discursive context. Where there is both strong ontological and methodological compatibility within a team (Technical – the bottom right corner of Table 3.1), discussions are basically technical, focusing on details concerning how commonly understood objects and processes are to be studied, according to commonly understood methods. Where there is strong ontological compatibility but little or no methodological compatibility (Ontological – top right corner of Table 3.1), we expect the discourse to be more abstract and general, with coherent discussions about the characteristics of the objects of study being possible but concrete discussions regarding how to carry out the research, including how to fit together work from different disciplines, being more difficult.

Similarly, where ontological compatibility is absent, methodological compatibility may nonetheless provide a platform for researchers to communicate about

Table 3.1 Mapping the complexity of interdisciplinary team-level discourses

Methodological compatibility	*Ontological compatibility*		
	Absent	*Weak*	*Strong*
Absent	**Political**	Political/Ontological	**Ontological**
Weak	Political/ Methodological	**Confusion & Creativity**	Ontological/ Technical
Strong	**Methodological**	Methodological/ Technical	**Technical**

how to conduct the research (Methodological – bottom left corner of Table 3.1) even if they are unable to discuss the details of their respective study objects. Here the task of the team is basically to somehow combine multiple, potentially incommensurable discipline-specific representations that cannot be directly compared with each other, in order to develop a coherent, complex picture of the collaborative study object.

Whereas each of these types of discursive context promises some form of common ground, in situations where there is neither ontological nor methodological compatibility present (Political – top left corner of Table 3.1) there is no common scientific basis upon which discussion can proceed. In these situations the capacity to influence the course of a discussion is political; it can be based only on credibility that 'resides in institutional position or has its source in purely personal qualities' (O'Neill 1993: 126; Farrell 2009 [2005], 2008a). As was discussed earlier, with regard to ontological and methodological diversity, it has been our experience that such political debates can happen in both mono- and interdisciplinary settings. However, in SES research projects, where physical and social scientists are *expected* to collaborate, both the likelihood that the discourse will become political and the stakes involved in this happening are higher, since the content of the research will depend on the outcomes of this interdisciplinary discourse.

Finally, where both ontological and methodological compatibility are present but weak (the centre of Table 3.1), there is basis for dialogue, room for learning, as well as plenty of room for misunderstanding. We have labelled this type of discursive context 'Confusion & Creativity'. Here, new ways of thinking about and doing research will need to be developed by the team specifically for the SES research project in question in order for the work to proceed. Since there are only weak links, they will need to be strengthened to support the execution of solid work, while at the same time their presence means that the group has a common basis for beginning the collaborative work of interdisciplinary integration. Here, effective teamwork and careful attention to processes and methods of collaboration become critical for the success of the entire project. For example, the attitude of researchers based within a dominant or gatekeeper discipline, with whom all team members *must* collaborate, can set the tone for all collaborative relationships, since establishing alliances with them is the only clear reference point for choosing negotiation strategies.

Teamwork dialectics: the alien, the ally and the other

This leads us to the question of how an SES research project team can make the most of the interdisciplinarity at its disposal. First, it seems that a general spirit of discursive ethics – where the collaborators enter the discourse with a willingness to listen to each other and to negotiate (see Habermas 1984, 1987, 1996; O'Hara 1996) – is needed if team-level discourse about interdisciplinary methods is to be constructive. From there forward, the specific challenges will depend, in large part, on the project objectives and the composition of the project team.

As a general rule, acknowledging differences within the group can be viewed as a first step towards opening up possibilities to formally discuss the character of those differences. However, if there is no common ontological or methodological ground whatsoever, contributing researchers may still find it very difficult to work together. Here, shared purpose and goodwill towards the collaboration would seem to be exceptionally important.[10] Using the heuristic of an alien/ally dialectical relationship (Figure 3.2) to explore a spectrum of potential collaboration styles, we can begin to discuss the character of these collaborative dynamics in a formalized manner while avoiding the fool's errand of trying to specify an infinite and indeterminate set of possible situations.

For our purposes, anyone who has a viewpoint or way of knowing that I cannot understand at all can be understood to be alien to me. Someone whose viewpoint or way of knowing is unfamiliar but accessible to me may be farther away from my position than an ally, whom I understand well and with whom I agree, but closer than an alien. We call this middle position 'the other' and propose that interdisciplinary integration can take place – and perhaps is even most effective – among 'others', while only multidisciplinary collaboration is possible among aliens, and transdisciplinary work, a subject with which we do not concern ourselves directly in this chapter, is attributed to teams made up of allies.[11]

Ancient and Renaissance intellectuals from around the world regularly engaged with big, deep questions as individuals. However, they were operating in a world where there was little or no distinction between disciplines and where substantially less knowledge needed to be processed. By contrast, in recent centuries reductionism has increased the depth at which scientists are able to investigate any single topic, yielding an explosion in understanding of natural forces and systems that helped foster the Industrial Revolution. This has also led to a situation where the most detailed and specialized scientific knowledge is, today, sequestered within what Clark (Chapter 5 of this book) calls the diamond mines of academia. We see the work of putting together these sequestered bodies of knowledge, without losing access to their depth, as one of the major challenges associated with developing SES research methodologies.

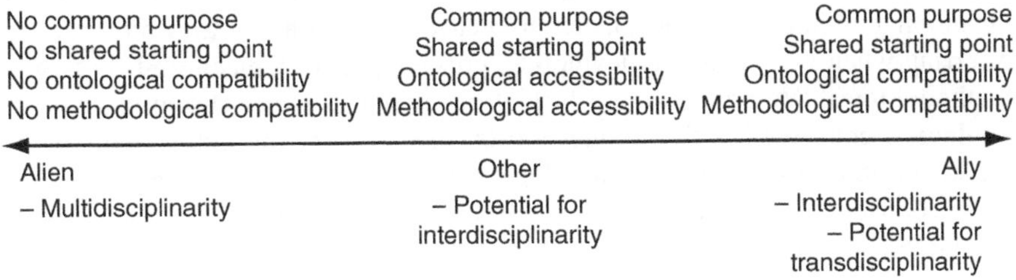

Figure 3.2 A spectrum of alien/ally teamwork dialectic possibilities.

Moving towards and working with ontological compatibility

We propose that in order to move beyond multidisciplinary collation – whether based on trust, opportunism or some other coordination principle – some degree of ontological compatibility needs to be achieved within the research team; aliens need to become others. Take, for example, a project with four contributing disciplines where each individual or team writes one discipline-specific sub-report. Typically, these are prepared independently and then combined by the project coordinator. This form of collaboration can be accomplished within a group made up of researchers who experience each others as aliens, but it is not integrative. However, having alienation as a starting point need not be a negative thing. For example, it may be that the need to achieve shared understanding among a team of aliens, with people coming from very different disciplines, forces the team to clarify the underlying assumptions that every discipline inevitably brings to the table. Instead of being breezed over, hidden assumptions may be met with naive questions that push participants to explain themselves.

If ontological compatibility within a team increases, effective communication can help a team to develop this, nourishing and further strengthening it. When this happens, individuals who perhaps at first experienced each other as aliens can move closer to each other, transforming a multidisciplinary into an interdisciplinary collaboration. We have seen this work in practice and are convinced that it is possible to build strong, integrative ontological bridges within a project. However, it should be noted that a big investment is required to build them: explaining oneself in language that others and aliens can understand; listening to others and aliens, who seem to speak strange languages; and carefully, collaboratively questioning and clarifying both confusions and understandings. All this takes time, effort and dedication.

Moving towards and working with methodological compatibility

Interdisciplinary discourse is, by definition, the means by which teams of researchers develop the approaches and strategies that guide them in the work of combining not only discipline-specific research results but also the data and results associated with their collaborative work. It is this additional work of developing methods to coordinate project-level integration to which we are referring when we talk about developing concrete, project-specific SES research methodologies. We are making a formal distinction between disciplinary methodologies, concerned with the question of how to carry out components of the work, and interdisciplinary methodologies, concerned with how to make each of these contributions relevant to the overall purpose(s) of an SES research project. Here questions arise concerning not only which tools to use when, and how, but also how to organize them so that they are operating in concert.

These are new questions constituting a new methodological problematique located at the level of the interdisciplinary research complex, and ways forward may be surprising. For example, although they may seem to sit on opposite sides of the disciplinary spectrum, the methodological approaches of an ethnographer and a rotifer taxonomist are more compatible than one might imagine. Both are concerned with close study of a single object or class of objects and with developing not only a detailed picture of the object's attributes but also a holistic understanding of the overall object and its relationships with its environment. Without taking the time to explore a team's methodological compatibilities, these two contributing researchers could easily see only the ontological incompatibility of their very different fields of study, missing an opportunity to improve the overall interdisciplinary balance of the team's work.

SES research asks additional, interdisciplinary questions, which require careful attention to how the pieces of an interdisciplinary puzzle are put together, such as how human exploitation is impacting on organisms by changing the structure of their habitat (Armstrong *et al.* 2009). These questions can be addressed only through collaboration that is taking place at the level of research design – that is to say, through interdisciplinary methodology. Here the team of researchers must sit together and develop something new: something relevant to their shared object. Just as social scientists wishing to study the human social and political aspects of the mega-site contamination in Bitterfeld (illustrative case II, p. 42) cannot do so without the cooperation and assistance of hydrogeologists and chemists, the economist trying to map human impacts on deep-sea ecosystems cannot do so without the cooperation of geologists, oceanographers and biologists, because contributions from physical scientists are needed to determine appropriate options for developing meaningful representations of the social science aspect of the problem. At the same time, both physical and social scientists still need to use their own methodologies if they are to make sensible contributions to the collaborative work (Benn *et al.* 2010). Finally, if the product of these collaborations is to be relevant to the research questions of the project, team members cannot just choose whatever interdisciplinary methods they like, without asking questions about the relationships that these methods have to the ontologies of the contributing disciplines and to those of the overall project.

Managing consequences of team structures for project outcome

Once a team has developed some appreciation for its interdisciplinary structure, decisions need to be taken regarding how the opportunities and challenges associated with the specific structure at hand are going to be met. While there are bound to be numerous effective strategies that can bring an SES research project forward with methodology development, if we return to the six attributes of SES research that we presented earlier in the chapter, two of them seem to us to be particularly important to keep in mind when proceeding with this work: (1) dominance and gatekeeper disciplines; and (2) the potential dual role of a team's social scientists. In Tables 3.2.a and 3.2.b we juxtapose our list of discursive context types (based on the array of possible ontological and methodological diversity combinations and associated alien–ally dynamics) with some reflections on the special roles that gatekeeper disciplines and social scientists can play in determining the character and content of an SES research team's discussions.

Dominance and gatekeeper discipline dynamics can be understood to influence interdisciplinary discourse in at least two important ways. First, and most generally, gatekeepers will, by definition, have proprietary control over data generated within their discipline. And, depending on the degree of ontological compatibility within the team, gatekeepers will also have more or less control over interpreting the meaning of these proprietary data, because data's meaning is based on the place of those data within the system being studied (i.e. upon ontology). Second, depending on the degree of methodological compatibility within the team, gatekeepers may also exercise considerable control over analyses that rely on their propriety data, since the implications of a given set of data for theoretical insight can be meaningfully interpreted only through informed reference to the methods that have been used to generate them.

The contribution that social scientists can make to interdisciplinary methodology design can also be expected to vary, depending on the discursive context within which teamwork is taking place. Where ontological and methodological compatibility are high (i.e. a technical discursive context and an alliance-friendly teamwork dynamic), formal attention to discourse design is not likely to be necessary. On balance, where both are low (i.e. a political discursive context and an alienation teamwork dynamic), discourse design support from social scientists trained in the study of human behaviour could, for example, help to bring distant 'alien' team members towards 'other' relationships. In some instances their skills might even be called upon to help identify and mediate political conflicts that could inhibit not only project completion but also interdisciplinary integration. In a political discursive context, for example, since there is no basis in technical criteria, a gatekeeper has to make decisions about how to share access to key data and analysis based on non-scientific criteria, such as personal trust. Here, formal discourse design interventions from social scientists can help ensure that it is the project's research aims, rather than politics, that regulate how the group is building up its collaborative representations.

Dealing with gatekeepers and dominance

Up to this point we have been talking about ontological and methodological compatibility in a rather monolithic way. However, the reality at project level is usually quite different. Almost by definition, SES research projects bring together not only multiple disciplines but also contributors working in different domains of science, some inclined towards mathematical modelling, others towards relational or comparative studies, and yet others towards deep, close study of specific objects or classes of objects. In the light of this diversity, it seems more appropriate to us to talk about nested levels of interdisciplinary collaboration as opposed to presuming that the endgame is a flat structure. For example, in fisheries management there might be an initial attempt at interdisciplinary collaboration between marine ecologists, geologists and oceanographers

Table 3.2a Gatekeeper discipline dynamics

Alien/ally teamwork dialectic		*Discursive context*	*Gatekeeper discipline control of data*	*Gatekeeper discipline control of data analysis*
Methodological compatibility	*Ontological compatibility*		*Ontology-related work*	*Methodology-related work*
Absent	Absent	Political	**Complete**	**Complete**
Weak	Absent	Political/methodological	**Complete**	Moderate
Strong	Absent	Methodological	**Complete**	Limited
Absent	Weak	Political/ontological	Moderate	**Complete**
Weak	Weak	Confusion & Creativity	Moderate	Moderate
Strong	Weak	Methodological/technical	Moderate	Limited
Absent	Strong	Ontological	Limited	**Complete**
Weak	Strong	Ontological/technical	Limited	Moderate
Strong	Strong	Technical	Limited	Limited

Table 3.2b The dual role of social sciences (5)

Alien/ally teamwork dialectic		*Discursive context*	*Methodological role for social sciences*
Methodological compatibility	*Ontological compatibility*		*Interdisciplinary methodology- related work*
Absent	Absent	Political	• advise on design of discursive forum; • identify and moderate conflicts; • foster ontology discourse; • foster methodology discourse.
Weak	Absent	Political/methodological	• advise on design of discursive forum; • identify and moderate conflicts; • foster ontology discourse.
Strong	Absent	Methodological	• advise on design of discursive forum; • foster ontology discourse.
Absent	Weak	Political/ontological	• advise on design of discursive forum; • identify and moderate conflicts; • foster methodology discourse.
Weak	Weak	Confusion & Creativity	• advise on design of discursive forum; • identify and moderate conflicts; • foster ontology discourse • foster methodology discourse • identify opportunities for creative collaboration.
Strong	Weak	Methodological/technical	• foster ontology discourse.
Absent	Strong	Ontological	• advise on design of discursive forum; • foster methodology discourse.
Weak	Strong	Ontological/technical	• foster methodology discourse.
Strong	Strong	Technical	• no special role.

which pulls together a picture of the basic characteristics of a fishery system, and a second level where social-economic and legal research is added to the mix. Although they may not be able to connect directly with the results of the individual physical science disciplinary conceptions of the study object, socio-economic and legal researchers, who are concerned basically with the fishery as a study object, can link their discipline-specific work to the interdisciplinary research product of the first team's collaborations – a physical representation of the fishery.

While this layered structure may be key for generating integrative interdisciplinary research, it can also stand in the way of integration if, for example, participants associated with a discipline that is privileged by the project's dominance – for example, oceanographers or geologists in a deep-sea study – either choose not to cooperate with the team or are unable to make their contributions accessible to other team members. Here we find that the work of Watzlawick *et al.* (1967) concerning the pragmatics of human communication offers some helpful guidance. Building on the work of Bateson (1972), they define five axioms of human communication, which they propose need to be recognized and taken into account if two individuals are to establish functioning communication: (1) one cannot not communicate; (2) every communication has a content and relationship aspect such that the latter classifies the former and is therefore a metacommunication; (3) the nature of a relationship is dependent on the punctuation of the partners' communication procedures [both expressive and perceptual]; (4) human communication involves both digital [quantitative] and analogic [qualitative] modalities; and (5) inter-human communication procedures are either symmetric or complementary, depending on whether the relationship of the partners is based on parity or differences (Watzlawick *et al.* 1967). While we imagine that attention to all five of these axioms, and to a range of other communications theories, might be useful for helping to organize communication within an interdisciplinary research project, we focus here only on the first axiom – one cannot not communicate – as it seems to us to offer a promising way of moving a group from the domain of alienation to that of other regard or even alliance.

Working from the basis that all behaviour is also a form of communication – a view that fits well with Maturana and Varela's concept of structural coupling (mentioned on p. 46) – Watzlawick *et al.* (1967) suggest that the quality of communication can be improved and logjams overcome when people communicate about how they are communicating. We do not mean to propose this as a panacea for overcoming all difficulties that may arise with interdisciplinary teamwork. However, particularly with respect to potential problems associated with dominance and gatekeeper disciplines, formal acknowledgement that communication is difficult constitutes an important step towards making it possible to transform aliens into others. Providing space and time for communicating about the communication can give outliers a forum for airing their confusion and frustration in lieu of just letting off steam during coffee breaks. In addition, making this a formal work activity can bring the need to reach out to the attention of otherwise naive but well-meaning gatekeepers and dominance-privileged members of the team. While such an approach is less likely to impact the behaviours of a recalcitrant gatekeeper concerned mainly with protecting their turf, or a myopic dominance-privileged participant who sees only their own discipline as important, in cases where there is the will to collaborate – that is to say, in most cases – we believe this small step can open up substantial opportunities.

Acknowledging the potential dual role of social science

The question of how human beings go about coordinating their activities is a basic research topic for sociologists, anthropologists, political scientists and economists. That is to say, all the methodological questions outlined so far in this chapter can also be understood as empirical social science research topics. While such study may not always be of interest to, or even fall within the competences of, the social scientists on a given research team, there is nonetheless likely to be a store of knowledge among them that can be drawn upon to help organize and design team-level coordination. Methodological contributions from social scientists might take various forms. Some that we have seen and practised include casual advice and suggestions about how to communicate; planned and organized social science reflection sessions where the social aspects of methodological decisions can be discussed; and explicit involvement of social science expertise in design of project management tools and interdisciplinary communications principles. The precise details of what social scientists may be able to add to a specific project will depend, of course, on the scientists and the project in question. However, as with communicating about communicating, from our experience it would seem that some kind of formal acknowledgement of this potential dual role of social scientists can open up substantial opportunities for improved collaborations and more integrated collaborative results.

Giving attention to the character of team discussions regarding how the methodologies of various contributing disciplines can be effectively coordinated seems to us to be central to the work of developing project-specific interdisciplinary SES research methodologies. However, engaging social scientists in this methodological role may not bring only advantages. For example, a degree of tension is to be expected simply because social scientists will be observing the behaviours of team members. Furthermore, their work may raise issues that some team members prefer not to discuss, such as, for example, how dominance and gatekeeper status may be hindering progress towards achieving project aims. In addition, 'human relations' is a subject with which all team members have extensive personal experience, whereas chemistry or physics is likely to be known in detail only to team members with disciplinary expertise in these fields. Of course, all team members can and should contribute towards making decisions about how interdisciplinary integration is to be achieved. However, in our experience it is sometimes difficult to impress upon physical scientists the fact that there is a meaningful difference between their personal reflections on their own life experiences and the theoretical and empirical work of social scientists concerned with similar issues. Since this is, in principle, a problem of ontological incompatibility, some work on moving from aliens to others may be required before social scientists can begin making formal methodological contributions that draw on their expertise.

An applied look at making methodologies

Since we are concerned with generalized guidelines for developing project-specific methodologies, our discussion has so far been somewhat abstract. In order to bring this to the practical level, we can consider how our general suggestions might be applied to the two illustrative cases presented in this chapter. We begin this process by considering the discursive contexts within which these two strands of SES research have been carried out.

Looking first at the set of research projects concerning the loss of biodiversity, while there was considerable disciplinary diversity, there was also some degree of both methodological and ontological compatibility and usually a clear project-level ontology of ecosystem-based study. Here we find a discursive context that we would call 'Confusion & Creativity', with fairly good accessibility throughout the group being tempered by the presence of substantial differences in both ontology and methodology. In the light of both the challenges and the results reported in this chapter, this categorization seems to us to provide a

Table 3.3a Team-level discursive context: biodiversity loss research

Methodological compatibility (3)	*Ontological compatibility*		
	Absent	*Weak*	*Strong*
Absent	Political	Political/Ontological	Ontological
Weak	Political/ Methodological	**Confusion & Creativity**	Ontological/ Technical
Strong	Methodological	Methodological/ Technical	Technical

Table 3.3b Team-level discursive context: mega-sites remediation research

Methodological compatibility (3)	*Ontological compatibility*		
	Absent	*Weak*	*Strong*
Absent	Political	Political/Ontological	Ontological
Weak	**Political/ Methodological**	Confusion & Creativity	Ontological/ Technical
Strong	Methodological	Methodological/ Technical	Technical

fair description of the discursive contexts within which the members of these teams were operating.

With respect to the second illustrative case, concerning research on mega-contamination site remediation, here we found a weak common orientation around the general problematique of contamination remediation, basic differences in project research objectives and considerable ontological incompatibility between social and physical scientific inquiries. This, combined with common reference to scientific research methods across the physical and social sciences, leads us to classify the discursive context of these collaborations as 'political/methodological'. Recalling the focus on methodological links between social and physical aspects of the problem, as reflected, for example, in the computer modelling of potential future flooding patterns, and the substantial influence of gatekeepers, this classification also seems to correspond well with the situation it is intended to describe.

Next we can consider what capacities for cooperation can be observed using our alien/ally heuristic to look at the two interdisciplinary settings. In the cases of biodiversity loss research (Figure 3.3), a common purpose and shared starting point were present in all the projects discussed above: (1) understanding what is driving the loss of biodiversity, and (2) identifying ways to halt it. This seems to give an interdisciplinary team a head start, as there is a basic shared understanding regarding the 'why' of the work even if there are still many different perspectives on what is to be studied and how. This initial 'other', as opposed to alien, status of the participants seems to provide a basis for constructive dialogue, easing the way for communication on points of difference and also about the overall quality and character of communication within the project team. While substantial ontological incompatibility was present, this was complemented by pockets of strong methodological compatibility and a layered structure of nested collaboration steps, which seemed to help to increase overall ontological compatibility over time. Finally, basic principles for good scientific method help to ensure that there is a minimal degree of methodological compatibility, upon which further understanding can be built. Here our heuristic suggests a relatively promising starting point for integrative collaboration that seems to fit well with the more or less positive results seen in the studies reported upon in this chapter.

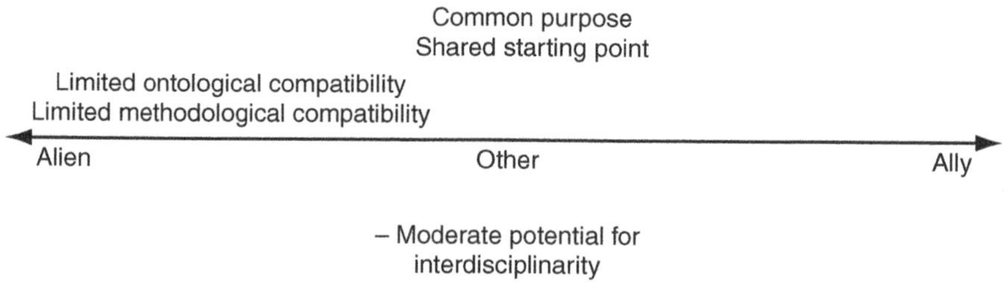

Figure 3.3 Biodiversity loss research projects general alien/ally dialectic.

By contrast, in the case of research concerning mega-site remediation in Bitterfeld (Figure 3.4), while there was a clear common purpose in terms of wishing to provide means to help remediate and manage the mega-contamination at the site, already at the level of starting points the social and physical scientific studies begin to diverge, with a physical science focus on technology development and social science work focused more on questions of impacts of the contamination on humans. In addition, while the ontological compatibility between the hydrogeology and the chemistry of the physical scientists was strong, social research questions not directly related to the physical science of contaminant migration and remediation – that is to say, concerning other study objects – were not pursued at length or in depth. While basic principles for good scientific method provided for a minimal degree of methodological compatibility, this can be understood to have served mainly to keep the project from tipping totally into the domain of alienation. Here too our heuristic seems to fit well with the results in the illustrative case, which eventually produced, as its major social science-relevant output, a hydrogeology-based simulation model of potential human exposure to flooding-related contamination.

Having considered the basic interdisciplinary structure of the two cases, we can now move on to consider how a team's capacity to achieve interdisciplinary integration might be improved through careful attention to the special roles that gatekeepers and social scientists could play in either facilitating or obstructing development of a project team's interdisciplinary methodologies.

On p. 59 we proposed the 'Confusion & Creativity' label to describe the discursive context of our illustrative biodiversity loss research projects; represented in Table 3.4a. Here we have a combination of weak ontological and weak methodological compatibility, where constructive discourse is possible but is by no means guaranteed. We would expect that ontological accessibility would make debate and dialogue about the interpretation of key data sets possible and that the methodological accessibility would enable debate and dialogue concerning the implications that these (or indeed other) data may have for interdisciplinary project-level analysis. Here we expect there to be generally open relations but also a lot of muddling through, in a rather fuzzy environment, where no one has a clear upper hand or overriding perspective. We would expect that careful attention to structuring team-level interactions could have a substantial positive influence on the team's ability to produce integrative work.

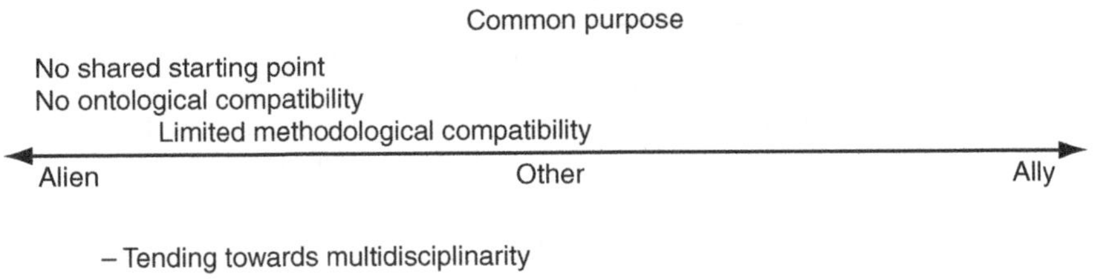

Figure 3.4 Mega-sites remediation research general alien/ally dialectic.

Table 3.4a Biodiversity loss research discursive context: Confusion & Creativity

	Ontology-related work	*Methodology-related work*
Dominance and gatekeeper discipline dynamics	Moderate control of data	Moderate control of analysis
Methodological role for social sciences	• advise on design of discursive forum; • identify and moderate conflicts; • identify opportunities for creative collaboration.	
	• foster ontology discourse.	• foster methodology discourse.

Moving next to the illustrative case of the research concerning remediation of the mega-site contamination in Bitterfeld, we have characterized this discursive context as 'Political/Methodological'. This characterization reflects a situation with weak methodological and little or no ontological compatibility. Here, because of their ontological distance from other members of the interdisciplinary team, gatekeepers could be expected to have complete control not only over their proprietary data but also over its interpretation, which is closely related to the ontology that underpins its characterization. The presence of a certain degree of methodological compatibility can be expected to make debate concerning interpretation of results possible. However, with regard to analysis and interdisciplinary integration, the range of available options is limited by decisions taking place deep within the gatekeeper disciplines of hydrogeology and chemistry. Here, gatekeepers have the potential to make or break a project. Since their impact will depend on how the project team manages this situation, the special role of social scientists is potentially very important.

On the basis of these two brief methodological treatments of our illustrative cases, we can now make a few tentative observations: (1) the six attributes identified at the outset of this chapter can be applied in a systematic manner that yields salient and plausible information about the general characteristics of two seemingly quite different SES research project areas; and (2) when applied in an analytical manner – here through reference to the question of how discursive contexts and alien/ally teamwork dialectics influence an SES research project's methodological discourse – they can provide practical insights into how interdisciplinary SES research collaborations might be made both more integrative and more effective.

Table 3.4b Mega-sites and Bitterfeld discursive context: Political/Methodological

	Ontology-related work	*Methodology-related work*
Dominance and gatekeeper discipline dynamics	Complete control of data	Complete control of analysis
Methodological role for social sciences	• advise on design of discursive forum; • identify and moderate conflicts.	
	• foster ontology discourse.	

Institutional, training and validation issues

Up to now, our review has provided two things that we believe can be helpful for designing and carrying out effective interdisciplinary methodology work within SES research projects: (1) some ontological categories (our six attributes) and some initial guidelines (e.g. dealing with gatekeepers, creating 'others') for thinking about how to organize the work of project-specific methodology development; and (2) an appreciation for how significantly this work is influenced by the discursive contexts of the interdisciplinary mixes of disciplines within which it is carried out. In this final substantive section of the chapter we turn our attention to some additional factors related to the institutional and professional context within which this work is carried out: factors that we suggest should also be kept in mind by research teams and institutions concerned with SES research methodology development.

Taken as distinct from the work itself, the professional context within which scientific research is carried out in modern academia can be distinguished into three broad categories: (1) institutional – research is conducted within a social work environment in which access to research funds are limited, which is oriented towards the production of patents and papers, and where career development is tightly related to the principle of 'publish or perish'; (2) education and training – discipline-based university pedagogy, apprentice-style training and general orientation towards discipline-specific specialization reinforce discipline-based skills development and orientation; and (3) validation – Type I error avoidance based on falsification as the ideal and discipline-based peer review as the adjudicator of quality. While decisions about the details of scientific work take place largely within a project, these three contextual factors can be presumed to influence the behaviours of the participating researchers.

As is noted elsewhere in this book (in the chapters by Barry and Farrell, Clark, Ravetz, Santaoja *et al.* and Vatn), the institutional, training and validation systems of modern academia are not designed to support the kind of work that we have proposed is required for carrying out SES research. This means that interdisciplinary methodology development needs to include formal attention not only to questions of methodology but also to the question of how professional context is impacting on an SES research team's work. Since our focus in this chapter remains methodological, as we turn our attention to these social context issues our discussion will remain weighted towards the most explicitly methodology-related of these three categories, namely validation, which we address last and in the greatest detail.[12]

Institutional issues

Although it is now widely accepted that interdisciplinary work is the appropriate approach for SES research, at the moment there are still no formal guidelines for how to support this kind of work institutionally. A small number of anthologies and handbooks now address the practical questions of how to carry out this kind of work (Hirsch Hadorn *et al.* 2008; Waltner-Toews *et al.* 2008; Brown *et al.* 2010). However, these reflect mainly how different groups of researchers are engaging with these challenges in their own work. Since methodologies will always be developed within some institutional context, even in situations where there is strong methodological and ontological compatibility across a team, absence of supportive institutional conditions will inevitably make successful development of project-appropriate interdisciplinary methodologies difficult, if not impossible. For example, something as simple as finding the time required to think through and discuss interdisciplinary research methodology options can be very difficult in an institutional environment that only recognizes discipline-specific work.

In addition, while this is beginning to change, vehicles for publishing interdisciplinary research are still rare, and even where it is possible, publication in these journals tends not to be recognized as high-quality scientific work within disciplinary communities. This means that interdisciplinary researchers need to spend additional time writing, so they can continue to publish within a specific discipline while also contributing towards publications concerning interdisciplinary project work. Within current institutional structures, writing up work on interdisciplinary research is a luxury. If it is to be encouraged, then either researchers need to be given extra time and funding to support this 'luxury' work, or institutional structures need to be adjusted so that this work is included within basic job descriptions, promotion evaluations and funding awards. At present, researchers who 'waste' time on interdisciplinary projects and publications run the risk of not making good progress in their careers and of not getting grants within their primary discipline. While efforts to increase ontological and methodological openness and compatibility may lead to more willingness and ability to collaborate at an interdisciplinary level, it is also necessary to ensure that the institutions within which this work is taking place are evolving in a way that allows these practices to flourish.

Training issues

While good institutional support and good methodological design are always important for executing good research, it is also important to keep in mind that research, be it discipline based or interdisciplinary, is carried out by people – people who have been trained and educated to address certain problems in certain ways, most of which have not included any formal discussion of interdisciplinary research. This means that, in addition to the institutional issues raised above, both senior and junior scientists involved in SES research need different training and education. Currently, interdisciplinary training is mostly 'on the job', as individual researchers gain experience within projects, negotiate coordination challenges and come to understand basic principles of other disciplines. The main training strategy is usually 'muddling through'. While there is much to be said for going with one's instincts when tools and options are limited, unless this is eventually followed up with more standardized procedures for skills development, it can hardly be viewed as scientific training. However, determining what standards should be applied here is complicated. For example, particularly in SES research, lack of a diploma does not determine whether or not someone has expertise in a given field. If an economist works for many years in close collaboration with ecologists, then there is bound to be – indeed, there will need to be – a certain amount of cross-training taking place. In addition, many SES researchers (including two of the three authors of this chapter) have formal education in more than one discipline. These researchers have an additional but uncertified skill of being able to think across disciplines. Although there is no standard procedure for acquiring this skill, it can be quite useful in an interdisciplinary setting, providing ready-made bridges within an ontologically and methodologically diverse interdisciplinary discourse.

In the end, openness to the different contributions available within an interdisciplinary research team depends at least as much on the overall approach of the team as it does on the abilities of any one individual. Here the very idea of disciplinarity becomes a bit confusing, and perhaps even limiting. We do not mean to suggest that discipline-specific training and education should be abolished – quite the contrary. However, it would seem that special training in effective communication and teamwork, and perhaps also in a secondary discipline, should be part of the formal education process for scientists pursuing a career in SES research, much the same as scientific writing, which is taught as a general skill. Extending this thinking a bit further, we might imagine the field of SES research in the future as comprising a range of types of scientists: some trained to go deeper and deeper into a specific disciplinary subject; some trained to think broadly, at the level of the SES; some specifically trained in SES research methodology; and all trained to engage effectively with the challenges of communicating across multiple discipline-specific frames of reference. Clark suggests in Chapter 5 of this book that in order to address the pressing social ecological problems of our time, it seems we would do well to play to and support the collaborative side of the human character.

Validation issues

Although the need for rigorous ways to adjudicate the quality of interdisciplinary research results seems clear, progress towards creating the required techniques and procedures has only just begun. One of the few empirical studies of this problem, conducted by Boix Mansilla and Gardner (2003), has looked at how a targeted sample of interdisciplinary researchers at leading US institutions view the question of interdisciplinary research quality adjudication. They identify

> three realms in which to discern the acceptability of interdisciplinary work: (1) the degree to which new insights relate to antecedent disciplinary knowledge, (2) the sensible balance reached in weaving perspectives together, and (3) the effectiveness with which a particular piece of work advances understanding and inquiry.
>
> (ibid.: 11)

We find Boix Mansilla and Gardner's (2003) three measures helpful for understanding the kinds of adjudications that can be made about the quality of interdisciplinary research. However, we also believe that the ontology of such methodological validation processes is still seriously under-theorized (see also Boix Mansilla *et al.* 2006). For example, in all five of the studies referred to in Tables 3.5a and 3.5b (including the one presented in this chapter), it was found that interdisciplinary researchers paid very little direct attention to validation issues. The researchers interviewed by Boix Mansilla and Gardner (2003), who were specifically asked to reflect on this, were almost all in agreement that this is a difficult issue requiring further study: problems cited, which are echoed in all the other studies cited in Tables 3.5a and 3.5b, included inappropriate peer review, constraints on career development opportunities, and time constraints associated with the need to maintain status within one's primary discipline.[13]

While it is still too early to talk about definitive validation measures, by drawing on our own observations and on recommendations made by Birnbaum-More *et al.* (1990), Boix Mansilla and Gardner (2003), Boix Mansilla *et al.* (2006) and Klein (2008) we can identify a list of at least three factors that seem to be important for generating high-quality interdisciplinary research (listed in

Table 3.5a Factors that seem to be important for generating high-quality interdisciplinary research

1 Hospitable institutions	
Birnbaum-More *et al.* (1990)	The environment external to the research team (consisting of institutional and societal considerations)
Boix Mansilla *et al.* (2006)	Establishing social conditions for good work
Farrell *et al.* (this chapter)	Institutional support
2 Characteristics of the team	
Birnbaum-More *et al.* (1990)	The characteristics of the research team
Boix Mansilla *et al.* (2006)	Establishing social conditions for good work Focusing on 'the right shared problem'
Klein (2008)	Iteration in a comprehensive and transparent system Interactions of social and cognitive factors in collaboration
Farrell *et al.* (this chapter)	Common purpose Shared starting point Moving towards ontological compatibility Moving towards methodological compatibility Managing the special roles of gatekeepers and social scientists
3 Characteristics of the participants	
Birnbaum-More *et al.* (1990)	Characteristics of the individual participants in the research
Klein (2008)	Management, leadership, and coaching
Farrell *et al.* (this chapter)	Appropriate education and training

Table 3.5b Factors that seem to be important for assessing the quality of outcomes

1 Effective synthesis	
Boix Mansilla and Gardner (2003)	The sensible balance reached in weaving perspectives together
Boix Mansilla *et al.* (2006)	Reaching effective syntheses.
Klein (2008)	Variability of goals Variability of criteria and indicators
Farrell *et al.* (this chapter)	Integration rather than collation
2 Academic and applied impacts	
Birnbaum-More *et al.* (1990)	The impacts interdisciplinary research has on the systems used and the new knowledge created
Boix Mansilla and Gardner (2003)	The degree to which new insights relate to antecedent disciplinary knowledge The effectiveness with which a particular piece of work advances understanding and inquiry
Boix-Mansilla *et al.* (2006)	Meeting multiple disciplinary standards
Klein (2008)	Leveraging of integration Effectiveness and impact

Table 3.5a) and two that seem to be important for assessing the quality of outcomes (listed in Table 3.5b).

Unlike traditional discipline-specific validation criteria, which tend to focus on the data and analytics of a scientific work, there seems to be a consensus among these studies that the composition of the research team, the characteristics of their work environments and their relations to discipline-specific science are important factors mediating the quality of interdisciplinary research. The substantial overlap between the recommendations of these various studies suggests that, while interdisciplinary research methodologies may themselves be highly project or problem specific, their quality control can be generalized. To the extent that these criteria are at least pointing in the right direction, advancing work on the validation of SES research is going to require a fundamental shift in how we think about quality control in science. Within disciplines, the quality of scientific work can be evaluated against what Ravetz (1971: 157–162) refers to as 'criteria of adequacy' – is it right? does it fit with the existing knowledge frames? – whereas decisions regarding what to research are governed through reference to what he calls 'value criteria' – is it a good idea to study this topic? is this study useful to society? Once evaluations move outside the confines of a disciplinary frame, value criteria (is this useful?) are likely to arise again and again as an interdisciplinary team makes choices about how to fit together various contributions in order to address a common question. However, value criteria are derived through social and political as opposed to scientific processes (Latour and Woolgar 1979; Kuhn 1970 [1962]: postscript; Ravetz 1971, 1990; Gould 2003). This means that criteria for adjudicating the quality of interdisciplinary research must somehow take into account the presence of these value judgements. Here it seems that the concept of post-normal science, introduced and developed by Funtowicz and Ravetz (1990a, 1991, 1993), which addresses the problem of quality control in science for policy, may turn out to be a helpful conceptual tool for developing formal criteria for interdisciplinary research validation. At the very least it is worth investigating, since it is one of the very few methodological discourses that directly address these problems of the politics of interdisciplinary science (see Farrell 2008a).

Pitfalls in the road to validation

Although we are optimistic that useful general criteria can be developed for validating and judging the quality of SES research project results, since this work is still in its infancy it is important also to take note of some potential pitfalls that may lie ahead. Two that we can already see clearly on the horizon are: (1) complacency masquerading as collaboration – where high levels of trust within a team, which would seem to be a good thing, leave each disciplinary contributor with complete freedom to develop their part of the work as they see fit, without exposing it either to disciplinary or to interdisciplinary critique; and (2) formalism without ontological reference – where heavy reliance on methodological compatibility and common formalizations, such as mathematical models (which make it easy to combine data across disciplines), leads researchers to overlook the unique relationships that each model has to the empirical data with which it is associated. Such over-reliance on methodological compatibility might, for example, obscure lower-order differences between the dynamics of different study objects, thereby excluding relevant information about how the different modelled systems are likely to interact with one and other in the real world.

Conclusions

At the beginning of this chapter we set out to shed some light on the question 'How does one do interdisciplinary research?' Starting from the presumption that SES research is, by definition, interdisciplinary work, on the basis of two illustrative examples from our own research experience – research on biodiversity loss and study of the remediation options for the mega-contaminated site in Bitterfeld, Germany – and reference to a number of other studies, we identified six key attributes – (1) complexity, (2) ontological diversity, (3) methodological diversity, (4) dominance and gatekeeper disciplines, (5) a dual role for social science, and (6) team research – that we propose are common to all SES research projects and should be taken into account when developing SES research methodologies.

By identifying a set of attributes common to all SES research projects, we were then able to set about the work of beginning to formalize our discussion of SES research methodology development. Taking each of these attributes in turn, we considered what they add to an interdisciplinary research setting, in terms of both opportunities and obstacles. We then proposed one possible way in which these six attributes could be used as a basis for informing how a research team approaches the work of interdisciplinary methodology development: first characterizing the project's discursive context and then using this information to inform strategies concerning how to manage team dynamics associated with, on the one hand, dominance and gatekeeper disciplines and, on the other, the special role of social science in the work of designing team-level discourse. We expect that SES research teams that experiment with the tools we have presented here will come up with additional attributes, be they general or specific to their projects, and other ways of using them to inform their collaborative work. The specific approach we have presented here is meant to be suggestive only.

Finally, having identified the professional work context as an additional factor influencing the way in which SES research methodologies are developed, we turned our attentions to considering three issues related to how and where SES research fits within the wider context of international competitive academic research. Here we identified three key contextual domains – institutional, training and education, and validation – and proposed a tentative set of criteria for monitoring quality within the validation domain that we hope may prove helpful to researchers, reviewers and funders wishing to judge the quality of SES research project plans, outputs and achievements.

The topic we set out to address in this chapter is complex and ungainly, and until recently has been studied only rarely. We are aware that our treatment of it is, at times, cumbersome and meandering. However, much the same as with the empirical cases that we study in the developing field of SES research, we believe that the stakes are too high to let the uncertainty associated with our presently limited knowledge hold us back from beginning to develop better understandings of the complex relationships between SES research and the methodological and social environments within which it is carried out. The illustrations, heuristics and guidelines that we have presented here are intended to open up rather than to resolve discussion and we hope that readers concerned with the question of how to develop SES research methodologies will find, among the many loose ends and open questions, opportunities for further critique and elaboration.

Notes

1 We use the term 'physical science' here in lieu of the more common term 'natural science' as we are working on the basis that social sciences are also concerned with the study of natural, albeit anthropomorphic and anthropogenic, phenomena.
2 Since SES research projects share many attributes with other forms of interdisciplinary research and even, at times, with team-based monodisciplinary research, we will frequently discuss things here that are not exclusively relevant to our topic; we hope that these reflections may also prove useful to researchers concerned with other problematiques.
3 HERMES: Hotspot Ecosystem Research on the Margins of European Seas. See www.eu-hermes.net.
4 OASIS: OceaAnic Seamounts: an Integrated Study. See www1.uni-hamburg.de/OASIS/.
5 MacMan: MACulinea Butterflies of the Habitats Directive and European Red List as

Indicators and Tools for Habitat Conservation and MANagement. See http://macman-project.net/page.php?P=2 for further information.

6 For an exception, see Farrell (2008b).

7 While a large-scale social–physical science collaboration concerning the development of a tool for managing the mega-site in Bitterfeld was attempted within the research project SAFIRA II (see Farrell 2008c), the Bitterfeld case was eventually dropped from the list of sites being studied (see www.ufz.de/index.php?de=13244 for more information on this component of the project).

8 The core of SES research project often includes some form of sophisticated computer modelling, and modellers, who share the ontology of computer language and model building, can form a group unto themselves, despite disciplinary distinctions.

9 This has begun to change in recent years but there is still a heavy physical science bias to be observed with respect to both study objects and research approaches in this field; see, for example, project listings at leading social-ecological systems research institutes such as the Stockholm Resilience Centre (www.stockholmresilience.org), the Institute for Social Ecological Research (www.isoe.de/english/), the Potsdam Institute for Climate Impact Research (www.pik-potsdam.de) and the Social Ecological Systems group at the Australian Commonwealth Scientific and Industrial Research Organisation (CSIRO) (www.csiro.au/science/ComplexSocial-EcologicalSystems.html).

10 Personalities and personal and professional approaches to collaboration will of course also help to shape a team's methodology discourse. However, in the interest of maintaining our focus here we will leave these actor-oriented issues to the side. Nonetheless, these are expected to be every bit as important for SES research methodology design as any of the structure-oriented issues that occupy our attentions here.

11 While we do not wish to dismiss transdisciplinary work as unimportant or inapplicable to SES research, we occupy ourselves here with the problem of achieving interdisciplinary integration because we see it as a challenging task in its own right and presume it to be a necessary precondition for effective transdisciplinary research.

12 Readers will find more detailed discussions on institutional issues in Chapters 5, 6 and 11 of this book, by Clark, Barry and Farrell, and Vatn respectively, and on educational and training issues in Chapters 6 and 9, by Barry and Farrell and Santaoja *et al.* respectively.

13 In a similar but more tightly specified pilot survey of interdisciplinary researchers, Rhoten and Parker (2004) found more optimism among young respondents with regard to the career development opportunities that come with interdisciplinarity work. However, they also conclude that 'many still feel the tension between the scientific promise of the interdisciplinary path and the academic prospect of the tenure track' (ibid.: 2046).

References

Armstrong, C.W., A.J. Grehan, V. Kahui, E. Mikkelsen, S. Reithe and S. van den Hove. 2009. 'Bioeconomic modeling and the management of cold-water coral resources.' *Oceanography* 22(1): 86–91.

Banzhaf, E. ed. 1999. *Bitterfeld/Wolfen als Beispiel für den Wandel einer Industrieregion in den neuen Bundesländern: Untersuchung von Flächennutzungsänderungen der beiden Städte und Umstrukturierungen ansgewählter Altindustriestandorte*. Leipzig: UFZ – Umweltforschungszentrum Leipzig-Halle.

Banzhaf, E. and H.D. Kasperidus eds. 1998. *Erfassung und Auswertung der Landnutzung und ihrer Veränderungen mit Methoden der Fernerkundung und geographischen Informationssystemen im Raum Leipzig-Halle-Bitterfeld*. UFZ-Bericht Nr. 2/1998. Leipzig: UFZ-Umweltforschungszentrum Leipzig-Halle.

Bateson, G. 1972. *Steps to an Ecology of Mind*. London: Jason Aronson.

Benn, A.R., Weaver, P.P., Billet, D.S.M., van den Hove, S. and Murdock, A.P. 2010. 'Human activities on the deep seafloor in the North East Atlantic: an assessment of spatial extent'. *PLoS ONE* 5(9): e12730.

Bertalanffy, L. von. 1950. 'An outline of general system theory.' *British Journal for the Philosophy of Science* 1(2): 134–165.

Birnbaum-More, P.H., F.A. Rossini and D.R. Baldwin eds. 1990. *International Research Management: Studies in Interdisciplinary Methods from Business, Government, and Academia.* New York: Oxford University Press.

Boix Mansilla, V. and H. Gardner. 2003. 'Assessing interdisciplinary work at the frontier: an empirical exploration of "symptoms of quality".' In *Rethinking Interdisciplinarity*, an online seminar supported by the CNRS project Society of Information.

Boix Mansilla, V., I. Feller and H. Gardner. 2006. 'Quality assessment in interdisciplinary research and education.' *Research Evaluation* 15(1): 69–74.

Brown, V.A., J.A. Harris and J.Y. Russell eds. 2010. *Tackling Wicked Problems through the Transdisciplinary Imagination.* London: Earthscan.

Bruce, A., C. Lyall, J. Tait and R. Williams. 2004. 'Interdisciplinary integration in Europe: the case of the Fifth Framework Programme.' *Futures* 36(4): 457–470.

Carson, R. 1963. *Silent Spring.* London: Hamish Hamilton.

Costanza, R. 1989. 'What is ecological economics?' *Ecological Economics* 1(1): 1–7.

Farrell, K.N. 2004. 'Recapturing fugitive power: epistemology, complexity and democracy.' *Local Environment* 9(5): 469–479.

Farrell, K.N. 2008a. 'The politics of science and sustainable development: Marcuse's new science in the 21st century.' *Capitalism Nature Socialism* 19(4): 68–83.

Farrell, K.N. 2008b. 'Castles in the sand: structuring the big back loops with reliably volatile sub-systems.' Paper presented at the Eighth International Conference of the European Society for Ecological Economics (ESEE 2009), 'Transformation, Innovation and Adaptation for Sustainability: Integrating Natural and Social Sciences', University of Ljubljana, 29 June – 2 July.

Farrell, K.N. 2008c. 'One should never look directly into the Sun: Final Scientific Report of the European Union Marie Curie Research Project Accountability and Legitimacy of Governance Institutions that support Viable Environments (EU EIF – 024688: ALIVE).' Leipzig: Helmholtz Centre for Environmental Research – UFZ.

Farrell, K.N. 2009 [2005]. *Making Good Decisions Well: A Theory of Collective Ecological Management.* Aachen, Germany: Shaker Verlag.

Farrell, K.N., R. Kemp, F. Hinterberger, C. Rammel and R. Ziegler. 2005. 'From * for * to governance for sustainable development in Europe: what is at stake for further research?' *International Journal of Sustainable Development* 8(1/2): 127–150.

Farrell, K.N., M. Martienssen, J.E. Armstrong and M. Schirmer. 2007. 'Managing mega-contamination sites: coping with fundamental complexity by shifting orientation away from management and control, toward coping with transition.' Paper presented at the Seventh Biennial Conference of the European Society for Ecological Economics 'Integrating Natural and Social Sciences for Sustainability', Leipzig, 5–8 June.

Flämig, E., G. Krezeminski, S. Hermann, M. Herget and F. Quasdorf. 2007. 'GINSEK – Gemeinsames Integriertes Stadtentwicklungskonzept Bitterfeld, Wolfen, Greppin 2005/2006.' Berlin/Stadt Wolfen, Stadt Bitterfeld, Gemeinde Greppin: Eichstädt/Emge, Architekten und Stadtplaner.

Funtowicz, S.O. and J.R. Ravetz. 1991. 'A new scientific methodology for global environmental issues.' In *Ecological Economics: The Science and Management of Sustainability*, ed. R. Costanza. New York: Columbia University Press.

Funtowicz, S.O. and J.R. Ravetz. 1990a. *Uncertainty and Quality in Science for Policy*. Dordrecht, the Netherlands: Kluwer Academic.

Funtowicz, S.O. and J.R. Ravetz. 1993. 'Science for the post-normal age.' *Futures* 25(7): 739–755.

Funtowicz, S. and J.R. Ravetz. 1994. 'The worth of a songbird: ecological economics as a post-normal science.' *Ecological Economics* 10(3): 197–207.

Gould, S.J. 2003. *The Hedgehog, the Fox and the Magister's Pox: Mending and Minding the Misconceived Gap between Science and Humanities*. London: Jonathan Cape.

Habermas, J. 1984. *The Theory of Communicative Action*, vol. 1: *Reason and the Rationalization of Society*. London: Heinemann.

Habermas, J. 1987. *The Theory of Communicative Action*, vol. 2: *Lifeworld and System: A Critique of Functionalist Reason*. Cambridge: Polity Press.

Habermas, J. 1996. *Between Facts and Norms: Contributions to a Discourse Theory of Law and Democracy*. Cambridge, MA: MIT Press.

Hannemann, C., S. Kabisch and C. Weiske eds. 2002. *Neue Länder – Neue Sitten? Transformationsprozesse in Städten und Regionen Ostdeutschlands*. Berlin: Schelsky & Jeep.

Heidrich, S., M. Schirmer, H. Weiss, P. Wycisk, J. Grossmann and A. Kaschla. 2004. 'Regionally contaminated aquifers: toxicological relevance and remediation options (Bitterfeld case study).' *Toxicology* 205: 143–155.

Herbarth, O., M. Bauer, U. Franck, P. Krumbiegel, M. Rehwagen, U. Rolle-Kampczyk and H. Weiss. 2005. 'Effect of remediation measures on exposure and liver detoxification capacity of children.' In *Environmental Exposure and Health*, ed. M.M. Aral, C.A. Brebbia, M.L. Maslia and T. Sinks. Southampton: WIT Press.

Hervida, A. 2003. *Zur Mobilität von Fluoren und Phenol unter Milieubedingungen der Bergbaufolgelandschaft: Dissertation zur Erlangung des Grades eines Doktors der Naturwissenschaften im Fachbereich Geowissenschaften an der Freien Universität Berlin*. Berlin: Verlag im Internet.

Hirsch Hadorn, G., D. Bradley, C. Pohl, S. Rist and U. Wiesmann. 2006. 'Implications of transdisciplinarity for sustainability research.' *Ecological Economics* 60(1): 119–128.

Hirsch Hadorn, G., H. Hoffmann-Riem, S. Biber-Klemm, W. Grossenbacher-Mansuy, D. Joye, C. Pohl, U. Wiesmann and E. Zemp eds. 2008. *Handbook of Transdisciplinary Research*. Heidelberg: Springer.

Jasanoff, S. and B. Wynne. 1998. 'Science and decisionmaking.' In *Human Choice and Climate Change*, vol. 1: *The Societal Framework*, ed. S. Rayner and E.L. Malone. Columbus, OH: Battelle Press.

Kabisch, S. 2003. 'Stadtumbau in Weißwasser aus Bewohnerperspektive.' *Wohnbund Informationen* 2/2003 Themenheft: Stadtumbau Ost/West: 16–18.

Kabisch, S. and S. Linke. 2002. 'Now we have a future, people can also speak of the past: living next to an opencast mine.' In *Remediation of Abandoned Surface Coal Mining Sites*, ed. A. Murdoch, U. Stottmeister, C. Kennedy and H. Klapper. Heidelberg: Springer.

Kasimir, P. and B. Friede. 2003. 'Vergleich der Wassergüte vor, während und nach dem Sommerhochwasser in der sachsen-anhaltinischen Elbe.' Paper presented at Statusseminar des BMBF-Ad-hoc-Verbundprojektes Schadstoffbelastung im Mulde- und Elbe-Einzugsgebiet nach dem Augusthochwasser 2002, Ergebnisse und Forschungsbedarf, Freiberg, Germany, 27–29 August.

Kates, R.W., W.C. Clark, R. Corell, J.M. Hall, C.C. Jaeger, I. Lowe, J.J. McCarthy, H.J.

Schellnhuber, B. Bolin, N.M. Dickson, S. Faucheux, G.C. Gallopin, A. Grübler, B. Huntley, J. Jäger, N.S. Jodha, R.E. Kasperson, A. Mabogunje, P. Matson, H. Mooney, B. Moore III, T. O'Riordan and U. Svedin. 2001. 'Sustainability science.' *Science* 292(5517): 641–642.

Klein, J.T. 2008. 'Evaluation of interdisciplinary and transdisciplinary research: a literature review.' *American Journal of Preventive Medicine* 35(2S): S116–S123.

Kuhn, T.S. 1970 [1962]. *The Structure of Scientific Revolutions*, 2nd ed. Chicago: University of Chicago Press.

Lange, I.M. and J. Schreck eds. 1959. *Des Sieges Gewissheit: Ein Volksbuch vom Aufbau der Deutschen Demokratischen Republik.* Berlin: Deutsche Demokratische Republik.

Latour, B. and S. Woolgar. 1979. *Laboratory Life: The Social Construction of Scientific Facts*. London: Sage.

Lawrence, R.J. and C. Després. 2004. 'Futures of transdisciplinarity.' *Futures* 36(4): 397–405.

Maturana, H.R. 1978. 'Cognition.' In *Wahrnehmung und Kommunikation*, ed. P.M. Hejl, W.K. Köck and G. Roth. Frankfurt am Main: Peter Lang.

Maturana, H.R. and F. Varela. 1980 [1972] 'Autopoiesis: the organization of the living' (originally published as *De máquinas y seres vivos*. Santiago: Editorial Universitaria), part 2 of *Autopoiesis and Cognition: The Realization of the Living*, ed. H.R. Maturana and F.G. Varela. Dordrecht, the Netherlands: Reidel.

Max-Neef, M.A. 2005. 'Foundations of transdisciplinarity.' *Ecological Economics* 53(1): 5–16.

Mayumi, K. and M. Giampietro. 2006. 'The epistemological challenge of self-modifying systems: governance and sustainability in the post-normal science era.' *Ecological Economics* 57(3): 382–399.

Meadowcroft, J., K.N. Farrell and J. Spangenberg. 2005. 'Governance for sustainable development: developing a framework for sustainability governance in the European Union.' *International Journal of Sustainable Development* 8(1/2): 3–11.

Mühlenberg, H. and M. Kurt. 1991. *Panikblüte*. Leipzig: Forum Verlag Leipzig.

Nicolescu, B. 1999. *Transdisciplinaritatea*. Bucharest: Polirom.

Norgaard, R.B. 1989. 'The case for methodological pluralism.' *Ecological Economics* 1(1): 37–57.

Norgaard, R.B. 2004. 'Learning and knowing collectively.' *Ecological Economics* 49(2): 231–242.

Nowotny, H., P. Scott and M. Gibbons. 2001. *Re-thinking Science: Knowledge and the Public in an Age of Uncertainty*. Cambridge: Polity Press.

O'Hara, S.U. 1996. 'Discursive ethics in ecosystems valuation and environmental policy.' *Ecological Economics* 16(2): 95–107.

O'Neill, J. 1993. *Ecology, Policy and Politics: Human Well-Being and the Natural World.* London: Routledge.

Pielke, R.A. Jr. 2007. *The Honest Broker: Making Sense of Science in Policy and Politics*. Cambridge: Cambridge University Press.

Prigogine, I. 1997. *The End of Certainty: Time, Chaos, and the New Laws of Nature.* New York: The Free Press.

Rank, G., K. Kardel, W. Pälchen and A. Greif. 2003. 'Schadstoffbelastungen im Mulde- und Elbe-Einzugsgebiet nach dem Augusthochwasser 2002.' Paper presented at Statusseminar des BMBF-Ad-hoc-Verbundprojektes Schadstoffbelastung im Mulde- und Elbe-Einzugsgebiet nach dem Augusthochwasser 2002, Ergebnisse und Forschungsbedarf, Freiberg, Germany, 27–29 August.

Ravetz, J.R. 1971. *Scientific Knowledge and Its Social Problems*. Oxford: Clarendon Press.

Ravetz, J.R. 1990. *The Merger of Knowledge with Power: Essays in Critical Science*. London: Mansell.

Rhoten, D. and A. Parker. 2004. 'Risks and rewards of an interdisciplinary research path.' *Science* 306(5704): 2046.

Ring, I. ed. 1997. *Nachhaltige Entwicklung in Industrie- und Bergbauregionen: eine Chance für den Südraum Leipzig?* Leipzig: B.G. Teubner Verlagsgesellschaft.

Schiller, J., R. Manstetten, B. Klauer, P. Steuer, H. Unnerstall, H. Wittmer and B. Hansjürgens. 2006. *Herausforderung Programmforschung: Konzeption, Organisation und Evaluation problemorientierter Umweltforschung*. Marburg, Germany: Metropolis-Verlag.

Schirmer, M., K. Lyon, J.E. Armstrong and K.N. Farrell. 2012. 'A socio-ecological adaptive approach to contaminated mega-site management: from "control and correct" to "coping with change".' *Journal of Contaminant Hydrology* 127(1–4): 101–109.

Schrödinger, E. 1948 [1944]. *What Is Life?* Cambridge: Cambridge University Press.

Schultze, M., A. van der Veen and K. Friese. 2003. 'Die Überflutung des Goitschesees und ihre Folgen.' Paper presented at Statusseminar des BMBF-Ad-hoc-Verbundprojektes Schadstoffbelastung im Mulde- und Elbe-Einzugsgebiet nach dem Augusthochwasser 2002, Ergebnisse und Forschungsbedarf, Freiberg, Germany, 27–29 August.

Sousa, T. and T. Domingos. 2004. 'Phase transitions in macroscopic thermodynamics and neoclassical microeconomics.' Paper presented at the Eighth Biennial Conference of the International Society for Ecological Economics, 'Challenging Boundaries: Economics, Ecology and Governance,' Montréal, 11–14 July.

Thompson Klein, J. 1990. *Interdisciplinarity: History, Theory, and Practice*. Detroit: Wayne State University Press.

Thompson Klein, J., W. Grossenbacher-Mansuy, R. Häberli, A. Bill, R.W. Scholz and M. Welti eds. 2000. *Transdisciplinarity: Joint Problem Solving among Science, Technology, and Society*. Basel: Birkhäuser Basel (Springer).

Tümpling, W. von, M. Rode, O. Büttner, M. Baborowski, M. Böhme, C. Gläßer, B. Sonnabend, M. Matthies, M. Schulz, J. Schanze, U. Walz and A. Sauer. 2006. 'Entwicklung eines Schadstoffausbreitungsmodells zur stoffbezogenen Risikoanalyse und -bewertung extremer Hochwasserereignisse am Beispiel des Landkreises und der Stadt Bitterfeld.' *Umweltwissenschaften und Schadstoff-Forschung* 18(2): 129–131.

van den Hove, S. 2001. 'Participatory approaches to environmental policy-making: the European Commission Climate Policy Process as a case study.' *Ecological Economics* 33(3): 457–472.

van den Hove, S. 2004. 'Review of FP5 Biodiversity Research Projects to Assess Current and Potential Policy Impact.' Brussels: European Commission Research Directorate-General Unit DI-4 'Biodiversity and Ecosystems'.

van den Hove, S. 2007. 'A rationale for science–policy interfaces.' *Futures* 39(7): 807–826.

Varela, F.G., H.R. Maturana and R. Uribe. 1974. 'Autopoiesis: the organization of living systems, its characterization and a model.' *BioSystems* 5(4): 187–196.

Waltner-Toews, D., J.J. Kay and N.M.E. Lister eds. 2008. *The Ecosystem Approach: Complexity, Uncertainty, and Managing for Sustainability*. New York: Columbia University Press.

Watzlawick, P., J. Beavin Bavelas and D.D. Jackson. 1967. *Pragmatics of Human Communication: A Study of Interactional Patterns, Pathologies, and Paradoxes*. New York: W.W. Norton.

Weiss, H., F.D. Kopinke, P. Popp and L. Wünsche. 1998. 'In situ remediation research in a complexly contaminated aquifer: the SAFIRA test site at Bitterfeld, Germany.' In *Evaluation of Demonstrated and Emerging Remedial Action Technologies for the Treatment of Contaminated Land and Groundwater (Phase III): 1998 Special Session Treatment Walls and Permeable Reactive Barriers*. United States Environmental Protection Agency.

Whitehead, A.N. 1978. *Process and Reality: An Essay in Cosmology*. New York: The Free Press.

4 The maturing of the structural contradictions of modern European science

An exploratory sketch

Jerome R. Ravetz

Introduction: the problem

Although the scientific press is still full of exciting new discoveries, there is a widespread sense that all is not well in the world of modern European science (including science-based technology). The most obvious symptoms are a continuing shortfall in recruitment, along with continued public distrust (notably in the United Kingdom and the United States), scandals in both commercialized science (pharmaceuticals) and high-prestige research, and now steadily increasing competition from Asia in many key areas. To the extent that global pollution and climate change are the results of the modern, science-based systems of industrialization, then the pragmatic argument that 'science is good and true because it is successful' has been seriously weakened. None of these symptoms marks the end of science as we have known it; there are very many talented and dedicated scientists whose work still contributes to human betterment. But these problems show no sign of going away, and they undeniably merit serious attention. Making sense of these scattered phenomena is not easy. To some extent as an experiment, I have chosen to use an historical approach here, going through some key issues, most of which have been present in modern European science since its creation some 400 years ago.

In an earlier work, *Scientific Knowledge and Its Social Problems* (Ravetz 1971: 31–68), I identified several pathologies of what I then called 'industrialized science'. These observations were of a science that is entrepreneurial, shoddy, reckless or dirty; and I also observed the risk of runaway technology, developed through the application of industrial science in the absence of effective societal controls. Although in the early 1970s these were just barely visible, over the edge of the horizon, they have since become recognized as serious issues. In the intervening thirty-five years it has become possible to discern the structural features of the scientific enterprise within which those pathologies have flourished, and to discern some new ones that have emerged.

Here I analyse these pathologies in terms of 'contradictions' – meaning a tension whose resolution, or a problem whose solution, is impossible in the terms of the currently accepted frameworks. Contradictions evolve *with* the system they affect. They can be less salient at the outset, and can indeed be suppressed for a long time. But they can eventually 'mature' and then they require resolution, lest they damage or destroy the whole system. A good example of how I am using the term 'contradiction' here can be seen in the political sphere, in the system of slavery in the early United States of America; there, a civil war was needed to resolve the constitutional issue, and even after the constitutional issue was resolved, with passage of the Thirteenth, Fourteenth and Fifteenth Amendments between 1865 and 1870, which banned slavery, first in principle and then in practice, the situation festered as a social issue for nearly another century before a fundamental resolution was attempted. Slavery is a good example of a structural contradiction, particularly the system of slavery employed in the early United States, as it was built into the written Constitution as well as residing within the social life of the nation.

Here I will sketch a set of structural contradictions in European science, as a preliminary to the achievement of a theoretical understanding of how they have arisen and how they might be resolved. This is very much 'work in progress', subject to revision at all degrees of depth at any time. The aim here is to open, rather than to close, the discussion, and the treatments presented below are sketches of the problems at hand – their resolution seeming to be a challenge that lies still ahead.

The contradictions

Listed roughly (but not exactly) in the order of their appearance in the development of science, the contradictions are: knowledge and power; knowledge and ignorance; the True and the Good; consequences; quality; innovation and property; elitism/democracy; corruption in research; image and audience; societal context; reality; and safety. Many of these contradictions were present at the origins of modern science and were suppressed in the intervening centuries. They have now matured and become urgent.

Any growing movement suppresses its contradictions, and modern science was no exception. We may take Thomas Kuhn's (1970 [1962]) insight about 'normal science', which is reduced to 'puzzle-solving within a paradigm', as a metaphor for the whole modern scientific enterprise. Success is achieved in the short run so long as problems can be successfully set and solved. For Kuhn, the lesson of history was that in each field the 'anomalies' – puzzles that defy solution – always arise sooner or later. And when they can no longer be 'suppressed or evaded', the field is ripe for a revolutionary change of paradigm. Modern science as a whole is bigger, more powerful, more hopeful and more dangerous than the particular fields that Kuhn studied. I use the concept of 'contradiction', which has richer connotations than Kuhn's 'anomalies'; but the key insight is the same.

Knowledge and power

The relation of natural knowledge with state power was acknowledged as a problematic issue by both Francis Bacon and René Descartes, but then forgotten. For a long time it was believed that 'pure science' would produce a 'fountain of facts', thereby claiming credit for the good applications while blaming 'society' for the bad. The possibility of corruption of the knowledge-creation process by entanglement with institutional power was gradually recognized again with the emergence of 'big science' after World War II. Now the dominant industrialization and militarization of research produces urgent issues of quality and morale. These are compounded by the involvement of science in what many see as the global exploitation of the world's vulnerable peoples and species (as in biopiracy and 'terminator' seeds). The manipulation and debasement of policy-related science by recent regimes in the United States may be doing lasting damage to science as well as to policy.

What Bacon envisioned as a marriage of knowledge and power is instead becoming a merger, between very unequal partners; therein lies the contradiction of knowledge and power.

Knowledge and ignorance

The relegation and denial of ignorance was central to the programme of the 'new philosophy' of the seventeenth century. This, rather than atomism, was the core of its 'metaphysical barbarism', as it ruptured a tradition of philosophical wisdom extending back to Socrates. Ever since then, this 'ignorance of ignorance' has been maintained by all science curricula and training programmes, and by most philosophers. Education in science is now far more dogmatic than education in theology; useful tools are taught as incontrovertible facts.

One consequence has been a general incompetence in the management of uncertainty in scientific information, which has resulted in the widespread occurrence of misleadingly precise numerical expressions of imprecise empirical dynamics. The NUSAP system, created originally by Silvio Funtowicz and myself (Funtowicz and Ravetz 1990), and its descendants, attempt to rectify this defect by supplying scientists with procedures and protocols for documenting and declaring the systematic ignorances and uncertainties in their data and analyses. These procedures and protocols are tools for the management of uncertainty (van der Sluijs *et al.* 2005). They can be very helpful for scientists and policy-makers alike when their use is complemented by the appropriate craft skills regarding how to use them. As yet, few scientists seem to appreciate the need for such tools and skills. Instead of openly discussing the systemic ignorance about some problems, debates on policy issues are distorted by a general incomprehension of how it is that two equally competent scientists can disagree on a given point. Now, with the growing recognition of policy-critical uncertainties and 'unknown unknowns' of all sorts, ignorance has come back with a vengeance: awareness of its importance is being promoted with all possible motives.

The contradiction between unreflective knowledge and ignored ignorance diminishes the quality of the search for knowledge itself.

The True and the Good

In its long struggle against the institutions of theology, science claimed for itself the achievement of the True and the Good in this world. Among philosophers, the idea of a universal True has been in retreat for more than a century, although science teaching has not yet caught up with the change. In science we have only just now begun learning how our knowledge and our ignorance are shaped by values. This shaping results from the necessity to make choices between 'sensitivity' and 'selectivity' in all statistical tests. The necessary choice between the errors of excess sensitivity and of excess selectivity determines which results are 'not significant' and hence rejected and forgotten. Thus, our ignorance as well as our knowledge is influenced by the values that shape research. In addition, the management of 'outliers', which cannot be reduced to any rule but involves individual judgements, shows how there is a touch of the post-normal even in the most normal of science. All this awareness of the conditioning of knowledge has led to great confusion about the True, especially among those who grew up with a simplistic belief in Facts and the Scientific Method.

As to the Good, it is compromised not merely in the applications of science but also in the very activities that we might describe as doing science. What I have previously called shoddy, reckless and dirty science are not to be ignored. The sufferings of sentient beings (non-human and human alike) in the name of research have previously been justified on the grounds that science is pursuing Truth in the interest of the greater Good. Now that the True and the Good of science are being called into question, the activities themselves need to be justified. One approach is to invoke a new ethic of compassion in science, but this has few roots in traditional practice or understanding. The loss of conviction that science is essentially involved with the True and the Good cannot help but affect morale, upon which both recruitment and quality assurance critically depend.

The contradiction between the old absolutist vision of science and the new realities of this human institution will require considerable maturity for its resolution.

Consequences

The possibility of adverse, usually 'unintended' consequences of the applications of science was also recognized by Descartes and Bacon, but suppressed thereafter. Not until the use of poison gas in World War I was it even imagined that science could do evil. Now the examples of what we might call 'Muddle and Malevolence' crowd in. There remains today the overriding threat of annihilation through nuclear warfare; in the civil sector we have the corresponding threats of global climate change, computer malware and science-based pollutants of all sorts (personal and environmental). To these we add the prospect of the disruptions soon to be produced by the nascent 'converging' technologies of mind and matter. Under what conditions could there be an effective official reassurance that a new technology is 'safe' or 'safe enough'? If the prospect of such successful reassurances is called into question, then the politics of innovation and technology development takes on a new form.

The genuine positive claims regarding the benefits of science are now in contradiction with its unintended, perhaps uncontrollable, negative consequences.

Quality

Bacon decried the very low quality of scholarship and invention of his time, and believed that he could remedy it by an administrative and moral reform. Quality assurance in research science has always depended on the high quality (technical and moral) of its leadership, as there can be no external body of expert critics and quality assessors for 'pure' or 'basic' research.

But research science's informal system of self-regulation is now under increasing strain from the conditions of 'mega-science'. Research and technology development, both civil and military, are increasingly affected by hype and fantasy (GM crops, stem cells, 'Star Wars'), as all scientific discovery promises immediate commercial profit or military advantage. Low-quality information technology is being used as a primer platform for corruption, as in electoral systems in the United States and in public-sector IT systems in the United Kingdom. The extremely powerful high-quality information technology, lauded as faster and more powerful than human thought, has produced bizarre consequences. Research scientists may find themselves unable to judge the quality of their own work because they cannot understand the sophisticated computer programs that analyse their data. And the enormous computer-based financial industry has created masses of 'products', speculative packages of securities, which are useful for rampant speculation but are incomprehensible to evaluators. Extending considerations of quality to science-based industry, we find a very dangerous situation in which the systematic pillaging of the planet (fisheries, rainforests, aquifers) seems to be beyond the ability of anyone to control, and the edifice of incomprehensible computer-based financial 'products' may yet come crashing down with more dire consequences than nuclear war.

The need for effective quality assurance, originally met through the social practices of science, has now come into contradiction with the contemporary social processes governing the production and utilization of commodified power/knowledge.

Innovation and property

Reconciling the needs of scientific innovation and personal intellectual property was first accomplished by devices such as challenges (where a mathematical problem, already solved by the challenger, became their property if no one else could solve it), encryption, and sealed notes claiming propriety. Then a two-stream system emerged: patents ensured that the market would reimburse inventors (or at least patent-holders), and peer-reviewed journals ensured that prestige-rent in the form of citations would accrue to discoverers. Each world had its appropriate etiquette and ethics, and their overlaps could be managed. Now the boundary has become indistinct. With the increasing commodification of knowledge, even past discoveries are now seriously defended in the American courts as the private property of their first user, creating retroactive entitlement to royalty payments from all other users.

In mega-science, researchers lose the intellectual property of their discoveries, which are handed over to the institutions where they work. Their status becomes less that of skilled craftsman and more that of industrial worker.

The contradiction between the need for distinct streams of discovery and invention, and the inevitable blurring of just that distinction in the current management of innovation as property, can easily lead to corruption and paralysis in research.

Elitism and democracy

While the contradiction between elitism and democracy might at first seem out of place in this list, the demand for 'science for the people' was raised unsuccessfully in earlier revolutions (the English, the French); then, under Stalin, the populist charlatan Lysenko destroyed Soviet biology. In spite of professions of democratic sentiments, science is still part of elite culture. The very language of science – explicit, logical, formalized and technically esoteric – requires a style of thinking that is almost totally restricted to those with a lengthy (and expensive) education. It contrasts sharply with the informal, partly tacit, situated and anecdotal knowledge used by those less favoured people who actually keep our systems running (as in the 'Murphy's law' literature). When philosophical doctrines presented as science collide with deeply held popular beliefs, there arises a dangerous reaction, most recently and notably, for example, the rise of creationism in the United States. On the political side the lack of ways to ensure the democratic accountability of the powerful institutions of industrialized science now comes onto the agenda for debates and action. The failure of attempts to introduce GM crops in Europe, in the face of Green activism and public resistance, was the first notable event in the new politics of science. We also find boycotts (of immunization) and adoption of officially disapproved products and processes (organic food, complementary and alternative medicine).

The contradiction between the democratic pretensions of contemporary science and its actual elitist role, in a still very unequal society, can lead to new forms of contestation for which the institutions of science are ill prepared.

Corruption in research

Science has never been immune from human frailty. Battles over 'priority' (securing intellectual property) have been, at times, fierce and vicious. Sir Isaac Newton himself secretly masterminded a report by the Royal Society on the invention of the calculus in which his rival Leibniz was traduced. But generally, science has required, and achieved, exceptional integrity in its work. This includes the intellectual integrity of researchers not yielding to the temptations of quick and easy answers, and the ethical integrity of referees and assessors, giving fair judgements and respecting the property of colleagues. However, under the conditions of mega-science, 'entrepreneurial science' is the enforced norm and there are many new perils of corruption. The prospects and rewards of instant success, combined with the hype, uncertainty and even fantasy of so many projects, create new strains on the ethical standards of scientists. On the one hand, the widespread manipulation of research and of published results by commercial sponsors (notably drug companies), and the complicity of some regulatory agencies, can no longer be ignored or denied. On the other hand, here forms of corruption are endemic to the system of knowledge designed for profit, power and privilege. Campaigns to eradicate them encounter the same difficulties as analogous campaigns in the commercial or political spheres. The sheer magnitude of these new mega-science structures makes it difficult to see the corruptions coming, and almost impossible for any one single scientist to oppose them on their own.

Here the contradiction is that the integrity that had previously been assumed to define the scientific endeavour, a gentleman's enterprise, has now become a social cause needing to be defended against a host of systemic corrupting pressures.

Image and audience

By its very nature, scientific research cannot guarantee to produce an immediate return, and so it has always needed the promise of eventual reward to its patrons: either individuals, institutions or the state. Maintaining a sympathetic audience so as to secure resources, recruits and protection has depended on a sincerely projected image of science as the unique provider of the means to achieve human happiness in this world. That image has been increasingly compromised by the complication of science's relationship with power, with its mixed consequences. The hype for civil nuclear power as a safe technology, discredited by the tragedy of Chernobyl, and recent scandals of science-based consumer industries (BSE; the covering up of problems associated with harmful pharmaceuticals; the promoting of junk food with its huge dosages of sugar, salt and fat) are all examples of situations where science's image as problem-solver is contradicted by its role as creator of new problems. As an example of the new self-contradictory image, a film like *The Constant Gardener* is no more an exposé of corrupt drugs trials by science-based multinationals than *The Sopranos* is an exposé of the folkways of New Jersey gangsters. In both cases the evil is an uncontroversial plausible background element of the plot. Michael Crichton's muckraking-science novels are best-sellers. 'Trust me, I'm a scientist' has become an ironic motto in the United Kingdom. In the United States, science is dragged down with government and industry in the universal cynicism of the public.

Science is caught in the contradiction between the need for an accepted positive image, and the negative reactions of an increasingly sceptical public that is all too aware of the difference between the projected image and the experienced reality.

Societal context

Historically, the context for the growth of European science was the successive phases of expansion of European empires: from the Renaissance onwards, on to the present. Through its expertise in the means of production and in the means of conquest, science was fully engaged in the process of European empire-building, and shared its ideologies (including racism and sexism). Now economic power is moving eastwards, and Euro-American science, especially in its industrial aspects, is beginning to show signs of ageing. The ebbing of local recruitment (and the increasing dependence on Asia for new scientific personnel) is one obvious sign of this condition. Euro-American science could be in a process of hollowing out that is analogous to what has already happened with manufacturing industry and information technology.

Here the contradiction is between the historic role of science as an engine for European imperial power, and its present condition as an integral part of the industrial base that is being recaptured by the East. Given the crucial importance of science in the modern knowledge economy, this contradiction has serious consequences for the European imperial project of the past half-millennium.

Reality

Perhaps the deepest contradiction in modern European science derives from the drastically reductionist, 'atomistic' reality imposed by the 'new philosophy' of the seventeenth century. In a remarkable transformation, this ancient heresy quite suddenly became accepted educated common sense in North-West Europe. This Epicurean metaphysics, denying all things non-material, rigorously excluded both the Aristotelian 'final causes' and the enhanced realities of the Stoic craft-magical tradition. This revived cosmology was later claimed to be a truth, deduced from science, although many of the greatest early modern scientists inhabited a much richer reality. After centuries of dominance, it is now being challenged. Its truncated reality is rejected by Western biblical commitments and Eastern philosophies alike. This sometimes happens within science ('Gaia') and sometimes among its consumers (creationism, complementary medicine). Traditionalist scientists feel themselves engulfed in a rising tide of 'irrationalism'.

They acutely experience the contradiction between the inherited unquestionable metaphysical framework of reductive modern science and the confusing and complex common-sense experiences of its publics.

Safety

Although this is the most recent contradiction, more than any other, it expresses the predicament of the tradition of modern European science. Thanks largely to science, life is (at least for the time being) safer (at least for the rich minority) than ever before in history. 'The Safe' has now become an absolute for public policy, taking its place alongside 'the Just'. But the manifold contradictions in 'the Safe' cannot be kept concealed and they are not yet supported by a quality control system like the ones responsible for ensuring 'the Just'. For practical policy, the question becomes 'How safe is safe enough?', and since safety cannot be measured, the question is itself a conundrum. Safety cannot be reduced to risk, for it is pragmatic, contextual, recursive and ethical. The decisive question is not whether a quantity measuring a risk is zero or 'acceptable', but whether the institutions managing the hazard are competent and trustworthy.

Governments are caught in a policy contradiction: they need to demonstrate a commitment to safety before their electorate, while economic progress, or indeed national economic survival, demands high-tech innovation, which is inescapably dangerous. Some of the recent loss of public trust in governments and their scientists is a result of failure to resolve this contradiction of governance in the scientific age.

Reactions

Some of these contradictions are now presenting urgent challenges. What are we to make of them? Doing more science along the present lines will not resolve them. Indeed, the 'converging' science-technologies that are described by the acronym GRAINN (genomics, robotics, artificial intelligence, nanotechnology and neuroscience), laudable as they are in their own terms, can serve as case studies in the aggravation of the maturing structural contradictions of science rather than as a means to their resolution.

The problem is not one of the failings of individual scientists, either in their motivation or their probity; we can assume that they are doing their best to bring new knowledge and power to humanity. The problem is at the system level. If these inherited structural contradictions have matured, independently of the wills and even of the awareness of the individuals caught up in them, they must now, finally, be addressed directly.

Contradictions need not have destructive outcomes; the success of nonviolence in places like South Africa and Northern Ireland shows that creative resolutions can be achieved. However, the contradictions of modern European science have not yet given rise to a coherent movement for reform or protest. Thus, even the trailblazing ETC Group, which militantly opposes a wide range of abuses and sponsors the 'Captain Hook Awards' for biopiracy, awarded to leading multinationals and governments, focuses entirely on the guilty institutions and has not yet broadened the scope of its critique into the realm of positive alternative action.[1] Projects like Vandana Shiva's Navdanya Biodiversity and

Conservation Farm seed saver and demonstration farm at Dehra Dun[2] do point towards a brighter future, embracing the potential for creative resolution of these contradictions, but as yet they are still few and far between, and have minimal influence on the research science world.

The concept of post-normal science, highlighting uncertainty and value-loading in policy-related science, and calling for an extension of the peer community beyond its traditional elite base, has cut through the inherited false consciousness of science and has provided an initial basis for systematic criticism. It opens up a new workspace for theorizing and analysis at the cutting edge of these contradictions, inviting critical reflection and action; but there remains here much work to be done if the contradictions that post-normal science reveals are to be resolved through creative solutions rather than through degeneration and destruction.

Official responses

It is also impossible for me to predict how these multiple systemic contradictions will sort themselves out or be sorted out. There are, however, already some encouraging responses. Taking note of developments in my own context, the United Kingdom, most impressive is that the leaders of the British scientific establishment are today mainly quite post-normal in deed, if not in word. Starting with Bob May's master-coup in bringing transparency and openness to government scientific advice in the wake of the BSE debacle, he and others have supported a variety of initiatives for 'upstream engagement' which at least aims to achieve the democratization of science. Also, the British have taken the lead among the scientists of developed nations in warning about climate change, and the Royal Society recommends 'integrated, safe and responsible' development for novel technologies like nanotechnology. More broadly, at the level of the European Union the European Commission has ambitious programmes in 'Science in Society', fostering public engagement with science and research. The initiatives fostered by this programme provide an invaluable forum for the rapidly growing world of reflection and criticism gathering momentum within the post-normal approach.

Universities all over the world are modifying their programmes to train up experts in the management of these new problems and in new strategies for their resolution. A special initiative, again from my own immediate context in the United Kingdom, is the two institutes funded by James Martin in the University of Oxford, which are explicitly dedicated to exploring the problems that will become urgent in the near future. Although it remains true that (as Sydney Brenner once said) 'there is no Nobel Prize for Safety', the sciences I call 'SHEE' (safety, health, environment, ethics) do seem to be advancing under the banner of 'the precautionary principle'. Organizations like Pugwash and Scientists for Global Responsibility raise ethical awareness among researchers.[3] Research communities like the Society for Social Studies of Science promote awareness and improved understanding of the both the bright and the 'shadow' sides of science, and the United Kingdom's Chief Scientist, Sir David King, has proposed an ethical code for science, an idea previously restricted to the idealistic fringe. The dialogue between orthodox medicine and complementary and alternative medicine, with all its implications for society and reality, continues and deepens. It is even possible now to get Healing on the UK National Health Service!

Societal responses

Complementary to these developments on the 'established' side of social structures and institutions, there are growing movements of opposition to the increasingly common abuses of science committed in the pursuit of profit, power and privilege. The previous mass campaigns against GM crops in Europe still cause governments to proceed with caution in promoting innovation. Other pressure group campaigns have exposed sources and consequences of the industrial production and distribution of pollutants and poisons, ranging from gender-bending chemicals to artificial sweeteners and just plain junk food. The fear that citizens would turn into nothing more than consumers has not materialized. Rather, citizen-consumers are beginning to show a healthy scepticism about all the established institutions and their claims of safety, and they know how to use their purchasing power. In retail marketing, 'organic' (bred largely by popular distrust of industry and the regulatory authorities), green and 'sustainable' are increasingly recognized labels. Within the worlds of science and learning, ethics is slowly becoming a salient concern. The various 'open' movements in software and in science are now starting to breach the silent barriers blocking access to knowledge, which have hitherto excluded all those who lack the support of rich institutions. The combination of cheap computers, the Internet and the 'wiki' movement on the one hand and this new socio-political awareness of the issues raised in the post-normal science discourse on the other could well lead to a 'democratization of knowledge' of the sort that past reformers of science strove in vain to achieve. In classical Marxist terms, the new 'social relations of production' in IT involve many workers whose level of skill and sophistication is commensurate with that of their bosses, and who can innovate in the social (as with 'shareware') as well as the technical sphere. And on the issue of reality, the 'common sense' of Victorian physics and neo-classical economics has become rather antique in the face of cosmic-scale speculation, micro-scale engineering and systems thinking.

This transformation requires patience; after all, it took a full century before any scientists except for cranks and rebels accepted that the Earth is spinning like a top and also floating through the heavens.

Awareness

Having got this far, I must offer some speculation on which dimension of the complex social system of science might provide the crucial element(s) for setting in motion the processes that could lead to resolution of these structural contradictions of European science. At the moment I favour 'awareness' as the starting point. This is partly from my post-normal background, recognizing Thomas Kuhn as the philosopher who, however confusedly, identified the anti-human tendencies of 'normal science'. Kuhn's myopic puzzle-solving 'normal' scientist is strongly reminiscent of the captive children in a novel by John Hersey, *The Child Buyer* (1960), who were kept manacled and blinded so that they could more efficiently solve mathematical problems for Defense. The 'objective' and 'value-free' character of science, so lauded by its apologists over the generations, justified a teaching style that produced puzzle-solvers who described their actions in the third-person passive voice, and who were prevented from ever seeing a problem that lacked a unique correct solution. Needless to say, many teachers performed such indoctrination in the sincere belief that it was liberating men's minds from theology and superstition; and perhaps, in its early days, it did. But the world moves on. I have done my bit for awareness in science, providing students with a list of questions asking what science means for them in my recent book *The No-Nonsense Guide to Science* (Ravetz 2006). But there is more to be done if these contradictions are to be fruitfully resolved, and it needs to be done by the next generation, with an awareness of systems, complexity and the many dimensions of reality that is appropriate for our times.

I should say that 'awareness' also characterizes the new radical political movements, starting with feminism and including Zapatistas and 'alternative' social change campaigns like the World Social Forum. Their strong base in the ex-colonial 'majority world' provides them with a keen awareness of the contradictions of European science, as they are not sheltered from its consequences by the diffused material affluence that Europeans have enjoyed up until now.

The contrast between these new movements and old-style Marxism should never be forgotten: where old-style Marxism was doomed by its belief in itself as 'The Science of Society', these new movements are making demands for a new social contract between science and society (Ravetz 1990). An enhanced self-awareness of science, with all its inherited contradictions, could help embattled scientists (for example in the United States) defend the integrity of science more effectively against the demagogues and kleptocrats who seem to be helping speed the onset of total system corruption. A renewed appreciation for the irreducible aspects of any valid scientific problem, and particularly of the big problems like climate change, water pollution, fisheries collapses, etc., could help scientists to begin building new methods for non-reductive twenty-first-century science. The 'complementary and alternative' therapies now being funded under the UK National Health Service are also about practising an enhanced awareness of ourselves as integrated systems of body–mind–spirit, integrated as well with the environmental systems that surround us.

Non-violence

However, awareness on its own can become sickly, leading to recursive levels of irony, introspection and even melancholy. Eventually, such unempowered awareness can grow beyond the restraining bonds of common sense and sanity. It needs a guide for action and a control that defines for it its boundaries, and for that I suggest the moral element non-violence.

If there is anything that is redemptive about the history of the century gone by, it is the rise of non-violence as a political and cultural force. I include under that heading the rise of compassion extended to ever-widening sets of beings outside the upper-class white males who had dominated European consciousness for so long previously. The great heroes of that century, Mahatma Gandhi, Martin Luther King Jr and Nelson Mandela, all showed that non-violence can truly transform politics in a way that ordinary methods cannot.

Rather than discuss non-violence at length here, I might just remark that during all the period discussed above in this chapter there was no discernible connection between science and non-violence. Of course, in historical perspective we can say that science helped to create a powerful means of production, enabling 'the human use of human beings' rather than the dehumanization of the many by the few. If we ask what a non-violent science would look like now, the guideposts are few. Gandhi, Schumacher and Vandana Shiva have spoken of it, but no one has yet articulated the vision in relation to the situation and powers of science today.

When one contemplates the insanity and evil wrought in the name of science by the Pentagon in the United States in the course of the 'war on terror', it would seem that a science based on non-violence is still very far away indeed. But if that be the case, let us face the prospect and draw our conclusions.

Valedictory

Do not expect a smooth ride! If the cultural hegemony of science were to be suddenly shattered, we could expect turmoil, confusion and excesses of all sorts. Contradictory tendencies would struggle for supremacy, and their internecine battles could be more intense and vicious than those against the common opponent; this is the lesson of reformations and revolutions in the past. Both creationism and aromatherapy reject reductionist science, but their differences are deep indeed.

In this chapter I have proposed that the progression of science into new situations in the twenty-first century has brought many of European science's inherent contradictions to the verge of maturity. Indeed, the main reason for my analysing these contradictions in European science is to help us become more effective in making their resolution creative and not destructive. It is not easy work and it may at times prove a treacherous path, but I think it is one that needs to be taken up; if we fail to act now, we may expect to soon enough to be acted upon. This essay, preliminary and tentative, is intended as a contribution to the endeavour.

Acknowledgements

My thanks to Silvio Funtowicz and to Kate Farrell for inspiration and dialogue.

Notes

1 www.etcgroup.org/en/.
2 www.navdanya.org.
3 See, respectively www.pugwash.org and www.sgr.org.uk.

References

Funtowicz, S.O. and J.R. Ravetz. 1990. *Uncertainty and Quality in Science for Policy*. Dordrecht, the Netherlands: Kluwer Academic.

Hersey, J. 1960. *The Child Buyer*. New York: Knopf Random House.

Kuhn, T.S. 1970 [1962]. *The Structure of Scientific Revolutions*, 2nd ed. Chicago: University of Chicago Press.

Ravetz, J. 2006. *The No-Nonsense Guide to Science*. Market Harborough, UK: New Internationalist.

Ravetz, J.R. 1971. *Scientific Knowledge and Its Social Problems*. Oxford: Clarendon Press.

Ravetz, J.R. 1990. *The Merger of Knowledge with Power: Essays in Critical Science*. London: Mansell.

van der Sluijs, J.P., M. Craye, S. Funtowicz, P. Kloprogge, J. Ravetz and J. Risbey. 2005. 'Combining quantitative and qualitative measures of uncertainty in model-based environmental assessment: the NUSAP system.' *Risk Analysis* 25(2): 481–492.

5 Beyond reductionism

Understanding the 'ecology' of human nature

Mary E. Clark

Introduction

This chapter is a plea to include human 'social ecology' in the dialogue between ecologists and economists in their efforts to rescue humanity from its current self-destructive path. Over the past 200 or so millennia – a brief moment in evolutionary time – our *Homo* ancestors migrated in waves of close-knit groups from Africa to all the diverse habitats on our planet. Unlike every other species, they did not require eons of genetic adaptation in order to adapt as they went. They survived because their big brains made them both inventive and able to share and pass along acquired knowledge across generations. Those big brains functioned by organizing that information into meaningful stories – often called 'religions' – that explained 'how' group life should proceed in a *particular* way, and 'why'. Thus were our many diverse cultures born. Because of their enormous survival value, these stories became 'sacred' to each group, protected by a deep emotional commitment that made them highly resistant to modification. Whenever the conditions of life changed, it thus became necessary to change the group's techniques for surviving. A change in conditions also demanded the deep psychological work of modifying the sacred story – not only about the proper patterns of daily life, but sometimes even about the very meaning of existence. Evolution has endowed us with brains potentially capable of carrying out both of these adaptive tasks, but technical adaptation is emotionally far easier than is changing our deepest metaphysical understandings. That requires a much deeper 'rewiring' of our brains – of our accepted precepts about how social life *ought* to be lived.

Relative to the past, however, technological developments during the nineteenth and twentieth centuries occurred at lightning speeds, leaving us today with environmental impacts and social upheavals on scales never before experienced. As the twenty-first century begins, this social reordering has 'globalized', affecting billions of people. Furthermore, unlike in much of the past, when change was limited, most often driven by local survival necessity, today it is driven by the West's ever-accelerating planet-wide exporting of new technologies and transnational institutions. Welcome or not, this whirlwind process imposes on all humanity a degree of social reorganizing and psychological restructuring on an unprecedented scale. This stress coincides with our species' burgeoning impact on Earth's ability to support our collective survival needs. We are creating two *converging* crises for ourselves: one social, one environmental. It is naive to suppose that new technologies will somehow 'rescue' us from either one. To do so ignores the emotional depth of the enormous collective cultural adjustments now facing us. The rapid rise in global terrorism and the fuzzy 'wars' now being waged against it are but the tip of the iceberg of what may come. Where do we turn for help?

Since the postulates of Western culture have largely created these crises, the West bears major responsibility for finding solutions. Ideally, we would turn to our 'centres of learning' for insights. Ever since the Greeks and Romans, learned academies – both religious and secular – have served as introspective sources of collective wisdom. Unfortunately, the modern academy, especially in the West, is fragmented into disciplinary boxes: *Unsere Akademie ist zerstreut.* Its disciplines, like the straw of the unfortunate Scarecrow who lost his stuffing, lie strewn about in meaningless disarray. University scholars daily troop off into their own disciplinary tunnels within the 'Academic Dwarfs' Diamond Mine' (Figure 5.1).

There, the 'top experts' from each discipline, using state-of-the-art technology, busily chip away at the 'cutting edge' of their tunnel, creating 'new knowledge'. But no one has a map of the overall mine. No one connects the totality of knowledge to see whether the 'whole' makes meaningful sense. It's a giant

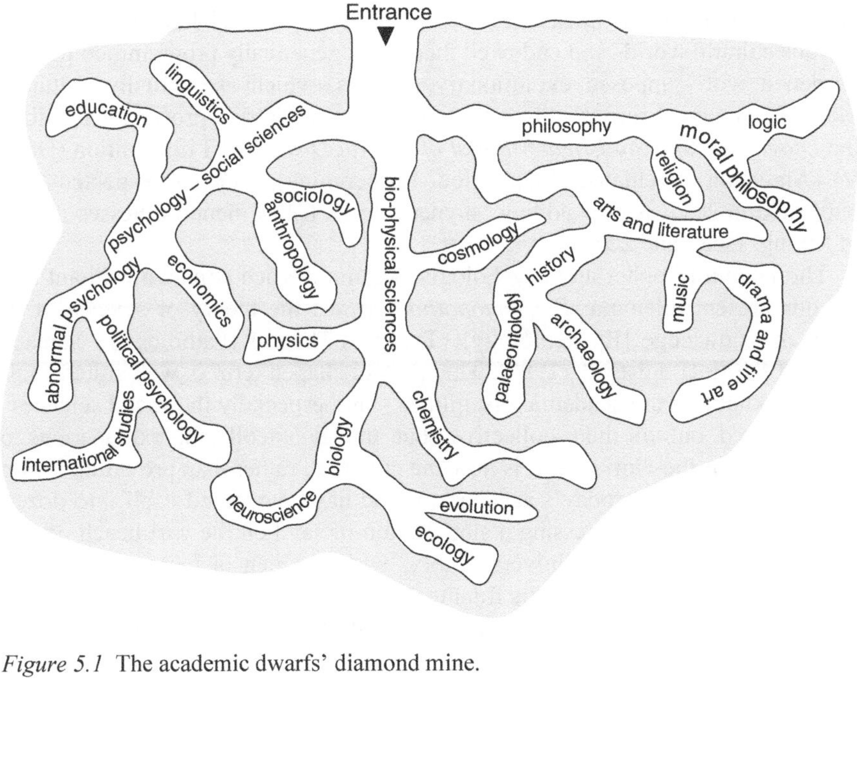

Figure 5.1 The academic dwarfs' diamond mine.

jigsaw puzzle with thousands of pieces but without an intellectual process for fitting them together.

Since the mid-twentieth century this fragmentation of knowledge has been compounded by two trends: (1) an increasing 'quantification' in our study of human behaviour; and (2) the mutation of universities from centres of learning to commercial corporations competing in the lucrative 'knowledge market'.

Trend 1

The tendency to 'scientize' all inquiry, to impose the mathematical methodologies of physics and chemistry on the social sciences in an attempt to create an 'aura of authority' for their theories, has so abstracted them from daily human experience as to render them meaningless (Clark and Holler 1986; Ravetz 1994). Economics, for example, invented a pair of unjustified presumptions about human nature. All social transactions, it argued, can be 'commoditized' (assigned a monetary value), even those between a mother and her infant, and each person's behaviour is intrinsically selfish – driven by calculating 'selfish genes'. These assumptions have been used to justify the universal establishment of competitive markets, which, not surprisingly, *impose* the very behaviours that are supposedly 'intrinsic'. Economic theory became a self-fulfilling prophecy; we now behave 'selfishly' because our economic institutions force us to. Modern political theory has also adopted the self-interest trappings of 'economic man', assuming that attaining control over others is the goal of all political behaviour (Sidanius and Pratto 1999; Saunders 2005). Psychological theory has also floundered. From Freud to Lacan, it has repeatedly abstracted humans from their various cultural worlds and endowed them with genetically programmed psyches burdened with supposed evolutionary demons, which are actually culturally induced! The most recent edition of American psychiatry's professional 'bible', the *Diagnostic and Statistical Manual of Mental Disorders*, Fifth Edition (DSM-V) (American Psychiatric Association, forthcoming), which is expected to be published in 2012, is now adding 'shyness' to its list of mental illnesses in need of 'fixing' (see Lane 2007)!

The late philosopher and psychologist Sigmund Koch coined a brilliant term for our present dilemma: *Epistemopathologistics*: the theory or science of the Basis of Knowledge {Epistemology} + Diseases Thereof {Pathology} + Management of Same {Logistics} (1999). This pretzel-shaped term is well suited to the Gordian knot that the academic disciplines – and especially the social sciences – have created out of their collective, but utterly uncollated, explanations of Humankind-in-the-Universe. It is now the case that, rather than providing a comprehensive overview, today's academic world has fragmented itself into dozens of 'disciplines' each addressing a single grain of sand on the vast beach of sand grains that comprise the Universe Story, within which is located our human story.[1] Attempts to deal with this fragmentation have led to the creation of hybrid disciplines such as 'ecological economics' and 'political psychology'. Yet even these fail to make sense of the whole picture. Koch's despairing observation on this Tower of Academic Babel, where no two disciplines speak the same language, is appropriate here: 'Decades of inquiry into the inquiry of others – and into germane processes inside my own head – have induced in me a sense of awe at the plenitude of our gift for the mismanagement of our own minds' (1999: 397). Social scientists, he says, are especially prone to '"epistemopathic" peregrinations of the inquiring impulse'. Figure 5.2 is my selected list of some of his Epistemopathies, largely rephrased (Koch 1999: 397–398). As Koch points out, this kind of 'culture-bound' thinking afflicts the entire academic world.

Epistemopathologistics pervades higher education, resulting in 'a meaningful thinking' (Koch 1999: 399). Academe today is largely *beside the point* as a corrective to the globally destructive institutions that constitute modern societies. Its dominant function, as I see it (and I think Koch would agree), is to train youths to become efficient robots, holding well-paying positions in rich societies whose self-destructive worldviews academe itself continues to ignore.

Trend 2

This brings us to the second factor contributing to this fragmentation of knowledge: the profound, yet unacknowledged, change in the social role of universities. After centuries of being storehouses of accumulated wisdom, guiding each

1. Extensive use of jargon, restricted to the field.
2. Tendency to so narrowly define one's field as to render the study beside the point.
3. Setting narrow boundary conditions, and then drawing conclusions that are presumed to be universally applicable.
4. Relying on narrowly conceived statistical analysis of a limited study, assuming it will be found to extrapolate to more complex situations.
5. Elaborating – and then blindly trusting in – preconceived 'rules of scientific enquiry' that, if 'correctly followed', would permit anyone to come to the same conclusions.
6. Willingness to accept as real a 'scientifically based' result, without any regard for 'traditional' wisdom or even one's own individual experience.
7. The above practice results in the *total abrogation* of the criterion that knowledge should *make sense*, and in an ultimate distrust of one's own experience. If a finding does make sense, one distrusts *it*.
8. Tendency to uncritically accept current methodologies, ignoring whether they are truly useful and ignoring alternative approaches. It becomes more important to be an 'accepted scientist' in a defined 'field' than to risk asking truly useful questions and seek appropriate means for answering them.

Figure 5.2 Koch's list of 'epistemopathies'.

new generation's elite graduates in their philosophical and moral understanding of 'humankind-in-the-universe', they morphed during the twentieth century into 'academic corporations' competing for prestige, grants and students (Greenberg 2007). The graduates' role today is to add even more to the alma mater's prestige and grants by becoming extremely clever, enormously efficient highly placed managers of the techno-economic machine – which is what global society as a whole is fast becoming.

This universal competition for status in an ever-steepening hierarchy of academic + economic + political power effectively blocks the possibility of correcting the global problems these very institutions create. With a few remarkable exceptions, Western universities, especially those in the United States, have become a crucial part of the problem. 'Rebellious' academics who seek cross-disciplinary dialogue are either replaced or, if tenured, are often underpaid and sequestered in an obscure corner of the campus.

My task in this chapter is to repair the disconnect between the institutionalized suppositions, within both academe and society at large, about the nature of humankind, and our *actual nature* – or at least as much about that nature as is now known. We are learning more every day! There are now helpful new insights that clarify the so-called nature versus nurture wars about what factors shape human minds and human behaviour. Much of it comes from new observations of brain development and brain activity under varying situations. Experience, not surprisingly, significantly shapes the structures of our brains, affecting how we think, feel and act. Fortunately, we now also know that we can 'overcome' past bad experiences by consciously 'rewiring' our brains, but this rewiring is not achieved simply by exhortations to exert personal 'will-power'. It requires compassionate guidance and lots of hard work. Brains may be 'resilient', but they are made resilient *only with the help of the culture around them.* Blaming, punishing, shaming, scolding, threatening – all are *highly* counterproductive, whether one is dealing with individual persons, or selected groups in a larger community, or an entire nation-state! Rather, it is the difficult cerebral and emotional process of 'rewiring' the problematic brains of *everyone involved* that is a prerequisite to establishing socio-political harmony. Indeed, it is those authoritarians who would punish, shame or threaten others whose own brains are most often in need of 'fixing'!

Such new insights should help us break free of the psychological straitjacket placed on us by our widespread assumptions of an incorrigibly selfish human nature. They should emotionally empower us to risk experimenting with new kinds of social institutions that better fulfil our natural longings for reciprocal compassion and mutual trust.[2] We need to profoundly revise our shared understanding of what we humans are *really* like; of how our 'emotional selves' are constructed; and of what makes us feel either 'secure' or 'insecure'. What are the processes of adaptive cultural change that will leave everyone feeling a personal sense of ownership and identity with the new collective image being built?

Only a deeper understanding of how our brains work, of how our minds both 'think' and 'feel', can help us successfully undertake the emotionally fraught task ahead. The totality of our collective project is to change our global and local institutions in ways that not only protect our planetary home but are seen as equitable by all societies, *yet* preserve our rich cultural diversity. Ensuring a multitude of cultural 'experiments' is essential for our species' future survival. Cultural diversity, even more than genetic diversity, is central to our species' continuing adaptability, an eternal well of wisdom to draw upon. Understanding our emotional selves better will make us more willing to preserve – and negotiate – our differences; to swap insights; and hence to adapt in a myriad of cultural patterns around the globe. The corporate capitalism that dominates a host of oversized, impersonal 'democracies' cannot be humanity's 'ultimate solution'.

Brain and culture

> Row, row, row our boat, jointly down the stream
> Thinkingly, caringly, lovingly, merrily, culture's but a dream.

Culture* is *each brain's 'real world'

'In the West, you have TV. In Afghanistan, we have genealogy.' This central Asian, by contrasting their distinctive social pastimes, underscored the huge disparity in cultural 'worlds' that can exist between two contemporaneous societies.

'Entertainment' serves the same social role in both – be it rehearsal of endless details of intricate family trees in Afghanistan and other tribal societies, or watching popular nightly television shows in the electronically wired societies of the West. Both are ways of framing and reinforcing what it means to be a 'human being' – but a human being in one particular culture. So although we intuitively feel a certain kinship with fellow humans in other cultures – and compassion for their suffering – we do not automatically share their vision of what is important in life, of what it *means* to be fully 'human' from their point of view. While the nature of physical pain is universally understood, the nature of that elusive bluebird called 'happiness' is not. Happiness and other similarly diffuse precepts such as 'justice', 'truth' and 'duty' – all necessary for living in human social groups – are culturally defined. They are embedded in the shared worldview that gossip, tradition and, in the modern West, the ubiquitous electronic media daily model and reinforce. They are reflected in the structure of a culture's social institutions: its schools, its economic relationships, its political processes and, formally or otherwise, its religions and the moral understandings they embody.

Cultural stories define the boundaries of behaviour and provide historical authority for why those boundaries exist. They map out social customs and habits, smooth daily encounters and forestall potential friction. Ideally, they create a secure, safe social environment. At the minimum, they create a 'known' world that is embedded in the neuronal connections of each human brain. They are indispensable to human existence. Each newborn infant's mind is physically constructed by the cultural patterns that child experiences. All information received by its sensory system is given shape and meaning, is fitted together into a comprehensible whole by the shared cultural story. So critical to survival is that story that it becomes the emotional centre of each person's life. Embedded in it are loyalties not only to those one personally knows, but also to those who share the same language, history, customs and beliefs. From the emotional brain's point of view, forcing someone to modify their personal worldview – to divorce themselves from that secure understanding – is tantamount to a death sentence. It can be a terrifying prospect. At the very least it requires a gut-wrenching effort that involves painfully rewiring large areas of the brain. (As one who made the quite minor cultural adjustment from California to the United Kingdom, I can attest to a few emotional hurdles that recurred over several years.)

Given how emotionally difficult it can be for an individual to migrate from one culture to another, we can begin to fathom how nearly impossible it is for a whole culture to reconceive its vision of itself-in-the-world. Not only does this require that each individual undergo a personal 'rewiring', it also requires that everyone agree on what the new cultural image, the new 'Real World', should be like. Even more intimidating, it often requires enormous group effort to replace outdated social institutions – from modifying the ways people make their living, all the way to revising concepts of family relationships and duties, a task that is especially difficult in tribally organized societies. Along with obvious emotional upheavals there may also be huge economic costs. Social adaptation is never easy. Not surprisingly, imposed revolutions can be violent in the extreme. We can begin to grasp the enormously powerful emotional impact that prophets, from the Buddha to Jesus and then Muhammad and most recently Gandhi, obviously have had.

Two brief examples of the difficulties of generating even minor social changes in the modern West will perhaps help. In the United States the purely social change of recognizing the legitimacy of same-sex marriages is hugely divisive, arousing enormous emotional resistance even though no one would be physically or financially harmed by such a change. (We can note that Iran's president, while on a visit to the United States, simply 'erased' the 'problem' from his country by proclaiming that 'there are no homosexuals in Iran'!) The other difficult change facing the United States (and the rest of the world) is the need to respond to global warming. This involves both costly modifications of social infrastructure and inconvenient changes in the daily habits of individuals. Until quite recently the fact of warming was flatly denied by the Bush government (not unlike the denial of the existence of homosexuality in Iran), thus blocking discussion at the political level. How the necessary adaptive changes should be implemented and how they will be funded remain outside the political conversation.

These examples of cultural resistance to change – one 'moral', the other 'economic' in its impact – model for us how profoundly difficult changing the collective 'mental world' of a culture can be. As Jared Diamond (2005) observed, history is filled with 'collapses' – from environmental disasters, to internal revolutions, to external invasions by hordes displaced from elsewhere. Unfortunately, he argued that such cultures often 'chose' to go extinct by deliberately refusing to attend to the environmental changes they were causing. He ignores the human mind's deeply ingrained resistance to reconstructing its comprehension of reality, of recognizing an 'inconvenient truth' and then undertaking the difficult task of 'rewriting' its sacred story. Even modern, supposedly 'scientifically based' cultures often manage this only *after* the sky has started to fall in. As Adlai Stevenson is supposed to have once said about his countrymen, 'We Americans never seem to see the handwriting on the wall until our backs are up against it.'

Today, our shared species-wide task is to clarify what it is about ourselves that is common to all humanity and what is specific to each culture. Oddly enough, this distinction has long been a point of dispute among professionals in conflict resolution, particularly those working at the intercultural level. The tribe of 'unifiers' argues that all human nature is basically the same, while the tribe of 'splitters' insists that culture determines everything.[3] Like the blind men describing an elephant, *both* are right – but each 'cultural tribe' of conflict resolvers is so 'blinded' by its own disciplinary insights that neither can 'see' how to resolve *their own dispute*! This is the irony of the West's academic tunnels. It is high time to incorporate some new insights about our emotional selves (from several disciplines) into our 'rational' descriptions of human nature; it is time to begin fitting the disparate pieces together – of attending to our 'epistemopathologies'!

Human genes, human brains and human experience

The premises on which this section of the chapter is based are as follows:

1 All behaviour begins in the brain – until recently, the 'black box' of psychology.
2 The hard-wired survival goals of our universally shared human genes cause each individual to seek *autonomy* of action, secure *attachment* to others, and a '*meaningful story*', shared with others, that provides a supportive social milieu – in other words, a culture.
3 The ideal 'goal' set by our genes is to achieve a *moral* brain that seeks to establish mutually supporting social relationships with others. We are *not* driven by 'selfish genes'.
4 Failure to experience a satisfactory social milieu in infancy creates extensive adaptive changes in the structural patterns of one's brain, instilling feelings of insecurity that block development of trust and empathy. Consequent anxiety for secure acceptance in a group can dominate an individual's behaviour.

In my book *In Search of Human Nature* (Clark 2002) I propose that all humans are genetically programmed to seek three basic psychological conditions for survival: autonomy of personal behaviour, attachment to a group and meaningfulness in life. Among these, *attachment* – being accepted by others – is by far the most critical for survival, and hence the most significant behaviourally. However, the developing human brain is *not* 'self-constructed'. Rather, it develops a 'secure' or 'insecure' outlook in response to the life events it experiences. From infancy on, what we most fear is being rejected or, worse, totally abandoned. If attachment is denied, we will often do almost anything to attain it. Our response to persistent neglect or rejection may take either of two forms: 'dissociation' – withdrawing into a private world, unwilling or unable to risk further feelings of rejection) – or 'retaliation' – using either deception (cheating or lying) or various forms of control (from authoritarian behaviour, to bullying, to outright physical violence) to obtain attention. By contrast, feeling accepted and valued by others imbues a sense of warmth and security.

The *moral burden* for an individual's behaviour, then, lies in the nexus of the reciprocal interactions between the autonomous acts of each developing individual and the social milieu it experiences, especially during, but not restricted to, its early development. Do these experiences add up to safe feelings of acceptance and security, or do they create a brain that is insecure, anxious and constantly vigilant? Both society and the individual play a role in how the latter's brain develops. Too often, the impact of society and its institutions – the 'culture' – is virtually ignored. The entire burden for pro-social behaviour is placed on the individual, regardless of life experiences which that person neither created nor controlled. Human compassion requires us to recognize and responsibly weigh both components of each person's behaviour, a task that 'the law' tends to do poorly. In this chapter I try to repair the great imbalance in our current assignment of this responsibility.

One corollary of what I am saying is that societies whose institutions fail to fulfil basic needs of individual members and small sub-groups, especially those for attachment and inclusion, will most likely experience disruptive behaviours that invite the use of coercion to maintain order. This coercion can easily exacerbate feelings of insecurity and loss of autonomy, and trigger further negative behaviour, incurring ever-spiralling costs to maintain order. Collapse may be inevitable if the causes of widespread disaffection are not corrected.

This leads to a second corollary, namely that these same emotional needs for autonomy, attachment, and meaning apply equally to *groups* within a larger community. Each group has its own customs, rules and beliefs on which its collective survival depends, and when groups interact, the integrity and security of all groups need to be respected if retaliation is to be avoided. This same emotional need for mutual respect extends beyond sub-groups within a community or region, to nation-states. Hans Blix, former chief UN weapons inspector during the search for weapons of mass destruction (WMDs) in Iraq, pointed out (2007) that small countries justifiably mistrust large nuclear powers that feel free to coerce them in multiple ways, while simultaneously disallowing them the right to build such weapons. This is but one case of 'fear for our autonomous survival' being the cause of resentment and potential retaliation. We must conclude,

I believe, that the same feelings of 'acceptance or rejection' apply across all social levels.

We can no longer limit our concept of international relations as being a matter of intimidation and threats, nor even of bribes and bargains, but rather need to see it as one of mutual, concrete human-to-human relationships, as proposed recently by Harold Saunders (2005).

At each of these levels of human interaction, whenever the security of a 'me' or an 'us' is potentially threatened by a 'you' or a 'them', emotions of insecurity are aroused, similar to those experienced by a small infant who feels endangered by an abusive parent. Understanding the causes and psycho-physiological impacts of our emotional states may be the most important task we humans face if we are to adapt with minimum pain, suffering and especially minimum violence, to the many global changes now facing us. Our overstressed planet can scarcely tolerate any further destruction brought on by the latter.

These observations impose upon us academics the moral duty of examining how cultures and their institutions affect the structure of the brains, and hence the behaviours, of their members. This project will surely be psychologically difficult, since it probes almost all aspects of a society, from the education of its children, to its distribution of wealth, to its power structure. People, as I have learned from experience, are very defensive, even about patently immoral features of their own society. (This touchiness applies even to us professors and the current 'theories' in our own disciplines!) We invent all kinds of rationalizations to defend the 'sacred story' that our own culture has constructed. Having to forgo or modify such stories creates feelings of insecurity similar to those of being abandoned by a parent. The 'world' on which *my* security depends is being threatened. Surprisingly, this can be true even in societies where a majority are suffering. Like 'bad parents', a bad social story that is familiar is emotionally far better than nothing! Oppressed groups within a nation-state will still send their sons and daughters to fight for its preservation against external forces. Borrowing from Reinhold Niebuhr (1960 [1932]), we may thus think of the world as constructed of fundamentally *moral* human beings living in and adapting as best they can to *immoral* societies.

Evidence that morality is intrinsic to primate brains

The claim by Richard Dawkins and some fellow biologists that genes are intrinsically 'selfish' was eagerly embraced by Western economic theorists, since it provided moral imprimatur for their claim that *competitive* free-market capitalism 'naturally promotes maximum efficiency' – and is therefore economically virtuous. Belief in an inevitable Hobbesian 'war of all against all' in the face of scarcity provided convenient legitimization of an economic order that was blatantly unjust by any ordinary moral standard. These same ideas were also used to legitimize the political and legal institutions designed to control the resulting social unrest generated by such extreme inequality: harsh laws and burgeoning prisons. 'Criminals' were conveniently seen as unredeemed products of our selfish genes, not as victims of institutions they did not create. This assumption is part of the hard-core belief in human self-centredness that I heard repeatedly from hundreds of students over the years: 'You can't change human nature; it is naturally greedy and selfish!' In the popular mind, innate morality is dismissed as evolutionarily impossible; therefore, genuine trust cannot exist.

Along with some others, I have long argued that we humans are not manipulated by 'selfish genes' but are *genetically* inclined to promote our individual survival by actively contributing to the survival of our group (Clark 1989, 2002). When spontaneous reciprocity fails to develop, it is because stresses intervene that block it. Nor does support for our group depend on the presumption that all group members share most of our genes, argued as the only possible evolutionary explanation by W.D. Hamilton (1963, 1975). Selfishness, per se, is not genetically wired; helping other humans is. Indeed, David Erdal (2005), who reports on superior human psychological and physical health in modern egalitarian, as against hierarchical, communities in Italy, argues that this is because we evolved in such cooperating, sharing egalitarian societies.

Evidence from other primates

Numerous recent studies both on other primates and on humans support this claim. Unlike some of their cousins, macaques in captivity can be rather feisty, yet in the wild they live in closely knit groups and spend hours per day grooming each other – a hygienic activity. Do they have some sort of 'tit-for-tat' accounting system: 'You scratch my back and I'll scratch yours'? Primatologists unexpectedly found that those who are doing the grooming have very low cortisol levels. Cortisol is the notorious adrenal hormone that soars in times of stress and is lowest during pleasurable moments. Against all predictions by sociobiologists and selfish-gene theorists, doing a service for another monkey rewards the *doer*, while the receiving monkey's cortisol levels remain unaffected. The 'helper' receives more psychological benefit than the 'helped' in this species, and the habit of reciprocal grooming keeps the group both healthy and bonded. A 'non-selfish-gene' theorist might suppose that natural selection is rewarding the hard-working groomer because her 'sacrifice' is actually strengthening group ties of cohesion, which in turn makes the whole group more likely to successfully reproduce its next generation. This apparent example of the importance of *group selection* in evolution puts one more monkey-wrench into the 'selfish gene' theory (Holden 2007).

A human example first reported in the *Washington Post* summarizes a series of psychological experiments and brain-imaging studies which show that the human brain has a built-in moral compass: 'many aspects of morality appear to be hard-wired in the brain'. For example, the neuropsychologist Jordan Grafman at the US National Institutes of Health showed that when volunteers chose to place 'the interests of others before their own, the generosity activated a primitive part of the brain that usually lights up in response to food or sex'.[4] These results imply that *empathy* and *helping others*, the basis of *morality*, must have existed in our earliest ancestors and may well be connected with the pleasurable actions of grooming among other primates, as described above.

Joshua Greene, a neuroscientist at Harvard, argues there is no single moral centre in the brain.

> [M]oral judgment does not appear to be a function of 'higher' cognition ... [n]or do moral judgments appear to be driven entirely by emotional responses. Rather, moral judgments appear to be produced by a complex network of brain areas subserving both emotional and 'cognitive' processes.
>
> (2005: quotation from p. 17 of draft)

Greene's work implies, in humans, a cognitive overlay in moral decision-making that allows us to invent 'reasons' to justify our moral choices. This newly evolved capacity has both advantages and disadvantages. If we modify our perception of 'moral' when we discover that some once approved behaviour in fact has had bad outcomes – 'Spare the rod, spoil the child', for example – then the cognitive overlay becomes an advantage. We learn the error of our earlier assumptions. But equally, 'reasoning' allows us to invent a moral argument for an immoral act in the first place and to justify it by a 'rational' moral claim. We can – and often do – override our innate moral instincts for socio-political purposes.

The claim of innate moral tendencies in primates other than humans is a subject that arouses great resistance among many philosophers. In a recent book, Frans de Waal (2006), the world's best-known primatologist, describes the mountains of evidence for reciprocal morality among various primates, while a group of moral philosophers critique his conclusions. Whereas both Charles Darwin and Frans de Waal claim that moral instincts are innate, a product of natural selection, Thomas Huxley (Darwin's spokesman), some modern evolutionists and most philosophers insist that morality is a 'veneer', a cultural invention needed to correct what they insist are our *real* inborn tendencies: war, rape, cheating and inveterate selfishness. But as we shall see, the innate potential for moral behaviour is indeed universal. Its full expression, however, depends on what each individual brain experiences during the completion of its development after birth.

These studies on primate brain function have two extremely important consequences for our self-understanding. First, the presumption of 'innate selfishness' in all individuals – so ardently promoted by 'selfish-gene' evolutionists, and eagerly adopted by mainstream economists – is unfounded. Evolution did *not* create self-centred primates; it created empathic, caring creatures, anxious to belong to and be valued by *a group*. The propensity to repair social relations after rifts is widely present in all primate species. It is surely time to banish competition between individuals from its central place in our understanding of the evolution of social primates and to incorporate empathic reciprocal valuing into our basic model of intrinsic primate behaviour. This will require the dismantling of the many rationalized arguments invented to justify all competitive behaviour as 'natural', but that is another story, one I have addressed in detail elsewhere (Clark 2002: esp. chs 6 and 7).

The second important consequence is the impact our contemporary social institutions have on how our brains develop. Foremost among these is the way we raise our infants in the first crucial years after birth, about which there has been an explosion of new information in the past decade. We do not all arrive at adulthood with the same emotional and moral equipment.

Early brain development: we are all 'preemies'

Compared to other mammals, human babies are born nine to twelve months too soon, utterly helpless. Their half-developed brains rapidly complete their development, however, and by age 4 a child's brain is already 85 per cent of its adult size (Perry and Szalavitz 2006: figure 1, in the appendix on page 247).

During that brief time the major neuronal pathways of the burgeoning cerebral hemispheres are laid down – and the patterns they form are shaped by each infant's experience. I draw mainly on the work of Dr Bruce D. Perry, a child psychiatrist who works with seriously disturbed children, and of Professor Allan N. Schore, a neuroscientist who studies infant attachment.

'In 1987,' Perry writes, 'child psychiatry had not yet embraced the neurosciences. Unfortunately, the prevailing view of children and trauma at the time – *one that persists to a large degree to this day* – is that "children are resilient"' (Perry and Szalavitz 2007: 18, emphasis added): 'Children are resilient. They will be fine' (ibid.: 38). It is still widely assumed that very young children are not affected by witnessing violence, mutilation and devastation, or even experiencing abuse and neglect. Nothing is further from the truth. Whenever an infant has a profound traumatic experience – such as abuse by a trusted adult, or abandonment – its right hemisphere (RH) records the details of the incident, which are passed along to the limbic storage centre. The child becomes emotionally sensitized to similar events. When such events are repeated, a permanent state of anxiety known as *hypervigilance* develops. Temporary mental 'states' turn into permanent 'traits'. Children are not resilient. They won't be 'fine', say Perry and Szalavitz. '[C]hildren are more vulnerable to trauma than adults.... Resilient children are made, not born' (ibid.: 38). By 'made', Perry and Szalavitz mean that youngsters must be given therapeutic help, whether by parents or professionals, in order to reconstruct the organization of their brains and thus overcome the panic, terror and trauma that reminders of a past negative experience spontaneously call forth. This is a form of post-traumatic stress disorder (PTSD) permanently imprinted into the neuronal pathways of an infant's brain.

Even today, disturbed children, depending on their symptoms, are being diagnosed with various 'mental' afflictions, such as attention deficit hyperactivity disorder (ADHD), while the underlying social causes of their behavioural problems go unrecognized. Misdiagnosis of brain trauma is *still* very common. Instances include the readiness by professionals to prescribe mood-changing drugs to control disruptive behaviours in young children and, within the military, by the unwillingness of those in charge to acknowledge the depth of brain trauma experienced during combat. PTSD is real – and can happen at any age. It does *not* 'go away' on its own. Every hypersensitized human emotional system requires a long period of safe interaction with compassionate 'others' in order to defuse the automated fear response in its neuronal pathways. Rewiring brain patterns is a long, slow process that can seldom be accomplished simply by application of self-generated 'will-power'. It requires positive empathic support from a circle of trusted others.

As Perry and Szalavitz further note, as recently as 1995 the brain scan of a young child raised in a dog cage for five years was diagnosed by neurologists (who did not bother to inquire about his home life) as evidence of a 'genetic defect'. The scan revealed an atrophied brain with a tiny cerebral cortex whose ventricles were filled with fluid where there should have been nerve cells. (Years of therapy restored his brain.) As Perry and Szalavitz repeatedly imply throughout their book, 'The brain is an historical organ, a reflection of our personal histories' (2007: 128).

To this day there is widespread institutional and cultural *denial* of this now-demonstrated fact. In American society, inept child care is a major cause of many social problems that begin in infancy, in the privacy of troubled homes.

Another recent major contributor to our understanding of human brain development is the already-mentioned neuroscientist Allan N. Schore, who has followed the neonatal brain development of infants in the course of their interactions with their mothers (2005). His simultaneous brain images of interacting mothers and infants reveal 'mirroring patterns' between their brains. They 'light up' in the same places – as if in 'conversation'. Whatever emotional mood one of them is feeling, the other is mimicking simultaneously. Schore can actually visualize the personal history of an infant's brain being shaped by the quality of its social experiences.

Schore's work clearly demonstrates how our early experiences set the stage for *secure* or *insecure* psyches throughout life. Especially critical is the early development of the emotional right hemisphere of an infant's brain. At birth, the cerebral hemispheres have scarcely begun to develop. Only the brainstem, which controls critical survival functions, and its associated limbic system are fully active. The latter is a large, unconscious emotional processing area that interacts with the endocrine system, which in turn regulates body chemistry. All three are essential for survival – and they all function more or less automatically, in accordance with whether we are secure and safe, or in distress or danger.

After birth, the limbic system begins to receive conscious signals from the rapidly developing RH, where emotional information about the infant's daily experiences is being tallied. The RH evaluates the 'good/bad' quality of each event and passes significant (memorable) information along to the limbic system, where it is permanently stored. Highly traumatic, life-threatening experiences are particularly recorded. This experience-dependent construction of the right brain/limbic neuronal pathways thus creates the emotion-laden 'historical brain', which later triggers varying levels of protective, defensive reactions, such as those described in traumatized children by Perry and Szalavitz.

With these new, non-invasive techniques, Schore has shown how the developing infant's brain is simultaneously responding to the brain of its mother as the two are interacting. The emotion-dedicated RH of the infant is developing a reciprocal 'emotional bond' with the same region of the mother's brain. If the bond is positive, the baby's RH grows rapidly, resulting from their ongoing 'proto-conversation'. The infant feels secure, learns to trust and by around the twelfth month of life starts to actively explore its world. Only then does the laggard left hemisphere (LH), with its capacity for language, verbal memory and logical thinking begin to develop. Emotions come first!

Schore's data show that attentive maternal–infant interaction creates a well-adjusted, secure baby capable of maturing with feelings of self-confidence. By contrast, an infant that has experienced abusive behaviour or – even *worse* – prolonged periods of neglect, being left to cry without comfort or attention, becomes extremely insecure and *potentially unable to form trusting relationships*. The fact that a 'bad' response is better than no response at all speaks to the enormous importance of some sort of human interaction in the crucially critical early development of the human brain. A neglected brain may never become fully 'human' and is often deprived of a sound basis for moral sensitivity. There are 'successes', however. I know one case where late learning did work, but the adoptive parental input was profound, patient and extremely wise. And Perry, after years of therapy with the boy kept in a cage, whose cortical hemispheres had failed to develop, was able to correct the damage, enabling him to attend college (Perry and Szalavitz 2007: ch. 6).

Schore reports a high incidence of borderline personality disorder (BPD) in toddlers who were abused in infancy. Their hypersensitized RH sends fear-laden signals to the brainstem. The child lives in a state of hyperarousal, marked by extremes of agitation: crying, screaming, even vomiting. Blood pressure and heart rate are high. As the 'fight-or-flight' system takes over, the child becomes *hypervigilant*, constantly focused on the possibility of danger, unable to concentrate. This is Nature's attempt to ensure survival of a helpless creature that has 'learned' to sense danger in everything. An alternative state, reported by numerous researchers, including Perry (1997, 1999), is one of depressive withdrawal, or *dissociation*, in the presence of threat. In survival terms, one is trying to escape interacting with others by becoming mentally 'not present' (Clark 2002: ch. 6).

Surprisingly, in most cases of infant abuse or neglect the later-developing 'rational' LH is far less affected than the 'emotional' RH. Provided a child has sufficient opportunity to physically explore its surroundings and to experience language, its IQ may scarcely be affected, even after severe emotional deprivation. If seriously neglected or abused as an infant, a high-IQ adult may remain deficient in emotional sensitivity, misinterpret social signals, be unable to empathize with others and be easily roused to anger. Emotional deficits formed in the first couple of years become more or less permanent when, at around age 3, the brain prunes away unused neuronal pathways, preserving only those that have been most strongly reinforced. Intense therapy, however, can compensate greatly, as Perry has shown.

This severe pruning of an excessive number of neuronal connections in human brains occurs twice during development: once during the toddler stage and again during puberty. By adulthood, our major emotional and cognitive patterns, our 'personalities', are solidly in place. The fact that deep emotional insecurity may be hidden by learned behaviours, however, creates a lifelong potential for outbursts of antisocial behaviour under conditions of stress, or whenever such behaviour becomes socially approved. People may learn social skills to compensate for their emotional deficits, but permanent restructuring of their deep-rooted, insecure affect patterns requires prolonged compassionate therapy similar to that for the PTSD that can affect soldiers and others who experience terrifying incidents.

The impact of 'ecology' on the psychic security of infants and adults

We now arrive at the responsibility of societies as a whole in the development of morally competent individual citizens. Western – and particularly American – society, with its highly individualistic notions of human nature, assigns total responsibility for social behaviour to the individual. It is tacitly assumed that conscious 'will-power', arising from the rational LH, can override all reflex negative emotional signals emanating from the RH, in all situations and regardless of prior developmental experience. Such absolute control is assumed by most legal systems, and is demanded by those in authority. This cavalier assumption, I believe, requires revisiting. It lets cultures off the hook.

The correct aetiological identification of the 'berserk states' exhibited by many returnees from Vietnam finally resulted in PTSD becoming recognized as an acquired mental illness outside an individual's control. No amount of 'will-power' can prevent the triggering of spontaneous flashback behaviours. Brain restructuring – through prolonged therapy, often undertaken in the supportive company of fellow sufferers – is necessary for recovery. These uncontrollable reactions, it was finally realized, are survival responses brains spontaneously generate following repeated exposure to deadly danger.[5]

It is long past time that we extended this insight to all other human experiences of profound endangerment. Mistreatment – or worse, abandonment – in infancy is scarcely an infant's fault any more than PTSD is among individuals in the military. However, in many contemporary societies, especially the United States, far too many parents have little or no outside social support and lack personal knowledge about an infant's emotional needs. Even those who *wish* to be attentive parents may, if they are economically unable to stay at home or afford truly adequate day care, be forced to use affect-deficient alternatives, where infants receive little or no emotional support. Physical safety is too often the sole consideration: 'Is the child fed, changed and kept from bodily harm?' This is all the law requires, and is all that the boy in the dog cage experienced.

Armies of such emotionally neglected children enter social life at constant risk of making relational errors, their secret deficiencies hidden from view by their normally developing language skills and 'passable' coping behaviours for the simplest social interactions. But they remain insecure, inept at reading the emotions of others. Often they are socially shunned. They may be neglected by peers, or become non-cooperative 'troublemakers', perhaps given drugs to control their behaviour. In either case, their underdeveloped affect processing states not only remain unaddressed but are often made worse. Other children, raised in a pervasively competitive atmosphere, readily make fun of the withdrawn 'losers', exacerbating their feelings of rejection, while the adult world punishes the angry misfits as 'bullies'. In either situation the child's underlying emotional insecurities are ignored – and often made worse. The belief that punishment will correct underlying psychological deficits is one of the cruellest delusions from which most contemporary societies suffer.

It is seldom appreciated how allowing such maladaptive conditions of child development to persist generates enormous and growing overheads in modern societies. One instance where such costs are becoming recognized is an organization called FIGHT CRIME: INVEST IN KIDS.[6] Founded in 1996, it now exists in ten US states. Those involved include sheriffs, prosecutors, victims of violence and youth-violence experts. Police are the ones who are called to investigate 'disturbed' families, where they often observe young children in possible danger of abuse or neglect, only to find themselves, a few short years later, arresting those same children for serious crimes. They postulated a connection and began to gather data. When mothers in families at risk received parent coaching from a state-supported agency, the rate of infant abuse and neglect dropped by about 50 per cent. And the arrests of youths at age 15 from such families dropped by about 60 per cent. It's the old adage: a stitch in time saves nine. In the case of Oregon, it turns out that one dollar spent by the state on in-home parent coaching saves taxpayers five dollars later on, in avoided costs for criminal investigations, court costs, incarceration and the belated psychological healing that could have been provided years before. Indeed, the enormous socio-economic inequalities in American society, one of the steepest among all developed countries, generate the highest per capita costs for the expensive social overheads that are incurred.[7] Addressing the social causes, embedded in American institutions, of such 'crimes' as drug use, gang fighting and the like not only would be a collectively moral act but would be economically rewarding. Why aren't modern economists studying this?

It is now clear that culturally accepted social institutions – such as competition and the justification of massive social inequality – can, and do, affect the psychic security of infants, and of the adults they become. One final important finding in recent years is that the conditions one generation of infants experiences – whether secure or insecure – result in the same process being repeated in the next generation (see Fraiberg *et al.* 1975; Fraiberg 1980; Lieberman *et al.* 2005). Bruce Perry was asked during a National Public Radio discussion on 'sick societies' (National Public Radio 1996) whether a whole society could become 'crazy' – in reference to a period of hideous social mayhem in Russia that lasted from the reign of Ivan the Terrible to Peter the Great, around 1550–1700. Perry replied, 'The answer is "Yes".' The initial psychosocial and monetary 'costs' of revising social institutions to eliminate their gross inequalities and associated evil consequences would soon be paid back in an enormously more efficient economy and a psychologically far more pleasant 'social ecology'. (Details of how to overcome the political and psychological barriers to implementing such profound change must be left for a future paper.)

Group identities in today's world

Our brains did not evolve to live in today's mega-societies but in small, mobile groups of a few dozen, tied by kinship and trade to neighbouring groups. Even that level of social complexity was enough to create a very large brain. Today, most of us know, personally, perhaps a few thousand people – most rather casually. People we interact with and count as significant friends or family may number a few hundred. Yet most of us now live in urban areas comprising a few thousand to a million or more people. We cannot personally know everyone else, yet we all 'identify' with, and feel loyalty towards, that which we all share: the same 'ecological space'. Daniel Kemmis, former mayor of Missoula, Montana, has written with considerable insight about how the sharing of a particular 'place' by a random group of people automatically creates a common identity (1990, 1995). For example, my small town of Cottage Grove, Oregon (with a population of less than 10,000), possesses a powerfully shared historical identity despite the heterogeneity of its citizens, a fact that has won it recognition, twice, as one of the United States' ten most livable cities.

Similar feelings of identity exist towards one's state and region. Indeed, national identities in the modern world have, if anything, gained in strength during the past century. In a Chautauqua lecture on 'fanaticism', the theologian Martin E. Marty noted that in 1976 the two-hundredth anniversary of the signing of the Declaration of Independence happened to fall on a Sunday. He commented that in all the nation's churches, if anyone had happened to have sent the sanctuary flag – the Stars and Stripes – out for cleaning, the whole congregation would have taken notice. Even removing the Cross or the Star of David would stir up less concern. 'Be careful of this kind of symbol,' he warned, noting that the French philosopher Jacques Ellul had said, 'It is because the modern state has become sacred that once again forces like fascism were made possible' (Marty 1994). Is it perhaps our hyperindividualism – the very lack of numerous strong, person-to-person relationships in giant modern societies – that allows such intense nationalisms to arise? Are not most of us perhaps emotionally more isolated than ever before in human history?

Marty was illuminating humankind's deep need for 'identity' – for a meaningful social 'self'. In a sense, all 'identities' have a religious quality. When a group feels its identity is threatened, it becomes fearful. It circles the wagons, draws boundaries, and becomes 'exclusive' – a word Carl Sandburg once called 'the ugliest word in the English language' (Marty 1994).

We are all familiar with class and ethnic 'exclusivity' within societies – with how psychologically painful it is for those who feel excluded. In most societies, outright oppression is now legally proscribed. The shame of colonization, of the Nazi Holocaust and of slavery in the United States sensitized humanity to such blatant political inequality. Yet equally blatant economic inequality persists globally, and the psychological and physical trauma it imposes remains in political limbo (Wilkinson 2005).

What sort of psychological security does 'national identity' afford to an individual human being? Components are language, some sort of political-economic order, a definition of 'justice' and an historic memory – in short, a meaningful framework for one's daily life. Existential meaning is found in emotional attachments – to symbols such as a flag or anthem, and to collectively recalled 'glories and traumas', whose significance is often embodied in past and present national leaders (Volkan 2004). So strong has this 'identity need' become in the United States in recent decades that there has been growth in adherence to highly emotive religions. One wonders whether the concurrent decline in religious observance in Europe may be due to increased social supports there.

In the United States, as I recently discovered when speaking to a local group of relatively sophisticated retired professionals, there is a powerful tendency to be highly protective of 'our' nation's identity and its underpinning ideologies. Just because I pointed out the global problems we all face and the necessity for adapting our national institutions, I was met by a firestorm of defensive, half-shouted responses. Somehow, I had 'attacked' the Constitution, 'belittled' the military and didn't understand that 'our whole problem is our school system'. I had mentioned none of these things. These were emotional outbursts to a perceived threat to their (individually quite diverse) 'American identity'! The possibility of having to adapt social institutions created a wall of resistance. Not one offer of a possible solution. Simply: 'shoot the messenger'.

The convergent emergence of global warming, oil depletion, population pressures and other environmental stressors is occurring at a time when historic cultural identities around the world are being threatened by economic globalization under rules imposed from outside – mainly by the United States and other 'developed' nations. This, more than any other global trend, accounts for the advent of 'terrorism', which in turn has triggered inappropriate retaliatory military responses that only exacerbate the psychological fears which first initiated the terrorism. Humankind as a whole seems to have lost touch with its collective moral compass. Global 'social ecology' has become toxic.

Overriding our moral instincts: society's role

Conventional academic approaches to the study of human moral behaviour tend to utilize contrived situations. One common example involves a runaway train that will kill ten people unless the bystander pulls a switch to deflect it onto another track, where it will kill 'only' one person. Such 'body count' thinking works 'cleanly' – unless, of course, the unlucky person on the second track happens to be a baby, or the bystander's father! As was discussed earlier in the chapter, the 'emotional' brain is what really counts in life. It is the seat of our moral decision-making, and how it responds in a new situation depends on what past secure and insecure experiences have imprinted themselves on it.

To the extent that we behave 'morally' because we fear others' disapproval, we are acting out of our need not to be rejected by society as a whole, another of our emotional RH reflexes. It is not compassion that moves us, but need for acceptance. This, of course, contributes to order-keeping in small village communities where there is no 'police force' to maintain order. Such communities, however, usually have much stronger, compassion-based relationships among their members, where the feelings of others are constantly part of people's awareness. Life is mentally lived in the others' moccasins, and one's social acceptance is seldom in doubt. Moral behaviour is more natural reciprocity than onerous adherence to rules. As neuroscience now explains, such conditions lead to a socially positive emotional state (see Rogoff 2003 for a cross-cultural analysis of these ideas).

To sum up, then, the strength of one's urge to assist another person depends heavily on how strongly one's innate tendencies for trust, compassion and 'gifting' (one might call them the Mother Teresa trio) have been reinforced by personal life experiences. Have our attempts to bond with others been (1) openly welcomed and reciprocated? Or have they been (2) conditional, dependent on our achieving some goal set by another (such as 'getting top grades', or 'tidying up my room', or 'winning a game')? Or, worst of all, have they been (3) shunned altogether – do we feel rejected, abandoned? The relative frequency of someone's answers to these three types of past personal experiences, I suggest, reflects the quality of the moral instinct, to trust or not to trust, that past experience has wired into their emotional brain. Rejection anxiety is surely high in contemporary US culture, owing to the pervasive competitive rankings found in almost all life settings, something advertisers exploit to the hilt but both 'rational' economists and family psychologists mostly ignore.

In modern urban life the quality of our encounters with others is increasingly depersonalized. Walking down a crowded sidewalk, some people are automatically attentive to others around them, moving aside slightly, perhaps making eye contact, even smiling, saying 'hello'. Many others come charging straight ahead, often clutching a cell phone and shouting into the air, oblivious of the fact that they are not in a telephone booth. Those belonging to the latter group are increasingly common in our electronically wired society. In stores, checkers and other employees are likely to be treated by 'the public' as robots rather than as human beings with names and histories. (Some manage to 'reciprocate' by carrying on conversations among themselves while serving clients.) The human quality of interpersonal encounters is receding rapidly.

What does this have to do with 'morality'? In a way: everything. Our dominant – though unarticulated – social context is one that focuses inward, on individual identity, *at the expense of others*. My sidewalk vignette is about 'unknown-others-in-a-crowded-space'. People as human beings disappear from consciousness. It's a powerful symptom of the hardening of the American RH towards others – too often even towards family and siblings.[8] We imprint on children extremes of self-centredness; we promote competitive behaviours; we institute ranks – Grade Point Averages and honour rolls in school, sports championships, extreme variation in job salaries. Of course, there are 'rules' of honesty and sportsmanship to fend off mayhem, but social rank matters deeply to personal identity. High rank comes from being *more* 'accepted', *more* socially 'valued' and therefore *more* 'secure'. In a competitive hierarchy, however, status becomes fragile, always at risk of being lost.

What goes unmentioned in Western society as a whole (even by most psychologists) is that this highly conditional nature of one's personal psychic security is engraved in one's RH. Ours in many ways is a hypervigilant society, where individuals live anxious lives filled with constant stress, constantly patrolling the social perimeter around them for signs of rejection, and hungry for reassurance. And, I suggest, this is as true for corporate CEOs or college professors, with their frequently overblown (defensive) egos, as it is of the members of street gangs in inner cities. In a competitive mobile hierarchy of extremes of status, few are truly emotionally 'safe'.

In recent years, considerable interest has arisen over how easily most people can be coaxed into extreme exclusionary behaviours by persons in authority. Most psychologists are familiar with the story of Iowa's third-grade teacher Jane Elliott (Elliott *et al.* 1992), who devised an 'experience of oppression' for her class after Martin Luther King Jr was assassinated (Peters 1987; Tappan 2005, 2006). Her 'blue eyes' versus 'brown eyes' experiment worked in an almost shocking way, though of course she carefully debriefed the children after both groups had experienced the 'power' of dominance and the 'shame' of rejection. The greatest lesson, as Elliott had intended, was that the emotional rewards of dominance become repulsive once one has personally experienced the pain of being socially scorned. (The moral centres of their brains had been activated!) After decades of repeating her initial experiment in schools and adult institutional settings, Elliott has consistently reported identical findings. For children, it takes only five minutes to establish extremes of dominance, reflected in upright, confident posture and facial expressions to match, and of submission, reflected in crestfallen expressions and hunched, hangdog posture. Among multiple adult groups the responses were virtually the same, although it sometimes took ten minutes for them to become established.[9]

Similar responses to 'authority' were found during experiments conducted with American university students during the 1970s by Stanley Milgram (1974) and Philip Zimbardo (Haney *et al.* 1973; Zimbardo 2007). In both cases, perfectly decent student volunteers were instructed by a professor to perform physically or psychologically harmful acts on others. In Milgram's case the 'others' were actually confederates who faked the physical harm of electric shocks seemingly inflicted on them by the willing students. But in Zimbardo's experiment the humiliating treatment that those labelled 'guards' decided to inflict on their 'prisoners' – all fellow undergraduate students at Stanford University – became all too real. The experiment was terminated after a week when Zimbardo realized, in horror, what was actually happening: how readily the 'guards' were abusing their 'prisoners' and how deeply affected the latter had become. The power of the experimental situation was enormously greater than expected (Zimbardo 2007: 40–228)!

The ease with which Zimbardo's student 'prison guards' – all members of the 1960s and 1970s hippie era of love-ins and supposed 'resistance to authority' – turned into abusive tormentors of their 'prisoner' classmates bespeaks the depths to which an authoritarian cultural milieu affects even those of us who are conscientiously trying to fight off its effects. Zimbardo calls this psychological force the 'System'. I translate this to mean our culture's assumptions about 'human nature' and a 'natural social order' – the underlying worldview that justifies our inequitable social institutions. We live and work in rule-based hierarchies, the psychological near-equivalent of the US Post Office. But acknowledging this aloud makes us uncomfortable, defensive (Clark 2002: 15–26).

For most people it is emotionally unsettling to criticize the institutions of their own culture. It feels 'unpatriotic' – akin to being ashamed of one's parents. Our personal identities are wrapped up in family, local community and nationality – and that loyalty has a solid place in the structure of our emotional brains. For example, when living in Britain for over a decade I regularly used to find unbidden tears rolling down my cheeks at the sight of an American flag waving on the screen at the start of a movie. Even at the time, I was surprised, as I was not homesick, or particularly given to patriotic fervour. And on visits home to San Francisco I had a deep emotional response to the sight, taste and feel of the ocean fog blowing across my face, so completely different from the sulphurous stuff that burdened English cities in those days of coal burning. One's identification with people and place – with 'home' – goes very deep.

Add to place, and the cultural perceptions of social order, the critical shared moments in one's national history, also embedded as identifiers in the RH/limbic sensitivities of every member of a society (albeit to varying degrees), and you have a formidably powerful, cerebrally embedded 'map of collective identity' to modify, if a group or nation finds itself compelled to alter the basic structure of its institutions in order to adapt to a changing world. It's like a personality makeover but on a national scale!

No wonder politics is such an emotionally explosive topic. No wonder it is hard to create change, to get societies to adapt to new circumstances. Consider the leaders of nations that are in conflict at secret peace talks, trying to seek an end to violence. The problem they face is not just 'the other' across the table; it is the millions of others back home, each of whom must also be persuaded to go along with the proposed new way of 'interacting in the world'. The task is somewhat similar to that of the psychiatrist treating a person with PTSD. The process requires a gradual 'analysis' that 'de-wires' particular neuronal pathways (perhaps an analogous task to removing the detonator from a landmine – you have to know your subject well and handle it very gently). Once all the people have been 'defused', they need help establishing a new wiring system, with a new emotional pattern, devoid of the old fears: a better-adapted – and hence more secure – state of mind.

There is not space here to detail this process, but increasingly those who study healing from conflict are making headway. A few well-known professionals among the many in the field include John Burton (1990), Vamik Volkan (2000), John Paul Lederach (2005) and Ervin Staub (2006). Out of their work, and that of many others, it is becoming increasingly evident that violence *in all its forms* is counter-productive to human problem-solving and adaptive social change. Both the aggressors and the threatened are equally damaged. A few examples will suffice.

Tony Lagouranis, a US Army interrogator in Iraq, who was taught the use of torture, tells how he found it both abhorrent and unproductive. Coercion, violent or otherwise, legal or illegal, seldom if ever improves a bad social situation, and often exacerbates it. Any form of violence as social control works only up to a point. If prolonged, it exhausts both victims and perpetrators – and leaves both in a state of moral exhaustion. Action that is not specifically designed to achieve trusting relationships is ultimately counter-productive. Lagouranis describes how empathy – an honest concern for the welfare of 'the other', even an enemy – works far better than intimidation and fear (Lagouranis and Mikaelian 2007: 243). For further insights into the negative consequences of the use of torture, see Huggins *et al.* (2002), Haritos-Fatouros (2003) and the film *Your Neighbour's Son: The Making of a Torturer*, which is based on Mika Haritos-Fatouros's work showing the process of desensitization that takes place during the training of soldiers and police personnel in the practices of torturer.

At this point we can take a page from the Arabs themselves. Saudi Arabia has recently found a way to rehabilitate some of the al-Qaeda youth who have become a problem within Saudi society itself. An aggressive crackdown was begun. Although amnesty was promised to any who turned themselves in, few responded. As the jails filled with apprehended, non-repentant youths, the authorities introduced a psychological counselling regimen. This entailed group discussions with clerics, who used Islamic teaching to refute any religious rationales for acts of terrorism, plus one-on-one meetings with psychologists and with family members, who urged their beloved son or daughter to return home. One-third of those in prison have been rehabilitated so far. The reason many had joined in the first place was loneliness, especially among those living abroad, away from their families. They sought out other Muslims, making themselves easy targets for al-Qaeda operatives. Like so much else that is wrong with the world, terrorism results from feelings of social rejection – a failure of human attachment at one or another social level (Henry 2007).

Moving beyond helplessness

I conclude this chapter by briefly noting some ways we humans are in fact able to actively reconstruct our damaged emotional selves, thus opening the path for positive adaptive change in response to our burgeoning global crises. The first comprises techniques for personal reshaping of our individual minds. The second is a brief case history of a community that is currently discovering how to totally reconstruct its own social relationships following collapse of the larger economic world around it. Together they demonstrate the possibility of escape from 'evil' in all its nefarious forms. It is our 'social ecology', not the genes we were born with, that created both our global crises and the insecurities now wired into our own heads. The following offers ways for overcoming today's less than ideal emotional responses to the insecurities we all face.

Taking personal charge

'Will-power' – the reining in of one's personal emotions – is what societies from time immemorial have demanded of their citizens as the antidote to antisocial emotional outbursts. By placing the onus for group harmony on individuals, regardless of the quality of their social experiences, social groups have adroitly sidestepped collective responsibility for creating a healthy 'social ecology', a cultural milieu that automatically nurtures individual mental security.

Self-control, or 'will-power', however, is not something one is born with. It is socially shaped, either by local customs (attentive child-rearing etc.) or by specific social training practices. It cannot be ordered into existence simply by passing laws or decrees. In the absence of a psychologically nurturing upbringing, the acquisition of 'will-power' necessitates a lengthy self-retraining of one's own brain. This skill must be taught to us by others; it does not spontaneously develop on its own. 'Will-power' requires developing a *conscious attentiveness* to the functioning of one's own mind, a prerequisite for consciously processing emotion-laden information, rather than reflexively responding to it. Attentiveness takes place in the prefrontal cortex, the so-called executive region of the brain, an area activated during deep prayer, and especially during meditation as practised by trained Buddhist monks. Both prayer and meditation are means of creating an attentive mind. Today, the development of parallel 'attention-focusing' skills is being taught by modern psychiatrists to patients afflicted with uncontrollable compulsive behaviours.[10] All of these techniques are ways of taking conscious control of our emotional experiences.

Modern neuroscience now confirms that all these self-generated training techniques actually reshape the neuronal connections in this 'executive brain centre', greatly increasing our capacity to modulate our emotional responses to the world around us. The question is whether societies around the globe will adopt the supportive training programmes necessary. Will 'social ecologies' modify their institutions sufficiently to provide the level of 'will-power' training needed to meet the coming planetary stresses with thoughtful deliberation rather than disorganized violence?

Recreating traumatized societies

By the end of the twentieth century, most of South America's economies were in collapse – a combination of weak governments and widespread corruption by the capital-owning classes. One of the worst-hit countries was Argentina, especially around Buenos Aires. By 2001–2002, dozens of factories were no longer turning out goods. Owners had 'cashed in' on all the capital they could – to invest more lucratively overseas. In the meantime, their employees, all owed unpaid back wages for months, even years, were left behind, still living in the neighbourhoods of the closed factories, with nowhere to turn for a livelihood.

Sin patrón ('Without a boss')[11] is the story of how workers from several dozen of these abandoned factories managed to form legally constituted worker cooperatives and reorganize themselves into democratically administered, egalitarian corporations. They drew on the varied strengths of their individual members to find new clients, buy raw materials, design products and get the machines up and running. Told by the Lavaca Collective (2007), an openly structured umbrella organization, the combined stories of these worker-groups offer profound insights into how distressed communities can create collective solutions to shared problems, inventing their own moral compass to guide them along the way. In almost all cases these new businesses have found solid support within the communities in which they are located. Indeed, the reciprocity between workers and communities predicts a far smoother, more inclusive culture-wide adaptation to coming global changes than was previously possible. These stories from Argentina offer insights into the numerous hurdles to be faced anywhere during profound social change, and of the variety of inventive means by which different small groups can proceed along the way. Simple awareness of their accomplishments surely lends strength to the rest of us on how to tackle the many-faceted problems ahead. No one discipline has 'the answer'!

My summarizing comment is this. Only those social-change processes that incorporate a compassionate awareness of the fears and insecurities imprinted on *all participants* (from individuals to nations) by their respective traumatic histories can provide the necessary *mental* healing that will allow our species to survive into the future. Compassion – too often ignored by 'social ecologists' – is essential at all levels: between parents and children; between ethnic groups within a larger community; and between all the world's nations. All human brains work in basically similar ways. Coercion per se never 'fixes' damaged brains, and, as I have argued elsewhere, retributive justice – effectively, 'vengeance' – may make one group feel 'better' but ultimately heals nothing (Clark 2005). As Gandhi said, 'An eye for an eye only makes everyone blind.' It certainly dehumanizes all of humanity – and in the end accomplishes nothing. Coercion, retribution, punishment – in the long run, all are counter-productive. Eventually, trust and attachment and mutual security must be re-established – the central components of the moral impulses we are all initially born with.

In the long run, compassion and human fellowship are far more powerful forces than all the weapons in the world. The question is, will we, as a species, come to recognize this before it is too late?

Notes

1 'The Universe Story' (Swimme and Berry 1992) was Thomas Berry and Brian Swimme's brave effort to pull philosophy, the sciences and humanities together into a single, existential whole. To date, no more comprehensive effort has come forth.

2 New Age literature is now promoting numerous models, some imaginary, others already in existence – ways cultures can become simultaneously more humane and ecologically sustainable. Almost none of it is incorporated into academic curricula. Examples of such change are cited at the end of Clark (2002) and are regularly found in *YES!* magazine. Several more are cited at the end of this chapter.

3 Among the tribe of 'unifiers' are the followers of John Burton (1990), a major founder of modern conflict resolution, who insists that human nature is a universally shared entity; we all experience the same basic human emotions. Among the 'splitters' are Kevin Avruch and Peter Black (1991), anthropologists who tend to interpret all conflict through the lenses of individual cultures.

4 Quotations are from the article by Vedantam (2007). See also the report by Harbaugh *et al.* (2007).

5 See Mahedy (1986) for a personal account of the struggle to obtain formal recognition of the nature and causes of PTSD. See also Lt. Col. Dave Grossman's (1996) insights into the psychological changes wrought by 'killing' on members of the military. They parallel the traumas described by James Gilligan (1996) among the youths growing up in American inner cities.

6 'Fight Crime: Invest in Kids' is an umbrella organization for the several state-based community groups across the United States focusing on the social roots of rising levels of crime. Local state offices produce various resource materials filled with statistics, analyses and helpful contact information. In Oregon their address is 17675 SW Farmington Road, PMB# 336 Beaverton, OR 97007. Ph. (503) 649-2068. Website: www.fightcrime.org/or.

7 For extensive analysis of the social overheads incurred by societies with gross inequality in economic well-being, see Richard Wilkinson (2005) and also David Erdal's unpublished manuuscript (2005) 'Effects of Living in an Egalitarian Environment'. He argues that humans evolved in cooperating, sharing, egalitarian societies, and demonstrates increased longevity etc. in egalitarian as against ranked modern Italian societies. Erdal is based in the School of Psychology, University of St Andrews, UK.

8 A friend in Marin County, California, described a middle-class family, a mother with two teenagers who each had their own room with a TV set. When dinner was ready, they emerged from their rooms, picked up their TV trays and disappeared again. That was 'family life'.

9 See PBS Frontline video FRON309K, filmed partly in 1970 and partly fifteen years later, and Peters (1987).

10 For Buddhist insights into self-modification, see the Dalai Lama and Daniel Goleman (2003), the Dalai Lama (2005) and Hanh (2007). For modern psychological intervention, see Schwartz and Begley (2002).

11 This amazing story deserves to be widely known in the North. First written by the Lavaca Collective in 2004, its English translation bears a foreword by Naomi Klein and Avi Lewis. Further information on the movement appeared in *YES!* magazine, Summer 2007 (ISSN 1089-6651).

References

American Psychiatric Association, The. Forthcoming. *Diagnostic and Statistical Manual of Mental Disorders*, 5th ed. (DSM-V). Arlington, VA: American Psychiatric Association.

Avruch, K. and P.W. Black. 1991. 'The culture question and conflict resolution.' *Peace and Change* 16(1): 22–45.

Blix, H. 2007. Interview: morning edition, 6 September. National Public Radio (USA).

Burton, J. 1990. *Conflict: Human Needs Theory*. New York: St Martin's Press.

Clark, M.E. 1989. *Ariadne's Thread: The Search for New Modes of Thinking*. London: Macmillan.

Clark, M.E. 2002. *In Search of Human Nature*. London: Routledge.

Clark, M.E. 2005. 'Skinner vs the prophets: human nature and our concepts of justice.' *Contemporary Justice Review* 8(2): 163–176.

Clark, M.E. and L.D. Holler. 1986. 'Teaching science within the limits of science.' *Journal of College Science Teaching* 16(8–9): 56–57.

Dalai Lama, His Holiness the. 2005. *The Universe in a Single Atom*. New York: Morgan Road Books.

Dalai Lama, His Holiness the and D. Goleman. 2003. *Destructive Emotions: How Can We Overcome Them?* New York: Bantam Dell.

de Waal, F. 2006. *Primates and Philosophers: How Morality Evolved*. Princeton, NJ: Princeton University Press.

Diamond, J. 2005. *Collapse: How Societies Choose to Fail or Succeed*. New York: Viking.

Elliott, J., W. Peters and C. Cobb. 1992. 'A class divided' [video recording], PBS Video FRON309K. New Haven, CT: Yale University Films for Frontline.

Erdal, D. 2005. 'Effects of living in an egalitarian environment.' Unpublished MS, School of Psychology, University of St Andrews, St Andrews, UK.

Fraiberg, S. ed. 1980. *Clinical Studies in Infant Mental Health*. New York: Basic Books.

Fraiberg, S., E. Adelson and V. Shapiro. 1975. 'Ghosts in the nursery: a psychoanalytic approach to the problem of impared infant–mother relationships.' *Journal of the American Academy of Child Psychiatry* 14(3): 387–421.

Gilligan, J. 1996. *Violence: Our Deadly Epidemic and Its Causes*. New York: Putnam.

Greenberg, D.S. 2007. 'On the road to academic greatness: a parable.' *Science* 317(8543): 1328–1329.

Greene, J.D. 2005. 'Cognitive neuroscience and the structure of the moral mind.' In *Innateness and the Structure of the Mind*, vol. 1, ed. S. Laurence, P. Carruthers and S. Stich. Oxford: Oxford University Press.

Grossman, D. 1996. *On Killing: The Psychological Cost of Learning to Kill in War and Society*. Boston: Little, Brown.

Hamilton, W.D. 1963. 'The evolution of altruistic behavior.' *American Naturalist* 97(896): 354–356.

Hamilton, W.D. 1975. 'Innate social aptitudes of man: an approach from evolutionary genetics.' In *Biosocial Anthropology*, ed. R. Fox. New York: John Wiley.

Haney, C., C. Banks and P. Zimbardo. 1973. 'Interpersonal dynamics in a simulated prison.' *International Journal of Criminology and Penology* 1: 69–97.

Hanh, T.N. 2007. *Buddha Mind, Buddha Body*. Berkeley, CA: Parallax Press.

Harbaugh, W.T., U. Mayr and D.R. Burghart. 2007. 'Neural responses to taxation and voluntary giving reveal motives for charitable donations.' *Science* 316(5831): 1622–1625.

Haritos-Fatouros, M. 2003. *The Psychological Origins of Institutionalized Torture*. London: Routledge.

Henry, T. 2007. 'Get out of jihad free.' *Atlantic Monthly* June: 39–40.

Holden, C. 2007. 'Better to give than to receive.' *Science* 316(5282): 1105.

Huggins, M.K., M. Haritos-Fatouros and P.G. Zimbardo. 2002. *Violence Workers: Police Torturers and Murderers Reconstruct Brazilian Atrocities*. Berkeley, CA: University of California Press.

Kemmis, D. 1990. *Community and the Politics of Place*. Norman: University of Oklahoma Press.

Kemmis, D. 1995. *The Good City, the Good Life: Renewing the Sense of Community*. Boston: Houghton Mifflin.

Koch, S. 1999. *Psychology in Human Context: Essays in Dissidence and Reconstruction*. Chicago: University of Chicago Press.

Lagouranis, T. and A. Mikaelian. 2007. *Fear Up Harsh*. New York: NAL Caliber Books.

Lane, C. 2007. *Shyness: How Normal Behavior Became a Sickness*. New Haven, CT: Yale University Press.

Lavaca Collective, The. 2007. *Sin patrón*. Chicago: Haymarket Books.

Lederach, J.P. 2005. *The Moral Imagination*. Oxford: Oxford University Press.

Lieberman, A.F., E. Padrón, P. van Horn and W.W. Harris. 2005. 'Angels in the nursery: the intergenerational transmission of benevolent parental influences.' *Infant Mental Health Journal* 26(6): 504–520.

Mahedy, W.P. 1986. *Out of the Night: The Spiritual Journey of Vietnam Vets*. New York: Ballantine.

Marty, M.E. 1994. 'What is fanaticism?' Chautauqua audiotape 94-11. Chautauqua, NY: Chautauqua Institute.

Milgram, S. 1974. *Obedience to Authority*. New York: Harper & Row.

National Public Radio. 1996. 'Sick societies'. *Talk of the Nation*, 9 December. National Public Radio (USA).

Niebuhr, R. 1960 [1932]. *Moral Man and Immoral Society: A Study in Ethics and Politics*. New York: Scribners.

Perry, B.D. 1997. 'Incubated in terror: neurodevelopmental factors in the "cycle of violence".' In *Children, Youth and Violence: The Search for Solutions*, ed. J. Osofsky. New York: Guilford Press.

Perry, B.D. 1999. 'Memories of fear: how the brain stores and retrieves physiologic states, feelings, behaviors and thoughts from traumatic events.' In *Splintered Reflections: Images of the Body in Trauma*, ed. J. Goodwin and R. Artias. New York: Basic Books.

Perry, B.D. and M. Szalavitz. 2006. *The Boy Who Was Raised as a Dog: What Traumatized Children Can Teach Us about Loss, Love, and Healing*. New York: Basic Books.

Peters, W. 1987. *Class Divided: Then and Now*. New Haven, CT: Yale University Press.

Ravetz, J.R. 1994. 'Economics as an elite folk-science: the suppression of uncertainty.' *Journal of Post-Keynesian Economics* 17(2): 165–184.

Rogoff, B. 2003. *The Cultural Nature of Human Development*. Oxford: Oxford University Press.

Saunders, H.H. 2005. *Politics Is About Relationship: A Blueprint for the Citizens' Century*. New York: Palgrave Macmillan.

Schore, A.N. 2005. Material on early childhood attachment presented at a lecture at the Oregon Psychoanalytic Center, 8 December, Oregon Health and Sciences University, Portland.

Schwartz, J.M. and S. Begley. 2002. *The Mind and the Brain: Neuroplasticity and the Power of Mental Force*. New York: HarperCollins.

Sidanius, J. and F. Pratto. 1999. *Social Dominance: An Intergroup Theory of Social Hierarchy and Oppression*. New York: Cambridge University Press.

Staub, E. 2006. 'Reconciliation after genocide, mass killing, or intractable conflict: understanding the roots of violence, psychological recovery, and steps toward a general theory.' *Political Psychology* 27(6): 867–894.

Swimme, B. and T. Berry. 1992. *The Universe Story: From the Primordial Flaring Forth to the Ecozoic Era: A Celebration of the Unfolding of the Cosmos*. London: Harper Collins.

Tappan, M. 2005. 'Domination, subordination, and the dialogical self: identity development and the politics of "ideological becoming".' *Culture and Psychology* 11(1): 47–75.

Tappan, M. 2006. 'Reframing internalized oppression and internalized domination: from the psychological to the sociocultural.' *Teachers College Record* 108(10): 2115–2144.

Vedantam, S. 2007. 'If it feels good to be good, it might be only natural: new findings suggest that good impulses "are basic to the brain".' *Washington Post*, 28 May.

Volkan, V. 2000. 'The tree model: a comprehensive psychopolitical approach to unofficial diplomacy and the reduction of ethnic tension.' *Mind and Human Interaction* 10(3): 142–210.

Volkan, V. 2004. *Blind Trust: Large Groups and Their Leaders in Times of Crisis and Terror*. Charlottesville, VA: Pitchstone.

Wilkinson, R. 2005. *The Impact of Inequality: How to Make Sick Societies Healthier*. New York: The New Press.

Zimbardo, P.G. 2007. *The Lucifer Effect: Understanding How Good People Turn Evil*. New York: Random House.

Part II

Life after reductionism

Exemplary ecological economics beyond reductionism, in practice

6 Building a career in the epistemological no man's land

John Barry and Katharine N. Farrell

Introduction

At the 2007 Conference of the European Society for Ecological Economics, Professor Malte Faber's keynote speech was entitled 'How to be an ecological economist'. In that lecture (Faber 2008), Professor Faber, himself originally an 'ordinary' economist, reflected upon a career's worth of experiences with the personal and professional challenges that arise as one reaches beyond the reductive boundaries of an individual academic discipline in an effort to conduct ecological economics research. In keeping with the discussion that Faber and others of his and the preceding generation (see also Boulding 1991; Max-Neef 2005; Røpke 1999, 2002, 2004; Walker and Holling, Chapter 10 of this book) have opened up, our aim in this chapter is to explore what is required of both the scholars and the institutions involved in conducting research that is concerned with *interactions between economic and ecological systems* – work that requires one to stand across the two disciplines of ecology and economics, often with very little institutional support underneath.

While our subject is, in principle, a matter of ecological economics methodology, we believe that the challenges associated with building an academic career in ecological economics are also matters relevant for the study of twenty-first-century environmental governance (Barry 2007).[1] This is because we consider accurately perceiving and appropriately responding to ecological economic situations to be central to good environmental governance. That is to say, we see the balancing act required for developing ecological economics scholarly work as having an important place within environmental governance, not only in terms of providing information, interpretations and recommendations but also in terms of the scholars' participation in the collective work of developing expectations and aspirations regarding societies' relations with their environments. On this basis we take up our exploration of scholarly practice in what we call the epistemological and methodological no man's land of interdisciplinary sustainability research. We do so not only as scholars of method or with respect to our personal experiences but also as political scientists.

Although ecological economics is practised within and across a wide variety of institutional settings, we focus here on the setting of university education and research, in part because it is the setting with which we are most familiar and in part because we see the university system as a trend-setting institution.[2]

We begin by presenting some background on the specific topic of the political theory-oriented ecological economics PhD thesis that we prepared together, as student and supervisor, locating it within the larger domain of ecological economics through Giampietro and Mayumi's discussion of the requisite abilities for ecological economics. On the basis of this discussion we develop some minimum standards that we believe must be met if one aims to conduct the kind of fundamentally integrative ecological economic research and analysis that Max-Neef (2005) has tagged as 'strong interdisciplinarity', where not only data and results but also theory and explanations are built up between the traditional disciplinary domains. On the basis of this discussion we identify two quid pro quo, conditions that needed to be met or confronted if the work was to proceed at all: self-reflection and complex comprehension. In the next two sections we then consider some of the specific challenges that we encountered as we set out to conduct this kind of strongly interdisciplinary (ibid.) work within a traditional university setting. While our account is of our own experiences, we are exploring them here not only from a personal but also from a social science perspective, posing the question: what institutional settings and social practices may be required of universities if they are expected to support this kind of academic work?

Finally, on the basis of both our personal and our professional assessments we develop some practical recommendations regarding how ecological economics education and research might be better supported within university settings.

From our perspective as scholars of political science, working on issues that we classify as ecological political economy (EPE), we discuss and analyse what it means for a political scientist to think and work across disciplinary boundaries within the current globally dominant Western-style university system, where the ruling constitutive research, learning and incentive structures (and also significant aspects of the culture of social sciences more generally) largely work against, rather than in support of, interdisciplinary (and multi-authored) research.

While our account may at times seem a little self-indulgent, our aim here is not to present ourselves as woebegone misfits or heroic outsiders. Rather, we wish to present a scholarly argument illustrating that inasmuch as environmental governance requires that the institutions governing human societies need to change, this need does not stop at the doors of the academy. That is to say, we propose that overcoming the substantial institutional and personal challenges that continue to face researchers concerned with ecological economics questions demands not only individual effort and creativity but also collective action and political commitment to institutional and cultural change *within the academy*.

Our focus on the institutional setting of university education and research takes up this domain of study as one among many that together comprise the complex system of global environmental governance. We maintain that, on the one hand, the move beyond reductive disciplinary boundaries is a necessary step that must be taken in order to conduct ecological economics research, while, on the other hand, existing European-style university structures (which are the globally dominant structures for research organization) present substantial institutional obstacles and methodological challenges to taking this step.

Our argument presumes that social institutions, including the institution of university education and research, are impacted by and impact upon ecological economic situations and dynamics (Norgaard 1988; Özkaynak *et al.* 2002; Farrell 2007) and that the configuration of these institutions may be more or less useful for sustainable development (Dryzek 1987; Dietz *et al.* 2003; Olsson *et al.* 2006; Ostrom 2005; Young 2002; Biermann *et al.* 2007).

We are setting out to contribute to a discourse addressed by several other contributors to this book, concerning the empirical question of how revisions to the institutions of university education and research might contribute not only to the production of better science but also to the execution of better environmental governance. Our arguments are intended to give suggestions regarding what might constitute good environmental governance of university education and research, and they are informed by our experience within and our expert opinions regarding the current structure of this system. We see this work as an active and engaged part of the collective task of developing understanding and taking action to address ecological economic challenges.

Practically speaking, we consider here how scholarly work within university systems might be reorganized to be more useful for addressing ecological economic issues. In doing so, we touch upon issues that are intimately related to questions that are taboo within 'the academy' regarding the relationship between power and knowledge (in a Foucauldian sense) and the sanctity of facts. Here we are speaking not only as scholars but also as workers – as individuals employed within the *academy*. In this respect, in addition to being an assessment of an empirical political science problematique – let us call it the ecological political economy of environmental science – our comments will, from time to time, also take on a more normative, moral and even at times ethical tone.

Contextualizing ecological political economy

Our overall approach to the thesis discussed in this chapter was engagement with the following dilemma: in spite of substantial evidence indicating that there are good reasons to make radical changes in international systems of economic production and consumption, there has been, and there continues to be, a surprising inability exhibited in global human society (as a whole) to develop effective strategies for halting and reversing the recent (meaning during the past 300 years) trend of human-caused, largely economically driven, ecological system destruction. Here we propose that one possible contributing factor may be a lack of sufficient and suitable epistemological (interrogative) and integrative analytical (picture-building) capacity within the international system of university science.

As we began our journey together as student and supervisor, one of the first things we did was to distil the research question of the thesis down to one sentence:

> Having identified the tension between scientific and political understandings of environmental problems to be one of the obstacles facing societies of human beings aspiring to achieve sustainable development, I am working to develop new democratic theory that can help to resolve these tensions, in an effort to support the development of more sustainable human societies.

Although we did not know it at the time, this question struck to the very heart of ecological economics, raising issues regarding how the purpose of economic activity is determined and regarding the epistemology of ecological economics problems and the methodologies used to explore them. The point of departure for our work was puzzlement over the persistent use of monetary proxy values to represent the economic worth of ecological goods and services in economic analysis, despite a general scientific consensus that these values could not possibly be correct (Constanza *et al.* 1997; Norgaard *et al.* 1998; Daly 1998). One of the central tasks of the thesis work was to develop an alternative to the use of monetary valuation in environmental management decision-making. This eventually took the form of new environmental governance political theory, which we see as a contribution to the discourse on EPE (Gale and M'Gonigle 2000), and the groundwork for that new theory was laid by developing a systematic critique of the pragmatic defence of monetary valuation (Farrell 2007, 2009 [2005]). Since almost no one, not even Costanza *et al.* (1997), defends the practice of monetary valuation on purely theoretical grounds, it became clear to us that the persistence of this practice must somehow be related to its defence on pragmatic grounds, wherein it is maintained that monetary valuations of priceless ecosystem goods and services, while technically incorrect, are nonetheless useful:

> The figure [arrived at by Costanza *et al.* 1997] of 33 trillion dollars screams at us to save what natural capital is left. There are evident physical consequences of excessive human expansion that scream the same message without need of explicit valuation. But for those who only hear dollars, let us scream now and then in dollars! It is a crude and inaccurate measure, but I think it is more than just 'a bad underestimate of infinity'. For decision making, valuing natural services at infinity is not a great advance over valuing them at zero.
>
> (Daly 1998: 22–23)

Exploring the respective ecological economics and environmental politics literatures concerning monetary and non-monetary environmental valuation, we developed a heuristic framework for what we came to call ecological political economy (Figure 6.1), which we understand to comprise three inextricable domains of interdependence, all equally fundamental for understanding and articulating the economic worth of ecological phenomena (now commonly referred to as ecosystems services).[3]

In order to develop an EPE critique of the pragmatic defence of monetary valuation, we set out to understand a series of questions situated within several different disciplinary frames. With respect to ecology, working from the basis that

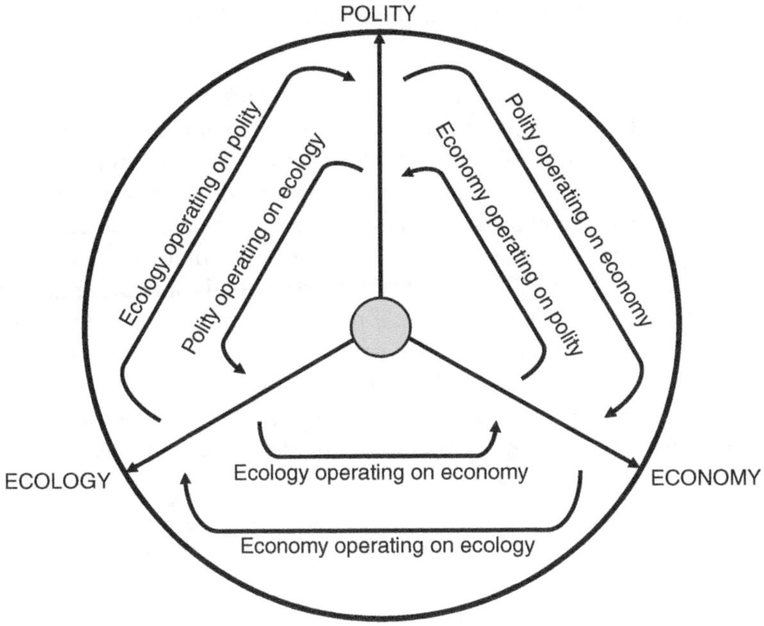

Figure 6.1 An picture of ecological political economy (source: adapted from Farrell 2009 [2005]: 19).

Note
Credit is due here to Juan Sanchez-García, whose informal lecture on the future of ecological economics given during the 2003 Tenerife ESEE conference inspired this visualization.

construing the economic contribution made by ecosystems cannot be done without construing what and how that contributing is constituted we asked: what are the most basic necessary conditions for being alive? This led us into study of open systems thermodynamics, General System Theory, systems ecology and biology. With respect to economy, we asked: what is it about estimated, stand-in monetary values that makes them unsuitable as input data for economic analysis and decision-making? This led us into study of basic micro- and macroeconomics, decision theory, impact assessment and post-normal science. And with respect to polity, we set out to understand how and why this pragmatic defence of an obviously incorrect practice continues to enjoy such wide acceptance. This led us into study of political and social theory, cognitive science and anthropology. Finally, as we worked our way through these three questions we found ourselves confronted with a fourth: what role does the perspective of the scientist play in framing these politically influential arguments that are eventually presented as science? For example, the failure of monetary valuation to serve the purpose for which it is intended – to improve the ecological economic quality of environmental policy decision-making – can be understood as a detriment to the common good, because the promised contribution to development of good environmental policy serves a common interest of the entire community of human beings.

Politics and institutions: the fourth requisite ability of ecological economics

Within the broader domain of ecological economics, the research that we carried out can be understood to address what Giampietro and Mayumi have referred to as the fourth requisite ability of ecological economics. Quoting from a flyer announcing the 1987 Barcelona meeting, which was one of the first gatherings of the group of scholars who eventually established the International Society for Ecological Economics (ISEE),[4] Giampietro and Mayumi remind us that the original motivation for establishing this field was fundamentally interdisciplinary: 'Without an ecological foundation, economic policy is blind and unsustainable; without an economic foundation, ecological policy is impractical; that's why the leaders in these fields and many others have joined ISEE' (2001: 2). In an effort to interpret what this means for practice, they propose four requisite 'abilities' necessary for conducting ecological economic inquiry. The first three are as follows:

> [1] [t]he ability to understand and scientifically represent ecological processes...;
> [2] [t]he ability to understand and scientifically represent socioeconomic processes...;
> [3] [t]he ability to integrate the two systems of scientific representations in a way that makes possible to improve both understanding and representing the predicament of sustainability in a holistic way.
>
> (Giampietro and Mayumi 2001: 2)

The fourth is the ability to describe, understand and engage with the processes through which humans *translate* understandings of the predicament of sustainability into collective action.

While command of the first three abilities certainly requires interdisciplinary science, command of the fourth requires an extension of the ecological economic analysis in two new directions: first, into the realm of institutional and constitutional theory; and second, into a reflexive stance where the role of the ecological economic researcher, *within the governance processes that they are themselves describing*, is explicitly problematized. That is to say, we take here the position that political theory-oriented ecological economists (such as we are) must explicitly study and consider both the objective political forums where collective action on ecological economic questions is authorized and the impacts associated with their own place within the wider collective system of ecological economic activities of the societies of which they are part.

In so far as this is the case, new strategies for training and supporting the work of scholars who attempt the interdisciplinary ecological economics balancing act are urgently required, not because any one scholar or specific field of work deserves to be 'taken care of', but on scientific grounds, because it is only through careful attention to phenomena that are balanced between the disciplines that core objects of ecological economic interest can be observed, described and understood (i.e. known) (Clark 1989; Vatn, Chapter 11 of this book; Faber 2008; Max-Neef 2005).

A fine line between reporting on experience and developing political theory

We are very aware that there is a fine line between presenting a simple account of personal reflections on our shared experiences and a formal attempt to grapple with the theoretical political science and ecological political economy methodology implications that we, as experts, glean from these experiences. However, we believe that the distinction can and should be made when discussing ecological economics methodology, bearing in mind that, regardless of the topic being studied, it is not possible to fully disentangle personal, professional and political perspectives from one another.

We have adopted this reflexive approach because we are interested in better understanding how the configuration of knowledge production institutions within a given society supports (or fails to support) that society's endeavours to describe, understand and engage with the processes through which humans (including ecological economists) translate understanding of the predicament of sustainability into collective action – Giampietro and Mayumi's (2001) fourth requisite ability of ecological economics. Since it is one of the primary knowledge production institutions of global human society, in spite of the fact that it is our place of work, it seems quite obvious to us that the structure of the *academy*, and particularly of the international university system that is its model, must be a focal point of interest for any such inquiry.

Working on this question compels us to reflect upon our own position within the academy, not only on personal and professional basis, as is ordinarily the case, but also on theoretical and methodological grounds. This is because the specific case of 'conditions necessary for conducting robust transdisciplinary ecological economics research' is embedded within the larger set of 'conditions necessary for the humane and ecologically viable operation of the global economic system'.

Complex comprehension of complex problems

Understanding and evaluating any ecological economics problem entails describing, if only at a most basic level, the structure and dynamics of the ecological system(s) within which the relevant economic processes are embedded. It also entails, again, even if only at a most basic level, describing the structure and dynamics of the human system(s) within which these same economic processes are embedded. It is simply not possible to clearly engage a basic ecological economics question through reliance upon any one single disciplinary frame and it is often the case that more than just these two are required. Investigation of such topics requires interdisciplinarity not only with respect to cooperation in analysis but also with respect to the fundamental conceptualizations of the research (Max-Neef 2005; Faber 2008) and one's intellectual orientation towards the chosen research question or questions.

With its centre of gravity firmly fixed in the domain of interdisciplinarity, ecological economics rests in an epistemological and methodological no man's land. A fortiori, it is impossible for one discipline to provide a 'solution' to an ecological economics problem or question. We would go so far as to suggest that a 'problem–solution' approach is itself deeply problematic when considering ecological economics generally, and certainly with respect to the kinds of ecological political economy questions that concern us here. As Røpke (2002: 11) puts it, the original transdisciplinarity vision for the ecological economics venture calls, at its root, for work that goes 'beyond one discipline just [subsuming] another discipline under its own perspective'.

In this chapter we are working from the basis that the inability of the *academy* to make space for the epistemologically complex work of ecological economics is not merely a parochial concern for affected scientists wishing to secure a comfortable position within the university establishment. Following Clark (Chapter 5 of this book) and Giampietro and Mayumi (2001), we see this also, if not primarily, as a collective social problem, certainly for the global academic community and perhaps even for humanity as a whole. In so far as we accept that it is precisely such epistemologically complex research that is required if scientists are to understand and effectively engage with the most pressing ecological economics problems of the early twenty-first century, creating conditions conducive to conducting that research must be understood as a collective social project. Having navigated our way together through a stretch of this no man's land, we have chosen to approach the topic here by critically reflecting upon our shared experience as student and supervisor. In reviewing how our expectations and practices needed to be revised along the way, we hope to be able to offer some small insights into what is required of the scholars who venture into this new domain and of the academic institutions that constitute their professional work environments.

In our experience, we found that producing an ecological political economy PhD thesis that could still pass muster within the discipline of political theory required a great deal from us both. While determination, camaraderie and creativity helped to compensate for a lack of institutional understanding and support for our approach, we are convinced that the strain on individuals is too great and the chances of success are too slim to leave the future of this type of epistemologically complex research up to the good fortune and personal sacrifice of individual students and supervisors. If this is an area of research that needs to grow (and we believe that it does), then it is an area of research that deserves to have at its disposal the basic institutional supports that are traditionally available for disciplinary research: access to departmental infrastructures; provisions for training and development of students and staff; formal incorporation within university calendars, symposia and research programmes; etc.

Stepping into no man's land

In the preceding section of this chapter we have taken it as given that ecological economics does not fit neatly within the existing university education and research structures. In order to proceed further with our argument, we need to unpack that proposition a bit and consider: what is it that makes ecological economics so hard to map onto any single one of the traditional academic disciplines? Can this be changed? Should this be changed? And what is it about the academy that makes it so hard to fit ecological economics within its structure?

It is not difficult to understand why ecological economics does not neatly slot into the already well-established disciplinary silos of the university. This has to do, inter alia, with the range of issues, including cross-cutting issues such as scale dependency of social and physical dynamics; the great variety of types of investigative data (qualitative and quantitative, generated from within different disciplines, concerning various materials and life forms and compiled according to a variety of data collection and formatting standards); the diversity of methodological approaches; and the complexity of interactions between scientific, empirical, policy and normative dimensions of the ecological economics research problematique. Simply put, ecological economics, as we discovered in the course of preparing together an ecological economics dissertation, can cover, within a single sentence, paragraph or conversation, everything from the ultimate meaning of 'life' for human and non-human entities to the logistics of how to carry out an interview or phrase a key statement within an environmental impact assessment.

Scholars wishing to pursue ecological economics research face the intellectual challenge of making sense out of the potentially overwhelming range of subjects, topics, issues, schools of thought, debates, etc. that ecological economics sees as its 'subject area' (if such a term is even appropriate). In our case we grappled with questions about the epistemological framing of risk; about how to test ecological economics hypotheses; and the ideological and normative (often hidden or occluded) power of the very language (and grammar – understood as the rules of language use) we use to describe phenomena and prescribe engagement with them; about how we, as social scientists, might best approach natural scientists and engineers in order to engage in interdisciplinary collaborations; concerning what political and economic institutional structures might best support the move from ecological economics theory into practice (and back again!); to what degree the accuracy and legitimacy of ecological economics assessment are interrelated; where the results of our work should be published if our aim is to contribute to the project of ecological economics; where if our aim is to contribute to advancement of our careers; where if it is both, and what we should do when the two conflict; and so on. With so many options and so many relations in play, decisions regarding where any given ecological economics project belongs within the university are by no means easy to make.

While a certain amount of what might be called 'intellectual dyspraxia' seems to be necessary for effective engagement with any strong interdisciplinary research question, the range and spectrum of ecological economics subjects means that answering even the most basic questions of *what* to research and *how* to research it can be overwhelming. Losing one's way and losing heart and enthusiasm in this no man's land seems to be part of the process of finding one's way (Faber 2008; Santaoja *et al.* in Chapter 9 of this book). Discovering the new, uncharted areas that we encountered while researching and supervising this ecological economics PhD felt to us, at times, like pioneering exploration: exciting, frustrating, risky and enjoyable, sometimes all at the same time. The novelty of ecological economics as a research subject meant that the PhD we created together was the very first of its type at our university. As a result of this, there was no pre-existing research within the faculty, nor were there appropriate supervisory mechanisms in place for supporting the interdisciplinarity of the work of the thesis. And even as good-willed and enthusiastic partners in this project (supervisor and student), we ourselves were still coming to the topic from very different epistemological and disciplinary positions: on the one hand, from a disciplined political studies background with a specialization in green political theory and experience with official and non-governmental politics, and on the other, from a mixed academic background that included biochemistry, political science and environmental engineering, combined with a professional career that included experiences ranging from environmental activism to regulatory compliance control carried out in collaboration with production line managers and accountants in private enterprises.

In the face of these various personal, institutional and academic challenges, working together on this PhD thesis was a bit like exploring a strange new landscape in which we regularly disagreed over what to call or name all the new features and objects that we were discovering. This called for substantial goodwill on the part of both teacher and student, which we were fortunate to have in abundance because we both care passionately about the thesis topic. However, we can imagine that things might have turned out quite differently if we had had only our expertise and our institutional positioning to draw upon as resources. This leaves us to wonder how many promising ecological economics theses have never been written simply because the favourable conditions needed to make them possible were not present. What new and valuable understanding do we lack today as a result?

Work that is meant to be meaningful

While the normative character of any work intended to address environmental issues is a theme in its own right (see Becker and Jahn 1999; Forsyth 2003; Martinez-Alier 2002; Diaw and Kusumanto 2005), we found ourselves facing special demands specifically associated with our wish to produce work that is meaningful for contemporary environmental governance debates. Of course, we presume that most scholarly work is intended to speak to some social discourse, and so the dilemma is not ours alone. What we are getting at here is a will to produce meaningful research in a manner that is more akin to Marx's famous dictum: 'The philosophers have only interpreted the world in various ways, the point however is to change it' (Marx 1978 [1845]).[5] For scholars concerned with addressing real-world problems like the deterioration of our planet's environmental life support systems, the task at hand is not only to understand the world but also to *change* it. With the thesis work we carried out, we sought to go beyond simply describing and interpreting how environmental governance 'is' to prescribing how it 'ought to be'. But we also added to our agenda the dimension (not unique to ecological economics, but certainly one of its defining features) of moving beyond prescribing change to suggesting how to implement that change.

There are not only ethical but also empirical implications associated with this kind of normativity. Insights are *meant* to be made available for practice, but their implementation and further development in practice are relevant not only for political action but also for further scholarly assessment of the appropriateness of recommendations. Since the work is always going to be serving one or another political perspective, in order to remain ethical, research projects concerned with EPE should, from the outset, clearly answer questions regarding for whom and to what political end the work is being conducted. However, meeting this ethical demand is not without its risks. With fear of 'engaged research' that has 'heterodox' and challenging political, ethical and economic consequences, when such work is placed before academic peers it is often negatively branded as being ideologically motivated and partial. In failing to be 'objective', such work is demeaning one of the unique selling points of the university, its status as a site of impartial, objective knowledge production.[6]

Our own experience as a case study

In the European-style university system, which is designed to reward and support discipline-specific research and results, carrying out the epistemological bridge work that lies at the heart of ecological economics inquiry also requires bridging the institutional structures that support these various pertinent epistemological domains. However, the gravitational pull of dominant paradigms and accepted or 'normal' patterns of knowledge production in traditional university settings is strong. In our case we found that working at the boundaries between disciplines required both strong personal commitment to the work and a willingness to face the risk of being ostracized, both socially and financially. Put another way: in order to develop the dissertation *Making Good Decisions Well* (Farrell 2009 [2005]), we had to exert a great deal of effort in order to place ourselves in a highly exposed and insecure position within the academy. For an established scholar, this is risky; for a student it is, at best, a gamble.

While there are now a few major ecological economics centres associated with universities,[7] and an increasing number of environmental studies departments that include ecological economics in their curricula, many ecological economists working within university settings still live a sort of double academic life, having a discipline-specific institutional home in economics or ecology, or sometimes geography, anthropology or science and technology policy studies, and conducting their ecological economics work alongside bread-and-butter disciplinary work that relates more specifically to their institutional home. To a degree, this arrangement is perfectly reasonable. Since ecological economics is more than just one single discipline, it makes little sense to try to limit the work to a single field of its own (Norgaard 1989; Martinez-Alier 1999). Nonetheless, the situation highlights the fact that there remain clear institutional barriers to establishing this kind of work within the *academy* (see Max-Neef 2005; Clark 1989; Clark in Chapter 5 of this book). Upon venturing into this no man's land, one becomes, at least for some time, disciplinarily homeless (Max-Neef 2005).

We encountered this homelessness ourselves and it seems to us, in hindsight, that it was largely due to the structure of the arguments that we were building. Within *Making Good Decisions Well* (Farrell 2009 [2005]) there are core arguments that have been built using pieces of political science and ecological economics theory, which employ principles from far-from-equilibrium thermodynamics, categorizations drawn from cognitive science, and logical elements of argumentation drawn from evolutionary theory and philosophy. In order to gather together all these various threads together into one coherent fabric, we consulted with a great variety of experts, teachers and critics. Fortunately for us, the experts whom we approached (both inside and outside of our university) were willing to talk with us and to give critical and instructive comments on our work. However, because we came to them as homeless people they did so out of goodwill, not because our request fell within their formal responsibilities. Perhaps they felt that our work might be relevant or interesting for them, but it was certainly not among their duties to reply to our enquiries. That is to say, they had to make an extra effort, above and beyond their ordinary work, to provide their comments. Of course, these colleagues might have found our questions to be a source of new ideas (we would like to think so, in any case), but their decisions to engage with us were decisions to take on extra unpaid work and to go against the grain of the academic system.

Lest we be accused of condemning the academy as an institution unfit for the purposes of ecological economics, we hasten to point out that the very birth and growth of the field is itself a testament to the capacity of the modern academy to produce new forms of knowledge. But it is also a testament to the endurance, courage and commitment of those who dared to be different and who were willing and able to become intellectual pioneers. We do not mean to suggest that this is an all-or-nothing situation, where everything must change or nothing can be accomplished. Instead, we are looking to invoke and employ the spirit of continuing self-refinement that has always been part of the academic endeavour. The current organization of the academy, with its epistemological no man's lands and disciplinary diamond mines (Clark in Chapter 5 of this book), is not inevitable. Indeed, even the currently dominant disciplinary character of the university system has not always been the case. The very name *university* has its origins in the idea that these institutions should be centres for the development of universal knowledge, and nearly as soon as there came to be formal institutionalization of what we might today define as disciplines – coming largely with the industrialization and specialization of science in the nineteenth century – calls for interdisciplinary collaboration began. For example, an appeal for interdisciplinary studies can be found in Cardinal Newman's (1999 [1854]) classic text *The Idea of a University*, where, long before the overspecialization and hermetic separating of different knowledges that we encounter today, it was nonetheless possible for him to note:

> I have said that all branches of knowledge are connected together, because the subject-matter of knowledge is intimately united in itself, as being the acts and the work of the Creator. Hence it is that the Sciences, into which our knowledge may be said to be cast, have multiplied bearings one on another, and an internal sympathy, and admit, or rather demand, comparison and adjustment. They complete, correct, balance each other. This consideration, if well-founded, must be taken into account, not only as regards the attainment of truth, which is their common end, but as regards the influence which they exercise upon those whose education consists in the study of them. I have said already, that to give undue prominence to one is to be unjust to another; to neglect or supersede these is to divert those from their proper object. It is to unsettle the boundary lines between science and science, to disturb their action, to destroy the harmony which binds them together. Such a proceeding will have a corresponding effect when introduced into a place of education. There is no science but tells a different tale, when viewed as a portion of a whole, from what it is likely to suggest when taken by itself, without the safeguard, as I may call it, of others.
>
> (ibid.: 92)

And even as early as Kant we find discussion of potential problems associated with poorly executed interdisciplinarity: 'We do not enlarge but disfigure the sciences when we lose sight of their respective limits and allow them to run into one another' (2005 [1787]: 15).

That is to say, the questions we raise here concerning life in the no man's land of ecological economics are questions that seem to us to have always stood before the academy and the scientists who comprise it. In conducting this critical ontology of ourselves, as Foucault (1984: 47) describes it, we are returning to one of the earliest tasks of the modern scholar: considering what it means to enlighten.

Mapping the edges of no man's land

Working with the concept of post-normal science introduced by Funtowicz and Ravetz (1990a, 1991, 1992, 1993, 1994), we have been able to develop a 'rough working field guide' to the epistemological and methodological no man's land into which our research question led us. Post-normal science has given us both a terminology and a grammar that made it possible for us to communicate and understand each other more effectively. Being able to locate our political theory questions (regarding the balance of rights and duties of citizenship, work as a social practice and the power of knowledge in environmental politics) and our ecological economics questions (regarding the role of entropy in economic processes, the biophysical constraints associated with the material basis of economic activity and the biological character of the human subject) within the post-normal science frame helped us to develop a workable common language for discussing these key elements of the thesis. In addition, the sheer existence of this discourse and the high quality of much of the work contributing to it gave us courage and confidence. In our experience the importance of having access to this kind of information, of knowing that there was rigorous, high-quality scholarly work under way that concerned itself with our no man's land and our sometimes shaky epistemological and methodological bridges, should not be underestimated. When moving into a new and novel area of work, especially as a PhD student seeking to establish one's reputation and credentials, it is reassuring to discover that others (perhaps not many, but some, and some who are respected) have already scoped out the territory a bit and identified it as being worthy of further investigation.

Of particular interest for our study were the implications associated with the normative proposition that ecological economics research should find appropriate ways to incorporate public debate into the process of scientific assessment (Funtowicz and Ravetz 1990, 1994; Funtowicz and O'Connor 1999). This proposition reflects a tendency within ecological economics research that seems to us to be intimately related to Giampietro and Mayumi's fourth requisite ability, typified by what Funtowicz and Ravetz (1994) call its 'issue-driven' approach to science. Whereas under a curiosity-driven approach the topics of research for modern science were determined largely by scientists following their own curiosity and inspiration, the advent of large-scale industrialization in the late nineteenth century saw a shift towards a mission-driven approach, with research agendas being set largely by the aims of commercial enterprises and the demands of the world's militaries. And eventually, linked to the time when new environmental impact assessment issues came to the fore in the 1960s with reports like Rachel Carson's *Silent Spring* (1963), and later that of the World Commission on Environment and Development, *Our Common Future* (Brundtland 1987), we can now talk about issue-driven science, like ecological economics. Here the research agenda is set collaboratively, by scientists and non-scientist, based on common concerns, and the execution of good-quality scientific method moves from being based on the routinized application of a set of fixed technical procedures to being marked by flexible but still rigorous co-production of knowledge by an epistemologically pluralist (Healy 2003) community of laypersons, technical experts and holders of various kinds of relevant scientific and non-scientific knowledge.

Within the issue-driven frame of ecological economics one can see the ancient 'public mission', as it were, of science and knowledge work (re)emerging. We tend to forget that despite the relatively recent era of patentable and profitable intellectual property rights, of mandatory science–industry collaboration (driven by both formal government policy and financial need) and militarily supported technology development, and the ever-increasing focus on improving one's own academic standing through targeting publications to maximize one's impact factor profile, the work of science has always had an implicit 'public mission' to improve the world. Seen in this light, one of the opportunities coming along with the ecological problems of the twenty-first century is the chance to recover the public servant role of a science that has, in the course of massive science-supported industrialization, become in many ways no longer humanity's servant but its master (Marcuse 1991 [1964]; Max-Neef 2005; Farrell 2008). Here the socially engaged inter- and transdisciplinarity of ecological economics can be understood as a situation in which scholars are stepping back into the driver's seat of scientific knowledge production, self-consciously seeking to produce knowledge that can serve the specific social and political purposes associated with achieving ecological viable, economically productive and politically just systems of collective human action.

From the inside out: some reflections on our own experiences

Having laid out the ecological political economy theory context within which we propose to embed our discussion, in this subsection we present some admittedly subjective but, we think, nonetheless relevant reflections on how we have seen these issues arising in our own work, from the inside out, so to speak.

Student perspective: Katharine N. Farrell

FINDING ONE'S PLACE

In many respects one of the greatest challenges for me in conducting this research was that of finding my place. Being based in an interdisciplinary research institute (the Institute of Governance, Public Policy and Social Research, IGPPSR, was a partnership project between the university's schools of sociology, economics, politics and law), the idea that one could and should be operating across disciplines was accepted within my immediate environment. Looking back, I can imagine that without this sympathetic immediate environment the work would have been even more difficult, so this simple acceptance was certainly important. However, even with the shelter of interdisciplinary institutes like the IGPPSR, the overall university system still expects a scholar to have a home: people want to be able to assign a label; teams of researchers want a succinct description of what you propose to do; departments want people who can teach introductory courses. For an interdisciplinary scholar, acceptance beyond the bounds of such an institute, as a member of the wider community of the university, depends not only upon producing good science but also upon finding ways to consistently translate the interdisciplinary descriptions and analysis of one's work into one or another disciplinary language. This is an awkward position, tantamount to having to justify one's right to be.

While I was able to develop productive connections with my colleagues in the schools of politics, law, biology, philosophy, anthropology and economics (the main disciplines relevant for my work), establishing and maintaining these connections depended, in the first instance, at least as much on my interpersonal and social skills as it did on my capacities as a scholar. In addition, even where there was strong expression of interest from colleagues in these departments, a constant effort was required on my part just to maintain these relationships, since my presence was not a part of their ordinary departmental activities.

FINDING MENTORS

Unlike in many professions of the twentieth and twenty-first centuries, qualification as an academic is still today, much as it was centuries ago, very much a matter of apprenticeship; to find a master and to work for and with them, to watch them work and thereby develop a feel for the craft of research and science, is still the primary method of training. For this training method to work, mentoring is vital. One needs mentors to mimic, after which one can begin to model one's own style. However, when the chosen field of investigation is at the frontier of science and located in the no man's land of ecological political economy, it is not at all clear just who one's mentors should be.

In my case, as with most academics, my PhD thesis supervisor, a political theorist, with whom I am writing this chapter, was my primary mentor. But my research also included core scientific points of argument based within ecology, economics, cognitive sciences and philosophy. In these areas my supervisor, a political scientist, could not serve as my mentor. Setting out to find other established researchers with an understanding for these three additional core areas of study and an appreciation for my attempt to weave them all together was a research task in and of itself.

WORKING AT A FRONTIER WITH MULTIPLE MENTORS

A mentor is, in principle, someone who has been where you are heading, who can point out some of the pitfalls that might be lying ahead, who can critique and guide you in the development of techniques and methods, and who can encourage you that you are indeed heading in the right direction. However, when one is breaking new ground and moving into uncharted territory, the role of a mentor is slightly different. It becomes more like that of a wise friend who can suggest good principles but who can no better predict the future than can you. In the case of the research for this PhD thesis, which was concerned with the ecological political economy of disciplinary and interdisciplinary scientific research methods, my primary mentor was anchored within a discipline that informed the content and language of his guidance. His advice and examples had to be transposed *and* compiled with advice and examples from other mentors who also had their own intellectual homes in other, equally relevant but differently conceptualized, disciplines. Even if one is lucky enough to have a mentor with experience in bridging disciplines, they too will inevitably have their own style and strategies for combining information and interpretations from across the disciplines. And finally, there is the challenge here of mixing together the messages not only intellectually but also emotionally and socially, as each mentoring relationship inevitably has its own style and character. In such a context it takes substantial effort and probably a bit of luck to avoid becoming a 'jack of all trades, master of none'. And it takes dedicated and forward-looking mentors who are able to see the risks that a student is facing, who are willing to venture a way into this no man's land themselves and who are willing to commit to the work; it is very easy for a student of many to become the responsibility of no one.

Teacher perspective: John Barry

Taking on an interdisciplinary PhD student within the context of a discipline-focused higher education organization, buttressed by one's own disciplinary training and mindful of the discipline-specific reward and promotion system, is an exercise in trust, perseverance and, at times, hope over experience, with an expectation that everything will turn out right in the end. When one's institution is set up in such a way that it is in spite of rather than because of this institutional context that one carries on the supervisory relationship, the quality of the working relationship between student and supervisor is even more important that in the standard PhD learning context.

The sense of being a pioneer in a new area, while exciting, also at times raises issues of vulnerability in relation to one's academic judgement and occasionally places one outside of one's areas of competence. However uncomfortable this may be (and one should not underestimate the benefits of frequently being outside one's intellectual 'comfort zone'), I have found that one of the most important and necessary qualities for interdisciplinary supervision is honesty within the supervisory relationship: admitting that one is not sure of what is the 'right' path for the thesis. At times this honesty demands a leap of faith to 'let go' of the natural desire to render and translate the student's work into the more familiar language and idioms of one's home discipline.

On balance, this work demands a certain degree of candour, regarding for example the practical limitations of creating one's own esoteric language. The student must be given enough room to really develop their ideas while still being given the tools to successfully position themselves within the still heavily discipline-oriented institutional structures within which they will have to build their academic career. In supervising an ecological economics PhD, the supervisor must be willing to learn new intellectual languages and explore and become familiar with new bodies of knowledge. It is not merely intellectual curiosity that is required of both student and supervisor – which after all should be the hallmark of all research; also needed is the ability to couple it with a capacity to 'join the dots' of what at first seem like distinct and separate issues, arguments, schools of thought, authors and debates. And a shared acceptance of the 'pioneering' character and uniqueness of the research, accompanied by acknowledgement that this is challenging work, seems to be crucial to success.

One useful way to illustrate the special character of our shared experience is through reference to philosopher Alastair MacIntyre's well-known distinction between 'practices' and 'institutions'. For MacIntyre, 'practices' are forms of human collective and productive activity that have their own internal goods and standards by which they are judged. As he puts it (1981: 187), a practice is

> any coherent and complex form of socially established cooperative human activity through which goods internal to that form of activity are realized in the course of trying to achieve those standards of excellence which are appropriate to, and partly definitive of, that form of activity; with the result that human powers, and human conceptions of the ends and goods involved, are systematically extended.

Whereas institutions are human creations that have 'external goods' as their main motivation or standard by which they are judged – in the case of academia these standards include income, wealth, power, prestige or bureaucratic compliance – when viewed as a practice, supervision of a PhD has internal goods and virtues, such as co-producing new knowledge, training PhD students, enabling students to 'learn the craft' of academic work, and so on. MacIntyre alerts us to the danger that while institutions can support practices, they can also 'corrupt' them. In the context of supervising a pioneering PhD in ecological economics within a traditional university setting, we were in many respects left to work in isolation from our wider university institutional context. There were, for example, no regular ecological economics seminars and no other students or staff conducting ecological economics research.

Within this institutionally sparse setting, we found ourselves relying heavily on the quality of our 'practice' of teacher–student pedagogy, which became all the more important for guiding us in the development of the work, serving often as the main and at times our only referent for judging the quality of our work. When judgements about how to proceed, for example whether or not to pursue a certain line of inquiry, could not be based on external criteria because none of the academic institutions around us had positions on the questions that concerned us, we relied on good pedagogical practice to help us decide: are we treating each other with respect when we consider this question? Are we hearing? Are we acting with due regard for our respective roles as teacher and student? We cannot overemphasize how important a good working relationship and good interpersonal communication were for completing this PhD work successfully. We would even go so far as to call it absolutely central.

Challenges and recommendation

Both of us can testify to having often encountered one of Brutschin and Wiesmann's (2003) constitutive feelings of new and interdisciplinary research: that of being outside of one's 'comfort zone', of having to understand and renegotiate familiar terms and issues, now seen in a new light or from a different disciplinary perspective. Brutschin and Wiesmann (ibid.: 2, emphasis added) note the challenges associated with this special feature of transdisciplinary research when they write, 'On the personal level, the social competence of researchers taking part in transdisciplinary projects must be very high, *in order to sustain disorientation and question one's own disciplinary paradigms*.' This sense of risk, disorientation and novelty, which is part and parcel of conducting innovative research, means that more support than the 'standard issue' is needed if the work is to remain clear and focused: more time is need for gaining one's orientation and renegotiating understandings, more patience from supervisors who may at times be as confused as their very confused students, more resources for verifying and elaborating new understandings, and more down time, to allow our human brains to return to the restful world of the mundane after our sorties into this domain of cognitive chaos. And here it is important to be clear that we do not just mean financial or funding support, although that is still often lacking for the kind of strong transdisciplinary work we are talking about here. Here we also mean mentoring support (for both students *and* supervisors) and community support, to ensure a convivial research environment where such work is valued as an innovative and important contribution to the advance of science, rather than just being seen as somehow a bit 'odd' or off the beaten track.

An ethico-political imperative

Instead of viewing our work as merely idiosyncratic, we see our position, as ecological political economy scholars concerned with the place of purpose in environmental sciences for policy, to be somewhat like that of someone who is critically investigating racism within a racist context: we are critically investigating sustainability within the context of unsustainability. There is a strong argument for the ethical obligation of a scholar in such circumstances to disseminate their findings widely within and beyond the confines of the institutional and disciplinary context within which they are located, including going beyond the academy to engage with citizens, the policy and political community, the media, and so on. Increasingly, good environmental sciences scholarship is viewed in terms of 'making a difference', but this is still largely understood to refer only to the confines of knowledge production itself, with a key measure of success being the degree to which scientific advice has been taken up in practice (Tian 2004; Costanza 2003). The general standard used to compare the relative success of different scholars is still related to the high premium placed on the production of knowledge as a commodity, both in terms of patents and in terms of the self-referential (within the academy) obsession with the 'impact factor' of journal articles (Ravetz 1971; Costanza *et al.* 2004; Rhoten and Parker 2004) – an indicator that primarily confirms only that a scholar is functioning within the academic system in the approved manner.

This raises an extremely important question not only for ecological economists but for any scholar concerned with the complex human–non-human nature relationships of the twenty-first century: what is the role and what is the political/ethical obligation of a scholar researching pressing and urgent political subjects? Does the critical scholar of racism have a duty to get involved in anti-racist political activity, or do they, quite to the contrary, have a duty to remain outside the political debate, in order to protect the authority of their analysis? Does the scholar of sustainability have a duty to 'make a difference' by getting involved in political, media or other forms of activity outside their prescribed, assigned and 'normal' academic position? Is it really possible to do this kind of work without becoming embroiled in the associated politics, even if only as a silent accomplice upholding the status quo? Under such conditions, can one realistically expect to maintain a clear distinction between one's role as a researcher (or student or supervisor) and one's position as a citizen or potential political actor?

A duty of care imperative ...

The wider cultural and societal context within which we were working as we developed this thesis was marked by growing scientific, media and political concern over what has come to be understood as a multifaceted 'ecological crisis', particularly a growing appreciation for the impacts and implications of anthropogenic climate change. Since the persistent-seeming inability of European-style democratic institutions to effectively engage with these challenges was the focus of the thesis, we found that our scholarly work was intimately related to a major popular political discourse taking place around us in real time. We shared between us a disposition for combining normative theoretical reflection with real-world application, and felt a need to consider and engage with this wider cultural context.

As we have already intimated, we believe that any study of ecological political economy carries with it a de facto normative component. In our case, as the thesis we were working on developed, what we would call a 'politico-ethical imperative' emerged as an additional, praxis-oriented aim of the work. This imperative – to try to help address the environmental governance problems that we identified in the course of writing the thesis – was based on a realization that there are substantial policy and 'real-world' implications associated with how environmental science and interdisciplinary research are carried out within the university systems of the world. Even though the product of our collaboration was a theoretical dissertation, we could not ignore the putative significance of our findings for the ever-more urgent tasks associated with making the transition to sustainable societies. This imperative called upon us to integrate our work with this wider cultural context, or at least to develop a clear argument concerning what might constitute meaningful links between the related political debates taking place in our 'ecological economic cultural context'.

Particularly towards the end of the thesis work, there was a strong sense that a constitutive dimension of the thesis was this movement from theory to practice, which saw us independently and collaboratively involved in organizing special seminars and workshops, giving policy advice to government authorities and in some instances participating directly in political debates and formal electoral competitions. These activities, which were undertaken alongside the writing of this thesis, were nonetheless part of that work, the motivation for investing our time and effort being the translation of our insights into actions.

We see this push towards political action, within and beyond the university, as a characteristic of ecological political economy research. The special normative character of ecological economics specifically and environmental science more generally is reasonably obvious and has already been discussed at length by others (Becker and Jahn 1999; Funtowicz and Ravetz 1990, 1991, 1992, 1993, 1994; Costanza 1991). Basically, since environmental science is concerned with the quality of human environment relationships, each study chooses, whether implicitly or explicitly, a definition of environment and an ideal for what constitutes good-quality human relations with that environment. And each study is conducted in order to provide information that can improve the quality of human environment relations with respect to the stated (or implicit) ideal.

Similarly, when we propose to formally consider the politico-ethical obligations that we felt as researchers working on topics of pressing importance to the political communities in which we live, we raise the point not only as a personal account but also as a formal object of study relevant for developing a better understanding of how to achieve Giampietro and Mayumi's (2001) fourth requisite ability of ecological economics: to describe, understand and engage with the processes through which humans translate understandings of the predicament of sustainability into collective action. This imperative places a number of challenging questions onto the table for discussion: at what point (if at all) should a researcher go beyond the academic world of peer review publications, research reports and dissemination of results at conferences into the rather more disorderly world of politics, with its noisy ideological debates, sometimes indifferent and sometimes expert citizens, and sometimes ignorant, sometimes biased, sometimes highly informed and innovative policy-makers and politicians? How should the ecological economics researcher, for whom the impact of research is arguably as important as the results, engage with and disseminate their findings to a wider public? How should such a researcher respond to the inevitable politicization of their work, which is created to be used by political actors and policy-makers?

Duty, decisions and the fourth requisite ability of ecological economics

Traditionally, the call for academic discretion has been based on the presumption that a line between the politics and the science of a given issue could be drawn: that the two could be held, in practice (Weber 1947; Habermas 1980 [1971]) if not in principle, separate from one another; and we believe that this is often still the case. However, with respect to questions of ecological political economy, the purpose-setting systems of human societies are brought *within* the analytical frame. When we begin to study Giampietro and Mayumi's fourth requisite ability, our decisions as scholars regarding how the purpose-setting systems of human societies are conceptualized are inevitably political (Funtowicz and Ravetz 1997; Luks 1999; Funtowicz and O'Connor 1999; Farrell 2008). Martinez-Alier puts the problem as follows:

> Governance requires the integration into policy (whether greenhouse [gas] policy or European agricultural policy or local urban policies) of scientific and lay opinions, sometimes contradictory among themselves, relevant for different scales and different levels of reality. Who then has the power to decide the procedure for such integrated analysis? Who has the power to simplify complexity, ruling some languages of valuation out of order?
>
> (2002: 271)

Furthermore, he puts the task of addressing this problem squarely in the lap of political theorists:

> [T]he impossibility of an economic rationality (either based on the market or on central planning) which takes into account ecological side effects and uncertainties, and the impossibility, also, of deciding human affairs according to purely ecological planning, lead towards the politicization of the economy ... the economy and the ecology of humans are embedded in politics.
>
> (Martinez-Alier 1991: 134)

Since the thesis we developed together was concerned with understanding how and where scientific and other forms of knowledge inform decisions about human–environment relationships, from our perspective as scholars, interactions between citizenship and science were objects of study and analysis. However, at the same time these same questions stood before us as ethical and moral considerations: how and where should we take action to try to change conditions within our university, within our own academic disciplines of economics, political science and ecology, and within our immediate political contexts in Northern Ireland and Europe?

The place of the academy within an ecological economy

The exceptional character of our continuing struggle with the tension between scholarly rigour and duty to our various professional and political communities was particularly evident to us in our work with the concept of collective ecological management (CEM), which served as an organizing framework for the political theory of the thesis. The concept was initially formulated theoretically by one of us (Barry 1999) and then developed by the other (Farrell 2007, 2009 [2005]) in a way that brings out the duty of scholars of ecological management to move not only beyond the reductionism of single disciplines but also beyond the confines of the academy, to engage with the realpolitik consequences of their work.

Originally formulated within green political theory as an overarching critique of ecocentrism, CEM focuses attention on the role of institutions (such as the state and the market) in human–environment relationships and presumes that humans will always somehow actively manage their relations with their environments. Within the thesis reported upon here, the concept was developed in a number of directions and we do not have the space to review them all. What is important to our current argument is that we share, in our interpretation and elaboration of the concept, a rejection of a naive view that one sometimes finds within certain strands of economics, environmental politics and ecological thinking: that there is a 'solution' to human–nature problems which, once achieved, implies that a certain 'harmony' will almost automatically persist. As green political theorists we anticipate that successful institutions of environmental governance will need to be not static but changeable, able to continue responding to the inevitable changes that are only to be expected from the continuing process of evolving human–non-human relationships. To put it another way, we do not see sustainability as a goal but as a way of travelling.

The concept of CEM characterizes ecological governance as a complex set of political practices that make use of market, state and sub-state institutions and those associated with community, as well as combinations of them' (Barry 1999: 158). We understand human impacts on (or we might even say within) ecological systems to be ordinary and inevitable, and ask the question, how well do current practices manage these inevitable impacts, with respect to the needs of the ecosystems and of the human societies? In this light the question is not so much whether or not collective ecological management is taking place but rather how good the current system of collective ecological management is. Such assessment depends of course in large part upon what (if anything) a society has determined to be its collective aims for managing its relationship with the ecological systems within which it is embedded. However, determining appropriate aims is not purely a question of intent: first, since a society can quite easily have intentional aims that are incompatible with the needs of the ecosystems with which it is associated, and second, because even a society without any explicit aims for managing its ecological impacts has, nonetheless, implicit policies regarding how those impacts are to be managed, which are set by the aims of its political economy. Determining what should be the aims of a society's collective ecological management is both a political judgement regarding what that society desires and an empirical question of what the associated ecosystems can sustain. And since determining these aims is not a task that will someday be accomplished but an enduring and recurring feature of the activity 'collective ecological management', part of what must be determined when considering how to create good-quality collective ecological management is the procedures that are to be used to determine collective ecological management aims.

Ecological economics, in one way or another, is intended to contribute to each of these three CEM tasks – construing what are appropriate economic aims, construing what are appropriate ecological aims and construing what are appropriate procedures for determining aims – but it is mainly the third that concerns us as political theorists and scholars of ecological political economy. And our interest in this third task places us in the midst of a complex circle of causalities: as we continue to make recommendations about how the collective ecological management institutions within which we ourselves are operating might be changed, in order to improve their fitness for the purposes decided upon by a collective to which we belong and contribute, this places our own theoretical propositions within our frame of analytical observation (Funtowicz and Ravetz 1990; Funtowicz and O'Connor 1999).

The activities of CEM can be understood as the collaborative problematizing by human societies of their own role in the designing of their own futures and those of their environment(s):

> In a sense the collective ecological management strategy is on one level a democratic political procedure within which various ways of valuing the environment (and thus various relations and interests to and in the environment) can be raised, deliberated and incorporated into policy recommendations.
>
> (Barry 1999: 120)

The concept is introduced towards the close of Barry's (1999) book and remains somewhat under-theorized in that text. However, its broad conceptualization of self–other–environment relations fits well with the ecological economics presumption that human societies and their purpose setting systems are materially and ecologically embedded (Georgescu-Roegen 1971), and it provides us with a basis for developing political theory that responds to Martinez-Alier's observation that 'the economy and the ecology of humans are embedded in politics' (1991: 134). Rather than viewing the inevitable limitations of human perception (as manifest for example in our ignorance about the future or our limited knowledge of the present) as an insurmountable problem that must be tolerated but should be minimized (Habermas 1984, 1987), we see them as operational features of an ecologically embedded human cognition (see Berger and Luckmann 1991 [1967]; Dennett 1992; Douglas 1986; Foucault 2003 [1973]; Prigogine 1997; Wakefield 1990) that structure and regulate how we, as humans, perceive and engage with the ecological systems within which we are embedded (Luhmann 2004; Blühdorn 2000).

Because our understanding of our environment is always limited, humans are always deciding on how to relate to the environment without having full knowledge about the impacts of their behaviours (see Simon 1955, 1959). Instead of seeing conflicting conceptualizations of human–non-human nature relationships as reflecting differences of interest, or identity-based values, or an ethically diverse sets of opinions, we see them as different ways of perceiving and contributing to resolving the shared problems of collective ecological management. For example, we view value conflicts as a part of the complex multifaceted character of the ecological management collective, not as something that must be eliminated but as something that should be taken into account when proposing CEM operating procedures (Farrell 2007). Building on this interpretation, one of us (Farrell 2004) has proposed the democratic institutional innovation of epistemological representation, which was eventually elaborated, within the thesis, as part of a CEM framework, leading to proposals for design of new institutional configurations that could support epistemologically complex environmental governance.

The details of that proposal can be found in the thesis and associated paper (Farrell 2004, 2009 [2005]) and will not be discussed here. What is directly relevant to our present argument is the proposition underlying them: that where political decisions are substantively dependent upon scientific assessments, the technical choices that scientists make regarding what to include in their assessments – how to formulate their research questions, which of their results to report, where to report them, etc. – are also substantively political choices (Farrell 2008). In so far as they are, the work produced as a result of these choices deserves to be assessed not only for its scholarly rigour but also for its political legitimacy. We would even go so far as to say that it is the moral duty of the scientists working with these kinds of problems not only to work according to best scientific practice but also to behave as responsible citizens, attentive to the fact that they are acting within the political forum of collective ecological management.

For an example of what we mean here, let us take another look at the now common practice of using monetary value proxies to represent the economic worth of ecological phenomena (employed within both environmental economics and ecological economics). Although practically no one claims that these proxy values are correct (Costanza *et al.* 1997), they are widely used because they make it possible to slot environmental values directly into existing economic models and because they make it possible to produce what appear to be robust and convincing economic analyses of the costs of environmental degradation. That is to say, the products of monetary valuation (proxy units of value meant to represent the economic worth of ecological phenomena) have pragmatic and rhetorical value. Nicholas Stern's report *The Economics of Climate Change* (2006) and the more recent European Union-generated *Economics of Ecosystems and Biodiversity* report (Sukhdev 2008) are two prominent recent examples, but use of proxy monetary values is widespread, and reliance upon this type of data can be found in thousands of economics and policy papers, as well as within the reports of the Millennium Ecosystem Assessment (MA) and Intergovernmental Panel on Climate Change (IPCC). The choice to use monetary value proxies instead of developing new methods of ecological economic assessment that do not require monetary values is just that, a choice, and one that is not without consequences. Continued use of monetary proxies serves to reinforce a set of scientific assessment practices (and associated institutions) that make it difficult and risky to develop alternative approaches (Farrell 2007). While it is a decision taken in the course of carrying out one's ordinary work as, for example, an environmental economist, policy analyst or ecological economic systems modeller, the choice to use monetary proxies is a political and not only a scientific one.

Taken under conditions where one tends to see oneself not as a citizen but as an expert, such decisions reflect an extension of the domain of politics into the daily practice of science, presenting political theorists with an empirical challenge and ecological economists with an ethical one: what is an appropriate democratic duty of care with regard to the choices made about how to conduct policy-relevant ecological economics research projects – generally, with respect to the daily practice that constitutes this work, and specifically, with respect to the practice of creating and using monetary estimates as proxies for the economic worth of ecological phenomena?

In considering this problem we looked again to Barry's (1999) theory of collective ecological management, picking up on the concept of ecological stewardship, where he describes green citizenship as 'a praxis of citizens critically evaluating preferences and attempting to come to agreement on limits within which particular social–environmental relations may be pursued' (ibid.: 234). He proposes that these conditions call for an eco-aware ethics of use, offering a theoretical position that proceeds beyond the distinction between anthropocentrism and non-anthropocentrism. Instead, under Barry's use ethic, humans may be understood to hold custodial interests towards non-human nature, interests that can be manifested through ethical but nonetheless anthropocentric behaviours. This ethic favours a human to non-human nature relationship that is '[mutualist] symbiotic rather than parasitic'. Humans are understood to have a responsibility of 'ecological stewardship' (ibid.: 64), which he suggests may be operationalized through collective ecological management.

This use ethic can be understood as a sort of duty of care, and exercising such a duty requires that sufficient attention be given to understanding the basic attributes and requirements of its object, which in this case is the ecological economic systems of the planet: that is to say, understanding the sufficient conditions required for the viable forward-going simultaneous continuation of the ecological and the economic systems of human societies. However, that is not the final end of this duty, which also requires that, once construed, these sufficient conditions also be taken into account, if not ensured, in one's decisions and actions, in so far as those actions relate to one's participation in the forum of CEM.

As has been discussed in this chapter, and is also discussed in several other chapters of this book, within ecological economics it is taken as given that the development of an understanding of the dynamic relationships *between* the social and physical systems that comprise ecological economic systems is required. This means that we are talking about a duty that applies not only to individual scientists but also to the individuals who administer the academies of science. That is to say, in so far as the academy is expected to support the work of understanding common good problems in a democracy, there is also an ecological stewardship duty of care accruing to the administrators and directors of universities, a duty of care that calls upon them to give attention to the needs of researchers operating in the epistemological and methodological no man's land of ecological economics.

Re-establishing this direct link between one's professional responsibilities and one's responsibilities as a citizen brings us back full circle to the original principles of citizen duty under the Athenian model of democracy. In ancient Athens, citizen duties were intimately related to the citizen's role within wider Athenian society, as an educated man with certain specific training and responsibilities relating to trade, commerce and the military activities of the state (Finlay 1973; Headlam 1933).[8] In modern democracies this presumption of duty to the common good continues on in the principles of negligence and due diligence, which stipulate the social practice boundaries of a general duty of care that all individuals (including corporations) are expected to exercise towards other individuals. However, where negligence and due diligence set limits to what is acceptable, bounded by the mores of a society, ecological stewardship calls upon each citizen to actively take up an ethically informed social *practice* with their environment as a civic duty. It is a duty that calls upon the citizen to be proactive.

Barry relates this type of citizenship to the idea of work as social practice, proposing that '[t]he more [that] social-environmental purposive, transformative relations [behavings towards the environment] approach the ideal of a social practice, the more that use realizes the virtues of stewardship rather than exploitation' (1999: 240). Here we have the beginnings of a green political theory argument identifying a democratic duty of care that calls upon scholars to keep in mind how their own professional actions may impact upon CEM. In much the same way that we are expected to keep in mind the ethical issues associated with conducting experiments on live animals and human subjects because we have a duty of care to these individuals, we may also be expected to conduct science in a posture of ecological stewardship because we have a duty of care to the ecological systems of the planet.

Conclusions

Given the pressing need for what Max-Neef (2005) has called strongly interdisciplinary research (where not only the outputs but also the principles and concepts of various disciplines are combined), countries and institutions with relatively limited experience of the study of complex sustainability problems certainly have much to learn. However, it seems to us that many of the obstacles we encountered are more characteristic of university education in general than particularly symptomatic of the state of university education in the United Kingdom, including Northern Ireland.

From the different points of view of supervisor and student, and together as political science-oriented scholars of ecological political economy, we find that a greater recognition of the challenges and value of conducting good-quality interdisciplinary research is much needed, both in terms of advancing the practical effectiveness of human societies dealing with specific socio-ecological problems (i.e. developing policy related research) and in terms of internal (within the academy) recognition of the intellectual merits of such research. Good-quality execution of the interdisciplinary research typical of ecological economics – while differing in its scope, methodological approach and subject areas – has the same intellectual virtues and qualities as any journey of scholarly inquiry. However, the institutional rewards of conducting such research are few and far between. While there are some academic positions specifically related to ecological economics, mainly at research institutes, the vast majority of stable university positions remain firmly fixed within the disciplines, and a great many of the ecological economics-specific positions are themselves based within the twenty-first-century meta-disciplines of environmental science and mathematical modelling.

If the community of ecological economics scholars is agreed that politics is a relevant domain of ecological economic inquiry (and we think this can now be taken as given), then the fundamental work of ecological economics' political theorists and political scientists also needs to be supported. In part, this means providing a wider range of ecological economics positions within the academy, but it also means that the scholars and scientists who have become the establishment, in so far as they understand themselves to hold a duty of care for the ecological stewardship of the planet, need to consider how room for this work can be made within their disciplines and within the current institutional structures. This is not simply a question of whether or not a given scholar is eventually forced back within disciplinary boundaries in the course of seeking to establish their career. It is also a question of whether a scholar who has moved out into this no man's land can remain within the academy at all: of whether they can find a position where who and what they are is appreciated and valued (Ravetz 1971). And in the end it is a question of whether or not this line of inquiry can be developed within the academy at all.

In hindsight, our experience of writing and supervising an ecological economics political theory thesis can perhaps best be summarized in terms of living within, participating in and, hopefully, making some small contribution towards the intellectual process of a 'paradigm shift'. The 'no man's land' of ecological political economy is a messy, risky and uncertain interregnum between different paradigms of knowledge production. It is part of the project forged by the first generation of ecological economists, people like Nicholas Georgescu-Roegen, H.T. Odum, Kenneth Boulding, Mary E. Clark, K. William Kapp and C.S. Holling, who all pointed towards this new direction from within their respective disciplines of economics and ecology. As we work now, in the twenty-first century, to grapple with the questions that these pioneers placed before us, we venture into a completely new domain, one that first had to be imagined before it could be explored. At our disposal are some tools that these pioneers prepared for us, alongside those that we are crafting ourselves now as we go along. In the preceding pages we have argued that one of the most important ecological economics tools still to be crafted is academic research institutions that can support the execution of the interdisciplinary work that lies at the heart of this field of inquiry. We have left many threads hanging in the course of our account, which we hope may be taken up and developed by others, and we do not claim to have exhausted the topics raised here for discussion. Instead, we hope to have convinced our readers that the politics within ecological economics and the politics of ecological economics must be seen and addressed together, as related aspects of a single system of ecological political economy.

Notes

1 By 'environmental governance' we also mean governance for sustainable development/sustainability.

2 Following Hagedorn (2008), Olsson *et al.* (2006), Ostrom (2005), Young (2002) and Vatn (2005), we take it that different institutional configurations may be more or less conducive to sustainable development and we would, on that basis, expect that different challenges and different opportunities arise in other settings where interdisciplinary sustainability research is carried out, such as private research institutes, non-governmental organizations and public authorities and agencies. However, systematic exploration of this variety of settings, a sort of cross-institutional comparative analysis, while a promising follow-up to the work presented here, is beyond the scope of our current discussion.

3 We are indebted to Tommaso Luzzati for suggesting this term 'ecological political economy' and direct readers interested in exploring to topic further to consult Hinterberger *et al.* (1996) and Gale and M'Gonigle (2000).

4 See Røpke (2004) for a brief history of the early development of the field.

5 'Die Philosophen haben die Welt nur verschieden interpretiert, es kömmt drauf an, sie zu verändern' (Marx 1978 [1845]).

6 For reasons of space we here simply state, without argument, our view that this description of the academy and knowledge production is touchingly naive and betrays an innocence in its belief of the university as beyond politics and power that is itself ideological and deeply normative. While ignorance itself may or may not be ideological, to sustain the myth and the conditions that perpetuate a convenient ignorance of the constitutive role of power and politics in knowledge production is without doubt one of the most powerful ideological 'projects'.

7 For example, at the Gund Institute in Vermont, the Beijier Institute for Ecological Economics and the Stockholm Resilience Centre, both in Sweden, and the Institut de Ciència i Tecnologia Ambientals (ICTA) in Barcelona; and within the Commonwealth Scientific and Industrial Research Organisation (CSIRO) in Australia.

8 We hasten to emphasize that what is similar here is the principle that the duties of a citizen are duties related to their work, whatever that work may be, rather than the practices themselves, which in ancient Athens included a strict distinction between public patriarchy and private matriarchy.

References

Barry, J. 1999. *Rethinking Green Politics*. London: Sage.

Barry, J. 2007. 'Spires, plateaus and the infertile landscape of Education for Sustainable Development: re-invigorating the university through integrating community, campus and curriculum.' *International Journal of Innovation and Sustainable Development* 2(3/4): 433–452.

Becker, E. and T. Jahn eds. 1999. *Sustainability and the Social Sciences: A Cross-disciplinary Approach to Integrating Environmental Considerations into Theoretical Reorientation*. London: Zed Books.

Berger, P.L. and T. Luckmann. 1991 [1967]. *The Social Construction of Reality: A Treatise in the Sociology of Knowledge*. London: Penguin.

Biermann, F., P. Pattberg, H. van Asselt and F. Zelli. 2007. 'Fragmentation of global governance architectures: the case of climate policy.' Global Governance Working Paper 34. Amsterdam: Global Governance Project. Online, available at: www.glogov.org/images/doc/WP34.pdf (accessed April 2009).

Blühdorn, I. 2000. *Post-ecologist Politics: Social Theory and the Abdication of the Ecologist Paradigm*. London: Routledge.

Boulding, K.E. 1991. 'What do we want to sustain? Environmentalism and human evaluations.' In *Ecological Economics: The Science and Management of Sustainability*, ed. R. Costanza. New York: Columbia University Press.

Brundtland, G.H. ed. 1987. *Our Common Future: The World Commission on Environment and Development*. Oxford: Oxford University Press.

Brutschin, J. and U. Wiesmann. 2003. 'Transdisciplinary research in development cooperation: origins and paradigms.' In *Unity of Knowledge in Transdisciplinary Research for Sustainability: Encyclopedia of Life Support Systems (EOLSS)*, ed. G. Hirsch Hadorn. Oxford: EOLSS Publishers. Online, available at: www.eolss.net (accessed 20 October 2006).

Carson, R. 1963. *Silent Spring*. London: Hamish Hamilton.

Clark, M.E. 1989. *Ariadne's Thread: The Search for New Modes of Thinking*. London: Macmillan.

Costanza, R. 1991. *Ecological Economics: The Science and Management of Sustainability*. New York: Columbia University Press.

Costanza, R. 2003. 'A vision of the future of science: reintegrating the study of humans and the rest of nature.' *Futures* 35(6): 651–671.

Costanza, R., R. D'Arge, R. de Groot, S. Farber, M. Grasso, B. Hannon, K. Limburg, S. Naeem, R.V. O'Neill, J. Paruelo, R.G. Raskin, P. Sutton and M. van den Belt. 1997. 'The value of the world's ecosystem services and natural capital.' *Nature* 387: 253–260.

Costanza, R., D.I. Stern, B. Fisher, L. He and C. Ma. 2004. 'Influential publications in ecological economics: a citation analysis.' *Ecological Economics* 50(3–4): 261–292.

Daly, H.E. 1998. 'The return of Lauderdale's paradox.' *Ecological Economics* 25(1): 21–23.

Dennett, D.C. 1992. *Consciousness Explained*. London: Penguin Books.

Diaw, M.C. and T. Kusumanto. 2005. 'Scientists in social encounters: the case for an engaged practice of science.' In *The Equitable Forest: Diversity, Community, and Resource Management*, ed. C.J. Pierce Colfer. Washington, DC: Resources for the Future Press.

Dietz, T., E. Ostrom and P.C. Stern. 2003. 'The struggle to govern the commons.' *Science* 302(52): 1907–1912.

Douglas, M. 1986. *How Institutions Think*. Syracuse, NY: Syracuse University Press.

Dryzek, J.S. 1987. *Rational Ecology: Environment and Political Economy*. London: Basil Blackwell.

Faber, M. 2008. 'How to be an ecological economist.' *Ecological Economics* 66(1): 1–7.

Farrell, K.N. 2004. 'Recapturing fugitive power: epistemology, complexity and democracy.' *Local Environment* 9(5): 469–479.

Farrell, K.N. 2007. 'Living with living systems: the co-evolution of values and valuation.' *International Journal of Sustainable Development and World Ecology* 14(1): 14–26.

Farrell, K.N. 2008. 'The politics of science and sustainable development: Marcuse's new science in the 21st century.' *Capitalism Nature Socialism* 19(4): 68–83.

Farrell, K.N. 2009 [2005]. *Making Good Decisions Well: A Theory of Collective Ecological Management*. Aachen, Germany: Shaker Verlag.

Finlay, M.I. 1973. *Democracy Ancient and Modern*. London: Chatto & Windus.

Forsyth, T. 2003. *Critical Political Ecology: The Politics of Environmental Science*. London: Routledge.

Foucault, M. 1984. 'What is enlightenment?' In *The Foucault Reader: An Introduction to Foucault's Thought*, ed. P. Rabinow. London: Penguin.

Foucault, M. 2003 [1973]. *The Archaeology of Knowledge*. London: Routledge.

Funtowicz, S.O. and M. O'Connor. 1999. 'The passage from entropy to thermodynamic indeterminacy: a social and science epistemology for sustainabiliy.' In *Bioeconomics and Sustainability: Essays in Honor of Nicholas Georgescu-Roegen*, ed. K. Mayumi and J.M. Gowdy. Cheltenham, UK: Edward Elgar.

Funtowicz, S.O. and J.R. Ravetz. 1990. *Uncertainty and Quality in Science for Policy*. Dordrecht, the Netherlands: Kluwer Academic.

Funtowicz, S.O. and J.R. Ravetz. 1991. 'A new scientific methodology for global environmental issues.' In *Ecological Economics: The Science and Management of Sustainability*, ed. R. Costanza. New York: Columbia University Press.

Funtowicz, S.O. and J.R. Ravetz. 1992. 'The good, the true and the post-modern.' *Futures* 24(10): 963–976.

Funtowicz, S.O. and J.R. Ravetz. 1993. 'Science for the post-normal age.' *Futures* 25(7): 739–755.

Funtowicz, S. and J.R. Ravetz. 1994. 'The worth of a songbird: ecological economics as a post-normal science.' *Ecological Economics* 10(3): 197–207.

Funtowicz, S.O. and J.R. Ravetz. 1997. 'The poetry of thermodynamics: energy, entropy/exergy and quality.' *Futures* 29(9): 791–810.

Gale, F.P. and M.R. M'Gonigle eds. 2000. *Nature, Production, Power: Towards an Ecological Political Economy*. Cheltenham, UK: Edward Elgar.

Georgescu-Roegen, N. 1971. *The Entropy Law and the Economic Process*. Cambridge, MA: Harvard University Press.

Giampietro, M. and K. Mayumi. 2001. 'Integrated assessment of sustainability trade-offs: methodological challenges for ecological economics.' Paper presented at the conference 'Frontiers in Ecological Economics', Cambridge, 4–7 July.

Habermas, J. 1980 [1971]. *Toward a Rational Society: Student Protest, Science, and Politics*. London: Heinemann Educational.

Habermas, J. 1984. *The Theory of Communicative Action*, vol. 1: *Reason and the Rationalization of Society*. London: Heinemann.

Habermas, J. 1987. *The Theory of Communicative Action*, vol. 2: *Lifeworld and System: A Critique of Functionalist Reason*. Cambridge: Polity Press.

Hagedorn, K. 2008. 'Particular requirements for institutional analysis in nature-related sectors.' *European Review of Agricultural Economics* 35(3): 357–384.

Headlam, J.W. 1933. *Election by Lot at Athens*, 2nd ed. Cambridge: Cambridge University Press.

Healy, S. 2003. 'Epistemological pluralism and the "politics of choice".' *Futures* 35(7): 689–701.

Hinterberger, F., F. Luks and M. Stewen. 1996. *Ökologische Wirtschaftspolitik: Zwischen Ökodiktatur und Umweltkatastrophe*. Berlin: Birkhäuser Verlag.

Kant, I. 2005 [1787]. *The Critique of Pure Reason*, 2nd ed. Sioux Falls, SD: NuVision.

Luhmann, N. 2004. *Ökologische Kommunikation: Kann die moderne Gesellschaft sich auf ökologische Gefährdungen einstellen?*, 4th ed. Wiesbaden: Verlag für Sozialwissenschaften.

Luks, F. 1999. 'Post-normal science and the rhetoric of inquiry: deconstructing normal science?' *Futures* 31(7): 705–719.

MacIntyre, A. 1981. *After Virtue: A Study in Moral Theory*. Notre Dame, IN: University of Notre Dame Press.

Marcuse, H. 1991 [1964]. *One-Dimensional Man: Studies in the Ideology of Advanced Industrial Society*. London: Routledge.

Martinez-Alier, J. 1991. 'Ecological perception, environmental policy and distributional conflicts.' In *Ecological Economics: The Science and Management of Sustainability*, ed. R. Costanza. New York: Columbia University Press.

Martinez-Alier, J. 1999. 'From political economy to political ecology.' In *Bioeconomics and Sustainability: Essays in Honor of Nicholas Georgescu-Roegen*, ed. K. Mayumi and J.M. Gowdy. Cheltenham, UK: Edward Elgar.

Martinez-Alier, J. 2002. *The Environmentalism of the Poor*. Cheltenham, UK: Edward Elgar.

Marx, K. 1978 [1845]. 'Thesen über Feuerbach.' In Karl Marx und Friedrich Engels, *Werke*. Berlin: Marx-Engels-Lenin-Institut.

Max-Neef, M.A. 2005. 'Foundations of transdisciplinarity.' *Ecological Economics* 53(1): 5–16.

Newman, J.H. 1999 [1854]. *The Idea of a University*. Washington, DC: Regnery.

Norgaard, R.B. 1988. 'Sustainable development: a co-evolutionary view.' *Futures* 20(6): 606–620.

Norgaard, R.B. 1989. 'The case for methodological pluralism.' *Ecological Economics* 1(1): 37–57.

Norgaard, R.B., C. Bode and the Values Reading Group. 1998. 'Next, the value of God, and other reactions.' *Ecological Economics* 25(1): 37–39.

Olsson, P., L.H. Gunderson, S.R. Carpenter, P. Ryan, L. Lebel, C. Folke and C.S. Holling. 2006. 'Shooting the rapids: navigating transitions to adaptive governance of social-ecological systems.' *Ecology and Society* 11(1): 18. Online, available at: www.ecologyandsociety.org/vol11/iss1/art18/.

Ostrom, E. 2005. *Understanding Institutional Diversity*. Princeton, NJ: Princeton University Press.

Özkaynak, B., P. Devine and D. Rigby. 2002. 'Whither ecological economics?' *Environment and Pollution* 18(4): 317–335.

Prigogine, I. 1997. *The End of Certainty: Time, Chaos, and the New Laws of Nature*. New York: The Free Press.

Ravetz, J.R. 1971. *Scientific Knowledge and Its Social Problems*. Oxford: Clarendon Press.

Rhoten, D. and A. Parker. 2004. 'Risks and rewards of an interdisciplinary research path.' *Science* 306(5704): 2046.

Røpke, I. 1999. 'Prices are not worth much.' *Ecological Economics* 29(1): 45–46.

Røpke, I. 2002. 'Ecological economics: a special perspective? Preliminary reflections.' Paper presented at the Seventh Biennial Conference of the International Society for Ecological Economics, Sousse, Tunisia, 6–9 March.

Røpke, I. 2004. 'The early history of modern ecological economics.' *Ecological Economics* 50(3–4): 293–314.

Simon, H.A. 1955. 'A behavioural model of rational choice.' *Quarterly Journal of Economics* 69(1): 99–118.

Simon, H.A. 1959. 'Theories of decision-making in economics and behavioral science.' *American Economic Review* 49(3): 253–283.

Stern, N. 2006. *The Economics of Climate Change: The Stern Review*. Cambridge: Cambridge University Press (on behalf of Cabinet Office – HM Treasury).

Sukhdev, P. ed. 2008. *The Economics of Ecosystems and Biodiversity (TEEB)*. Cambridge: Banson.

Tian, S. 2004. 'Ecological economics as a policy science: rhetoric or commitment towards an improved decision-making process on sustainability.' *Ecological Economics* 48(1): 23–36.

Vatn, A. 2005. *Institutions and the Environment*. Cheltenham, UK: Edward Elgar.

Wakefield, N. 1990. *Postmodernism: The Twilight of the Real*. London: Pluto Press.

Weber, M. 1947. '"Objectivity" in social science and social policy.' In *Essays in Sociology*, ed. M. Weber. London: K. Paul, Trench, Trubner.

Young, O.R. 2002. *The Institutional Dimensions of Environmental Change: Fit, Interplay, and Scale*. Cambridge, MA: MIT Press.

7 How ecofeminists use complexity in ecological economics

Ariel Salleh, Mary Mellor and Katharine N. Farrell with Vandana Shiva

Introduction

KF: As the main editor of this collection, I'm especially pleased to be able to include this chapter on ecofeminism. Both its content and its format illustrate what it means to operate beyond reductionism. Here Ariel Salleh, Mary Mellor and I explore ecofeminism as an example of 'best practice' ecological economics – beyond reductionism. The chapter is an open-ended conversation with a few reflective comments from Vandana Shiva woven in as well. The text ranges across the themes of Nature and Labour, Holism and Value, Technology and Myth, Complexity Theory, and Dialectical Thinking. By working through the relationship between ecological economics and ecofeminism in this way, we are putting ecofeminism into practice in the here and now. We explore the ideas raised here together, in cooperation as companions. Ariel and Mary, since you have both been working with ecofeminist ideas for many years, perhaps we should begin by giving readers a brief introduction to the topic?

AS: OK, let's start with a little history. It was a French writer, Françoise d'Eaubonne, who first used the term 'ecofeminism' in her book *Le Féminisme ou la mort*, published in 1974. I am not sure how widely known this work was at the time, but the American theologian Rosemary Ruether published her influential ecofeminist text *New Woman, New Earth* (1975) not long after. This elaborated on the core proposition of ecofeminist thinking: that the subordination of women and degradation of the earth are deeply interlinked. There is a chapter outlining a chronology of the movement in my *Ecofeminism as Politics* (Salleh 1997) that reveals a great deal of international grassroots activity and many publications from women calling themselves ecofeminist from the mid-1970s on. Among these, Mary's book *Breaking the Boundaries* (Mellor 1992) was an important contribution; and Vandana's text *Ecofeminism*, co-authored with Maria Mies (Mies and Shiva 1993), was particularly useful in setting our politics against the backdrop of North–South relations and debates about 'development'.

MM: There is quite an overlap between ecofeminism and political economy when it comes to spelling out the connection between exploitation of women's labour and the abuse of natural resources. Women and the environment are both marginalized in their positions within the formal capitalist patriarchal economy. As economists have long recognized in theory, though not necessarily in practice, the environment is conceptualized as a 'free good'. Ecofeminists show that along with this, women's lives and work are also undervalued in economic terms – precisely by being 'naturalized' (Mellor 1997). Thus, the starting point of ecofeminist analysis is the materiality of much of what the world defines as 'women's work' (although it is not necessarily all done by women or done by all women). This theme is found in the work of some feminist economists too, though not all are ecofeminist thinkers.

KF: This basic ecofeminist assumption, that the subordination of women and the degradation of the planet are interrelated, has attracted quite sophisticated contributions from across the academic spectrum. I mean beyond the ecological economics and political economy work that Mary and I do, there is the political ecology, environmental ethics, and epistemology critiques that Ariel does; histories of science like Carolyn Merchant's *The Death of Nature* (1981), new theories in molecular biology, all the way through to Vandana's practical work with the Navdanya or Nine Seeds Biodiversity and Conservation Farm in Dehradun, and the Navdanya ecological education café in New Delhi (Shiva and Moser 1995).

AS: Kate, before we go any further, I think it's important to underline the fact that ecofeminists are not only concerned about women. Our political analysis is about how the subjection of women is used in an unjust and unsustainable globalized economy that destroys the lives of men, women, children, other species and biological systems across the globe. Many ecofeminists contest this as activists, but others draw on various academic disciplines to theorize the domination of humans and nature within an historical, institutional, political-economic and ecological context. Because ecofeminists are concerned to redraw conceptual connections that have become lost over the centuries, most ecofeminist writing is transdisciplinary work.

Nature and labour

KF: That's interesting, because interdisciplinarity is exactly what attracted me to ecological economics. But it is also what eventually led me to discover ecofeminism, with its basic respect for the web of relationships that makes up the human–economic–ecology complex, a system with reproductive and regenerative capacities right at the centre of it. Yes, this is a big part of how I see these two fields of ecological economics and ecofeminism complementing each other. To me it seems that ecofeminism is an example of ecological economics 'done well': it shows clearly just why moving beyond reductionism is a must for ecological economists and it takes that task in hand, in both theory and practice.

In her essay 'Reduction and Regeneration: A Crisis in Science', Vandana Shiva (1993) explicitly connected the ecofeminist focus on regeneration and reproduction with the call for a new science beyond the artifice of what she called Cartesianism. Many scientists are now starting to rise to that challenge, with complexity research becoming ever more popular and participatory and interdisciplinary – even art science is becoming acceptable (Farrell *et al.*, Chapter 3 of this book; Edwards 2008).[1] But I also have a feeling that these new approaches are not always all they appear to be, that they are sometimes superficial window dressing or opportunistic instrumentalizations, and that the basic issues that Vandana raised in 1993 remain unaddressed. When I spoke with her about this, Vandana said that she thinks reductionist science has become more dominant since she wrote *Ecofeminism* with Maria Mies: 'For example, the reductionism of the green revolution has been taken to deeper levels with the gene revolution' (email interview with Katharine N. Farrell, 2007). Asked what is behind this, she added:

> I believe that the reason dominant science has failed to move beyond reductionism, and instead has become more reductionist, is because of the increasing influence of business and industry on science. Reductionism facilitates easier exploitation and also neutralizes ethical ecological assessment. It suits capital's agenda of maximization of profits.
>
> (ibid.)

AS: Today, the partnership of capitalism and science is very solid and Vandana faces it as an activist fighting to protect Indian women's traditional knowledge in medicine and agriculture from the biopiracy of pharmaceutical corporations. While I was looking at genetically modified organisms (GMOs) as a member of the Australian government's Gene Technology Ethics Committee, it occurred to me that a whole paradigm shift from reductionist molecular biology to dynamic genomics is being held back, in part, by Anglo-Saxon patent law (Salleh 2006a). Researchers in dynamic genomics have replaced the notion of a discrete unitary 'gene' with an understanding of genetic determination as a fluid, interactive process dependent on the interplay of many forces in the cellular environment (Weasel 1997: 49–59). In this respect, the 'thing' nominated by a corporation for sale as a countable and thus patentable 'unit' of altered DNA is just a convenient fiction. This throws a different light on efforts to discredit researchers in dynamic genomics. It suggests an orchestrated defence of reductionism that specifically seeks to keep it at the centre of science.

This point has been discussed at length by ecofeminist and feminist scholars for many years. The fact is that the ruling global elites of our time are well served by reductive, static, idealized constructs. Merchant's account of the European witch-hunts and the burning of midwives – during the period that was called the Baconian Enlightenment – links the appropriation of women's knowledge with the move to mechanical models in science and the rise of a bureaucratically administered state. In our time, this reductionist, mechanistic tendency has transmuted into a form of management teaching guided by analogies from cybernetic systems theory.

In contrast to Descartes' formulae and Bacon's influential methodologies for 'mastering' the earth, ecofeminist reasoning exemplifies a grounded 'embodied materialist' analysis at ease with the active generativity of nature and with the complexity that results from recognition of these energies. I am thinking of Vandana's case for protecting biodiversity in ways that enhance cultural diversity; or Mary's multidimensional analysis of caring, time, and money value; or my own current focus, on the particular qualities of labour that enable men and women to provision themselves sustainably (Salleh 2009). Each of these standpoints exposes how socially constructed sex-gender differences enter into and distort both academic discourses and the insights arising from them. In making this critique, the ecofeminist analysis is transdisciplinary. The reductionism of simplistic dualisms – like masculinity versus femininity, natural versus social, material versus ideological – is replaced by a perception of the humanity–nature metabolism that is dynamic and integrative.[2]

MM: I would add that ecofeminist political economy sees scientific and economic theories as abstracted from the embodied needs and limits of human existence embedded in nature. For example, what I call 'body work' must be done where the body is located and within the framework of its temporality, the daily cycle of rest and replenishment, the life cycle, and the timescales of disease. Human beings live in cycles of biological (birth, growth and death) and ecological time (absorption and renewal). Reductive economics and science ignore the holistic basis of human existence, largely because this is gendered. Reductive approaches do not 'see' the under-labouring work of women's unpaid or underpaid labour (which I call imposed altruism) or the work of nature.

KF: And since this imposed altruism is both immoral, exploitive and a materially essential part of the international economic system, modes of inquiry that ignore it are comfortable for those in power?

MM: Indeed, and if this fact is overlooked in the rush to move beyond reductionism, the whole point of the ecofeminist analysis can be misconstrued. For example, ecofeminism is often seen as arguing that women are intrinsically closer to nature because of their nourishing and caring roles; or that they are somehow morally superior because of the work that they do. Yet so-called women's work can be done by men, women or children. The critical point is that this work creates and recreates the labour force that is absorbed into the formal economy. Economists abstract this labour for their calculations while ignoring the means by which it is generated and leaving the rest of the human condition – youth, sickness, death – outside of their focus on production.

Part of the reason why body work remains invisible in economics is that it does not fit the schedules of paid work, since it must conform to the needs of biological time. By leaving so much of human existence outside of the boundaries of the economy, all the processes of regeneration and replenishment are also ignored. To put this in a way that highlights the first premise of an ecofeminist political economy: that is, it is by doing body work that women – or other workers within regenerative processes – gain an understanding of the fact that all human activities have to take account of natural conditions, limits and uncertainties, because humans are immanent rather than transcendent in relation to the natural world. Thus, ecofeminists like Veronika Bennholdt-Thomsen and Maria Mies (1999) describe the valued capitalist patriarchal production economy as merely the tip of a great iceberg, while below the waterline is the invisible reproduction economy: the world of unpaid domestic work, subsistence farming and the free gift of natural resources. Similarly, for the ecofeminist economist Hazel Henderson (1996) the market sector or valued economy is described as being like the icing on a layered cake. Economists in their reductive way are therefore studying a very small, boundaried and limited notion of 'the economy'.

AS: People with a 'view from below' are more able to see how the humanity–nature metabolism is both dynamic and integrative. Materialist ecofeminists such as ourselves recognize the source of an alternative epistemology in the reproductive labour sector. What Mary calls 'body work' and I call 'meta-industrial labour' equips humans cognitively for managing complex interlocking open-ended systems (Salleh 1997, 2004). In non-industrial domestic settings these terms cover the regenerative work of birthing, maintaining, and socializing new human generations. In non-industrialized societies at the geographic periphery, this reproductive labour includes agricultural provisioning as well, a topic that is covered very well in Vandana's writing.

Daily, such work balances and harmonizes a mix of biological, economic and cultural processes, each with its distinct scale and temporal frame. In most cultures, reproductive labour tends to be allocated by sex-gender, with women undertaking the bulk of regenerative tasks. And while it is true that class differences exist, and that not all women engage in such labour to the same extent, the global majority of women are heavily involved in it. Men too gain skills for sustainability when they break with the dominant urban role model and begin to share reproductive work. Peasant farming and indigenous gathering are regenerative economic practices regardless of whether they are practised by men or by women. The materialist ecofeminist argument is thus definitely not a statement about intrinsic or 'essentialized' differences between men and women. To the contrary, ecofeminists emphasize that sex-gender behaviour styles are socially constructed, and that men, women and transgender individuals develop their attitudes and capacities in an ever-changing historical milieu.

KF: I'm glad you emphasize that it is socially imposed roles that limit the lives of most women *and* men and that these are embedded in historically evolved institutional structures. This is a really important thing to get across to readers, I think, because I expect many of them will have assumed that ecofeminism is based on a kind of biological determinism.

AS: If ecofeminists believed sex-gender differences to be biological or fixed in nature, then there would be no point in our interrogating unjust power relations or advocating a transformative politics, because change would be impossible. But just as we believe that individuals actively make history, we believe they can unmake oppressive social relations and arbitrarily constructed methodologies. Three decades ago, a feminist revolution invited men and women to throw off restrictive sex-gender roles. But not all men and women have risen to the challenge of personal autonomy that this calls for. In fact, in recent years there has been something of a backlash against the feminist vision. Many men, and a handful of 'privileged' women, have retreated behind the individualistic and competitive ethos of the neo-liberal boardroom, the military, the sports field, and behind the defensive languages of technoscience.

A failure to evolve beyond Western objectivism has left many in politics, science and economics without any understanding of how hands-on labour with natural processes can give rise to a fresh, non-ideological rationality. Instead, mainstream disciplines develop in a linear direction, oriented to more of the same productivist, market logic – one that undermines the very material basis of life itself. The international crises of global warming and food scarcity are results of this disembedded logic.

Holism and value

KF: What I am hearing is that a holistic perspective beyond dualism is not just better but necessary, to address core ecological economic questions like 'what is the value of natural processes for sustainable development' (Faber *et al.* 1996)? Are you saying that failure to take concrete steps beyond reductionism is failure to create the necessary conditions for addressing sustainable development and livelihood?

AS: Well yes, but here I think it is worth highlighting this distinction between what the establishment calls 'sustainable development' and what ecofeminists call 'livelihood'. Since the Brundtland Commission and on through the 1992 Earth Summit in Rio de Janeiro, the sustainable development paradigm has been gradually absorbed into and watered down by the capitalist patriarchal system. This process continues in Davos 'think tank' meetings, in the World Trade Organization (WTO), in the work for Millennium Development Goals (MDGs) and in the Intergovernmental Panel on Climate Change (IPCC). As a form of 'repressive tolerance', the pursuit of so-called sustainable development perpetuates both social injustices and environmental damage; free trade in genetically engineered crops is one case in point, trading in carbon emissions is another. This is why ecofeminists prefer the economic term 'livelihood' and put forward subsistence models of provisioning. Eco-sufficient models are socially and environmentally embedded, not for profit, and resonant with cultural autonomy (Salleh 2009).

Choosing the term 'livelihood' is a major step beyond reductionism. It means that the whole system of social and environmental relationships that make up the daily life of ordinary people on all continents gets to be considered. A livelihood-oriented approach to ecological economics is complex enough to internalize all the metabolic flows that need to be taken into account in questions like: 'What is the value of natural processes?' By contrast, corporate-driven 'sustainable development' solutions are usually linear and one-dimensional, and generate externalities that have to be fixed later on.

KF: Ariel, what you're saying fits very well with another comment that Vandana made to me in the 2007 email interview mentioned earlier:

> If ecological phenomena are viewed in a reductionist framework, they will be valued in a reductionist way. That is why the full worth and value of ecological processes to livelihoods and sustainable development can only be assessed in a holistic framework.

Is it fair to say that, although the more holistic approach called for in ecological economics and ecofeminism alike doesn't guarantee the elimination of externalities, it has the advantage of putting onto the table, from the beginning, the question of how external effects will be handled?

MM: I would agree, and as feminist economists have pointed out, orthodox economics is precisely 'not holistic', but rather a theory written by men and for men (Nelson 1996; Folbre and Bittman 2004). As a result, women themselves are externalized and pushed to the economic margins. Take the feminist economics perspective articulated by thinkers like Susan Feiner, Marianne Ferber and Julie Nelson concerning the inadequacy of the mainstream concept of 'economic man' (Ferber and Nelson 1993; Feiner 1999). As they say, it is the product of an ahistoric, atomized approach to the understanding of human existence. And to be fair, some ecological economists have made the same observation (Siebenhüner 2000; van den Bergh *et al.* 2000).

In both ecological economics and ecofeminism, the call to move beyond reductionism and to integrate arbitrarily externalized effects is answered, at least in part, by drawing attention to the difference between quantitative and qualitative ways of describing and understanding human–ecosystem relationships. One of the earliest arguments regarding links between ecology and economics was made in the early twentieth century by the Scottish scientist Frederick Soddy (1926). He argued that all life and human activities depended upon energy and called for efforts to develop a sustainable economy in energy terms. In the early 1970s, Nicholas Georgescu-Roegen and Herman Daly again raised the issue of energy in economic systems and questioned the growth model at the heart of conventional economic theorizing (Merricks 1996; Georgescu-Roegen 1971; Daly 1973).

KF: Mary, you touch here on what I see as a fundamental connection between ecofeminism and ecological economics. I found out about Soddy from Joan

Martinez-Alier's text *Ecological Economics* (Martinez-Alier with Schlüpmann 1987). Having now worked my way through numerous writings from Georgescu-Roegen, I'm convinced that his concerns about the flow of energy in economic systems were fundamentally related to his argument that culture and tradition, including conflict and oppression, are basic factors that structure and regulate processes of economic production (Georgescu-Roegen 1966, 1971: 362, 1976).

MM: Yes, it is clear that the importance of ecosystems for human economic functioning has been raised increasingly since Soddy's work, culminating in the current concern with climate change and peak oil. However, ecological economists rarely recognize the links between the marginalization and exploitation of the natural world and the marginalization and exploitation of women's labour.

KF: I'm not entirely sure about that, especially in the work of Georgescu-Roegen but also more generally within ecological economics. I would say that relationships between (1) technological development, (2) belief, culture and social custom, and (3) the material/energetic constraints associated with the ecological embeddedness of human economies do play a central role.

MM: To speak of human embeddedness is one thing, but without a specific analysis of gender difference, ecological economics risks importing distorting masculine-identified gendered assumptions into its theories and proposals. This is why ecofeminist work is offered as a fundamental challenge to the discipline. As noted already, feminist economics has also sought to challenge neo-classical economic thought and explore economic issues as they relate to women's work, and women's marginalization and exclusion. I would name here Marilyn Waring (1989), Marianne Ferber and Julie Nelson (1993), Edith Kuiper and Jolande Sap (1995), Susan Feiner (1999) and Nancy Folbre (2001). Beyond this, there are notable examples of feminist economists linking women, the environment, and development: Rosi Braidotti, Ewa Charkiewicz, Sabine Häusler and Saskia Wieringa (Braidotti *et al.* 1994), Wendy Harcourt (1994) and Ellie Perkins (1997).

AS: Even so, there are distinct political and methodological positions on economics and the environment in this literature by women, a sort of continuum from a mainstream liberal feminism to a more culturally reflexive and transformative ecofeminism. But some conception of care-giving or reproductive labour will be central to all. In my view, what is critical is how this reproductive labour dovetails into an analysis of humanity–nature relations as a whole.

MM: True, some feminist economists have been slow to weigh up development from an ecological angle, being largely preoccupied with how gender inequality may constrain or facilitate economic growth (Benería *et al.* 2000). Then there is the quality-of-life literature growing out of Amartya Sen's work and supported by Bina Agarwal, Jane Humphries and Ingrid Robeyns (Agarwal *et al.* 2003). In it one can see the beginnings of a more holistic conceptualization of an environmentally embedded human economy. But as you say, an ecofeminist political economy tends to be even broader. Ecofeminists look at gender, class and racism in the articulation of ecologically unsustainable and socially unjust patterns of domination within human societies (Mellor 2006a). From this perspective, promises of 'equal opportunities' are vacuous if they rely on the further exploitation of the natural world. Ecofeminism works from the basis that humanity is part of a dynamic, interactive ecological process that cannot manipulate at will or without consequences (Mellor 2005).

Susan Donath writes of there being at least two economies – and two kinds of economics. In place of mainstream economics with its 'single story' of competitive production and exchange in markets, she calls for a 'distinctively feminist economics' based on 'the other economy' of care, reciprocity, the direct production and maintenance of human beings (2000). What in the West has become known as 'the economy' is carved out of the complexity of the whole of human and non-human existence (Mellor 1997). This valued economy provides only products and services that are profitable. A schematic summary of the two economies (Table 7.1) amplifies its origins in the reductionist 'self versus other' logic of the Cartesian mindset.

Marilyn Waring (1989) observes that what is unvalued or undervalued by the international 'malestream' economy is the resilience of the ecosystem, the unpaid and unrecognized domestic work of women, and the social reciprocity of communal societies and non-market economies (Table 7.1). What is left entirely out of consideration is the wider life of the body and the human and natural life cycles. There is no space for the young, the old, the sick, the tired, the unhappy. In relation to this absence of gender literacy in ecological economics, Sabine O'Hara comments:

> What may emerge as the core components of well-being may be exactly those functions rendered invisible by current value systems – the sustaining services provided in households, communities and nature that sustain the very social and environmental context within which we all live.
>
> (1999: 87)

Table 7.1 Two economies

Highly valued	*Low/no value*
Economic 'man'	Women's work
Market value	Subsistence
Personal wealth	Social reciprocity
Labour/intellect	Body
Skills/tradeable knowledge	Feelings, emotions, wisdom
Able-bodied workers	Sick, needy, old, young
Exploitable resources	Ecosystems, wild nature

Technology and myth

KF: I see strong synergy between the core questions of ecological economics and ecofeminism – not only because the subordination of women and degradation of the environment are interrelated but also because this domination and exploitation has common origins in masculinist systems of social organization. You are pointing to common underlying structural causes here, and I would like to tease these out if we can. The call to move beyond reductionism is often accompanied by critiques of technical rationalism and arithmetic fetishism.[3] Does ecofeminist engagement with mythology, storytelling, identity and image contribute to the alternative?

AS: I sense an old dichotomy behind your question, Kate, in the rather sex-gender loaded imagery of 'hard science' versus 'soft' literature. And this evokes for me the occasional trivialization of ecofeminism as having to do with 'cultural feminism', myths and nature goddesses. An example of this sort of misrepresentation happened with the publication of Vandana's early work *Staying Alive* (Shiva 1989). Her empirical analysis of the Green Revolution and its disastrous impacts on both farm productivity and the fabric of rural life in India set out table after table of observational data – like fertilizer use by gender, calorific intake by gender, etc. However, a pro-development elite rejected her integrative transdisciplinary use of science and avoided the powerful post-colonial thrust of her argument. A complex explanatory model was treated reductively and converted from a materialist into an idealist analysis extrapolated from her reference to the Indian cultural symbol of Prakriti, a traditional feminine metaphor for the life force. The hard science versus soft culture dualism is a potent hegemonic tool, and it demonstrates clearly how the social reductionism of masculine versus feminine sex-gender stereotypes is deeply interlinked with epistemological reductionism.

KF: Fair enough, and I think you are absolutely right here, Ariel. The presumption that one is discussing either quantitative or qualitative issues is itself a reductive way of thinking. So what I'm hearing from you is that ecofeminism is not about dropping the quantitative analysis but about placing it within a qualitative context, where the meaning of relationships can be discussed. Vandana put it to me this way in my 2007 email interview with her: 'Ecofeminism moves beyond reductionism by highlighting the integrity of ecosystem and organisms. This integrity is also captured in ideas of the sacred. Mythology, storytelling and image contribute to the imagination of a sacred earth, peopled by diverse living beings.'

MM: But Kate, I think Ariel has a point there, about being careful not to affirm the sex-gender loaded imagery of 'hard science' versus 'soft literature'. Ecofeminists have approached their holistic views in many different ways: poetry, song, myth as well as more analytic approaches such as ecofeminist political economy. The main distinction I would make is between 'immanence' and 'transcendence'. Reductive instrumental and technical rationalism has assumed that human beings have a transcendent 'God's-eye view' that can reveal universal and replicable truths. Ecofeminists understand that human knowledge is always immanent, situated within a complex framework of interactive dynamics. A holistic science would acknowledge that such complexity creates uncertainty and incomplete knowledge. This does not mean that we cannot take a reasoned approach. I would argue for a critical immanent realism that frames all knowledge in the immanence and uncertainty of human existence.

AS: Very much so, and my debates with Marxists and social ecologists have argued against 'transcendent' and essentialist readings of 'humanity' or 'the proletariat' with its future mission. My (albeit eco-socialist) ecofeminist position is that the social alternative is already with us here and now, immanent within reproductive labour (Salleh 2006b).

KF: The humility of what Mary calls 'an immanence-based perspective' seems to me to be an important part of ecofeminist theory and method. I can also see a connection here between the arrogance of 'a transcendence-based perspective' and violence against women and nature. When I look back at Vandana's comment in light of what you are both saying about this dualism, it seems me to fit very closely with my understanding of the thinking behind Georgescu-Roegen's flow/fund model (1971). He spent a lot of time in setting out this theory, meticulously discussing the relationship between qualitative and quantitative aspects of economic processes. I don't think that he ever managed to work out a full thesis on the role of tradition and belief in the regulation of economic processes, regarding what he called *Anschauung* (perspective), but I think he was definitely heading in that sociological direction (Farrell and Mayumi 2009).

AS: Kate, I don't feel qualified to comment on this aspect of Georgescu-Roegen. But it sounds as though there may be a fantastic future paper, if not a book, in there for you. My rather general interest in his writing has been with its potential to break down the humanity versus nature dualism – a major reductionist stricture on our thinking. Just like the hard versus soft dualism, such oversimplifications help exclude and control whatever is external to the 'idealized masculine ego' on which Western knowledge disciplines are hinged. Techniques for construction and diminishment of the 'other' (woman, native, child, animal) go back a long way. I've always been drawn to the Frankfurt School and its analysis of ancient Greece, where the invention of mathematics was bound up with this drive to mastery.[4] Today, in the world of hard science, numbers are still fetishized and used aggressively to construct plausibility for the designs of those with power to control the direction of societies. Thus, Jerome Ravetz (1994) speaks of neo-classical economics as an 'elite folk science' or myth serving to guide and reassure an educated ruling class. As Ravetz notes, implicit cultural and political agendas have a corrupting effect on knowledge production because they introduce mixed messages. Deconstructive ecofeminist readings of texts in science and economics expose the source of these layered meanings in unresolved sex-gendered attitudes, and the institutional contradictions that arise from them.

Getting back to Kate's focus on technology versus myth: it's a long time since Herbert Marcuse was in fashion, but his critique of the technological a priori is more relevant than ever today. And it was actually this thesis which set me thinking as an ecofeminist. The critical sociologists identified masculine power with positivism, hard science and the control of nature. My own thinking about this culture of instrumental reason began as a young woman in the 1970s, as I reflected on the contraceptive pill. Indeed, I predicted that the reductionist extraction of sex from the context of reproductive relations would both liberate women as individual managers of their own physiology, and yet reinforce the politically regressive dissociation of humanity from nature. And so it happened: the linchpin of Western patriarchal culture was shored up yet again (Salleh 1981).

Few inventions illustrate the technological a priori as foundational modern myth better than the practice of genetic engineering. The pharmaceutical industry is a major driver of the global economy, and from the very beginning, women have observed just how capitalist patriarchal interests shape it. Scholars like Ruth Hubbard, Evelyn Fox Keller, and Vandana of course, have maintained that the project to re-engineer life is saturated with sex-gender ideology and unconscious libidinal fears (Hubbard and Wald 1993; Fox Keller 2000; Shiva and Moser 1995). A reductionist denial of human (read men's) continuity with generative nature is very apparent in the practice of genetic engineering and, as already noted, the same dissociation recurs in legal instruments designed to deal with this 'new science'.

The idealist arithmetized programme of 'information technology' applied in molecular biology has allowed scientists to treat nature as a storehouse of computer codes, transcribing the secrets of life by means of a numbered 'master' molecule, DNA. The computer metaphor conveys precision and control; but is this highly reductive vision of the gene really fundamental science? The theory of genetic determinism, a simplistic model called the Central Dogma (even by its own authors), disconnects DNA from its dynamic biological context (Watson and Crick 1953).[5] Here a gene is described as unchanging over time, determining one specific function or trait and not affected by environmental conditions. The alternative theoretical position in genetics emphasizes complexity and more or less reverses these assumptions: a single DNA sequence does not determine a single protein but may code for several proteins, and because of interactions at many levels of cellular biochemistry it is not always possible to predict what will be produced (Wan Ho 1998).

Given this degree of complexity and uncertainty, the insertion of alien DNA into plant or animal cells leaves a great deal to chance. Moreover, Peter Wills (2002) points out that thinking ecologically about genomics means envisaging interrelationships and systems which operate over at least five levels: 'evolutionary processes, ecological networks, genetic mechanisms within organisms, protein interactions in cells, and cellular metabolism'. Epistemological concerns such as these make a nonsense of international legal instruments like the Cartagena Protocol and even the precautionary principle, which has been read so loosely. But the point of this digression into genetic engineering is to draw a parallel between the social construction of models in science and in economics. Against these statements regarding the complexity of genomics, the linear causal theory of genetic determinism, with its master gene, shows a remarkable resemblance to classical economics with its self-maximizing rational individual (male) actor.

KF: And then this brings us back to your earlier points about the obsession with control being linked to an idealized masculine ego.

AS: For sure, in fact, the conventional genetic engineering conceptualization of the reproductive process precisely mirrors the idealized structure of what ecofeminists name the iceberg model, whereby the market operates in seeming independence of the complex material web of reproductive labours that constitute its base. The identity of a piece of DNA is 'projected on to it as a fixed essence' in the act of legal patenting, just as a child constituted by a woman's body spends the rest of its life carrying a man's name. The material flows that guide the unfolding of an organism's DNA receive no formal recognition.

A related contradiction, based on legal reductionism, occurs with the idea of 'coexistence' – that is, the notion that GM and non-GM crops might live side by side in the farmer's field without interacting and reproducing as living species do. A debate on coexistence has taken place on every continent, but in Australia the co-mingling of corporate interest, law and science took shape in the astonishing proposal that a bureaucratic 'policy principle' should suffice to contain the 'identity' of a GM organism once released into the environment (GTSC 2003). This arrogant absurdity is a residue of the Western denial of human identity as part of nature.

If the ancients first authored the hierarchy of man over nature, disciplinary rigour was necessary to formalize the disconnection. Mathematics has served as one such instrument of reductionism, enabling living substances to be represented and manipulated as abstract indicators – with disastrous ecological consequences.

KF: Here I think that ecological economics, or at least Georgescu-Roegen, tries to address the how and why. In his major work, Georgescu-Roegen specifically referred to this practice of abstracting as 'economy of thought' (1971: 28–35). He was struggling with the uses and abuses of abstraction, noting that it has enabled ever more clear and efficient argument and logic, while at the same time leading thinkers to ignore huge amounts of relevant information about reality: 'wholesale arithmetization is impossible ... there is valid knowledge even without arithmetization, and ... mock arithmetization is dangerous if peddled as genuine' (ibid.: 15). In her text *The Death of Nature*, Carolyn Merchant (1981) presents what seems to me to be a very similar argument, that the concept of a dead nature is related to a mythology that glorifies technological fixes and atomization.

AS: The technology of arithmetization has been invaluable in maintaining the capitalist patriarchal economic, scientific and legal view of nature as inert and unitary. Accounting systems, in turn, have assisted with the commodification and distribution of this dead nature as 'product'. Measurement fits with a given way of conceptualizing the world, with a *Weltanschauung* that recalls and reiterates the image of a wild and dangerous nature that – like women's troublesome bodies – must be disciplined by 'men's reason'. In Freud's words, civilization began with 'renunciation of the senses' (1974: 90).

MM: In political economic terms, of course, it is through broader institutional mechanisms of instrumental violence, including nepotism, colonialism and market systems, that the capitalist patriarchal economy controls the sources of sustenance for the majority of the world's people as well as other species. People have little choice but to engage with this economy if they want to survive. Distorted patterns of ownership and control and unequal currency values mean that labour and resources can be bought cheaply. No moral responsibility is taken by the beneficiaries of this economy, as all negative outcomes are put down to abstract 'market forces'.

KF: It seems to me that these injustices are what ecological economists have been trying to get to grips with – in Tenerife, for example, when the 2003 Congress of the European Society of Ecological Economics stated:

> As ecological economists, we are convinced that the pursuit of sustainable development is only possible in a world of equitable cooperation and mutual trust. Unilateral military and economic action by a dominant superpower undermines the very preconditions for sustainable development.
>
> (Fifth International Conference of ESEE 2003)

Your ecofeminist interrogation of the discipline implies that it must deepen its concepts in a transdisciplinary way, one that allows it to reach below 'the iceberg' – and begin to test its own constructs.

AS: The ESEE statement about 'appropriation and control of resources like oil' slides over the energetic resourcing of women as unpaid reproductive labour. Ecological economists cannot explain the global economy without grasping the pivotal role of women's embodied labours within it. When political literacy is rounded out with gender literacy, phrases like 'equitable cooperation and mutual trust' get to sound rather hollow. Ecofeminists call for sex-gender 'reflexivity' among ecological economists; for if men and women stay silent about structural violence practised in the name of economics, then they support it by default.

Complexity theory

KF: Kenneth Boulding wrote, '[T]he statement that such and such a policy is "economically" advisable but "politically" impossible ... should have no more or fewer moral implications than the statement that a certain policy is agriculturally desirable but industrially undesirable' (1950: 4). I have tried to take up this question – of where and how the lines between politics and science are drawn – as an empirical topic of investigation. To do this, I build on the works of Silvio Funtowicz and Jerry Ravetz, using their concept of 'postnormal science' (1990a, 1991, 1992, 1993, 1997), and also draw upon complexity theory more generally.

I depict ecological, political, and economic processes and the relationships between them as a complex whole: interrelated, interdependent, co-determining and irreducible (Figure 7.1).

When I asked Vandana to comment on this, here is what she had to say (in my email interview with her in 2007):

> My work focuses on how the dominant system of economic globalization is destroying the environment (ecology), people's sustenance (economy), and democracy (polity). It also works on alternatives to protect ecosystems and create living economies and living democracy. These regenerative and mutually beneficial relationships constitute what I call Earth Democracy.

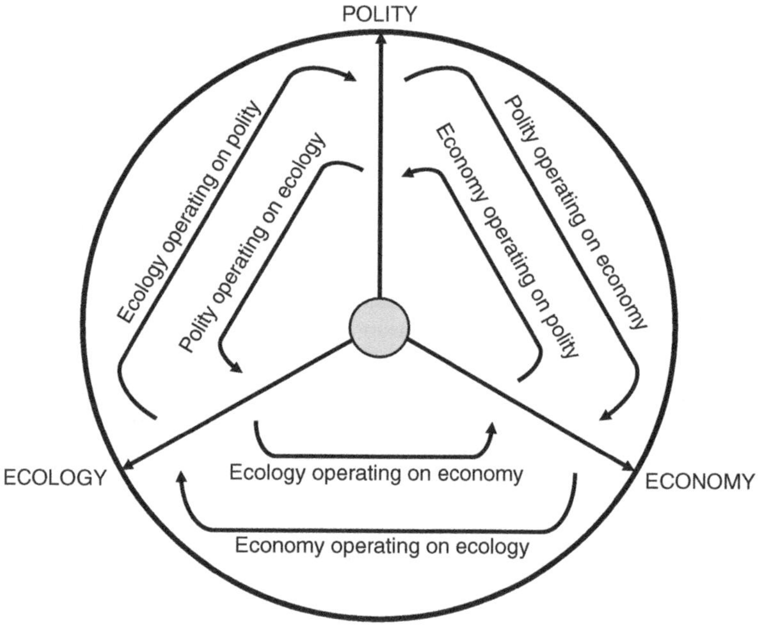

Figure 7.1 Ecological political economy (source: adapted from Farrell 2009 [2005]: 19).

Note
Credit is due here to Juan Sanchez-García, whose informal lecture on the future of ecological economics given during the 2003 Tenerife ESEE conference inspired this visualization.

MM: Well, Kate, I don't know what Boulding was after here, but I can say that ecofeminist political economy points to the gendered structures at the intersection of ecology and economy, where every day women and men deal with the consequences of human embodiedness and embeddedness (Mellor 2006b). Too often, ecological economists reveal themselves to be at a loss for adequate analytical tools to bridge the social, the economic and the biological. What is needed is an analysis of the mechanisms of dominance (capitalism, patriarchy, racism, colonialism) that enable transcendent forms of the economic to be constructed.

AS: One way to expose the pre-conscious ontology of ecological economics – that is, its sociology of knowledge – is to ask why reductionism occurs in the first place. Is reduction perhaps an inevitable by-product of 'renunciation of the senses', of divisions between mental versus manual labour, of productive versus reproductive activities? As noted above, and in the chapters of this book contributed by the biologist Mary Clark and the economist Arild Vatn, the existence of separate disciplines in academia can be seen as serving the political and the epistemological status quo. In much the same way, the conceptual separation of sex-genders, classes, races and species serves the powerful by setting up subjugated groupings in competing political struggles with each other.

MM: And a division of labour happens even within our own academic discourses. Among feminist economists, Julie Nelson (2003) would be fairly unusual in giving attention to ecological questions. In fact, she joins the ecofeminist agenda when she maintains that a new feminist ontology is needed, though she also cautions against excessive philosophizing in face of the real-world disadvantages suffered by women.[6] Nelson wants economists to examine their beliefs about how the world works, as well as to recognize the centrality of emotion and caring in the discipline. Like ecofeminists, she criticizes the split between 'a material world that is assumed to be spiritless and a (possible) realm of meaning that is assumed to be bodiless'; and she emphasizes the 'living, novel, relational aspects of nature'.

KF: Georgescu-Roegen spoke at length on this topic but he never managed to provide a coherent thesis (1966, 1971, 1976: 71–102).

AS: Others have taken up this line of inquiry into how the economy is embedded in nature and developed it in new directions (Faber *et al.* 1998). Peter Söderbaum is another ecological economist looking for alternatives that 'go beyond Economic Man and make things that matter for women (like "unpaid work") visible in economic analyses'. But he does not further explore the profound economic implications of a gender analysis (2000: 130). Among the more promising of these is the discussion of livelihoods and environmentalism of the poor developed by Joan Martinez-Alier (2002) and, among others, by Wolfgang Sachs in his 'Jo'burg Memo' (2002).

As ecofeminists, we argue that artificial and idealized social categories can be overcome in the integrity of socially and environmentally embedded provisioning, and that reproductive labour exemplifies an empirically grounded form of complexity reasoning. However, in my view the emergence of 'complexity theory' per se, as an antidote to scientific reductionism, has not necessarily achieved that aim. Certainly, holistic methodologies are desirable, but what has become known as complexity in management and policy circles is often a formulaic sub-discipline of systems theory based on the reification of living humans and natural processes as abstract arithmetized variables.

The common assumption of some bureaucrats and even academics, that the social system functions like a machine, gives a scientistic aura to complexity analyses. However, the question of 'who' has the power to define where the boundaries of this socio-cybernetic system are drawn is not addressed. Moreover, social structures and individual actors are disembedded here from existing power relations and discussed in an ad hoc way as 'units of information'. The functionalist focus of the systems analytic approach to complexity means that by default it prioritizes integration over dissent. In this way it supports the established order. For the most part, systems theory is still echoing the paradigm of physics, as does the mainstream economics that would-be non-reductionist ecological economists are trying to get away from. Reductive application of cybernetics results in an ahistorical and apolitical sociology de-linked from its social and environmental conditions. Such a complexity analysis replicates the pseudo-objectivity of the scientific positivism that it would replace. It is the very antithesis of the self-conscious, culturally reflexive awareness that is materially embodied knowledge-making.

KF: However, within ecological economics and ecofeminism, I think there is a type of complexity reasoning that does force the question of 'who' defines the boundaries onto the table for discussion (Mayumi and Giampietro 2006; Giampietro *et al.* 2006; Giampietro *et al.*, Chapter 8 of this book).

AS: Perhaps the relation between ecofeminism and the standard approach to complexity theory is best envisaged as a Moebius formation. That is to say, ecofeminism is a sort of complexity theory (de facto) that is both materially grounded and intellectually critical. But ecofeminists will reject the ideological practice of complexity theory when it is used to manipulate living beings – human or natural – as abstract resources. To quote a sample of this engineering thought-style: 'For linked ecological/social/economic systems, slow variables, multi-stable behaviours, and stochasticity cause adaptive management to outperform optimization approaches that seek stable targets' (Holling 2001: 403). For whose benefit is this 'God's-eye view' type of management carried out? How does it speak to power and questions of social justice? Information is not the same thing as meaning.

KF: Would you concede, then, that there is a clear link between ecofeminism and ecological economics on the question of time? The incompatibility of mechanical 'clock time' and 'time as an endless flow' is central in Georgescu-Roegen's flow/fund model (1971) and Daly's elaborations of it

(1999), and also in more recent work by Mario Giampietro (2003), among others (e.g. Mellor 1997).

AS: Indeed, Kate, the complexity of time is important in both ecological economics and ecofeminism, although you will not find ecofeminists reducing time to mathematical indicators and formulae, as some ecological economists do. The sociologist Georges Gurvitch characterized domestic, local and rural groupings as engaged with a sense of past projected into the future. Thus, the time frame most relevant to reproductive labour – the true basis of ecological economics – is his category of 'enduring time' (Gurvitch 1964). As I put it in an earlier essay, living things are joined across time as well as space – an indwelling structure invisible to a science that prioritizes observation over all the other senses. As things stand, most scientific knowledge making is ruled by the technological a priori, and time as an endless flow is suppressed in favour of a measurable and manipulable clock time. Consider agroforestry, mining, nuclear weapons, road transport, genetic engineering, where the plan is mastery, but the timing of complex metabolic exchanges is disrupted and ecological disintegration results (Salleh 1997: 137).

MM: This incompatibility of timings is not accidental: the ability to ignore the epistemological contextuality of time is intimately related to the tendency to ignore the ecological and biological contextuality of the human economy, including the reproductive roles of women and ecosystems. The consequences of such ignorance are, indeed, disruption and disintegration of nature.

Dialectical thinking

KF: Ariel, you raise concerns about the static functionalist focus of the systems analytic approach to complexity and about use of complexity theory to manipulate living beings as abstract resources. This bothers me too. I refer to it as the Frankenstein syndrome: where complex systems modellers and the policy-makers and managers who take direction from them seem to be focused on how to develop more powerful tools of control – by mapping employee habits, anticipating market developments, controlling floods, and so on. Just as Frankenstein took the creation of a complex organism as an end in itself, without reflecting on the consequences, these modellers and the policy-makers using their tools seem to me to be more interested in whether the tool works than in whether or for whom it might be useful or dangerous.

On the other hand, many ecological economics writers who are thinking 'beyond reductionism' refer to the importance of dialectical thinking for understanding the interplay between ecological and economic processes. For example, not only Georgescu-Roegen (1971) but also Malte Faber, Reiner Manstetten and John Proops (Faber *et al.* 1996), Silvio Funtowicz and Jerry Ravetz (1993), Joan Martinez-Alier (1999a, b), Martin O'Connor (2000), Sabine O'Hara (1997), John O'Neill (1993) and Arild Vatn (2005), among many others, explicitly bring dialectical thinking into the discussion, and precisely at the point where attention shifts from the component to relations between components. Does dialectics also feature in your approach to ecological economics and ecofeminism?

AS: Taking ecological economics first, there is an 'objectivist' dialectic in Georgescu-Roegen's rejection of 'the mechanics of utility' and his remarkable insight into the metabolic co-evolution of natural and human systems. Funtowicz and Ravetz attend to a 'subjective' dialectic entailed in the social construction of disciplinary terms, and their internal contradictions. Martinez-Alier and O'Connor apply this in examining competing concepts of value. O'Neill and Vatn call for more awareness of historical context. All are moves towards dialectical reasoning. But only Sabine O'Hara on your list tackles the question of gender literacy and how its absence in turn collapses all economic theory back into reductionist thinking. In fact, without the gender literacy of ecofeminism, ecological economics can only proffer half-truths – that is, truths applicable to half of humanity. So, Kate, I enthusiastically join your anticipation of a convergence between ecofeminist holism and counter-reductive tendencies in ecological economics.

KF: I'm pleased to hear that, Ariel. Once again you bring me back to a realization which has come about in the course of working with you and Mary and Vandana on this chapter, that leaving explicit discussion of gender issues out of ecological economic analysis actually results in a whole set of highly relevant ecological economic dynamics being completely ignored. Slowly, I am beginning to understand what Vandana means by the following statement, taken from my email interview with her in 2007:

> Dialectical thinking for me plays out as constantly moving from ideas to actions, and actions to ideas. In social terms it implies a dialectics between research communities and grassroots communities. It also involves a dialectics of resistance to destruction and constructive action for sustainability.

This brings the discussion full circle to the original idea for the chapter, which was that ecofeminism offers an example of best-practice ecological economics. To pull out an old phrase that I used a lot when talking with mainstream mathematical economists, ecofeminism is encumbered by the constraints of empirical reality. And it is explicitly concerned with developing methods of analysis and action that cope with the irreducibility and interrelatedness of the real world of human and non-human relations.

AS: I wouldn't say ecofeminism is 'encumbered' by everyday reality, which sounds too much like Cartesian idealism to me, and the mindset of the serviced individual. If anything, I'd say that philosophers, mathematicians and lawyers are more likely to be 'encumbered' by constructs too far removed from the complexity of material processes. As a dialectical politics, ecofeminism has an inbuilt check on this 'unhinged abstraction', because it develops from a unity of theory and praxis; it is an empiricism par excellence.

The scientific method (as we know it) is designed to control living relationships. However, people who work hands-on in maintaining the life cycle and eco-systemic cycles do not define themselves as fundamentally separate from nature, and they tend not to build an oppositional ontology. The Aristotelian law of non-contradiction, A cannot = notA, is inadequate in a dialectical world where A may well be in the process of transforming into notA. Further, since mothers, peasants and gatherers do not wield much power and control, they do not perceive causality as unilinear. People working in open interactive systems understand that events can have multiple determinations at once. This means that those who do reproductive labour are more alert to externalities and the need for precaution to avoid entropy in nature (Salleh 1997: 133–149).

To come back to your point about the role of dialectical thinking in keeping complexity theory away from the Frankenstein syndrome, a focus on the subjective aspect of dialectical thinking underscores what is missing in managerial versions of complexity. Dialectical thought situates individuals in the historical and political processes of their time. It seeks accountability in asking, 'By whom and for whom?'

KF: Exactly! Bringing the observer into the descriptive frame.

AS: Yes, except who sets the parameters of the 'descriptive frame' and who has the power to 'bring the observer in'? Besides, the subjective dialectic involves more than this: it has an embodied or material depth dimension. Groupings oppressed by sex-gender, racism or class encounter more social deprivation and mixed messages than those who enjoy the benefits of a capitalist patriarchal society. But the anguish of living through such political contradictions in everyday life can actually empower individuals to take on corrupt power relations (Salleh 1994, 1997: 170–182). The analysis put forward by many ecofeminists was arrived at through just this kind of existential dialectic – as women began to realize how they were being treated as little more than a 'natural resource'.

Closing remarks

MM: Bringing all these epistemological threads back to the discipline of economics, overall, I find the complex and dialectical character of the ecofeminist problematic nicely summed up in Linda Lucas's review (2000: 119) of Ellie Perkins's special 1997 edition of *Ecological Economics*. She saw this as encapsulating four interrelated themes:

- how women's work and nature's work are invisible to economic practice because they lie outside the intellectual tradition and vision of the economics discipline;
- how this invisible work provides a free subsidy to the production sector;
- how because of this inside/outside problem neoclassical economics presents only a partial analysis of the economic world; and

- how time as a gendered concept is connected to the creation of economic space and the subsidized economy (see also Perkins and Kuiper 2005).

KF: We might say that the challenge of hearing subordinate voices is really about accepting the dialectical complexity of being and becoming, of production and reproduction (Prigogine 1980; Prigogine and Stengers 1984).

Notes

1 For example, see the journal *Glimpse* (www.glimpsejournal.com).
2 See also the argument for fluid complexity against dualism in Salleh (1984).
3 See, for example, Schrödinger (1948 [1944]), Gardner (1993 [1983], 1999), Clark (1989, 2002), Dennett (1992), Cilliers (1998, 2005) and Lewontin (2000).
4 For discussion of this relationship, see Horkheimer and Adorno (1944), Marcuse (1991 [1964]) and Adorno (1973).
5 It is worth noting that Rosalind Franklin, the woman scientist who produced the X-ray crystallography images that revealed the structure of DNA, was not included as a co-author of this paper. For more about her work and career, see www.ias.ac.in/womeninscience/Franklin.pdf.
6 Tony Lawson (1999) also attends to complexity in the subjective dimension, but his articulation risks ignoring women's subordination and exploitation.

References

Adorno, T. 1973. *Negative Dialectics*. London: Routledge.

Agarwal, B., J. Humphries and I. Robeyns. 2003. Special issue on Amartya Sen's Work and Ideas: A Gender Perspective. *Feminist Economics* 9(2/3).

Benería, L., M. Floro, C. Grown and M. MacDonald. 2000. Special issue on Globalization. *Feminist Economics* 6(3).

Bennholdt-Thomsen, V. and M. Mies. 1999. *The Subsistence Perspective*. London: Zed Books.

Boulding, K.E. 1950. *A Reconstruction of Economics*. London: Chapman & Hall.

Braidotti, R., E. Charkiewicz, S. Häusler and S. Wieringa. 1994. *Women, the Environment and Sustainable Development: Towards a Theoretical Synthesis*. London: Zed Books.

Cilliers, P. 1998. *Complexity and Postmodernism: Understanding Complex Systems*. London: Routledge.

Cilliers, P. 2005. 'Complexity, deconstruction and relativism.' *Theory, Culture and Society* 22(5): 255–267.

Clark, M.E. 1989. *Ariadne's Thread: The Search for New Modes of Thinking*. London: Macmillan.

Clark, M.E. 2002. *In Search of Human Nature*. London: Routledge.

Daly, H.E. 1973. *Toward a Steady-State Economy*. San Francisco: W.H. Freeman.

Daly, H.E. 1999. *Ecological Economics and the Ecology of Economics: Essays in Criticism*. Cheltenham, UK: Edward Elgar.

d'Eaubonne, F. 1974. *Le Féminisme ou la mort*. Paris: Payot.

Dennett, D.C. 1992. *Consciousness Explained*. London: Penguin.

Donath, S. 2000. 'The other economy: a suggestion for a distinctly feminist economics.' *Feminist Economics* 6(1): 115–123.

Edwards, D. 2008. *Artscience: Creativity in the Post-Google Generation.* Cambridge, MA: Harvard University Press.

Faber, M., R. Manstetten and J. Proops. 1996. *Ecological Economics: Concepts and Methods.* Cheltenham, UK: Edward Elgar.

Faber, M., S. Baumgärtner and J. Proops. 1998. 'All production is joint production: a thermodynamic analysis.' In *Sustainability and Firms: Technological Change and the Regulatory Environment*, ed. S. Faucheux, J. Gowdy and I. Nicolaï. Cheltenham, UK: Edward Elgar.

Farrell, K.N. 2009 [2005]. *Making Good Decisions Well: A Theory of Collective Ecological Management.* Aachen, Germany: Shaker Verlag.

Farrell, K.N. and K. Mayumi. 2009. 'Time horizons and electricity futures: an application of Nicholas Georgescu-Roegen's general theory of economic production.' *Energy* 34(3): 301–307.

Feiner, S. 1999. 'A portrait of *Homo economicus* as a young man.' In *The New Economic Criticism: Studies at the Intersection of Literature and Economics*, ed. M. Woodmansee and M. Osteen. London: Routledge.

Ferber, M.A. and J.A. Nelson. 1993. *Beyond Economic Man: Feminist Theory and Economics.* Chicago: University of Chicago Press.

Fifth International Conference of the ESEE. 2003. 'Statement by the Fifth International Conference of the European Society for Ecological Economics, concerning the commencement of war in Iraq.'

Folbre, N. 2001. *The Invisible Heart: Economics and Family Values.* New York: New Press.

Folbre, N. and M. Bittman. 2004. *Family Time: The Social Organization of Care.* London: Routledge.

Fox Keller, E. 2000. *The Century of the Gene.* Cambridge, MA: Harvard University Press.

Freud, S. 1974. *Moses and Monotheism.* London: Hogarth Press.

Funtowicz, S.O. and J.R. Ravetz. 1990. *Uncertainty and Quality in Science for Policy.* Dordrecht, the Netherlands: Kluwer Academic.

Funtowicz, S.O. and J.R. Ravetz. 1991. 'A new scientific methodology for global environmental issues.' In *Ecological Economics: The Science and Management of Sustainability*, ed. R. Costanza. New York: Columbia University Press.

Funtowicz, S.O. and J.R. Ravetz. 1992. 'The good, the true and the post-modern.' *Futures* 24(10): 963–976.

Funtowicz, S.O. and J.R. Ravetz. 1993. 'Science for the post-normal age.' *Futures* 25(7): 739–755.

Funtowicz, S.O. and J.R. Ravetz. 1997. 'The poetry of thermodynamics: energy, entropy/exergy and quality.' *Futures* 29(9): 791–810.

Gardner, H. 1993 [1983]. *Frames of Mind: The Theory of Multiple Intelligences*, 2nd ed. London: Fontana.

Gardner, H. 1999. *Intelligence Reframed: Multiple Intelligences for the 21st Century.* New York: Basic Books.

Gene Technology Scientific Committee: Ministerial Council (GTSC:MC). 2003. 'Briefing Papers for Public Consultation: Policy Principle on Co-existence.' Canberra: Department of Health.

Georgescu-Roegen, N. 1966. *Analytical Economics: Issues and Problems.* Cambridge, MA: Harvard University Press.

Georgescu-Roegen, N. 1971. *The Entropy Law and the Economic Process.* Cambridge, MA: Harvard University Press.

Georgescu-Roegen, N. 1976. *Energy and Economic Myths: Institutional and Analytical Economic Essays*. Oxford: Pergamon Press.

Giampietro, M. 2003. *Multi-scale Integrated Analysis of Agroecosystems*. Boca Raton, FL: CRC Press.

Giampietro, M., T.F.H. Allen and K. Mayumi. 2006. 'The epistemological predicament associated with purposive quantitative analysis.' *Ecological Complexity* 3(4): 307–327.

Gurvitch, G. 1964. *The Social Spectrum of Time*. Dordrecht, the Netherlands: Reidel.

Harcourt, W. ed. 1994. *Feminist Perspectives on Sustainable Development*. London: Zed Books.

Henderson, H. 1996. *Creating Alternative Futures: The End of Economics*. West Hartford, CT: Kumerian Press.

Holling, C.S. 2001. 'Understanding the complexity of economic, ecological, and social systems.' *Ecosystems* 4: 390–405.

Horkheimer, M. and T. Adorno. 1944. *Dialectic of Enlightenment*. London: Allen Lane.

Hubbard, R. and G. Wald. 1993. *Exploding the Gene Myth*. Boston: Beacon.

Kuiper, E. and Y. Sap. 1995. *Out of the Margin: Feminist Perspectives on Economics*. London: Routledge.

Lawson, T. 1999. 'Feminism, realism, and universalism.' *Feminist Economics* 5(2): 25–60.

Lewontin, R. 2000. *The Triple Helix: Gene, Organism, and Environment*. Cambridge, MA: Harvard University Press.

Lucas, L. 2000. Review of *Women, Ecology, and Economics*, ed. Ellie Perkins. *Feminist Economics* 6(2): 115–119.

Marcuse, H. 1991 [1964]. *One-Dimensional Man: Studies in the Ideology of Advanced Industrial Society*. London: Routledge.

Martinez-Alier, J. 1999a. 'From political economy to political ecology.' In *Bioeconomics and Sustainability: Essays in Honor of Nicholas Georgescu-Roegen*, ed. K. Mayumi and J.M. Gowdy. Cheltenham, UK: Edward Elgar.

Martinez-Alier, J. 1999b. 'The socio-ecological embeddedness of economic activity: the emergence of a transdisciplinary field.' In *Sustainability and the Social Sciences: A Cross-disciplinary Approach to Integrating Environmental Considerations into Theoretical Reorientation*, ed. E. Becker and T. Jahn. London: Zed Books.

Martinez-Alier, J. 2002. *The Environmentalism of the Poor*. Cheltenham, UK: Edward Elgar.

Martinez-Alier, J. with K. Schlüpmann. 1987. *Ecological Economics: Energy, Environment and Society*. Oxford: Basil Blackwell.

Mayumi, K. and M. Giampietro. 2006. 'The epistemological challenge of self-modifying systems: governance and sustainability in the post-normal science era.' *Ecological Economics* 57(3): 382–399.

Mellor, M. 1992. *Breaking the Boundaries: Towards a Feminist Green Socialism*. London: Virago.

Mellor, M. 1997. 'Women, nature and the social construction of "economic man".' *Ecological Economics* 20(2): 129–140.

Mellor, M. 2005. 'Socialism.' In *Political Theory and the Ecological Challenge*, ed. A. Dobson and R. Eckersley. Cambridge: Cambridge University Press.

Mellor, M. 2006a. 'Ecofeminism: linking gender and ecology.' In *Handbook on Environment and Society*, ed. J. Pretty, A. Ball, T. Benton, J. Guivant, D.R. Lee, D. Orr, M. Pfeffer and H.D. Ward. London: Sage.

Mellor, M. 2006b. 'Ecofeminist political economy.' *International Journal of Green Economics* 1(1/2): 139–150.

Merchant, C. 1981. *The Death of Nature: Women, Ecology, and the Scientific Revolution.* New York: Harper.

Merricks, L. 1996. *The World Made New: Frederick Soddy, Science, Politics, and Environment.* Oxford: Oxford University Press.

Mies, M. and V. Shiva. 1993. *Ecofeminism.* London: Zed Books.

Nelson, J. 1996. *Feminism, Objectivity and Economics.* London: Routledge.

Nelson, J. 2003. 'Once more with feeling: feminist economics and the ontological question.' *Feminist Economics* 9(1): 109–118.

O'Connor, M. 2000. 'Pathways for environmental evaluation: a walk in the (Hanging) Gardens of Babylon.' *Ecological Economics* 34(2): 175–193.

O'Hara, S.U. 1997. 'Toward a sustaining production theory.' *Ecological Economics* 20(2): 141–154.

O'Hara, S.U. 1999. 'Economics, ecology, and quality of life: who evaluates?' *Feminist Economics* 5(2): 83–90.

O'Neill, J. 1993. *Ecology, Policy and Politics: Human Well-Being and the Natural World.* London: Routledge.

Perkins, E. 1997. Special issue on 'Women, Ecology and Economics'. *Ecological Economics* 20(2).

Perkins, E. and E. Kuiper. 2005. Special issue on 'Explorations: Feminist Ecological Economics'. *Feminist Economics* 11(3): 107–148.

Prigogine, I. 1980. *From Being to Becoming.* San Francisco: W.H. Freeman.

Prigogine, I. and I. Stengers. 1984. *Order out of Chaos: Man's New Dialogue with Nature.* London: Heinemann.

Ravetz, J.R. 1994. 'Economics as an elite folk-science: the suppression of uncertainty.' *Journal of Post-Keynesian Economics* 17(2): 165–184.

Ruether, R. 1975. *New Woman, New Earth.* New York: Seabury.

Sachs, W. ed. 2002. *The Jo'burg Memo. Fairness in a Fragile World: A Memorandum for the World Summit on Sustainable Development.* Berlin: Heinrich Böll Foundation.

Salleh, A. 1981. 'Of Portnoy's Complaint and feminist problematics.' *Australian and New Zealand Journal of Sociology* 17(1): 4–13.

Salleh, A. 1984. 'Contribution to the critique of political epistemology.' *Thesis Eleven* 8: 23–43.

Salleh, A. 1994. 'Nature, women, labor, capital: living the deepest contradiction.' In *Is Capitalism Sustainable? Political Capital and the Politics of Ecology*, ed. M. O'Connor. New York: Guilford Press.

Salleh, A. 1997. *Ecofeminism as Politics.* London: Zed Books.

Salleh, A. 2004. 'Global alternatives and the meta-industrial class.' In *New Socialisms: Futures beyond Globalization*, ed. R. Albritton, S. Bell, J.R. Bell and R. Westra. London: Routledge.

Salleh, A. 2006a. '"Organised irresponsibility": contradictions in the Australian government's strategy for GM regulation.' *Environmental Politics* 15(3): 399–416.

Salleh, A. ed. 2006b. Symposium: 'Ecosocialist–Ecofeminist Dialogues' (special issue). *Capitalism Nature Socialism* 17(4): 32–124.

Salleh, A. ed. 2009. *Eco-Sufficiency and Global Justice.* London: Pluto Press.

Schrödinger, E. 1948 [1944]. *What Is Life?* Cambridge: Cambridge University Press.

Shiva, V. 1989. *Staying Alive: Women, Ecology and Development.* London: Zed Books.

Shiva, V. 1993. 'Reduction and regeneration: a crisis in science.' In *Ecofeminism*, ed. M. Mies and V. Shiva. London: Zed Books.

Shiva, V. and I. Moser eds. 1995. *Biopolitics.* London: Zed Books.

Siebenhüner, B. 2000. 'Homo sustinens: towards a new conception of humans for the science of sustainability.' *Ecological Economics* 32(1): 15–25.

Soddy, F. 1926. *Wealth, Virtual Wealth and Debt: The Solution of the Economic Paradox*. London: George Allen & Unwin.

Söderbaum, P. 2000. *Ecological Economics: A Political Economics Approach to Environment and Development*. London: Earthscan.

van den Bergh, J.C.J.M., A. Ferrer-i-Carbonell and G. Munda. 2000. 'Alternative models of individual behaviour and implications for environmental policy.' *Ecological Economics* 32(1): 43–61.

Vatn, A. 2005. *Institutions and the Environment*. Cheltenham, UK: Edward Elgar.

Wan Ho, M. 1998. *Genetic Engineering*. Bath: Gateway Books.

Waring, M. 1989. *If Women Counted: A New Feminist Economics*. London: Macmillan.

Watson, J. and F. Crick. 1953. 'A structure for deoxyribose nucleic acid.' *Nature* 171: 737–738.

Weasel, L. 1997. 'The cell in relation: an ecofeminist revision of cell and molecular biology.' *Women's Studies International Forum* 20(1): 49–59.

Wills, P. 2002. 'Biological complexity and genetic engineering.' Paper presented at the Environment, Culture and Community Conference, University of Queensland, 2–5 July.

8 Two conceptual tools for Multi-Scale Integrated Analysis of Societal and Ecosystem Metabolism (MuSIASEM)

'Multi-purpose grammars' and 'impredicative loop analysis'

Mario Giampietro, Kozo Mayumi and Jesus Ramos-Martin

Introduction

The epistemological predicament associated with the study of the evolution of living (complex adaptive) systems is generated by two peculiar characteristics: (1) they are operating simultaneously on different hierarchical levels of organization, and (2) they are becoming in time, at different paces, across these different levels (for an overview of these concepts, see Giampietro 2003; Giampietro *et al.* 2006a, b).

Therefore, scientists willing to do quantitative analyses of evolving systems have to face two key problems. The first is that of finding multiple useful descriptions of the same observed entity, which cannot be reduced to each other. In fact, these distinct descriptions are generated by different choices made by the observer to adopt either different scales or different criteria of observations. The second is the fact that the usefulness of all these non-equivalent descriptions and models depends on the interests of the storyteller – that is, the person or entity deciding about the relevance of the narrative and the goals of the analysis determining the usefulness of the results. Because of this fact, the validity of any model applied to a sustainability issue will sooner or later expire, either because the observed system will change or because the interest behind the observation – that is, the identity of the storyteller – will change. To make things worse, the validity of the different descriptions and models will expire at different rates.

These two problems can be stated in general terms in the following way:

1 When dealing with the issue of sustainability, scientists can only represent just one specific perception and experience of the reality at the time, and not 'the reality'. It is impossible to have a substantive representation of sustainability issues.
2 A quantitative model can only establish a causal relation over representation of events on the basis of what is encoded in a given set of records. It is impossible to establish in substantive terms a linear causation among all recordable events.

These two implications are summarized by the famous line of Box: 'All models are wrong, but some are useful' (1979: 424). The reliability of any prediction of any model depends on the validity of the underlying assumptions. Therefore, when one is analysing the sustainability of living systems (socio-economic systems, ecological systems and their interaction), the only reasonable approach is to perform a systematic 'semantic check' on the usefulness of the chosen models. When one is dealing with the need to check the validity of assumptions behind quantitative models, the real issue is not whether or not the model is right or wrong, but whether or not the narrative within which the model has been developed is relevant for the problem to be solved. This requires checking whether the chosen issue definition coincides with the perception that the social actors have of a given problem. This is to say, when one is handling quantitative analyses of sustainability, it is the semantic behind the chosen formalization that should be the first object of the quality check.

Two quotations can be used to make our point:

> I shall argue that the postulates of the [neo-]classical theory are applicable to a special case only and not to the general case, the situation which it assumes being a limiting point of the possible positions of equilibrium. Moreover, the characteristics of the special case assumed by the [neo-]classical theory happen not to be those of the economic society in which we actually live, with the result that its teaching is misleading and disastrous if we attempt to apply it to the facts of experience.
>
> (Keynes 1936: opening paragraph)

> [A]nalytic work begins with material provided by our vision of things, and this vision is ideological almost by definition.
>
> (Schumpeter 1954: 42)

The validity of a formal analysis depends on the validity of the relative 'perception' of the underlying issue. This perception is reflected by the selection of a relevant narrative about the issue to be addressed. It is only after having defined a narrative about a given state of affair that it becomes possible to develop a pertinent analysis that gives a useful quantitative representation (Giampietro *et al.* 2006b).

> The perception and representation must be coupled wisely. This implies that for scientific analyses, there is something that is worse than being wrong: being irrelevant. A scientific analysis may be wrong, but it may still use the right set of categories relative to an appropriate narrative. In such a situation sooner or later practitioners in the field will learn and produce better models. On the contrary, in the worse case, where the selection of narrative is wrong, the problem lies outside the realm of technical choices. Things do not work even superficially at the way they are supposed. The problem is a systemic lack of meaning on the analytical tools applied in relation to the situation at hand. There is insufficiency in the semiotic check.
>
> (Giampietro *et al.* 2006a)

Conversely, the standard approach of reductionism adopts the application of quantitative protocols for the optimization and the maximization of preselected objective functions. This approach is based on two 'tacit assumptions'. The first is that it is possible to characterize in quantitative terms very complex problems in terms of just a single numerical variable to be optimized. This translates into denying the existence of uncertainty and technical incommensurability (about models and representation) when handling complex set of indicators referring to different dimensions of analysis and scales. The second is that it is possible to reach agreement, among all those who will be affected by the policy selected by the model, about the choices made by the analyst. This translates into denying the existence of social incommensurability (about values and perception) when coming to the choice of the most appropriate issue definition, data input, objective functions and optimizing strategies (Giampietro *et al.* 2006b).

MuSIASEM as a response to this challenge

The approach known as Multi-Scale Integrated Analysis of Societal and Ecosystem Metabolism (MuSIASEM – originally proposed as MSIASM by Giampietro and Mayumi 2000, 2001; Giampietro 2003; Ramos-Martin *et al.* 2007; Giampietro *et al.* 2011; 2012) was developed in relation to the following goals, which are designed to provide data compilation and analysis that can and does reach beyond the limits of reductionism: (1) keeping the descriptive aspects separated from the normative aspects; (2) maintaining a balance between the two contrasting tasks of (i) compressing and (ii) keeping redundancy; (3) acknowledging from the beginning the unavoidable arbitrariness implied by the step of modelling; (4) providing a quality check on the chosen way of representing the interaction of human systems and socio-economic systems; and (5) including in the analysis the characteristics of the metabolic system determining the pattern of interaction, so that 'what to sustain', 'to what degree' and 'at which cost' are questions that can be incorporated into the analysis.

In their own ways, each of these goals serves the overall MuSIASEM purposes of facilitating empirically robust, socially relevant, ecologically realistic analysis of complex, irreducible ecological economic situations and their associated dynamics.

1 *Keeping the descriptive aspects separated from the normative aspects.* This is an important departure from the hidden strategy adopted by reductionism to deal with sustainability. Analyses developed within the paradigm of reductionism try to collapse the descriptive side – characterization of performance in relation to different indicators – and the normative side – definition of best course of action – into a single step, such as cost–benefit analysis, and optimizing models looking for 'the best' solution. Moreover, reductionism assumes that uncertainty and ignorance can be dealt with in substantive way by sound practices of science, such as more data, bigger computers and more sophisticated sensitivity analyses. As a consequence of

this fact, many researchers end up adopting only a limited set of narratives for their analysis, generating deterministic optimizing models without recognizing the implications of this fact. A simple example: a descriptive tool provides an analysis of trade-offs or, better, the dialectic tension associated with the issue of sustainability, whereas a normative tool simplifies the complexity of this unavoidable tension by providing a clear indication (based on a computation) of what is 'the best policy' to be implemented, given the model and the data set developed in the analysis. That is, when facing a sustainability dilemma of the type 'you have to lose something in order to retain something else' – for example, reducing emissions and consumption to reduce human impact on climate change – a normative approach would adopt Stern's review *The Economics of Climate Change* (2006) to find out what is the value to be assigned to an exponent of an equation to maximize the welfare of present and future generations. The MuSIASEM approach has as its goal to represent in an integrated way relevant changes in the performance of an investigated system, using an integrated set of different criteria and indicators reflecting the concerns expressed by social actors at different scales and in relation to different narratives. Unlike normative approaches, MuSIASEM does not to establish a ranking of importance or priority among contrasting or non-equivalent representations. That is, it requires an accompanying process to deal with the normative issues, such as, for example, Societal Multi-Criteria Evaluation (Munda 2004). For example, determining rankings of importance is a normative task, which is a social as opposed to a purely scientific responsibility.

2 *Maintaining a balance between the two contrasting tasks of (i) using typologies to represent individuals by filtering out details referring to special cases – compressing; and (ii) forgetting about Occam's razor: keeping as far as possible a mix of typologies of information that can be used for better characterizing special individuals operating in special situations – keeping redundancy*. This can be done by adopting a flexible integrated package of meta-models and indicators to be tailored, at the moment of the application, on the specificity of a given situation. This second task requires the introduction of the concept of 'multi-purpose grammars' (to be discussed shortly), getting away from reliance on working with just one scale and descriptive domain at the time. By adopting the concept of 'multi-purpose grammars', the MuSIASEM can be tailored to both (i) the type of problem to deal with – the issue definition can be based on selection à la carte of goals and relevant indicators; and (ii) the specific characteristics of the social and ecological system in which the investigated problem is occurring. In this way it becomes possible to provide a reliable characterization of the situation – when using scientific knowledge based on types – while reflecting, at the same time, the legitimate perspectives found among the social actors and considering the peculiarity of observed situations, which are all 'special' by definition.

3 *Acknowledging from the beginning the unavoidable arbitrariness implied by the step of modelling*. The MuSIASEM approach is based on a meta-model

of analysis: an expected set of relations between semantic and formal categories. This meta-model is used to characterize (i) the interrelation among parts and whole (inside the black box), and (ii) the interaction between social systems and ecosystems (the black box interacting with its context). This approach acknowledges that the same issue can have multiple legitimate formalizations, which can be dealt with by using a family of useful non-reducible models. Therefore, by default this approach entails, or requires, an explicit discussion among the scientists – the makers of the models – and the stakeholders – the users of the models – on the implications associated with any particular choice of a given formalization. The use of 'multi-purpose grammars' makes the process through which the scientists are deciding how to define 'what is' the whole, 'what is' the context, 'what is relevant among the parts' extremely transparent – that is, making apparent their interactions in the pre-analytical step where the narrative is selected. In particular, when one is addressing the issue of how to choose the categories determining 'what the system is' and 'what the system does', this approach includes the very identity of the storyteller in the perception/representation. Therefore, the analysis of the interaction of the society with its context includes 'the actual identity' of the society having a problem of sustainability among the co-evolving complex.

4 *Providing a quality check on the chosen way of representing the interaction of human systems and socio-economic systems.* This objective is obtained by checking for congruence over the non-equivalent representation of the interaction of parts and wholes and over societal systems and ecosystems: (i) across different scales, for example when representing the perceptions of individuals, households, communities, provinces, national states and global interactions; and (ii) across different descriptive domains, for example when focusing on different selections of relevant attributes: economic and social interactions (variables), biophysical interactions (variables) constrained by institutional settings. In order to do this congruence-checking, the MuSIASEM approach tracks exchanges of flows of energy, matter and added value among parts, wholes and contexts against a multilevel matrix of either funds or flows.

To study the biophysical roots of the economic process, Georgescu-Roegen (1971) proposed the adoption of a fund–flow model for representing, in biophysical terms, the socio-economic process of production and consumption of goods and services. This framework proposes a distinction between the categories used for the representation of flow and fund categories. *Flow categories* refers to elements disappearing over the duration of the representation (that enter but do not exit) and/or elements appearing over the duration of the representation (that exit without having entered) – for example, a new product. The term refers to matter and energy *in situ*, controlled matter and energy, and dissipated matter and energy. The pace of these flows is controlled by two types of factors: (1) external factors – for example, the accessibility of an adequate input flow from the environment or availability of a stock; and (2) internal factors – for example, the capability of processing the available flow during the relative conversion. *Fund categories* (capital, people and Ricardian land) refers to agents remaining 'the same' over the duration of the representations (that enter and exit the process); they are transforming input flows into output flows on the timescale of the representation. As was discussed before, in relation to the representation of metabolic networks, fund elements have to be able to preserve – during the duration of the analysis – the same definition of themselves as converters. As a consequence of this fact, they guarantee the validity of the definition of 'what is an input' and 'what is an output'. Two key characteristics of fund elements are that (i) they can only be used at a specified rate, and (ii) they must be periodically renewed. Therefore, *fund coordinates entail an overhead (for their own maintenance and reproduction) and entail a constraint on the relative rate of the flows associated with them (a range of value for the pace of conversion).*

Since they remain the same during the duration of the analysis, we can say that fund coordinates represent the set of attributes used by the analyst for defining *what the system is*. By contrast, flow coordinates represent the set of attributes used by the analyst for defining *what the system does*, when interacting with its context. In fact, the flow has to be made available by and has to disappear into the context of the system.

When we move our focus across levels, these compartments can be viewed as parts and/or wholes. The resulting set of non-equivalent representations of these flows is then forced into congruence across the considered levels within the multilevel matrix. Detailed examples of this will be presented in what follows. The total flow calculated for the whole (as resulting from its representation at *level n*) must be equal to the sum of the flows calculated for the parts (as resulting from their representation at *level n – 1*). This is congruence across levels and it must also hold when the respective definitions of parts and wholes employ different logics – say, economic flows versus biophysical flows.

The concept of multi-purpose grammar: a 'semantically open' system of accounting

Working on complexity dealing with the epistemological challenges associated with modelling life and evolution, Robert Rosen (1985, 1991, 1998) proposes a distinction between complexity and complicatedness. This distinction can be summarized as follows. *Complexity* is about an expected set of relations across semantics and syntax; it requires the ability to establish a coherent and effective link between semantic and formal categories. *Complicatedness* is about an expected set of relations within syntax; it requires the ability to establish a reliable link over formal categories within a given syntax (production rules).

Recalling the metaphor regarding the impossibility of summing apples and oranges, we can say that in order to be able to sum any set of members of a given equivalence class we have to, first of all, define the criteria used to define the 'legitimate type' (template) used for recognizing individual instances of the elements to be summed. This entails that (1) a chosen protocol of accounting is required in order to be able to define a quantitative assessment; but, at the same time, (2) the choice of protocol determines the appropriate use of the sums that are generated. For example, when dealing with apples and oranges, if we decide to calculate their aggregate weight, we will get a number that is not relevant for nutritionists but is relevant for the truck driver transporting them. On the other hand, if we sum them by using their aggregate nutritional content, we will get a number that is not relevant for either an economist studying the economic viability of their production or for the truck driver. Summing apples and oranges using their economic value generates a number that does not say anything about the space they occupy in a container. The more we aggregate items that can be described using different attributes by using a single category of equivalence – a single protocol of accounting – the more we increase the chance that the final number generated by this aggregation will prove irrelevant for an integrated analysis of sustainability. Unfortunately, the conventional analytical tools used so far in this field (e.g. economic accounting, energy accounting), which refer to individual disciplines and mono-scale analysis, and are used to generate quantitative analysis of sustainability, tend to share this problem.

In relation to this challenge, the MuSIASEM approach has been developed as a multi-purpose grammar that explicitly requires tailored definitions of categories (when selecting semantic categories, formal categories and proxy variables) based on the specificity of different 'problem structurings' – multi-objective analysis – and different contexts, making possible a selection of indicators à la carte. MuSIASEM can simultaneously analyse: (1) systemic features of the process of evolution generating indicators of 'senescence' and adaptability, related to the evolutionary fitness of the patterns of metabolism of socio-economic systems (when looking at the system from the inside); and (2) the implications of the size of the whole system in relation to its environment (when comparing the metabolism of socio-economic systems to the metabolism of the ecosystems embedding them).

Introducing the concept of simple 'grammar'

The conceptual tool of 'random grammars' – as a key tool for the possibility of having autopoiesis (Varela *et al.* 1974; Maturana and Varela 1980) in complex adaptive systems – has been proposed within the field of complex systems theory by Kauffman (1993). More in general, the concept of 'multi-purpose grammar' can be associated with a meta-system of accounting based on a flexible network of expected relations between semantic categories (e.g. relevant attributes of sustainability) and formal categories (names – indicators) generated by production rules that are applied to gathered data (tokens). When referring to the field of software development, a grammar entails a preliminary definition of (1) a taxonomy: the set of semantic categories and formal categories used in the grammar – the types of types that are used in the grammar; (2) vocabularies for the various categories included in the taxonomy: the attributes used to individuate or characterize the elements of the different sets (relevant meanings or information; names and tokens); and (3) production rules to be applied to formal categories using the distinction between 'tokens' and 'names'. Tokens are associated with a data set which must be assigned to the grammar for its operation (data input). Then the production rules are associated with the formal system of inference determining the values of 'names' starting from the data input. Finally, in order to be operational a grammar also requires, or entails, the existence of an agent (1) guided by a purpose and able to provide the required input – in terms of gathering an appropriate data set; and (2) able to perform the required computations.

Put it in another way: in order to operate a 'grammar', it is necessary to have a valid semantic input and a pertinent syntactic activity. As soon as the operator provides the 'right input' and the production rules are correctly executed, the grammar generates the relative set of formal outputs that are useful in relation to the given purpose – for example, in the case of spoken language, an intelligible sentence and, in our case, a set of relevant indicators.

In epistemological jargon we can say that a grammar helps to identify the right set of external referents (what has to be known and measured) for performing a giving quantitative assessment that has been judged to be useful in relation to a given purpose.

In conclusion, the concept of a grammar that we are using here entails three elements:

1 *the definition of a lexicon* – a finite universe of semantic and formal categories;
2 *the definition of a set of production rules* – a finite universe of semantic and syntactic rules, determining the structured set of relations which are to be applied to the elements of the various formal categories;
3 *an agent with the ability to apply this meta-tool to a specific situation, by providing the right set of external referents (the right set of data to be processed) and enough computational capability (in terms of memory and processing capacity)* – the agent operating the grammar must be able to provide a meaningful input of data and enough computational capability to store the required data and execute the production rules, in order to generate a formal output that will be useful for some purpose.

Even if from the previous definition the concept of grammar may still sound unfamiliar, we are using grammars all the time in our daily life – for instance, when using computers, even if just for simple applications (based on user-friendly software), such as buying online from Amazon.com, where software is used to interface the buyer with the company. The value of a given category of relevant costs – 'name = total to pay' – is determined by production rules: 'multiply the number of units of each item by the unit cost', and 'sum the various subtotals by referring to each item'. To operate this grammar, we need to provide input data (called 'tokens') for those categories requiring data. In this example, the tokens are: 'the set of items to buy' >> 'books' and 'CDs', 'the number of units for each item' >> 3 books and 6 CDs, and 'unit cost for each item' >> the cost in US dollars of each of these items. The underlying grammar can be used for generating different indicators (relevant attributes) – e.g. (1) total to pay; (2) the money spent on book purchases; (3) the money spent on CD purchases; (4) the ratio of money spent on book/money spent on CDs. This is to say, the same dataset can be used to generate different indicators, depending on what is relevant for the user.

An example of simple mono-purpose grammar

Grammars are crucial for performing an effective accounting for sustainability, and therefore they are at the basis of the generation of any sustainability oriented statistical databases. The assessments of 'primary energy consumption' found in international energy statistics such as those provided by the International Energy Agency (as in Figure 8.1) are an example of a simple mono-purpose grammar. That assessment is based on the application of a grammar characterized by, first, *a very limited lexicon*. The system of accounting used in international energy statistics does not deal with the whole set of energy transformations that can be found when looking at an economy. For example, solar energy, gravitational energy and food energy are not taken into account in these statistics. This grammar focuses only on a finite set of relevant categories of energy forms: (1) primary energy sources; (2) energy carriers; and (3) end uses or energy services (e.g. power generation, transport, residential). Because of these choices, this grammar deals only with commercial energy. Second, the grammar is characterized by *a very limited set of production rules*. This system of accounting deals

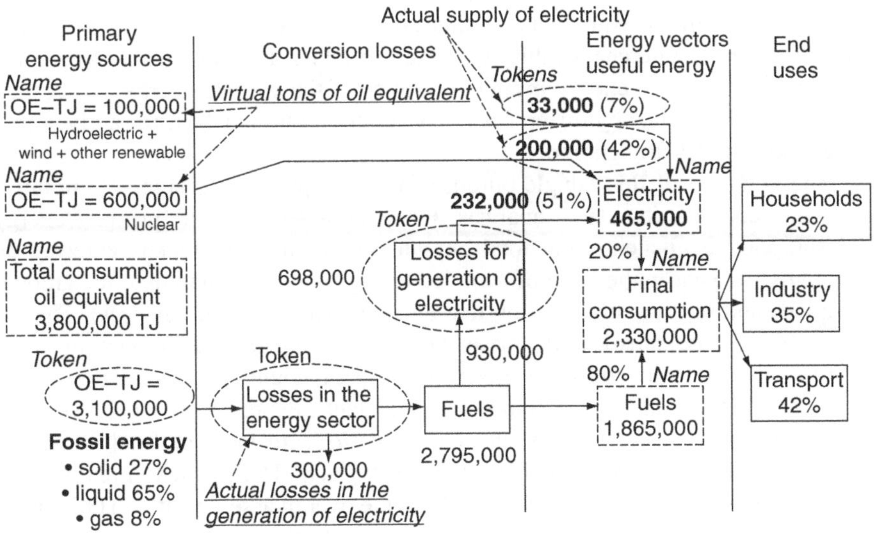

Figure 8.1 The simple grammar used to generate energy statistics.

only with the transformation associated with the generation of electricity [primary energy >> energy carriers]. When this generation is made using nuclear, hydroelectric and wind (here used to represent all other alternative sources not based on fossil energy), the actual amount of electricity generated becomes a token. The production rule is then used to define the assessment ('name') primary energy consumption. This production rule assumes a standard value for conversion losses associated with the generation of electricity from fossil fuels: 1 MJ of electricity supplied to the economy by an energy conversion that is not based on the consumption of fossil fuels is conventionally accounted as equivalent to 3 MJ of primary energy source, with fossil energy being used as the reference value – e.g. either tonnes of oil equivalent (TOE) or tonnes of coal equivalent (TCE). Third, *it is easy to operate since it adopts a simple production rules, but because of this, it has only limited usefulness.* In order to generate comparable assessments of 'primary energy consumption' (e.g. comparing the total consumption of France with the total consumption of Spain) – which is *the purpose of this grammar* – it is necessary to assume a standard general scheme of accounting – *a production rule* – that can handle a certain set of transformations taking place within the energy sector. The bias associated with the given purpose of the grammar – used to generate the 'primary energy consumption' indicator – entails a limited applicability for the numerical output. That is, the 'flat conversion factor' of a 3:1 ratio applied to account for 1 MJ of electricity produced without using fossil energy refers to a 'virtual' energy consumption of oil (or coal) *which has been not used* when generating 1 MJ of electricity in this way. Moreover, the same conversion of 3:1 is applied to all countries included in the statistics and cannot accurately account for country-specific variations. Ironically, this is not important, because for the given purpose – comparing the overall requirement of primary energy sources against a standard value 'primary energy consumption equivalent' – this error is irrelevant. This is why energy statistics can be interchangeably expressed in either TOE or TCE: because the carbon production to energy production ratios of the various energy sources are not included as data, any differences between the TOE and TCE for a given mix of energy sources are ignored.

The adoption of this 'single-purpose (or mono-purpose) grammar' implies a few shortcomings in related analysis. First, the assessment of 'primary energy consumption equivalent' (the total amount of virtual TOE that is entering an economy per year in the form of technical energy) does not map onto the amount of goods and services obtained by that economy (*final energy services*). That is, when using this statistical database we cannot compare the amount of 'final energy services' enjoyed by the citizens of different countries. Second, the assessment of 'primary energy consumption equivalent', expressed in TOE, found in energy statistics does not map onto *CO_2 emissions*. In fact, the final numerical assessment of consumption of TOE includes 'virtual' TOE, which in reality does not translate into real CO_2 emissions. Third, the overall assessment of TOE equivalent found in energy statistics cannot be related to the *amount of land required* to obtain this energy supply. It is completely useless for a comparison among countries where the purpose is to analyse the *pressure that the energy sector implies on land cover*. Fourth, the overall assessment of TOE does not make *a distinction between renewable and non-renewable primary energy sources*. Fifth, the overall assessment of TOE found in energy statistics is completely useless for a comparison among countries where the purpose is to analyse *the total requirement that the energy sector implies in terms of hours of work supply*.

A better-articulated, multi-purpose grammar could be used, starting from a given dataset, (1) to compare the energy metabolism of different countries in relation to a set of different benchmarks; and (2) to run 'what if' experiments by switching 'names' with 'tokens' and/or imposing different production rules (e.g. assuming technological changes). This is to say, there is information and understanding to be gained by adding new categories to the lexicon (tokens and names) from study of how to expand the set of indicators that a grammar used to represent an energy sector can handle. These additional categories and production rules could be added to the original data set as illustrated in Figure 8.2, making it possible to generate a wider set of indicators, including final energy services, CO_2 emissions, pressure that the energy sector implies on land cover, distinction between renewable and non-renewable energy supply, labour demand in the energy sector, and energy flows related to food security (Giampietro *et al.* 2012).

A more complex example of 'grammar' in action

The next example is given in Figure 8.2. It is a spreadsheet prepared with the popular software Microsoft Excel™ used to prepare a budget for a research project that has been funded by the European Commission. This particular application of a grammar has the purpose of establishing a useful relation between (1) the system of accounting of the university getting the money for the RTD project, and (2) the system of accounting required by the European Commission when providing financial support for the RTD project. In particular, this example focuses mainly on the person-months allocated in the project in order to handle the accounting of the relative costs.

In relation to our definition of grammar, we can recognize in Figure 8.2 both semantic categories and formal caregories. *Semantic categories*, such as 'personnel external contracts' and 'personnel staff salary', are related to the analogous definition of formal categories (names). In this example the semantic category 'personnel external contracts' is associated to two formal categories (names) – 'cost of post-doc' and 'cost of PhD student' – whereas the semantic category 'personnel staff salary' is associated to the two formal categories (names) 'cost of full professor' and 'cost of associate professor'. Other semantic categories would be 'direct expenses' versus 'indirect expenses', which are 'relevant information' since they are used by the university to handle the accounting of the money received from the EU Commission; and 'total funding RTD' and 'total funding management', used by the EU Commission to handle the money to be given to the university. *Formal categories* can be divided into 'names' and 'tokens'. For example, the value to be assigned to the 'name' 'cost of associate

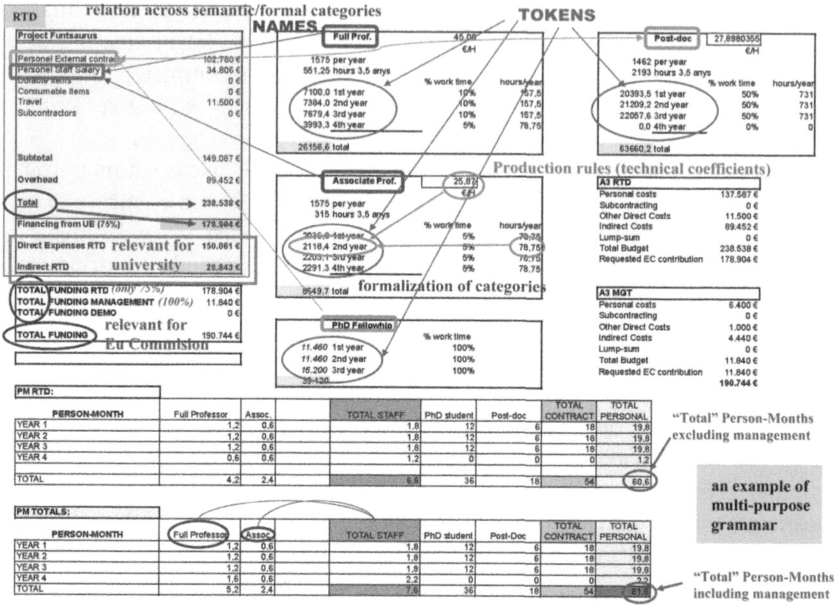

Figure 8.2 A multi-purpose grammar in action: the budget of a RTD project

professor' is determined by an expected relation (production rule) combining the values associated with the 'token' categories 'cost per hour', 'hours in a year', 'profile of distribution of hours over the four years'.

When looking at the overall analysis of costs for RTD activities (the box in the upper corner on the left), we can see the presence in that box of several 'totals' – names-categories mapping onto semantic categories. These different totals represent different formal outputs useful for different purposes. For example, there is an assessment of the total costs – €238.538 'no matter who pays for them' – which indicates the overall economic cost of this budget for EU taxpayers. There is a total referring to the financing from the European Union – €178.904 – but only in relation to RTD expenses. There is another total referring to the overall financing from the Union – €190.744 – which includes also the management costs. These are semantic categories relevant for the administrative office within the EU Commission. In a smaller box, located among the various totals, there is a 'logically distinct' division into categories. These categories are not relevant for the EU Commission, but they are relevant for the university receiving the money. These two categories will be used by the administration of the university for the handling of the money received from the Commission. For this reason, the distinction based on the semantic categories 'direct expenses' and 'indirect expenses', although meaningless for the EU Commission giving the money, is required to provide a useful output for the administrative offices of the university receiving the money.

The concept of 'multi-purpose grammars': using the same Microsoft Excel™ spreadsheet as a multi-purpose grammar

In this example the given spreadsheet can be used to generate different formal outputs – that is, assessments referring to different relevant categories – useful for a given purpose. So far, we specified the purpose of this particular application as follows: (1) *to establish a useful relation between the system of accounting of the university getting the money for the RTD project, and the system of accounting required by the European Commission providing financial support for RTD.* By applying this grammar it becomes possible to quantify, according to the rules adopted both by the European Commission and by the university receiving the money, the amount of money to be transferred from the EU Commission to a given university, the amount of money that a given research group can use for travels, the money that a PhD student will receive during this project, etc.

However, it is important to observe that the same grammar can also be used for different purposes, in this case (2) *to check the desirability and viability of a given project against an external definition of budget constraint.* For example, let's imagine that the given research group has been invited to become part of a consortium within an assigned overall budget. This means that now 'total financed by the EU Commission' is declared to be a 'token-category' and no longer a 'name-category'. In order to be able to decide whether or not it is desirable and feasible to be part of the given consortium under the given budget constraint, the group can use this very same grammar to visualize the 'option space' when allocating person-months over the given set of categories. Now the person-months of full professors, associated professors, post-docs and PhD students become 'names' categories (variables). By using this grammar one can study what combination of person-months across the categories included in the lexicon can be adopted given the limited budget.

The grammar can also be used (3) *to compare differences among universities operating in different countries in relation to economic costs of research.* For this purpose, what is relevant is the input data entered in the grammar before the application of the production rules. That is, this analysis refers to the values used for the 'token-categories'. Yet the grammar is still needed, since when dealing with a comparison among personnel costs, such a comparison among different countries has to be performed by looking at the cost 'per hour of working time' *across homogeneous semantic and formal categories* – that is, full professors with full professors, and PhD students with PhD students. In order to compare the same typology of token categories, we need to organize the relative data sets using the same grammars.

The grammar can also be used (4) *to compare differences among research groups in relation to the adoption of different strategies for use of financial resources.* For this purpose it is the overall profile of investments over different semantic categories of cost that can be used to look for benchmark values and peculiar situations. For example, when comparing a large number of budgets, all represented and characterized using the grammar illustrated in Figure 8.1, we can say that a particular research group that allocated 80 per cent of the total costs to travel would be an outlier of the sample.

The grammar can also be used (5) *to look for typical patterns (benchmark values) in the characteristics of the various sets of relations across different countries*. For example, is the difference as a percentage between the 'cost per hour' of a full professor and the 'cost per hour' of an assistant professor homogeneous over the sample? Can we find typologies of universities with very high costs per hour and those with very low costs per hour? For example, are there clusters of values for different 'token-categories' over the sample? Can we look for *typologies of RTD projects* in relation to the profile of allocation of the cost over the given lexicon? For example, when we deal with budgets in which 'cost of equipment' >> 'cost of personnel' we can conclude that the project is aimed at *technological development (engineering)*, whereas when we deal with budgets in which 'cost of equipment' << 'cost of personnel' we can conclude that the project is in *the social sciences or the humanities*.

In the next sections we will illustrate with practical examples how it is possible to use the concept of 'multi-purpose grammar' within the MuSIASEM approach, but we first need to define an additional conceptual tool: impredicative loop analysis.

The concept of impredicative loop analysis: a 'multi-scale' system of accounting

The very survival of metabolic systems is based on their ability to stabilize autocatalytic loops. They must be able to make available for their own consumption the flows of inputs they need to survive. The problem with the analysis of autocatalytic loops is that they are established across elements operating on different scales. Because of this, one has to abandon the myth that it is possible to analyse the sustainability of autocatalytic loops by using differential equations within a mono-scale analysis framework. That is to say, one must move beyond reductionism. The alternative proposed by MuSIASEM is to look for sets of useful typologies of parts and wholes (characterized in terms of the relative size and specific throughputs). These must generate a congruent set of flows, when one is considering the autocatalytic loop across non-equivalent descriptive domains, within the whole metabolic complex. This analysis of congruence across different scales is called 'impredicative loop analysis' (ILA) and can be defined as a check on the congruence between the metabolic characteristics of the whole ('size' and 'throughput') and the metabolic characteristics of lower-level parts (characterized also in terms of 'size' and 'throughput') which are expressing an expected set of relations.

An example of ILA will now be presented, referring to a hypothetical situation of 100 people living on a remote island. In this example the check refers to the given definition of the characteristics of the whole and the parts in relation to the possibility of establishing a dynamic budget of food energy. Using the basic rationale of metabolism, it is possible to associate a 'flow of required food' with a given amount of human activity. In order to have a feasible dynamic budget of food for these 100 people over a year, the amount of food to be consumed in that year must be produced within the amount of hours invested on this task during that year. The resulting biophysical constraint on the feasibility of this budget is represented by the fact that the hours of human activity allocated in food production are only a small fraction of the total of human activity, which determines the total food consumption of any type of human society. By adopting the concept of ILA, one can explore the severity of this constraint and study the interrelation between the characteristics of the parts and the characteristics of the whole.

Before getting into the example, we would like to make other two observations. With this framework it is possible to check a variety of different biophysical constraints referring to different dynamic budgets, oriented with respect to a variety of metabolized flows – for example, the requirement of food energy versus the relative supply; the requirement of commercial energy versus the relative supply; the requirement of water versus the relative supply. In the following example we deal only with one of the many metabolized flows – food energy – that can be used for an ILA. Here, the quantitative check on the congruence between requirement and supply necessarily reflects, or depends upon, the particular choices of formalization used to represent the flow in consumption and in production (the choice of a grammar and a given vocabulary for quantification).

Theoretical assumptions and basic rationale adopted in this example

The following ILA studies the stabilization of an autocatalytic loop of endosomatic (inside the body) energy: the output of useful energy from human activity is used to stabilize the input of food energy. Therefore, in this example the characterization of the autocatalytic loop is obtained in terms of a reciprocal 'entailment' of two resources: 'human activity' and 'food'. As was mentioned earlier, we will make use of Georgescu-Roegen's (1971) distinction between *flow coordinates (elements)* and *fund coordinates (elements)* for representing, in biophysical terms, the socio-economic process of production and consumption of goods and services. In the example that follows, human activity is the fund and food energy the flow.

Therefore, *the wear and tear on fund coordinates*, which makes their reproduction a necessary part of their continued use, *entails an overhead on the flow they are generating, while the throughput capacity of a fund constitutes a constraint on the relative rate of the flows associated with it.*

The term 'autocatalytic loop' indicates a positive feedback, a self-reinforcing chain of effects (the establishment of an egg–chicken pattern) generated by a part of the socio-economic process. This is what Ulanowicz (1986) calls a hypercycle, and in this example it is generated by the hours of human activity allocated in food production, which are generating more food energy than is being consumed. A viable dynamic budget of requirement and supply of food energy entails the ability to establish an autocatalytic loop in which (1) a given amount of human activity is capable of stabilizing a given flow of food energy – i.e. crops; and (2) the given flow of food energy is capable of stabilizing the original amount of human activity. An example of this view of the dynamic complex of relationships for our hypothetical society of 100 people living on a remote island is given in Figure 8.3.

Within this framework, our approach has the goal of establishing a relation between a particular characterization of this autocatalytic loop in relation to the whole (at *level n*), and in relation to the various elements of the socio-economic system, perceived and represented at a lower level (*level n – 1* and *level n – 2*), while at the same time checking the compatibility of the impact of this metabolism on the ecosystem embedding the society (at *level n + 1*).

The characterization of the elements (whole and parts) is obtained by using three types of variables. The first, (A), is an intensive variable characterizing the throughput (a flow per unit of size) – megajoules of food per hour of human activity per year – obtained by dividing the *flow* 'food energy' by the *fund* 'hours of human activity'. The second, (B), is a *fund* variable characterizing the size (for assessing the size of parts and wholes). In the following example, in our socio-economic system we can define the size of the whole in hours of human activity (THA = Total Human Activity) and the size of the parts (HA_i = Human Activity in the element *i*, specified using a category of human activity *i*). 'Hours of total human activity' is a variable directly related to population size and is

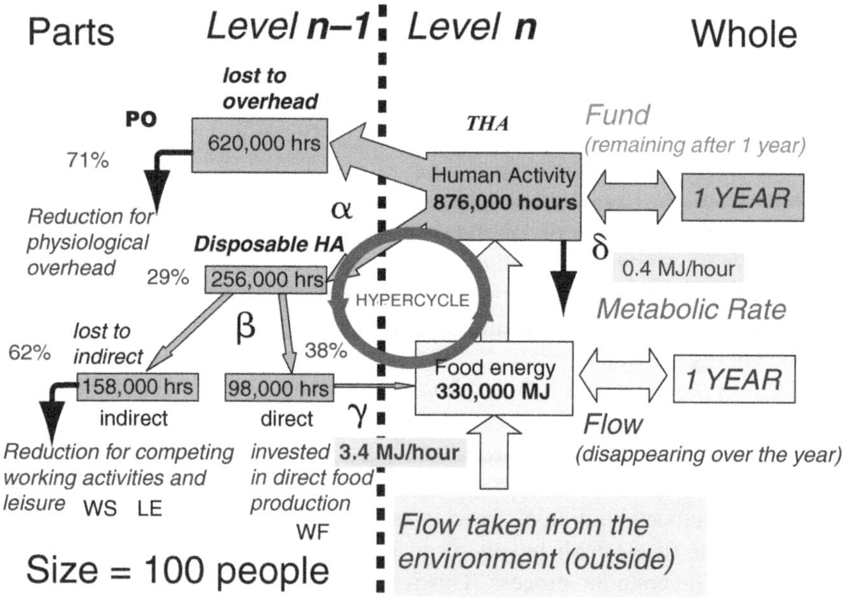

Figure 8.3 The impredicative loop between human activity (generating a flow of food energy) and food energy (supporting human activity).

affected by demographic changes. The third type of variable, (C), is a *flow* variable characterizing the amount of interaction with the context; in fact, the total amount of food energy to be metabolized by the society – expressed in megajoules of food energy – implies an interaction with an ecosystem that is generating such a flow.

In this simplified example we deal only with an integrated analysis of the endosomatic autocatalytic loop (= only human labour and human food) referring to a hypothetical society of 100 people on a remote island. The numbers given in this example are not the relevant part of the analysis per se. We are providing numbers – which can be easily followed by the reader – just to help the reader to better grasp the mechanism of accounting. *It is the forced relation among numbers (and the analysis of the mechanism generating this relation) that is the main issue here.* The same meta-mechanism of accounting, based on multi-purpose grammars, can be applied to exosomatic (outside the body) energy (e.g. fossil energy and technical capital), monetary flows (e.g. added value generation and human activity) and water (e.g. water flows and human activity), by adopting a different taxonomy of categories. Two goals are crucial in this approach. They refer to the ability of establishing: (1) a link between the characteristics of the societal metabolism as a whole (characteristics referring to the entire loop – *level n*) and the characteristics referring to lower-level elements and higher-level elements – *level n−2*, *level n−1* and *level n+1*; and (2) a meta-system of accounting which is capable of checking the viability of the dynamic budget of the metabolized flow (for more details on this approach, see Giampietro *et al.* 2011).

In this approach the accounting is addressing autocatalytic loops instead of using simple linear representations of flows – as is commonly done in the economic process (e.g. input–output analyses). Autocatalytic loops are a source of important epistemological problems – chicken–egg paradoxes – but this is the only way to study the mechanism of self-organization of autopoietic systems. In fact, it is well known that in complex adaptive systems the dissipation of useful energy must imply a feedback, which has to be used to enhance the adaptability of their system of control (Odum 1971; Ulanowicz 1986). This implies a dialectical tension between increases in 'efficiency' (doing better according to the shared experience referring to the window past–present) and increases in 'adaptability' (doing better when the present interaction will be different in the window present–future), which are impossible to capture within formal representation (for more on this point, see the book on the Jevons Paradox by Polimeni *et al.* 2008). In relation to the scientific challenge of how to effectively represent this tension, facing this task requires moving to a multi-scale analysis based on the adoption of innovative conceptual tools.

Technical assumptions and numerical data of this example

We hypothesize a society of 100 people that uses only flows of endosomatic energy (food and human labour) for stabilizing its own metabolism. In order to further simplify the analysis, we imagine that the society is operating on a remote island (for example, it is made up of survivors of a plane crash). We further imagine that its population structure reflects the value typical of a developed country and that the islanders have adopted the same social rules regulating access to the workforce as those enforced in most developed countries (that is, persons under 16 and those over 65 are not supposed to work). This implies a dependency ratio of about 50 per cent – that is, only 50 adults are involved in the production of goods and social services for the whole population. A few additional parameters are also needed to characterize societal metabolism.

Basic requirement of food. Using standard characteristics of a population typical of developed countries, we obtain an average demand of 9 MJ/day per capita of food, which translates into 330,000 MJ/year of food for the entire population.

Indicator of material standard of living. We assume that the only 'good' produced and consumed in this society (without market transactions) is the food providing nutrients in the diet. In relation to this assumption we can define, then, two possible levels of material standard of living, related to two different 'qualities' for the diet. The first possible diet is a *'low-quality diet' – Diet A*, which covers the total requirement of food energy (3,300 MJ/year per capita) using only cereals (a supply of only vegetal proteins). With a nutritional value of 14 MJ of energy per kilogram of cereal, this implies the need to produce 250 kg of cereals/year per capita. The second is a *'high-quality diet' – Diet B*, which covers 80 per cent of the requirement of food energy with cereals (190 kg per capita per year) and 20 per cent with beef meat (equivalent to 6.9 kg of meat per capital per year). Owing to the very high losses of conversion (to produce 1 kg of beef meat you have to feed the herd 12 kg of grains), this double conversion implies the additional production of 810 kg of cereals per year. That is, adopting a 'high-quality diet' (Diet B) requires the primary production of 1,000 kg of cereals per capita (rather than 250 kg/year with Diet A).

Indicator of technology. This reflects technological coefficients. In this case, (1) labour productivity is 1 kg of cereal per hour of labour, and (2) land productivity of cereal production is 1,000 kg of cereal per hectare.

Indicator of environmental loading. A very coarse indicator of environmental loading used in this example is the fraction 'land in production/total land of the island', since the land used for producing cereals implies the destruction of natural habitat (replaced with the monoculture of cereals). In our example the indicator of environmental loading is heavily affected by (1) population, (2) the type of diet followed by the population (material standard of living) and (3) the technology used – recalling the $I = PAT$ equation proposed by Ehrlich (1968). Assuming a total area for the island of 500 hectares, this implies an index of EL = 0.05 for Diet A and EL = 0.20 for Diet B (EL = environmental loading = hectares in production/total hectares of available in the island).

Supply of human activity. Let's assume that the required amount of food energy for a year (330,000 MJ/year) is available for the 100 people for the first year. With this assumption, and having the 100 people to start with, the conversion of this food into endosomatic energy implies (it is equivalent to) the availability of a total supply of human activity of 876,000 hours/year (=24 hours/day × 365 × 100 persons). To stabilize the resource human activity in the short term – by providing the required metabolic flow – it is necessary to invest an amount of working time capable of generating the supply of food also for the next year. However, the stability of this socio-economic system requires not only a certain investment of the fund Human Activity for food production, but also another investment of human activity for those tasks associated with maintenance and reproduction of the initial fund of Total Human Activity (THA). As was noted earlier, a fund element, by definition, requires an overhead for its own reproduction. This additional set of tasks must include sleeping, personal care, eating (at the individual/physiological level) plus a certain number of hours allocated in working out effective personal relations, giving birth to children and taking care of their education (at the household/societal level). This entails the existence of a 'societal overhead' on the fund Human Activity. That is to say, a certain fraction of the total hours of human activity will not be available for working at interacting with the context or environment – to generate food supply – since it must be dedicated to the reproduction of THA.

We can then define *a set of typologies of 'end uses' of human activity* which can be used to characterize the profile of investment of human activity within the dynamic budget of food energy, as illustrated in Figure 8.4. With MuSIASEM, unlike in reductive approaches to the analysis of sustainability assessment that shy away from the impredicative loop, the 'Physiological Overhead' associated with human activity and required for the reproduction of that fund is taken into

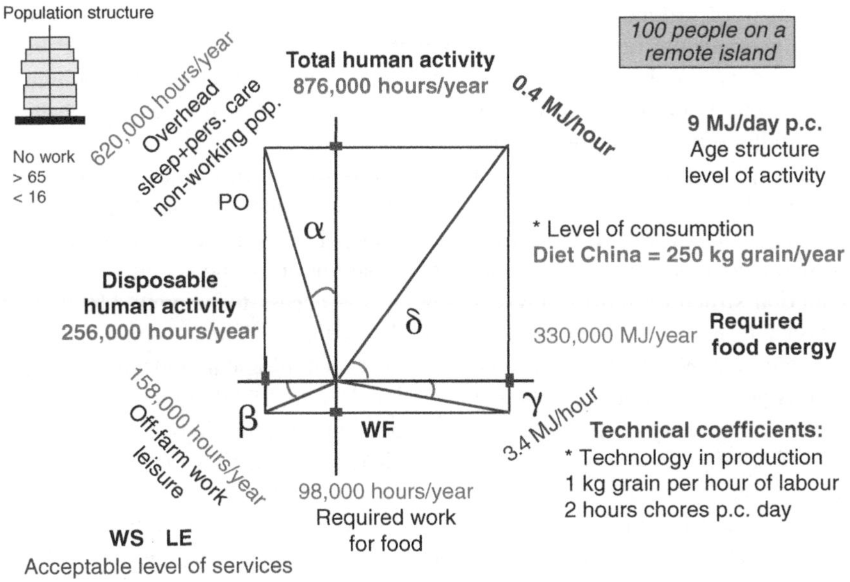

Figure 8.4 Impredicative loop analysis over the characteristics of the whole and the characteristics of the parts.

account. In any human society the largest part of human activity is not related to the stabilization of the flows metabolized in the societal metabolism (e.g. in this example producing food), but rather to 'Maintenance and Reproduction' of humans. This fixed overhead can be called Physiological Overhead (HA_{PO}) and includes (1) sleeping and personal care for everybody (in our example a flat value of 10 hours per day has been applied to all 100 people, leading to a first consumption of 365,000 hours per year out of the Total Human Activity available); and (2) activity of the non-working population (the remaining 14 hours per day of the elderly and children, which are important for the future stability of the society – to reproduce the fund element – but are not available – according to the social rule established before – for the production of the flow of food now. In relation to the available budget of Total Human Activity this implies an additional consumption of 255,000 hours per year ($14 \times 50 \times 365$) in non-productive activities. Altogether, the Physiological Overhead entails a consumption of 620,000 hours/per year of Human Activity.

This budget of human activity expressed at the societal level has to be divided between three tasks: (1) guaranteeing the production of the required food input (for avoiding starvation now) – 'Work for Food' ($HA_{WF)}$; (2) guaranteeing the people a good quality of life – 'Work for Services' (HA_{WS}); and (3) education and leisure, a required task for guaranteeing adaptability for society in the long term (HA_{EL}).

At this point we can get into the circular structure of the flows associated with the autocatalytic loop as shown in the lower part of Figure 8.4. The requirement of 330,000 MJ per year of endosomatic energy input (food at time *t*) entails the requirement of producing enough energy carriers (food at time $t+1$) in the following year. In the upper-right quadrant the value taken by the ratio between fund and flow variable is expressed in megajoules per hour (food energy/human activity), but it could have also been defined as 'kilograms of cereals per capita' by operating the relative conversions.

The impredicative loop analysis makes it possible, at this point, to look for a biophysical constraint on the level of productivity of labour in the element HA_{WF} (the hours of HA invested in 'working for food'). That is, IF we want to preserve the characteristics of the whole (the total consumption of the society, the actual population structure and the laws regulating the access to labour), THEN it is necessary to invest a given 'not-negotiable' fraction of 'Total Human Activity' in the end use 'Work for Food'. Based on the technological coefficient, in this case this amount of hours can be calculated as $HA_{WF}=98{,}000$ hours per year for Diet A. The severity of this constraint will depend on technology and the availability of natural resources. This in turn indicates the fraction of 'Total Human Activity' that can be allocated to the two end uses (1) 'Services' (HA_{WS}) and (2) 'Education and Leisure' (HA_{EL}). That is, the values taken by either HA_{WS} or HA_{EL} are not numbers that can be decided only according to social or political will. The circular nature of the autocatalytic loop (Figure 8.4) means that numerical values associated with the characterization of various identities, defining elements on different hierarchical levels (at the level of individual compartments

– extensive segments on the axis HA_i – and intensive variables – wideness of angles: throughput in HA_i), may all be changed. However, these changes must respect the constraint of congruence among flow variables and fund variables over the whole loop. These constraints are imposed on each other by the characteristics of the socio-ecological system and the size of the human economy (funds and flow and the intensive variables) used to characterize the various elements across levels (the parts in relation to the whole and the whole in relation to the parts). These constraints can be used to test the plausibility and the desirability of a given situation by coupling the use of multi-purpose grammars to the idea of checking the congruence of dynamic budgets of flows and funds defined across hierarchical levels.

Different formalizations of the budget within the same meta-model

Let us imagine now that we change, for example, some of the values used to characterize this autocatalytic loop of energy forms. For example, let us change the parameter 'material standard of living', which – in our simplified model – is expressed by the relevant attribute 'quality of the diet' (formalized in the two options Diet A or Diet B). The different mix of energy vectors in the two diets (vegetal versus animal proteins) implies a quantitative difference in the 'biophysical cost' of the diet expressed in terms both of a larger work requirement and of a larger environmental loading (higher demand for land). The same 330,000 MJ per year of food with this diet requires the production of 1,000 kg of grain per capita (because of the double conversion of grains into meat). As a consequence of this fact, whereas the production of cereals for a population relying totally on Diet A requires only 25,000 hours of labour and the destruction of 25 hectares of natural habitat ($EL_A = 0.05$), the production of cereals for a population relying totally on Diet B requires 100,000 hours of labour and the destruction of 100 hectares of natural habitat ($EL_B = 0.20$). Moreover, to this assessment we have to add a requirement of work hours for fixed chores. Fixed chores include preparation of meals, gathering of wood for cooking, fetching water, washing, and maintenance of food system infrastructures in this primitive society. In this simplified example we use the same flat value for the two diets = 73,000 hours per year (2 hours per capita per day $= 2 \times 365 \times 100$). This implies that if all the people of the island decide to follow Diet A, they will face a given requirement of 'Work for Food' of 98,000 hours per year. If they all decided to adopt Diet B, however, they would face a different requirement of 'Work for Food'. The relative size of the HA_{WF} compartment would be 173,000 hours per year. At this point, we can calculate, as the difference, the amount of 'Human Activity' that can be allocated to 'Social and Leisure' (Figure 8.5).

The combined size of the two compartments 'Services' (HA_{WS}) and 'Education and Leisure' (HA_{EL}) can be obtained by considering the difference between the amount of Disposable Human Activity (HA_{DS}) – 256,000 hours in this example – and the forced requirement of Work for Food (HA_{WF}) – 173,000 hours in this example. It is evident that the number of hours that the people living in

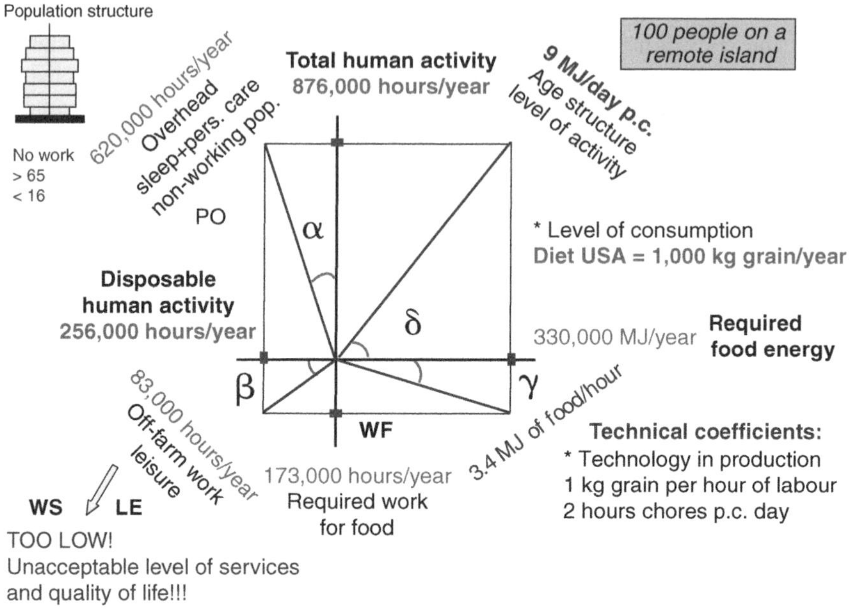

Figure 8.5 Impredicative loop analysis with different characteristics of parts indicating an unfeasible and undesirable state for the dynamic budget of food energy.

our island can dedicate to (1) 'Services' (HA_{WS}) – running social institutions and structures (schools, hospitals, courts of justice) – and (2) 'Education and Leisure' (HA_{EL}) – developing their individual potentialities in social interaction and personal enjoyment – is not only the result of their free choice. Rather, it is the result of a compromise between competing requirements of the resource 'Human Activity Disposable for Social Self-Organization' in relation to different tasks of the economic process, referring to the characteristics of individuals (e.g. types of human organisms) and social elements (e.g. types of households). However, without developing an 'ad hoc' grammar we cannot study the implications and the trade-offs of the reallocation of the spare hours between 'Services' (HA_{WS}) and 'Education and Leisure' (HA_{EL}). This can only be done (as will be illustrated in the next section) by using a multi-purpose grammar to formalize more in detail and across different levels the impredicative loop analysis of this example.

Going back to the overall analysis of the impredicative loop, assigning numerical values to social parameters such as population structure and dependency ratio for our hypothetical population (e.g. profile of distribution over age classes) affects the definition of key characteristics of the autocatalytic loop. That is, it translates into deciding which is a '*name*' and which is a '*token*' in the grammar. In this case, this means deciding whether or not the values taken by (1) the requirement of food energy (330,000 MJ/year) – that is, the throughput of the whole – and (2) the Societal Overhead on Human Activity – that is, the relative size of the compartment 'Physiological Overhead' (HA_{PO}=620,000 hours/year) – are parameters or dependent variables. The same applies to other numerical values associated with other socio-economic characteristics such as (1) material standard of living (Diet A or Diet B), and (2) technical coefficients in production (e.g. labour, land and water requirements for generating the required mix of energy vectors). Different characterizations of the material standard of living (the chosen quality of diet) used as 'token' will affect the size of the compartment 'Work for Food', when this is considered as a 'name'. That is, depending on the chosen diet, the forced allocation of hours in HA_{WF} can be either 98,000 or 173,000 hours per year. In the same way, differences in the characterization of the material standard of living, in this system of accounting, will also affect the level of environmental loading. In fact, requirements for land and water, as well as the possible generation of wastes, are all linked to the characterization of production. In our simple example we adopt a very coarse indicator for environmental loading (the fraction of colonized land over the total) generating the two values EL_A=0.05 and EL_B=0.20. This value can be linked, using technical coefficients, to the characteristics of the metabolic flow.

We are using the term 'internal biophysical constraints' to indicate the obvious fact that the amount of human activity that can be invested into the three end uses 'Physiological Overhead' (HA_{PO}), 'Work for Services' (HA_{WS}) and 'Education and Leisure' (HA_{EL}) depends only in part on the aspirations of the 100 people for a better quality of life in such a society. The survival of the whole system in the short term (the matching of the requirement of energy carriers input with an adequate supply of them – the dynamic budget of the flow resource) requires a non-negotiable amount of hours of Work for Food (HA_{WF}), which can imply forced choices. As is shown in Figure 8.5, depending on the characteristics of the autocatalytic loop, large investments of human activity in 'Services' (HA_{WS}) and 'Education and Leisure' (HA_{EL}) can become a luxury. For example, if the entire society (with the set of characteristics specified above) wants to adopt Diet B, then for them it will not be possible to invest more than 83,000 hours of human activity in the two end uses 'Services' (HA_{WS}) and 'Education and Leisure' (HA_{EL}) combined. On the other hand, if, together with a good diet, they also want a level of services typical of developed countries (requiring an HA_{WS} of around 170,000 hours per 100 people per year), they will have to 'pay' for it. This could imply resorting to some politically important rules reflecting cultural identity and ethical beliefs (what determines the Societal Overhead of Human Activity for Physiological Overhead). For example, to reach a new situation of congruence they could decide either to introduce child labour or increase the economically active population by forcing people over 65 to work. Alternatively, they could accept a certain degree of inequity in the society (a small fraction of people in the ruling social class eating diet B and a majority of ruled eating diet A). We can easily recognize that all these solutions are operating in many countries nowadays and were adopted in the past all over our planet.

The simple assumptions used in this example to bring the various assessments related to a dynamic budget of societal metabolism into congruence are of course not realistic (for example, nobody can eat a diet consisting only of cereals, and expected changes in the requirements of work are never linear). Moreover, by ignoring exosomatic energy we are not taking into account the effect of capital accumulation (e.g. potential use of animals, infrastructures, better technology and improvements in 'know-how' that can affect technical coefficients). Capital and flows of exosomatic energy are always relevant for reaching alternative feasible dynamic points of equilibrium of the endosomatic energy budget. A lexicon dealing only with the biophysical representation of endosomatic conversions of energy is not able to address either the economic dimension or the huge expansion of the option space provided by exosomatic energy conversion (technology). Economic variables – associated with the adoption of semantic and formal categories – are used to reflect the expression of human preferences within a given institutional setting (e.g. a market). These categories are logically independent from those used for an analysis reflecting biophysical transformations. This is to say that multi-scale integrated analysis can be applied to the study of modern society by adopting an integrated set of additional grammars to include and handle simultaneously the representation of economic and biophysical flows (e.g. Giampietro and Mayumi 2000, 2001; Giampietro 2003; Ramos-Martin *et al.* 2007; Giampietro *et al.* 2011, 2012).

ILA links characteristics defined across different levels and scales

After admitting its limitation, the example of the remote island clearly shows the potential of impredicative loop analysis. In that example it is possible to link the conditions determining the feasibility of the dynamic energy budget to the set of key parameters generally used in sustainability discussions. In particular, characterizing societal metabolism in terms of autocatalytic loops makes it possible to establish a 'relation' among changes occurring in parallel in various parameters and variables, which are reflecting patterns perceived on different levels and scales. For example, how much would the demand for land change if we changed the definition of the diet? What would happen to this society if demographic changes increased the dependency ratio or if a political reform affected the dependency ratio by changing workloads per year, or retirement age? By adopting this approach we can explore the viability domain of a dynamic budget (what combinations of values of variables and parameters are not feasible according to the reciprocal constraints imposed by the other variables and parameters) in relation to a lot of possible changes referring to different disciplinary fields of analysis.

For example, if the population pressure and the geography of the island imply that the requirement of 100 hectares of arable land for producing 100,000 kg of cereal is not available (for example if a large part of the 500 hectares of the island is too steep), the adoption of Diet B by 100 per cent of the population is simply not possible. The geographic characteristics of the island (e.g. defined at the *level* $n+2$) can in this way be related to the characteristics of the diet of individual members of the society (e.g. at the *level* $n-2$) going through the relation among parts (*level n − 1*) and whole (*level n*) considered in the ILA. This relation between land shortage and a poor diet is well known. It explains why, for example, crowded countries that used to depend heavily on the autocatalytic loop of endosomatic energy for their metabolism (such as India or China) have tended to adopt a vegetarian diet. However, without adopting a multi-scale integrated analysis it is not easy to individuate and analyse relations among characteristics affecting each other across levels. Remaining within disciplinary mono-scale analyses means that the relations that govern such choices are overlooked.

We can generalize the usefulness of MuSIASEM of autocatalytic loops by saying that the information used to characterize an impredicative loop associated with a given societal metabolism of a society translates into a definition of an integrated set of constraints over that value, which can be determined through reference to two integrated sets of variables (extensive and intensive variables). As is illustrated in the following section, this integrated set of constraints can be explored using a multi-purpose grammar capable of handling a series of formalizations of these constraints by referring to different views and different levels of analysis (individuals, households, the whole society, the environment in which the society is embedded).

Therefore, this approach can facilitate the discussion and the evaluation of possible alternative scenarios of development in terms of characterization of trade-off profiles. In fact, the congruence among the various numerical values of variables and parameters over the autocatalytic loop can be obtained by using different combinations of variable values. It is possible to drive the analysis with the value of parameters and/or with the value of variables defined at different hierarchical levels, making it possible to explore the relative effects in relation to different dimensions of performance, looking for possible viable solutions.

ILA makes it possible to deal with the implications of non-equivalent narratives

As was noted when discussing of the concept of multi-purpose grammars, considering simultaneous events occurring on different levels (adopting a multi-scale reading) can imply finding multiple directions of causation in our explanations. That is, the direction of causality will depend, first, on what we consider to be a 'time-independent' characteristic in the definition of the identity of parts and whole – the tokens. In this case the elements (parts and wholes within the impredicative loop) are characterized using attributes that are considered parameters. Second, the direction of causality will also depend on what we consider to be 'time-dependent' characteristics in the definitions of the identity of parts and whole – the names. In this case, the elements (parts and wholes within the impredicative loop) are characterized using attributes that are considered variables.

For example, in a given narrative, changes in technical coefficients are key factors driving changes in other system qualities: 'population grew because better technology made a larger food supply available' – the Malthusian explanation (Malthus 1778). In another narrative, changes in technical coefficients are driven by changes in other system qualities: 'technology changed because population growth required a larger food supply' – the Boserup explanation (Boserup 1965). These are two different narratives referring to the same impredicative loop. A formalization of a given narrative (a model representing a direction of causality) is only possible after the pre-analytical definition of what is a parameter and what is a variable. Therefore, when choosing a narrative, the analyst decides to explore the nature of a certain mechanism of causation (its possible dynamics) by ignoring the nature of others.

Whenever humans are facing the need to adjust the set of characteristics of an impredicative loop, they tend to go, first of all, for the 'silver bullet solution' able to provide win–win solutions. In this respect the idea of looking always for a technological fix can be seen as a remarkable hegemonization on the possible narratives that can be used in a debate over sustainability. The 'gospel' of Western civilization entails a standard solution to all kinds of dilemmas about sustainability: it maintains that sustainability has to be obtained not by changing human expectations and/or the identity of the storyteller, but, always and only, by looking for better technical coefficients. The storyteller is and has to remain at the centre of the universe and it is the external world that has to be adapted to its wants/identity. The 'silver bullet solution' in fact makes it possible to avoid facing conflicts among the various identities of the parts (social groups) making up an impredicative loop, when dealing with the metabolism of complex social systems. However, any solution based on adding more and better technology (a change in the characteristics related to intensive variables) does not come without side effects. It necessarily implies an adjustment over the various elements of the impredicative loop, and ultimately it will result in a change in the overall requirement of inputs and waste disposal of the relative societal metabolism with respect to its environment. It is well known that improvements related to a given characteristic defined in terms of an intensive variable (e.g. more efficiency in using a given resource for a task) often entail a worsening in relation to another characteristic defined in terms of an extensive variable (e.g. by-products or situations where the given resource will be used more for the original task and for also for other new tasks. A classic example of these sorts of side effects is the well-known Jevons' paradox (Polimeni *et al.* 2008).

Framing the discussion about future options within the framework of MuSIASEM over an impredicative loop implies that the various analysts are forced to consider, at the same time, several distinct effects (which requires the simultaneous use of non-equivalent models and variables to be represented) belonging to different descriptive domains.

There are characteristics of the autocatalytic loop that have a very short typical lag time for change, for example when adopting economic prices in the analysis. Other characteristics may have a lag time of changes of a few years, as in the case of analysis based on laws and technical coefficients, which can refer to a very location specific space-time scale (e.g. the yield of cereals at the plot level in a given year) or a large space-time domain (e.g. the efficiency of a gas turbine). Other characteristics, such as the dependency ratio (the ratio between non-working and working population) may reflect slower biophysical processes (those associated to demographic changes) having a time horizon of twenty years. Finally, there are other factors – such as regulations regarding compulsory schooling for children, or religious taboos – that reflect values related to the specific cultural identity of a society, which have an even slower pace of change (values and taboos tend to be very resilient in human systems). Ecological processes such as preservation of biodiversity also entail the adoption of space-time scales much larger than the one at which economic analysis can be operated.

Using the impredicative loop analysis of the dynamic budget of a remote island, we can explain the small body size of a population (after thousands of years of evolution) by saying that small body size maximizes the ratio Human Activity/Food consumed at the level of the whole socio-economic system. This is a result that can be considered as good, since it stabilizes the dynamic budget, at a given technology and level of natural resources. On the other hand, a small body size (and short lifespan) should be considered bad when other potential options arise. New possible narratives are added to the existing ones. For example, the option of trade and new technology make it possible for islanders to consume more food by escaping location-specific biophysical constraints – for example by attracting tourists to their island. However, in general terms we cannot expect that it will always be possible to decide in a substantive way what should be considered as the given option space – let alone deciding what priority should be given within an attributes set used to characterize the performance of a system.

We believe that by adopting a Multi-Scale Integrated Analysis of Impredicative Loops (MuSIASEM) for study of the interaction of human societies and ecosystems, we can enlarge the set of analytical tools that can be used to check the existence of non-equivalent constraints (lack of compatibility with economic, ecological, technical and social processes) affecting the viability of considered scenarios.

Combining the use of multi-purpose grammars with impredicative loop analysis: back to the example of 100 people on the remote island

In this section we provide an example of how it is possible to characterize the situation considered in the example of 100 people living in a remote island by addressing simultaneously different 'views' of performance, referring to different levels. This is possible by adopting the conceptual tool of 'multi-purpose grammar' discussed earlier (p. 184). One has to start by choosing a taxonomy – the types of types – that will be used to describe an expected relation over semantic and formal categories.

The 'multi-purpose grammar' we propose for dealing in quantitative terms with the example of the 100 people on the remote island is illustrated in

Figure 8.6. This is a copy of the Microsoft Excel™ spreadsheet used for the calculations. The different selections of categories can be divided into semantic categories (the categories used to make sense of the analysis) and formal categories (the categories used to provide a formal quantification). Then the formal categories are divided into tokens and names. The given selection must make it possible to use external referents (sources of empirical information) referring to elements represented at the different hierarchical levels across the impredicative loop.

Level of individuals (level n − 2)

We now present the selected taxonomy of this multi-purpose grammar, examples of how we use it and some of the associated implications.

Definition of the set of Types of Metabolic Systems. At this level we characterize the population as made up of a set of types of individuals. There are 6 chosen categories; this set is generated by a 3 × 2 matrix:

3 types for the age: (i) $x_1 < 16$; (ii) $16 < x_2 < 65$; (iii) $x_3 > 65$

2 types for the gender: (i) y_1, males; and (ii) y_2, females.

The size of the population – 100 people – has to be distributed over these 6 categories.

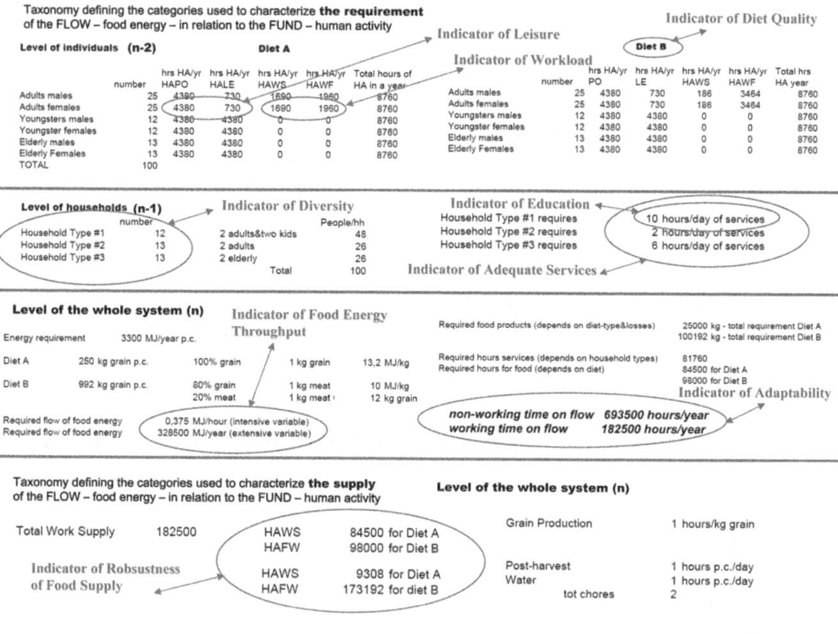

Figure 8.6 Taxonomy of the multi-purpose grammar used for the example.

The value of 100 people (instances of types) provides an overall value for the *fund* element Total Human Activity = 100 (people) × 8,760 (hours in a year) = 876,000 hours/year.

Changing the profile of distribution of the instances of people over the 6 categories will change the profile of distribution of hours over the set of categories of human activity.

Definition of the Categories of Human Activity. Each individual type allocates entirely its own endowment of Human Activity within the given set of 4 possible categories of human activity:

HA_{PO} = Physiological Overhead (sleeping, eating and personal care)

HA_{EL} = Education and Leisure (in this example applies only to adults)

HA_{WS} = Work for Services (in this example applied only to adults)

HA_{WF} = Work for Food (in this example applied only to adults)

The requirement of congruence implies that

$$THA = HA_{PO} + HA_{EL} + HA_{WS} + HA_{WF}$$

to be checked both at the level of each individual and at the level of the whole society.

Scenarios. There are two scenarios considered in the example, a scenario in which the society adopts Diet A and one based on the adoption of Diet B. These two scenarios entail a different allocation of the available *fund* element Human Activity over the profile of working activities.

Level of households (level n 1)

Definition of the types of households. At this level we characterize the population as made up of a set of household types, with 3 categories being chosen:

Type 1 – two adults + two children – size: 35,040 hours/year of HA (4 × 8,760)

Type 2 – two adults – size: 17,520 hours/year of HA (2 × 8,760)

Type 3 – two elderly people – size: 17,520 hours/year of HA (2 × 8,760)

The profile of distribution of instances of household types over this set of types has to generate an overall size in hours of THA *which is equal* to the overall size obtained by summing the size of the 100 individuals.

Depending on the distribution of adults over the set of household type each household type entails: (1) a certain amount of Human Activity which can be allocated in working time; and (2) a certain amount of Human Activity which is required in the category HA_{WF} (Work-for-Services).

Using this grammar we can also characterize (A) the diversity of household types at this level using the two parameters (i) number of types and (ii) the profile of distribution of the population of households over these types; and (B) the overall requirement of hours of work for services, depending on the profile of distribution of household profiles over the given set of types.

Level of the whole social system (level n)

Definition of the criteria of performance for the whole. At this level we have only one element – the whole – to be studied. Therefore, the information referring to this level cannot be organized in terms of a set of types. Rather, this information can be used to provide a characterization of the performance of the 'typology' of the social system to which the whole system belongs. This requires a semantic choice of pre-analytical definition of the relevant characteristics (attributes) of the 'typology of system', which should be used to evaluate this particular instance of society, when seen as a whole.

Since in this example we decided to ignore economic variables and characterize the social system made up by these 100 people as a metabolic system of food energy, constrained only by biophysical factors, we can adopt three indicators of performance which are relevant for discussing the sustainability of pre-industrial-type societies (they are discussed in Giampietro *et al.* 1993, 1997; Giampietro 1997):

1 *Adaptability* (long-term sustainability) – the ability of the system to use human activity in exploring new possible tasks and learning about 'itself interacting with the environment'. To this semantic category we associate the formal category: the ratio between the hours of 'human activity non-allocated in work on established tasks' and the hours of human activity 'allocated in work on established tasks' – using our definition of categories: $(HA_{PO}+HA_{EL})/(HA_{WF}+HA_{WS})$.
2 *Robustness of Food Supply* (short-term sustainability) – the ability of the system to use working human activity to face temporary shortages in the supply of food due to perturbations. This implies having an adequate buffer of working time, which in moments of crisis can be used to boost the production of food. Using our definition of categories, the relative indicator is $(HA_{WF}+HA_{WS})/HA_{WF}$.
3 *Food Energy Throughput* (steady-state picture) – the amount of energy that can be stabilized in the dynamic energetic budget, defining a scale/size for the process of self-organization of this society. This is a particularly relevant indicator of performance for pre-industrial societies – using our definition of categories: Flow of Food Energy per year. It is also useful for illustrating and tracing the shifting of burdens from one economy to another in a comparative analysis of multiple, related ecological economic systems.

Characterizing the requirement and the supply

The grammar presented so far makes it possible to define (1) the characteristics of the overall demand of food, (2) a requirement of hours in work for services, and (3) the various categories of human activity that will be used to generate a supply matching such a requirement. In order to verify whether or not such a matching is actually possible, we need additional information referring to the biophysical and technological constraints affecting the feasibility of the resulting dynamic budget of human activity and food energy. This information is given in two ways: (i) data and production rules required to convert the semantic categories used to define the 'Diet Quality' (high quality – Diet B; low quality – Diet A) into a quantitative assessment of the required flow of food items; and (ii) data and production rules required to convert the quantitative assessment of the food items making up the flow of food into a quantitative assessment of the required hours of work in the category HA_{WF} = Work for Food. This information is given in the lower part of Figure 8.6, which refers to the technical coefficients for the production of food and other work requirements.

The impredicative loop analysis across levels

A comparison of the two scenarios in relation to different indicators of performance, defined on different hierarchical levels, is provided in Figure 8.7.

In this particular example of integrated analysis – the visualization of the results is based on the very popular radar diagrams (also called spider web diagrams) which are used in marketing to characterize the performance of a given product, such as a car or a bike. This representation makes it possible to consider different dimensions of analysis (the economic criterion, safety criterion, mechanical performance criterion, comfort criterion, etc.). In more technical scientific jargon we can say that this radar diagram represents a Multi-Criteria Space (or a Multi-Objective Integrated Representation); for a review of options, see Gomiero and Giampietro (2005). In this example we use a method of contextualization called flag-model (Nijkamp and Vreeker 2000), in which different external referents – associated with names chosen for the multi-purpose grammar – can be used to obtain a meaningful comparison of the numerical value taken by each one of the indicators. The value taken by each one of the chosen variables can be contextualized against either target values and/or relevant reference points. Different colours can be assigned to different segments of the axes – e.g. green, for good; yellow, for acceptable; and red, for bad – to help obtain an overall image of the integrated analysis over the set of selected indicators, across the different hierarchical levels. Finally, the empty area in the middle of the graph refers to numerical values that are outside the 'feasibility domain'. This is to say, when a value goes below the minimum threshold of acceptable value – falling within the empty circle – this implies a collapse of the pattern of organization at the particular level to which the indicator of performance refers.

This comparison over the two scenarios will now be discussed level by level.

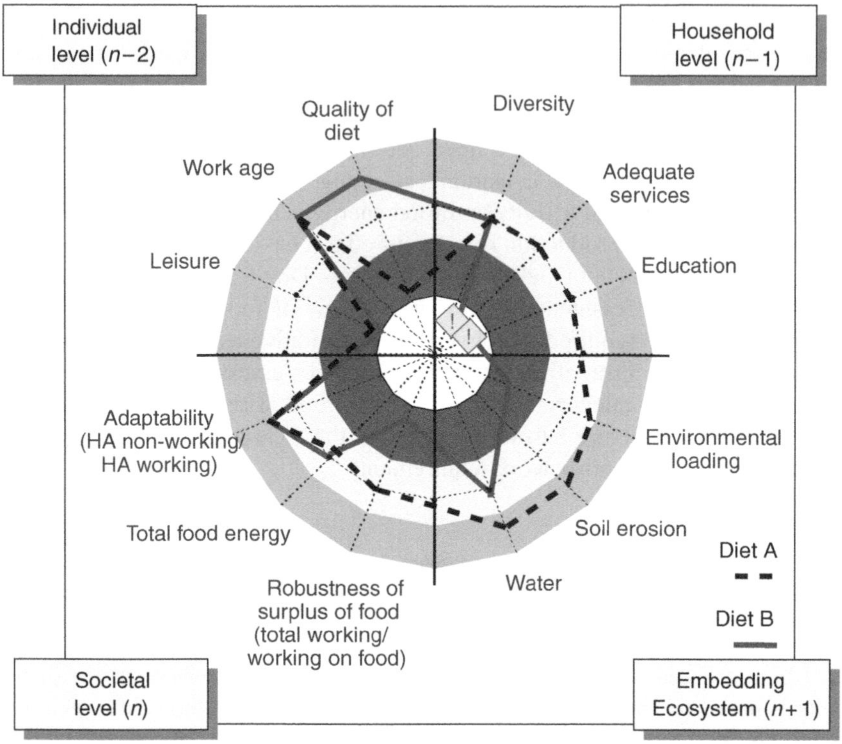

Figure 8.7 Characterization of the performance of the two scenarios across levels.

Level of individuals (level n − 2)

The three indicators used in the diagram (upper left quadrant) reflect the value taken by tokens associated with this indicator in the multi-purpose grammar. These indicators are all tokens, since we assumed that the 100 people arrived from a developed country and are keeping the value of 12 hours per capita per day as Physiological Overhead. For those aged over 65 and under 16, no working time is allowed.

In relation to the three categories:

1 Education and Leisure (semantic) – hours in HA_{EL} (formal) – the value has been fixed at a level of 2 hours/day of leisure per time. This implies a workload of 10 hours/day (3,650 hours/year). This is the maximum average workload admissible for obtaining useful work from human beings, a threshold not surpassed even in slave labour (Giampietro and Mayumi 2000).
2 Work Age (semantic) – the age bracket determining the possibility to work. In this example there is only one option, very favourable for individuals.
3 Quality of the Diet (semantic) – the value of this indicator has been assumed to be ‘High’ and ‘Low’ (formal) for the two scenarios (either Diet B or Diet A).

Level of households (level n 1)

The three indicators used in the diagram (upper-right quadrant) reflect the value taken by the *names* associated to this indicator in the multi-purpose grammar.

In this example these indicators are all names, since we assumed that the 100 people arrived from a developed country are keeping their original social rules, fighting against the biophysical constraints associated with the dynamic budget of food energy. In this fight, after guaranteeing the production of food they try to match also the requirement of services. Therefore, the production rules of the grammar first of all calculate the amount of Human Activity required to guarantee that there is enough food ($HA_{WF)}$ – according to the value resulting from the chosen diet (Diet A or Diet B) – and then allocate as much as possible of the remaining work supply to Work for Service (HA_{WS}).

As was observed in the previous section, according to the set of categories of human activity determining the overall work supply – defined at the *level* $n-2$ – it is not possible to further increase the actual work supply. The three indicators adopted for this level are:

1 *Diversity* (semantic) – the combination of the number of household types and the profile of distribution over the set (formal). In order to be useful, this indicator should be contextualized in relation to other typologies of pre-industrial societies. Since we are assuming that the 100 people are keeping the original pattern of a 'developed' society, the population is equally spread over the different three types, in spite of the fact that some of them – e.g. the elderly – are net consumers of energy (they require not only food but also working hours in service, without delivering anything in relation to these two categories). As a matter of fact, this pattern of a 'spread profile of distribution' represents a great burden on the dynamic budget – a burden that can only be maintained (i) in the scenario with a low diet quality, and (ii) by imposing a very severe 'workload' on the individual adults. For this reason, in actual pre-industrial societies it is normal to find a very skewed profile of distribution, with a very large fraction of those household types that provide a net surplus – e.g. farmers paying taxes – and a limited fraction of household types representing a net loss in food energy terms – e.g. in the form of a small amount of rulers rather than powerless elderly people.

2 *Adequate services* (semantic) – the ratio between: (i) the actual delivery of hours in HA_{WS} – supply; and (ii) the hours that would be required in HA_{WS} – the requirement (formal). From the figure it is clear that in relation to this indicator we have a situation of lack of feasibility, at this level, in the scenario, which is assuming a high-quality diet (Diet B).

3 *Education* (semantic) – the ratio between the actual delivery of hours of HA_{WS} which are allocated to education and the hours describing the requirement (formal). Also in relation to this indicator, it is clear that we have a situation of lack of feasibility, at the household level, in the scenario assuming a high-quality diet (Diet B).

Level of the whole social system (level n)

The criteria for this level (the lower left quadrant of Figure 8.7) have been already discussed on p. 208. Looking at Figure 8.7, we can see that the adoption of Diet B, with an excessive requirement of hours of work for food, not only makes it impossible to deliver enough work to cover the required service hours but also implies an excessive saturation of the requirement of available work just for delivering the required food supply. This translates into a clear fragility in case of perturbations over the dynamic budget.

Level of the ecosystem embedding the social system (level n + 1)

The copy of the Microsoft Excel™ spreadsheet illustrated in Figure 8.6 does not include information referring to the environmental loading. This requires the use of another set of categories referring to the use of the *fund* land. It is only when adopting a different multilevel matrix dealing with land use that it becomes possible to link it with the characterization of societal metabolism – referring to the *fund* human activity. In this way it becomes possible to study the interference that human activity entails on the metabolism of the ecosystems embedding the society. For reasons of space, the analysis and the grammar referring to land use are not presented here. The data reported in Figure 8.7 are briefly discussed when describing the analysis of the impredicative loop in relation to Environmental Loading.

The tension among levels within an impredicative loop in metabolic systems

The simple example of 100 people on a remote island indicates clearly the presence of a tension between the different definitions of performance adopted by the different metabolic units operating at different levels. In this example, maintaining a diversity of households is paid for by severe stress, in terms of workload, on the individuals. On the other hand, adopting a high-quality diet, while good for the individuals, could prove fatal for the system as a whole, entailing a failure to achieve a balanced dynamic budget. Note that the metabolic system has within the regulations of each level a certain margin of buffering. For example, if there is an emergency – another plane, full of babies, crashes, say – the individual level may be additionally squeezed. Even if already operating at the maximum level of stress in relation to the chosen categories [(i) Education and Leisure (semantic) and hours in HA_{EL} (formal) – at the minimum value of 2 hours/day], adults could still reduce their sleeping time – cutting into another category: the Physiological Overhead. In the same way, at the household level we can expect an adjustment either in the profile of distribution over the given household type, for example by reducing the number of households that are net consumers of hours in working time, or by changing the rules (definition of the set of types), requiring the people aged over 65 to contribute as much as possible to the chores associated with food supply.

To conclude the discussion of this example, we can say that in spite of the 'heroic simplifications' (Georgescu-Roegen 1971: 212) adopted in the quantification of the impredicative loop associated with the dynamic budget of food energy of 100 people on a remote island, it is possible to see clearly the integration power of this approach. Particularly important is the ability to check simultaneously the performance of the system at different levels. In this way it becomes possible to detect the level of stress affecting the different metabolic units at different levels in the system. This is important, since a socio-economic system can collapse at any one of its levels of organization. In the case of the Soviet Union, for example, a collapse took place at what we would call the household level, when the guards of the Berlin Wall simply stopped being 'guards of the Berlin Wall'. The macroeconomic parameters of the Soviet Union were not good, but they were not the cause of the sudden collapse of that system. It was the loss of 'feeling of belonging' to the socio-economic system, at the household level, that helped operationalize the collapse. In turn, this loss of a feeling of belonging was at least partly due to the fact that households in communist Europe were experiencing themselves as having a 'performance' (i.e. quality of life) much lower than households in Western Europe. If the Soviet Empire had been surrounded by countries with a much lower quality of life, probably it would have lasted much longer.

The vision of a tool kit of integrated analysis of sustainability based on the MuSIASEM multi-purpose grammar

So far we have been describing the approach as applied only to the dynamic budget of food energy of a simple society of 100 people living in a remote island. However, there are many applications of this approach for studying the metabolism of societies characterized by 'high exosomatic energy consumption' and 'low exosomatic energy consumption'. Addressing the relation between economic and biophysical flows across levels and scales follows the seminal idea of bioeconomics proposed by Georgescu-Roegen. In particular, in recent years we have tried to couple the analysis based on a lexicon of categories for the *fund* element Human Activity, with a lexicon of categories for the *fund* element Land. This makes it possible to establish an additional link between the changes in the characteristics of societal metabolism and the changes in the interference that human activity entails for the expected pattern of ecosystem metabolism.

Just to give an example of how this type of analysis can be made more complex by adding different levels and dimensions of analysis (which include also a multilevel matrix over the *fund* element 'land' to be used for land use analysis), we provide in what follows an overview of how the MuSIASEM approach can be used within a Participatory Integrated Assessment of sustainability issues. Obviously, we do not expect the reader to understand the overview of Figure 8.8 in all its details. The goal is rather that of providing an overview of how the various pieces can all be fitted together. In fact, Figure 8.8 contains

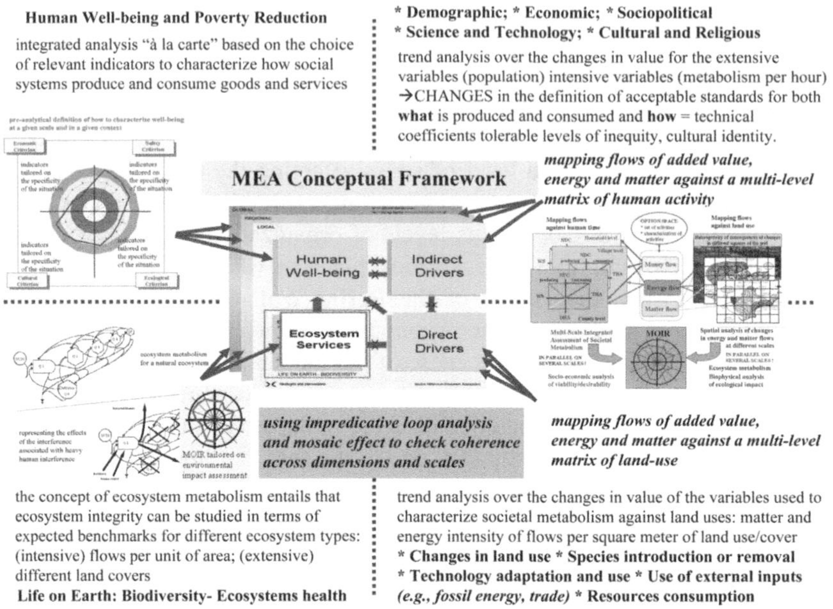

Figure 8.8 An overview of a tool kit of integrated analysis.

elements not presented above but used in other MuSIASEM applications, and shows where a tool under development is envisioned to be heading.

This particular application refers to a possible implementation of the conceptual framework adopted by Millennium Ecosystem Assessment.

Conclusions

As was discussed in the introduction, the special challenge associated with the concept of science for governance entails an important paradigm shift in the generation of quantitative analysis. In particular, we endorse here the call for a paradigm shift associated with the concept of 'post-normal science' (Funtowicz and Ravetz 1990, 1993; Funtowicz *et al.* 1998). Such a shift can be described as a movement away from the following list of assumptions:

Assumptions typical of the 'normal science' paradigm: Scientists must crunch numbers to individuate the best course of action.

1 It is possible to obtain a sound and reliable 'issue definition, problem structuring, and pre-analytical choice of narratives', which will be then agreed upon by those who use the results of the scientific analysis.
2 The role of the scientist is that of using a given 'issue definition, problem structuring, and pre-analytical choice of narratives' for generating models, analyses, data and indicators capable of determining the optimal choice.

3 An acceptable quality of the narratives and acceptable low levels of ignorance can be guaranteed by using more complicated models and larger computational power.

Assumptions that should be adopted in the 'post-normal science' paradigm: Scientists must crunch numbers to check the relevance and usefulness of the narratives.

1 It is necessary to build a different epistemological approach to deal with becoming systems which operate across different hierarchical levels on multiple scales.
2 It is necessary to look for innovative analytical approaches that can handle the unavoidable ambiguity implied by the use of non-equivalent descriptive domains (= integrated analysis dealing with different dimensions of sustainability) and with the evolving perceptions and representations of processes of becoming on multiple scales at different paces.
3 Quantitative analysis of sustainability should provide a qualitative check on the relevance and usefulness of the selected narratives and scenarios.

We believe that the two conceptual tools presented in this chapter, when used to perform a Multi-Scale Integrated Analysis of Societal and Ecosystem Metabolism, represent a step in the direction of this paradigm shift. However, these analytical tools, which are good for crunching numbers, should always be associated with participatory processes that can check the relevance of the narratives and scenarios associated with that number crunching – both in the step of issue definition ('upstreaming' stakeholder participation in the design of the science; see Wilsdon and Willis 2004) and in the step of deliberating which narratives and/or scenarios to keep, which to change and which new ones to add. Combining multi-purpose grammar and impredicative loop analysis with participation is an important next step in the development and application of this approach.

References

Boserup, E. 1965. *The Conditions of Agricultural Growth: The Economics of Agrarian Change under Population Pressure*. London: George Allen & Unwin.

Box, G.E.P. 1979. 'Robustness is the strategy of scientific model building.' In *Robustness in Statistics*, ed. R.L. Launer and G.N. Wilkinson. New York: Academic Press.

Ehrlich, P.R. 1968. *The Population Bomb*. New York: Ballantine Books.

Funtowicz, S.O. and J.R. Ravetz. 1990b. 'Post-normal science: a new science for new times.' *Scientific European* 266: 20–22.

Funtowicz, S.O. and J.R. Ravetz. 1993. 'Science for the post-normal age.' *Futures* 25(7): 739–755.

Funtowicz, S.O., J.R. Ravetz and M. O'Connor. 1998. 'Challenges in the use of science for sustainable development.' *International Journal of Sustainable Development* 1(1): 99–107.

Georgescu-Roegen, N. 1971. *The Entropy Law and the Economic Process*. Cambridge, MA: Harvard University Press.

Giampietro, M. 1997. 'Linking technology, natural resources, and the socioeconomic structure of human society: a theoretical model.' In *Advances in Human Ecology*, vol. 6, ed. L. Freese. Greenwich, CT: JAI Press.

Giampietro, M. 2003. *Multi-scale Integrated Analysis of Agroecosystems*. Boca Raton, FL: CRC Press.

Giampietro, M. and K. Mayumi. 2000. 'Societal metabolism part 1 of 2: introduction of the analytical tool in theory, examples, and validation of basic assumptions.' *Population and Environment* 22(2): 97–254.

Giampietro, M. and K. Mayumi. 2001. 'Societal metabolism part 2 of 2: specific applications to case studies.' *Population and Environment* 22(3): 257–352.

Giampietro, M., S.G.F. Bukkens and D. Pimentel. 1993. 'Labor productivity: a biophysical definition and assessment.' *Human Ecology* 21(3): 229–260.

Giampietro, M., S.G.F. Bukkens and D. Pimentel. 1997. 'Linking technology, natural resources, and the socioeconomic structure of human society: examples and applications.' In *Advances in Human Ecology*, vol. 6, ed. L. Freese. Greenwich, CT: JAI Press.

Giampietro, M., T.F.H. Allen and K. Mayumi. 2006a. 'Science for governance: the implications of the complexity revolution.' In *Interfaces between Science and Society*, ed. A. Guimarães-Pereira, S. Guedes Vaz and S. Tognetti. Sheffield: Greenleaf Publishing.

Giampietro, M., T.F.H. Allen and K. Mayumi. 2006b. 'The epistemological predicament associated with purposive quantitative analysis.' *Ecological Complexity* 3(4): 307–327.

Giampietro, M., Mayumi, K. and Sorman, A.H. 2011. *The Metabolic Pattern of Society: Where the economists fall short.* London: Routledge.

Giampietro, M., Mayumi, K. and Sorman, A.H. 2012 (in press). *Energy Analysis for a Sustainable Future: Multi-Scale Integrated Analysis of Societal and Ecosystem Metabolism*. London: Routledge.

Gomiero, T. and M. Giampietro. 2005. 'Graphic tools for data representation in integrated analysis of farming systems.' *International Journal of Global Environmental Issues* 5(3/4): 264–301.

Kauffman, S.A. 1993. *The Origins of Order: Self-Organization and Selection in Evolution*. New York: Oxford University Press.

Keynes, J.M. 1936. *The General Theory of Employment, Interest and Money*. London: Macmillan, for the Royal Economic Society.

Malthus, T.R. 1778. *An Essay on Population*. London.

Maturana, H.R. and F. Varela. 1980. *Autopoiesis and Cognition: The Realization of the Living*. Dordrecht, the Netherlands: D. Reidel.

Munda, G. 2004. 'Social Multi-Criteria Evaluation (SMCE): methodological foundations and operational consequences.' *European Journal of Operational Research* 158(3): 662–677.

Nijkamp, P. and R. Vreeker. 2000. 'Sustainability assessment of development scenarios: methodology and application to Thailand.' *Ecological Economics* 33(1): 7–27.

Odum, H.T. 1971. *Environment, Power and Society*. New York: John Wiley.

Polimeni, J., K. Mayumi, M. Giampietro and B. Alcott. 2008. *Jevons' Paradox: the Myth of Resource Efficiency Improvements*. London: Earthscan Research Edition.

Ramos-Martin, J., M. Giampietro and K. Mayumi. 2007. 'On China's exosomatic energy metabolism: an application of multi-scale integrated analysis of societal metabolism (MSIASM).' *Ecological Economics* 63(1): 174–191.

Rosen, R. 1985. *Anticipatory Systems: Philosophical, Mathematical and Methodological Foundations*. New York: Pergamon Press.

Rosen, R. 1991. *Life Itself: A Comprehensive Inquiry into the Nature, Origin and Fabrication of Life*. New York: Columbia University Press.
Rosen, R. 1998. *Essays on Life Itself*. New York: Columbia University Press.
Schumpeter, J.A. 1954. *History of Economic Analysis*. London: George Allen & Unwin.
Stern, N. 2006. *The Economics of Climate Change: The Stern Review*. Cambridge: Cambridge University Press (on behalf of Cabinet Office – HM Treasury).
Ulanowicz, R.E. 1986. *Growth and Development: Ecosystem Phenomenology*. New York: Springer.
Varela, F.G., H.R. Maturana and R. Uribe. 1974. 'Autopoiesis: the organization of living systems, its characterization and a model.' *BioSystems* 5(4): 187–196.
Wilsdon, J. and R. Willis. 2004. *See-through Science: Why Public Engagement Needs to Move Upstream*. London: Demos.

Part III

Into the woods

Mapping the challenges and the possibilities for continuing the development of methods that extend beyond reductionism

9 Looking for a place to anchor

Confusing thoughts along an interdisciplinary dissertation journey

Minna Santaoja, Raphael Treffny, Cordula Mertens and Catherine Jolibert with Katharine N. Farrell

Introduction

Writing a doctoral dissertation is always a challenge. There is probably no PhD candidate who has not struggled with formulating a good research question, writing a convincing research proposal, managing time and research design, coming up with a neat literature review, collecting suitable data, developing analysis and writing up results. Here, we will not go into detail about the challenge of making sense of the bits and pieces of data acquired over the years, which eventually leads to handing in a dissertation that brings a bit of something new into science. There is a multitude of books in which authors have made it their business to lend a hand to the confused minds of PhD students. This text here is about another kind of struggle, one that is growing increasingly common, as more and more PhD candidates are working on interdisciplinary or multidisciplinary research projects, particularly in the context of doing science for sustainable development (Kates *et al.* 2001; Farrell *et al.* 2005; Meadowcroft *et al.* 2005). The first part is written in the present tense, in the form of a sort of 'field report', and is then followed by reflections, analysis and lessons learned.

The ideas presented in this chapter are inspired by the experiences of nine PhD students working in an interdisciplinary European research project called GoverNat, in which we were struggling with the additional hurdles associated with creating an inter-, trans- or multidisciplinary dissertation that stays true to its own objectives while still attracting the benevolence of traditional academic institutions and peer reviewers. Our aim here is to sketch out the situations that we have encountered and to share the lessons that we have learned in the course of facing these challenges, in the hope that other students and their supervisors can benefit from our experience. At the close of this chapter we present a typology of some major challenges arising from interdisciplinary sustainability science work and, reflecting on our experiences, we make some suggestions about how they can be managed and even turned into opportunities.

We begin with a short introduction to the GoverNat research network and some background on our place within it, which we provide by noting our respective points of entry into the research network. Our varied backgrounds (biologist, ecologist, geographer, engineer turned social scientist) brought us to this shared research context from very different directions, and that alone has already created a lot of creative confusion among us. This diversity of backgrounds, we think, is a challenge special to sustainability science and one that others setting sail into these waters are also likely to encounter. In the main part of this chapter we discuss the challenges and opportunities that we have encountered. In addition to discussing the challenges of interdisciplinarity, we also talk, at times, about challenges associated with conducting intercultural research. We do this for two reasons: first, because it is part of our experience, since the research field for GoverNat covers all of Europe and each of us is conducting case study research in a country that is not our own; and second, because we understand cultural diversity to be a basic characteristic of the complex international regions that are the subjects of environmental governance. At times it has been hard for us to tell whether some troubles we have encountered are caused by the interdisciplinarity of our work or by doing research in another country, so we talk about both challenges as parts of the more general challenge of conducting interdisciplinary environmental science research. We conclude our chapter with some reflections on the strategies that we have each developed to address these challenges in our PhD work, present a typology of major challenges and provide a survival guide list for other PhD students and teachers setting out to work together on similarly complex sustainability science PhD projects.

The GoverNat project and our respective points of entry to interdisciplinarity

GoverNat is a four-year research and training project funded as a Marie Curie Research Training Network under the Sixth Framework Programme of the European Commission's Directorate-General for Research. Generally, GoverNat focuses on multilevel governance of natural resources, with the concrete aim of developing tools and processes for water and biodiversity governance in Europe. The project work is focused mainly on investigating progress and proceedings in the implementation of the European Union Water Framework Directive and Habitats and Birds Directives in various EU member states. In the call for PhD applications it was announced that the early-stage researchers wanting to join the project should ideally have an interdisciplinary background in social sciences. The project aimed to achieve a mix of academic upbringings, attracting and accepting as PhD candidates people with degrees and backgrounds from social and/or natural sciences. A brief overview of our own backgrounds and motivations illustrates the mix.

Four backgrounds and four motivations

Minna Santaoja (M.S.) likes to describe herself as an environmental social scientist who in her 'previous life' was an environmental engineer. After a couple of years of work experience in the field, she was not satisfied with the job opportunities offered by the technical education and took up studies in environmental policy to widen her understanding of environmental problems and their solutions. She finished the interdisciplinary Master's course at the University of Tampere in Finland in 2005 and was then working in research and other projects until joining GoverNat in April 2007. During her environmental policy studies, Minna also became active in environmental NGOs, which shaped her research interests towards public participation and the difficulties of integrating different kinds of knowledge and values in natural resource governance. She is currently employed by the Institute of Social Sciences at the University of Stuttgart in southern Germany. Finding her place in relation to the German sociological tradition, with such an interdisciplinary background as her foundation, has been a troublesome journey for Minna. Indeed, this is what sparked the initial discussion on the topic addressed in this chapter. She thought her interdisciplinary background matched perfectly with the aims of an interdisciplinary project like GoverNat until the reality revealed itself to be slightly more complicated.

Because of his strong interest in environment-related issues, Raphael Treffny (R.T.) decided to specialize in geography while still in high school. Wanting to learn more about the relationship between humans and the natural environment, Raphael conducted his studies with a mixed focus, including both physical and human geography. Eventually equipped with a first degree in geography, he still felt discontented with the explanations and solutions offered for understanding the relationship between social and natural reality, and decided to do an MSc in sustainable resource management. During the coursework, Raphael specialized in biodiversity as well as land and water management with a particular focus on participatory planning techniques. With this interdisciplinary background he felt perfectly prepared for the focus and the interdisciplinary nature of the GoverNat project. However, having been placed for a year in the Geography Department at Lancaster University, he has realized that the interdisciplinary nature of GoverNat poses challenges that he had not anticipated. This is especially the case when writing a dissertation that needs to get assessed by a review committee based within a particular discipline: when the core of the research cuts across various different disciplines, it seems that even the relatively safe harbour of an interdisciplinary field like geography leaves one exposed.

Cordula Mertens (C.M.) studied biology, focusing on zoology and plant ecology. Since the biology courses alone were a bit too one-sided for her interests, she took several language courses and chose history of science as an extra minor. So, next to her upbringing in a more natural-science-focused tradition, she had already had a taste of social sciences before joining GoverNat. After graduating from university, she worked as a volunteer at the Food and Agriculture Organization of the United Nations (FAO) with a project about traditional agricultural systems (GIAHS: Globally Important Agriculture Heritage Systems, an FAO initiative supported by the Global Environment Facility). Now Cordula is a member of the Environmental Social Science Research Group at St Istvan University in Gödöllő, Hungary, where there is a special emphasis on action research (Balázs *et al.* 2005; Reason and Bradbury 2006). Although she was aware from the start that she would be working on a social science PhD addressing the topic of natural resource management, and knew that combining social and natural science research was going to be demanding, Cordula has been surprised by the way natural science is spoken of in some social science circles. She regards natural and social science as complementary lines of inquiry and is disturbed by the way in which social and natural scientists seem so often to express frustration and disrespect towards each other, where they should try to respect each other's expertise in the respective field and look for a fruitful exchange in which all researchers could learn more and together contribute to solving problems.

Catherine Jolibert (C.J.) has a background in cell biology and physiology and a Master's degree in evolutionary biology and ecology. She has worked as a lecturer in ecology for an undergraduate degree course in the management and protection of nature, as a teacher in natural sciences at high school level, as one of the coordinators and also a contributing author for the 2002 *Rapport sur l'État de l'Environnement en France*, produced by the Institut Français de l'Environnement (IFEN), which covered thirty themes related to the environment, and finally as project manager for the French Ministry of Environment, before joining GoverNat. Catherine is working at the Institute of Environmental Science and Technology at the Universitat Autònoma de Barcelona. In her PhD she is focusing on the interactions between European biodiversity research communities and stakeholders, in an effort to help improve science–policy interfaces for biodiversity governance. She is therefore drawing on several disciplines, including social science ones. With an exclusively natural science training, Catherine has occasionally felt lost in the social science domain, but she sees the issue of loss of biodiversity as inherently interdisciplinary and views the challenges of this situation as something she is simply going to need to work with and manage.

Following rather different paths to the GoverNat project, all four of us thought of ourselves as rather a good match with the project aims. Now, in retrospect, that seems to highlight the different understandings we had concerning the task ahead of us. We were excited about doing a PhD as a part of a project with common aims, unaware of the turbulent discussions we would face regarding those aims. What followed for us was an initial disappointment upon realizing that instead of making things smooth, being part of an interdisciplinary sustainability science network seemed to make the PhD process even more demanding. In the following pages we describe the challenges we faced at the beginning of the GoverNat project, which eventually left us feeling empowered by our transformation from passive participants to owners of the process.

Opportunities and challenges in the GoverNat project

The GoverNat network, which is coordinated by the Helmholtz Centre for Environmental Research – UFZ in Leipzig, consists of ten partner institutes throughout Europe and several affiliated praxis partners. Besides the lead scientists at the partner institutes, there are nine early-stage researchers (PhD students, fellows) and three postdoctoral researchers (postdocs, fellows) in the programme.

The nine early-stage researchers are contributing work to the project at large but are also focused on their individual PhDs, and it is up to each fellow to design their work in such a way that the project tasks also serve their PhD aims. The PhD positions are funded for three years. The overall objective of GoverNat is to develop new solutions for multilevel environmental governance challenges and to facilitate their use by decision-makers in an enlarged European Union. Specifically, the project aims to contribute towards the design of new and improved environmental governance, and, since it is a research and training network, GoverNat aims to achieve this overall objective both by carrying out research and by training the GoverNat fellows in how to design legitimate and effective procedures and practices for environmental governance participation and communication between policy-makers, scientists and the general public.

GoverNat is a complex endeavour. It constitutes a mixture of research and training, operates across no fewer than seven countries, and has no fewer than thirteen different studies under way. It cannot be considered purely as a training network because it has a set of specific research objectives; neither can it be regarded fully as a research project because one of its primary tasks is training the GoverNat fellows. Throughout the course of the project there are a number of schools and training courses, and the fellows can also get training at the institutes where they are based. The topics that the fellows are investigating need to fit into the overall GoverNat research plan and the work needs to serve the project's overarching research objectives. Finally, the environmental governance systems in the various case study countries and in the European Union as a whole are being studied not only individually but also in comparison with each other.

While many challenges that we are facing in our work are just part and parcel of doing a PhD, we think there are several challenges that are directly related to the fact that we are working on sustainability science research topics that concern relationships between social and ecological systems. In the remainder of this section we discuss some of them in detail.

Working away from home: challenges in multicultural interdisciplinary environmental research

Marie Curie funding aims to promote the mobility of young researchers, which meant in practice that the GoverNat fellows had to move country. Doing research in a country other than one's own is becoming more and more common, especially in sustainability science. After all, the issues in sustainability science are often inherently international (for example, pollution does not respect borders) and therefore the research needs to be conducted in a way that takes global and international issues into account. In keeping with this international focus, although living in a foreign country many of the GoverNat fellows were attracted by the idea of including their home country within the comparative case studies for the project. Of course, it also makes sense to include the countries where we are working, but we found cultural differences arising as obstacles to empirical research, so that we were not always free to choose comparisons on purely scientific grounds. One is also limited by what is possible: what languages one can speak; where one can gain access to the people and information needed to carry out the study, etc. Time concerns also pop up here; three years is a tight schedule for any PhD, but it is especially short in a multicultural, interdisciplinary setting. For example, GoverNat fellows who did not speak the language of their host country well enough to conduct research in that language have had to devote a lot of time to language training. While these examples from our experiences as GoverNat scholars are very specific to our situation, they highlight a more general set of social and physical challenges that come with any interdisciplinary environmental and social science research work that sets out to compare and look at the relationships between different countries and cultures: taking cultural diversity into account is a practical as well as a conceptual matter.

While these kinds of challenges arise in various environmental science settings, say for example when Europeans are studying wildlife management systems in Africa, doing research in a country that is not your own poses particular challenges for the empirical work of social scientists. For example, being a foreigner, how do you explain and justify your research to local people? And how do you interpret their reactions and responses to your questions? In GoverNat this is further complicated by the fact that we are studying participatory processes, and understanding them requires that we get a clear idea of how people in the locality perceive these processes – that we develop close contact with local actors. Are we willing or able to engage in local debates and discourses? Are we ready and able to bring our research results back to the local community for corroboration and critique? To make decisions about which language and in what kind of format this should be done? Or are we content with just extracting material for our PhDs from these local communities and reporting about it to the European Union and the international scientific community? In this kind of work, such verification and discussion of research results seem to us to be necessary: first of all, because promise of due regard is required in order to build the trust that is needed to gain access to information about participation processes, but also because it is a matter of ethical treatment of our research subjects. While ethical treatment of research subjects is always an issue, in our case it is particularly important, because GoverNat plans to conduct policy experiments in the later stages of the project, based on the results and insights gained from the researchers' initial studies and their analysis of participation in European multilevel environmental governance. This raises ethical questions regarding how and on what grounds the researchers should proceed to make interventions that might lead to experiments, how the windows of opportunity for doing so may be located, and whether (and if so, when) it is ethical to use them.

As tricky as acquiring the data required for our multicultural and interdisciplinary GoverNat case studies is, interpreting those data and generating results and conclusions from data covering multiple disciplines, often gathered within a foreign setting, poses even more significant challenges. Can one actually trust one's data, or oneself with the responsibility of interpreting the data? Being an outsider to the country, its culture and the local setting may be an advantage: one may see things from a different perspective as compared with the locals, which does allow for new and innovative ways of interpreting what is going on. But at the same time we feel a need to stay true to the context in which we collect the data and we are obliged to fit our findings into the bigger European environmental governance picture. This means that alongside our basic research data, the country's history, its particular institutional regimes and political culture must also be taken into consideration. How much time does a researcher need to devote to background study in order to be able to interpret cross-country comparative interdisciplinary social-ecological research data correctly, or at least intelligibly and within its context(s)? How long does one have to live in a country in order to gain a basic understanding about what is going on?

Because of the cross-border nature of environmental problems, international cooperation has been an everyday reality to many environmental scientists for a while now. But as our example illustrates, it does not work by simply packing your bags and starting as usual in the new place. A due consideration of the new cultural context is necessary.

Learning interdisciplinary communication: our GoverNat experience

Since the fellows (PhD students and postdocs) in GoverNat do most of the research work in the project, the variety of backgrounds and skills that they bring to GoverNat has had a considerable impact on how the project is developing. Many of the motivations, aims and strategies of the research project were opened up for discussion during the early stages of the work, as we worked to get to know each other and our research subject. Discussions were held in order to gain a common understanding about the nature of the project and of how each of the fellows would be able to contribute to the undertaking in a fruitful way.

Originally, GoverNat was described as an interdisciplinary project that would combine concepts from economics, political and legal sciences, as well as from ecology, hydrology, philosophy and sociology. In the course of the process of developing GoverNat, less emphasis was put on the natural sciences, with a stronger focus on bringing together ideas from economics, political science, law, sociology and philosophy. The dual focus on nature and society was a point of attraction for us when we joined the project. Its conceptualization within the project has led to discussions among the fellows concerning how 'nature' can be understood, and the role of natural science in supporting our studies of the governance of natural resources. For example, among the four GoverNat PhD fellows writing this chapter, we all have some background in the natural sciences and would, of course, like to make use of this in our GoverNat research. To us it seems clear that this is appropriate, since natural environment and natural resources are an important part of what GoverNat is concerned with, but translating this into practical research work has proved difficult. We find that it is a mission impossible to convert 100 per cent from a natural into a social scientist in three years, and we are not even so sure that that is what we want to do. And whatever changes we make, they have to be working for us inside the three years, so that we also have the time to make a good PhD. In an interdisciplinary and multicultural project that addresses the interlinkages between nature and society there is enough material to sort through without having to add a whole new training on top. We think that there must be some kind of a middle ground where we can use the skills that we have already developed and learn additional skills specific to the interdisciplinary work that we aim to carry out.

As we searched together for this middle ground, the question of how 'nature' is conceptualized turned out to have a huge impact on the focus taken within each of our individual PhD projects and on our decisions about what methods would be necessary and adequate for obtaining suitable empirical data. Looking back, we can see that in confronting this question we were faced with a fundamental environmental policy problem: trying to determine whether we are evaluating natural resource governance from a process point of view (e.g. assessing the quality of different types and instances of participation) or from an outcome point of view (e.g. assessing the effectiveness of protection measures developed in participative settings). In the end, we could not find clear grounds within the GoverNat project plan for choosing one or the other approach, so we chose on the basis of our interests and abilities, often being unwilling to choose and looking at both the processes and their outcomes. Looking back, it seems that the need to simplify such complexity is something that every student interested in interdisciplinary problems must face in order to make a manageable PhD.

Finding a common framework

The original idea of the GoverNat project was to focus on governance processes, but many of the fellows felt that the governance processes as such had no meaning unless we also looked at the ecological outcomes of these processes. Here, the different ontologies behind the many different disciplinary perspectives that we brought to the project started to reveal themselves. The fellows with a natural science background felt that they could make a considerable contribution on this point and pushed the idea. People with backgrounds in social sciences felt that close study of the ecological outcomes of these processes would possibly fall outside the scope of the project and might require natural science research. However, this situation also revealed the confusion that can arise when people are working from different ontologies, since the fellows with a natural scientific background were clear about the social scientific nature of the project and did not expect to conduct empirical natural scientific research but rather to read reports and make use of the results from research done by other scientists. For our part, being four fellows with varying degrees of natural science training, we view our role in the GoverNat project as one of bridging the gap between natural science and social science, interpreting natural scientific data and results for social science purposes. However, this is a point that required considerable effort to communicate.

In order to ensure that comparable data were available for the project-wide European-level environmental governance analysis, the GoverNat research applies a common conceptual framework to all the individual research projects through which all the case studies in the various EU member states are to be analysed. Once we overcame the initial confusion about whether or not natural science research would be conducted, each fellow set out to develop their own research approach and plan, with their own unique interdisciplinary take and their own ontology of the relationships between nature, policy, civil society and economy. However, even with this framework as a reference, there was still a lot of confusion about how all the individual projects would fit together within it in order to produce the interdisciplinary and cross-country comparative analysis results.

Eventually, it was agreed that the GoverNat framework, which was substantially revised in the first year of the project, should not be applied strictly but should be employed as a theoretical heuristic, with implications for how the work of each of the fellows is structured. Not everybody felt able to place their own work within the framework, and not everybody felt comfortable with the assumption that our research would judge the quality of participatory governance processes or with the aim of conducting policy experiments. It was agreed that the experiments could be done also theoretically through interviews. In short, we found that our diversity of ontological perspectives on the GoverNat topic was accompanied by a diversity of epistemological perspectives regarding how the topic could be best understood and a diversity of methodological perspectives regarding how the research into the topic should itself be carried out.

'Nature' in social sciences

The purpose of developing a common framework for the GoverNat project was to facilitate interdisciplinary communication and the effective combination of research results coming from a range of disciplinary contexts. Eventually, a system theoretical model was taken as the basis of the new framework, and a focus on distinctions between economic, social, political and cultural systems was adopted. Fellows who had developed their approaches mainly as social science projects were able to place their work relatively easily within the framework, mostly at the interlinks between the different systems. However, the natural system, now included in the background, was not originally included in the revised framework, and the fellows with a natural science background felt that their work had somehow been written out of the plans. Even now, the particular approach adopted in the GoverNat framework does not recognize nature as a separate system but assumes that it is a background context for the four systems of society. This choice of how to conceptualize the relationship between human society and nature has posed a considerable problem for us, as fellows with a natural scientific background and orientation, and we have had difficulties adhering to the framework when doing the case studies. Upon reflection, we think this difficulty is related to the fact that we view 'nature', or the biophysical environment, as a primary object of study and as a change agent (albeit an unconscious one) in environmental governance. Being required always to subsume 'nature' into one of the various societal systems feels to us as though we are losing it in a social scientific void. We have each developed our own strategies for understanding the place and agency of biophysical systems in environmental governance but it still remains unclear to us what exactly it means to take the system of 'nature' into account in an analysis based on the GoverNat framework. We raise this point here because we think our struggle with understanding the place of 'nature' in environmental governance reflects a challenge that must be faced by any researchers concerned with the interdisciplinary study of complex social-ecological systems.

While there seemed to be an agreement within the project regarding the importance of biophysical systems and of understanding natural processes, since this is the vital basis for all human activities, natural scientific knowledge about the resources to be managed was not viewed as necessary for doing the research. In our view this led to a degree of imbalance in the interdisciplinary training that is taking place within the project, with natural-science-trained fellows being expected to learn about social science but social science fellows not being expected to increase their natural scientific knowledge regarding the objects of natural resource governance. While the social science orientation of GoverNat was more or less clear from the beginning, this perceived imbalance in the ontology of the project seems to us to have somewhat undermined its interdisciplinarity potential, with the interdisciplinary crew of GoverNat being somewhat split into two: between social and natural scientists. This split can even be seen in the bias of this chapter: the opportunity to participate in the joint effort of this writing was offered to all nine PhD and all three postdoc fellows, but all of us who have ended up contributing have either some sort of natural scientific background or a specific research interest relating to the bridging of the gap between natural and social science. So, we find that even here, in our attempt to problematize the topic of how social and physical scientific contributions are combined within GoverNat research, we again bump into the consequences of this diversity of ontologies, the diversity of conceptualizations of human–nature relationships, which seems to us to be a key part of the GoverNat and indeed of the sustainability science adventure.

Being a self-selected, natural-science-biased sub-set of the GoverNat fellows community, we can freely proceed to argue that research intended to provide solutions to fix something that is perceived by humans as being environmentally problematic has to have interdisciplinary collaboration between social and natural scientists at its core. This is because the causal chains behind environmental problems are both physically and socially complex. It is now generally accepted that the reductionism and monodisciplinary approaches that have contributed to the creation of these problems are not sufficient to solve them (Rhoten and Parker 2004), so we do not propose to argue that point here. But we find within GoverNat that we need to repeatedly emphasize the importance of understanding natural processes in analysing the consequences of environmental governance. The fundamental question here seems to be a philosophical one: whether there is a separate 'nature' outside society, or vice versa, a separate society outside nature. Mostly we have adopted ecosocial or hybrid views, where the two cannot be seen as separate, and this leads us unavoidably to interdisciplinary research, where we are now discovering fundamental theoretical as well as methodological problems that are still very far from being resolved.

The role of natural scientific knowledge within biodiversity governance is a primary point of interest for two of us: C.J. is looking at how European biodiversity research projects engage with stakeholders and is exploring what are the consequences of these engagements for biodiversity governance; M.S. is interested in the practices of the biodiversity knowledge networks and the role of amateur naturalists therein. In both contexts, special challenges associated with collecting the required data have arisen, with respect both to the specification of what data are required and regarding how to gain access to those data. For example, M.S. has discovered that the boundaries between amateurs and professionals, or laypeople and experts, on biodiversity are not at all as clear as might at first be expected. From our perspective, it seems that in social scientific research on natural resource management, the natural scientific knowledge being referenced is often assumed to be complete and correct. If it is viewed critically, it is because it is dominant in relation to other types of knowledge, because it is seen to be crowding out non-science knowledge. However, our experience as natural scientists and our discovery of these blurry lines between amateur naturalists and scientific experts call these presumptions into question. We do not assume that the natural scientific knowledge about our topics is either complete or necessarily correct, and we think this has implications for governance. It seems to us that an informed and critical understanding of available knowledge about the objects of environmental governance, about both the social and the natural processes involved, is required if one is to evaluate the quality of a given governance approach, since the governance tool needs to be appropriate for governing the objects that it targets (Farrell 2007: 15).

Although they are intertwined with human activities, in the end natural resource governance solutions are played out in very concrete terms, in the physical world, and they are subject to the laws of nature. To our thinking, the 'local' in multilevel governance includes not only the people involved in local governance but also local nature. Therefore, it would seem necessary to conceptualize nature here as also being an actor in the governance processes. In suggesting this, we are departing from mainstream disciplinary social sciences, but we are not without companions. We find that the route opened up by, say, Latour (2004, 2005) gives us a lot of options that are not available to us through more discipline-specific social science approaches. Our decision to treat 'nature' as an actor is a reflection of the interdisciplinary ontology that we have chosen to adopt in our research, where human–nature relationships are understood as complex, intertwined and reciprocal, and we propose that this ontology is important for analysing the human–nature interactions that lie at the heart of environmental governance. The following example of national park management illustrates this point.

Nature's role in natural resource management: a bark beetle outbreak in Bavaria

We see no way out of the trap in which we find ourselves; we must find a way to make our home between the natural and the social sciences, if these are the kinds of research questions we aim to address. Our view on the value of insights that can be gained through adopting such an ontology can be illustrated through reference to one of the case studies analysed within GoverNat: the 1995 bark beetle outbreak in the Bavarian Forest National Park. We propose that it is both reasonable and helpful to interpret the series of events in that case as an instance in which local nature stepped into the governance process as a powerful actor, significantly redefining relationships between stakeholders and substantially influencing the final outcome of the political debate.

In 1994–1995 a whole mountain ridge of spruce trees in the Bavarian Forest National Park, previously weakened by a severe storm, was attacked by bark beetles (*Ips typographus*). This national park was founded on the idea of protecting natural processes, with the aim of creating a primeval forest for the children and grandchildren of Bavarian residents, so the park administration decided not to intervene to stop the bark beetle's mass increase, since the bark beetle increase was a natural part of the forest's process of development. Seeing the dead grey-red furs of the mountain forests, local people were shocked by what they interpreted as the complete destruction of the forest. In the years 1996–1998 there were demonstrations against the national park administration by people opposed to the administration's decision not to intervene but to allow natural processes to go ahead, letting the old forest die. Alongside these protests, a discussion about enlarging the national park, initiated by the state government and Friends of the Earth Bavaria, began in 1996 – precisely at the time when the destruction of the old forest was most severe. There was strong opposition from the local community, but eventually, pressure from local interest groups and politicians at state and national levels led to a compromise: the park was enlarged but bark beetle management would continue in the new part of the park, in order to prevent destruction in the newly integrated areas. The state government, therefore, altered its original plans, putting the new part of the national park under only limited nature protection at first. This decision was a direct response to a political situation created by the decision to allow a normal course of deterioration and regeneration to take place in the older forest area within the park. Subsequently, the natural regrowth of the older forest in the park has changed its appearance, once again giving it the look of a 'Bavarian forest' that the local population expects – yet wilder and more natural than the old planted forest, so that the local population now increasingly identifies with the national park. Accompanying this change in appearance, which resulted from the forest going about its normal way of being a forest, the political controversy over the place of bark beetle management in the park management strategy has abated. In addition, since the middle of the 1990s communication between the national park administration and local stakeholders has significantly improved and today there is a general acceptance of the national park and cooperation between locals and park managers. Several programmes of the national park administration now specifically address local stakeholders, including special guided tours for the local population, and partnerships between the national park administration and the local tourism businesses.

Interpreting this case study as an instance of environmental governance, we propose that nature can in three ways be seen as a crucial actor influencing the decision-making process. First, the entirely natural destruction of the old forest by the mass increase in the bark beetle population triggered protest by local stakeholders, which forced the state government to make concessions and alter its plans regarding the enlargement of the national park. Second, the natural regrowth of the forest, which can now easily be seen after ten years, has soothed the fears of local people and quieted their protests. This can be understood as a factor helping to soften tensions and to make a resolution of the conflict between local people and the national park administration possible. Finally, the stakeholder consultation and community collaboration practices that are now part of the park management practice were developed as a response to stakeholder protests made during the period when there was controversy, which was spurred by the natural deterioration of the forest.

The idea that inanimate objects can be understood as actors is controversial but is also accepted within many areas of social science. For our purposes here we can refer to Latour's discussion of the idea, particularly as outlined in *Politics of Nature* (2004). Latour seeks a new definition for political ecology where the nature would not paralyse the politics, for in his thought we have never left the state of nature behind, and in order to aim for politics defined by progression towards a good common world, we need to understand the sciences as socializing non-humans. To give another example, using this approach Peltola (2006) has analysed a debate over the citing of a heating plant in Finland. Her analysis suggests that an esker, which was one possible location, assumed a crucial mediating role as a non-human political actor within the debate. The symbolic meanings of the esker as a part of the national landscape imagery contributed to the remoulding of the agenda of local energy production and opened up a way for new political choices, much in the same manner as in our bark beetle example. We do not mean to suggest that nature needs to be viewed as an intentional actor, but this does not stop us from viewing the natural dynamics of natural phenomena, like the deterioration of the old forest area in our example, as agents for change. Although there are precedents to the contrary (Latour 2004; Gunderson and Holling 2002), rigid academic distinctions between the natural and the social sciences seem to make it difficult to pay attention to the kinds of complex physical–social relationships that we feel are central to our understanding of environmental governance and natural resource management. We find it problematic to imagine that we should provide recommendations that are intended to generate a balance between nature and society but are based on dichotomizing them into two separate systems. Overcoming the strict limits of disciplinary distinctions would seem to allow for recognizing that constant change is an inherent characteristic not only within nature and within human relationships but also within relationships between humans and their environments. For us, one way to capture this recognition is to conceptualize nature as an actor within a set of complex human–nature relationship processes. It seems to us that understanding natural resource management challenges requires that we acknowledge and try to make sense of the blurred boundary between nature and human society, rather than avoiding it.

Interdisciplinary, transdisciplinary or out of discipline?

Within the GoverNat project, as in the wider sustainability science community, there seem to be a number of different interpretations of what interdisciplinarity actually means. For our purposes here, we suggest a working distinction between wide (between natural and social sciences) and narrow (within natural or within social sciences) interdisciplinarity. Such a separation allows us to make clearer the original aim of GoverNat, which was to conduct a form of narrow social science interdisciplinarity while drawing information input from natural sciences. Early confusion in the project highlighted an ambition, mainly stimulated by fellows with natural science backgrounds, towards wide interdisciplinarity. After the impossibility of fulfilling this ambition within GoverNat was accepted, the discussion has instead focused on reconciling different interpretations of how social science works with 'input from natural sciences', reflecting a narrow understanding of interdisciplinarity. Within the project there also seem to be differing levels of enthusiasm for embarking on interdisciplinary endeavours, and different views regarding what their aims should be. A guide to developing interdisciplinary research proposals distinguishes between two types of interdisciplinary research (Tait and Lyall 2007), one aiming to further the expertise and competence of academic disciplines themselves, for example through developments in methodology which enable new issues to be addressed or new disciplines or sub-disciplines to be formed, and the other being problem focused and addressing issues of social, technical and/or policy relevance, with less emphasis on discipline-related academic outcomes (see also Aram 2004). GoverNat, as a project, would seem to correspond to the latter, being designed to be policy-relevant research. For many of the fellows, this problem orientation is a source of motivation for our involvement in GoverNat, but we are still at a stage of our research careers where we need to prove ourselves, and for that, discipline-related outcomes are also important to us. On a day-to-day basis, as we prepare our PhD work, we are working within discipline-specific scholarly departments at universities and our research will eventually have to pass through a university review process. This raises a lot of uncertainties for us, because the criteria for evaluating problem-oriented and purely academic works are not always the same. Are the reviewers who will eventually judge our PhDs equipped to evaluate our interdisciplinary work?

In science, two developments seem to be going on in parallel: research is becoming more and more specialized, but at the same time there are calls for interdisciplinarity and a holistic understanding. The need for highly specific knowledge regarding detailed technical problems is ever more pertinent and must still be drawn from disciplinary research (Farrell *et al.* 2007). This is a source of inherent insecurity that seems to accompany the carrying out of interdisciplinary PhD work. As GoverNat PhDs, we ask ourselves questions like: even though working in an interdisciplinary project, should I still do a disciplinary PhD? How do I go about it, then, if my background is interdisciplinary or in another field? Is it even possible to be interdisciplinary on a single researcher level? It would mean that one would need to be deeply familiar with several disciplines and then combine them. Should I become a specialist, in one of the caverns of Mary Clark's diamond mine (Clark, Chapter 5 of this book), or a generalist – 'Jack of all trades, master of none'? Where do I belong, and is anyone going to appreciate my work? Where can I get a job after doing an interdisciplinary PhD, if academic recruitment is still based on disciplinary merit? One may need to find a compromise between one's own interests and scientific integrity on one hand, and practical issues relating to the requirements of PhD and the personal economic situation on the other.

Avoiding becoming undisciplined

An interdisciplinary background would seem to allow the easy connecting up of ideas and working between different perspectives, but this can also lead to the problem that one is all the time looking at the 'big picture', eventually being perhaps unable to focus, when the time comes, on a single, specific, answerable question. For some of us, we find that this may lead to the research remaining on a very descriptive and basically too general level. Focusing is necessary; it is not possible to write a PhD dissertation on the topic 'human–nature interactions in natural resource management'. Yet sustainability science and science for sustainable development also need people who are looking at the big picture. A specialist would probably come up with different answers to the same research questions that we are posing, but who is to say which is better? They are just different and as such, we think, also complementary. This leads us to wonder whether, in order to be able to do successful interdisciplinary work, we need to give up the idea of disciplinarity. Since the problems we are looking at do not contain themselves neatly within disciplines, this should be enough of a reason for us to take a wider perspective. But if we give up completely on the disciplines, then our work is not so much interdisciplinary as undisciplined, lacking the formalism that is expected of us as scholars and PhD candidates and that we think is needed to make sense of the topics we are studying.

The central challenge in interdisciplinary work to us seems to be that we need to get out of our comfort zones and work on a turf that is new to us. For a PhD candidate it feels a bit like shopping in the big supermarket of social scientific theories and having bits and pieces from here and there. You keep seeing attractive things on the shelves but are unable to take them with you since your basket appears to be full already. It is easy to get lost when everything seems to relate to everything, and one seems to have all the disciplines, theories and literature of social science available. How then to choose and proceed in one's work? It seems that even in interdisciplinary work you still need an academic home, and you are expected to demonstrate knowledge of the important thinkers in your field. Of course you can try to construct your own intellectual house, but that is far more difficult and risky. And the difficulty of choosing your home from among those already built is compounded by the fact that as a student, at the beginning of your academic career, you are not yet really equipped to do so. How are you to know what approaches are out there and what would suit your work? It is like being a cook without much experience: one does not know the basics – which flavours go nicely together, which are conflicting and where the possibilities of revealing something new and distinctive are to be found. To begin the process of exploring and developing a style, one needs to know at least a few recipes that can serve as a basis for developing one's own. These can come from established work and the guidance of supervisors, but those are likely to be discipline-based recipes and may not always include all the ingredients that one believes are important. On the other hand, each recipe, or disciplinary approach, is based on its own foundation texts and major thinkers. So here it would seem crucial to go to the original texts and make up one's own mind on them.

However, one cannot hope to learn all the texts of sociology, political science or philosophy in a year, at the start of a PhD, so rules are needed even for making initial choices about which ingredients to include. In making our first crucial decisions about how to begin sorting through all the available recipes and ingredients, we find that in the end we have only our basic research questions and perhaps a hunch based on preliminary empirical work to guide us.

The research question: an anchor in the storm

After a year or so of sailing the high seas of interdisciplinary ambiguity, we think it is time to settle anchor with a practical problem. From our experiences so far, it seems that when working between disciplinary boundaries, the formulation of the research question becomes crucially important. It provides a way to achieve focus and order amid the interdisciplinary swirl of ideas. In narrowing down the research question from a more general interest in a phenomenon like social-ecological systems, we find that it may be also beneficial to ask yourself, as with any PhD, what set you off on this quest. Once we could answer 'why' questions, what seemed like otherwise arbitrary choices in our research plans began to reveal their justifications. In this way the research question serves as a sort of a guide, helping one to determine which of the big thinkers encountered within the swirl are speaking to one's own specific topic and interests – which are the ones that can serve as points of reference as one works towards one's personal research goals. This, of course, brings up the need to deal with the normativity of one's work. We think that all research is somehow normative, since there is always, at the start, a choice of which question to try to answer; some things have to be fixed and left out of any empirical inquiry. But interdisciplinary sustainability science research is, by definition, fundamentally normative and this is something that we think it is best to face up to from the outset. We are trying to address practical problems, and to suggest solutions. As with any research, narrowing down a complex phenomenon into a defined research question can be painful, but it is necessary if one wants to proceed in the work. However, when the general topic is a sustainability science topic, like governance for sustainable development, that process of narrowing down is related both to the topic and to the normative aims of the research. Narrowing down the question is hopefully easier after a preliminary research phase (Tait and Lyall 2007), which should give one a better idea of the phenomenon to be studied and of its interesting characteristics. But the inevitable normative aspect of this work (Funtowicz and Ravetz 1991) also requires that we find ways to make scientifically valid assessments of politically charged issues. So the challenges of method, which we might hope to put off until after we have decided on our research questions, also arise at this early stage of the work, since the how, the what and the why need to be more or less collectively specified.

Supervision: a lighthouse on the shore

So far, it seems that there are a lot of challenges and obstacles before us in our PhD work, but, fortunately, we have not set out on this endeavour alone. In such unsteady waters, supervision seems to have an even more important and complicated role in an interdisciplinary PhD process than in the usual disciplinary process. We find ourselves asking questions like: is my supervisor equipped to instruct interdisciplinary work, or are they pushing me towards their own discipline? By contrast, if the supervisor is routinely doing interdisciplinary work and is him- or herself motivated mainly by policy-relevant problems, the supervisor might not be sufficiently sensitive to the concerns of a PhD candidate who needs to find an academic home and write a PhD thesis that can be appreciated in the traditional university evaluation process. Supervising an interdisciplinary project is demanding, and in this sense the GoverNat project is an experiment also for the senior researchers supervising the PhD candidates. As fellows, we believe that our supervisors should be open to new methods coming from different disciplines, be aware of the epistemological differences between the disciplines and be prepared to question the assumptions concerning their own disciplines (Lyall *et al.* 2008). If the expertise of the supervisor does not cover the whole field of the interdisciplinary work, the supervisor should help the student to form an external supervision team and encourage them to contact other relevant experts. At the same time, the supervisor should have realistic expectations towards the project and not expect the PhD candidate to read everything that is somehow connected to their topic. Every PhD student, whether disciplinary or interdisciplinary, will need help in structuring their dissertation, and when heading towards the evaluation stage it seems to us that the supervisor needs to find examiners who are expert on the topics that the student is addressing but who also sympathize with the idea of doing interdisciplinary work. So there is a lot in the interdisciplinary PhD journey that depends on how one's supervisor engages with the challenge.

Empirical data: a sandy shore to land on

Different disciplines (or traditions or schools) have different ideas about how research should be conducted, both generally and with respect to the role of theory in the work. From our experience so far, we think that a linear, theory-based deductive approach is probably not the best choice for the interdisciplinary work that we are conducting within GoverNat, where our focus is on discovering and explaining new phenomena, as opposed to trying to prove the existence of a phenomenon that has already been described by a theory. In interdisciplinary work it seems to us that the role of the theory is more that of a facilitator: helping us to answer our research questions. This implies a more inductive research process, where the theoretical aspect of the work is not fixed at the beginning but is chosen during and after defining the research question and further developed, together with the research ontology, epistemology and methodology. With a basic conceptual model built from these components, the big thinkers, upon whom one wants to lean and from whom one wants to learn, can be chosen. This is a comforting thought: theory is a choice; there is no one right theory for your PhD ready and waiting for you to find it in the swirl of the university library. The choice of theories is not arbitrary when it is serving a purpose (Funtowicz 2001), and so we think it is important to think carefully about what theories one will use.

Here, in addition to deduction and induction, a third research approach, called abduction (Bromley 2004), is emerging, which could also be helpful for the type of work done by the GoverNat fellows. Hiedanpää (2005) describes the approach as follows: begin with a surprising result, proceed to discern the rules and regularities that brought the result about, and conclude with a case for reform of the standard conditions, either to encourage or to discourage the surprising result – depending, of course, upon whether or not it is desirable. Abduction is thus both a critical and a creative process, which may be helpful for striking a good balance between the descriptive, analytical and normative elements of our work.

Your own convictions: a compass in the storm

Doubt lives in any PhD candidate's mind regarding the appropriate depth of inquiry: should I go all the way back to Aristotle, or is it enough to kick off from a contemporary thinker? For the research questions that we have posed within GoverNat, it would take several lifetimes just to read everything that is relevant to our studies! And there is not always just one valid theory on a question, even in natural sciences. Here we can take the example of light: light understood as photon particles can, for example, explain how energy is transformed in photosynthesis, whereas light taken as a wave explains colours, for example why leaves are green. But the relationship between light as a particle and light as a wave is still a source of debate within optical physics. A theory provides one possible perspective on an issue, but there are always others. Again, we find that coming back to specific research questions can help us to define which field and which theories are relevant to our studies and which are not. While a clear research question is important for any PhD study, for an interdisciplinary sustainability science PhD, where there are so many choices that need to be made about which fields and theories to use, it is absolutely vital.

If there is one thing we are certain about so far, it is that confusion seems to be an inherent dilemma in interdisciplinary work. In moderate amounts, confusion can be considered a good thing, fostering a creative state of mind, as long as it does not lead to an infinite regress of unhealthy confusion. In healthy doses, confusion pushes one to go back to scratch and ask, 'What the hell am I doing?' Such reflection can eventually lead to higher-quality work, leading to more conscious choices, but it may also lead to an existential crisis: what is an adequate level of reflection? When thinking about research ontologies, one drifts easily to fundamental questions about the nature of the world. What political and spiritual or religious convictions do I hold and to what extent do I have to be reflective about them? How much does my personal history affect the research I am doing and how much should I identify with my PhD topic? It would be rather painful reading if each sustainability science PhD were to start with a home-baked psychoanalysis: 'I was born in a small village…' Probably a minimum requirement for good-quality research in general is that you believe in what you are doing and have a clear idea of what you are trying to accomplish. In the case of interdisciplinary research for sustainable development, having a clearly defined research question may even turn out to be a determining factor in whether or not you are able to proceed with the work: a clear idea of where you are heading seems, in our experience, to be a way out of this sort of endless existential reflections.

A typology of interdisciplinary challenges encountered

Farrell *et al.* (2007b; and also Chapter 3 of this book) suggest that in interdisciplinary projects some discipline with core knowledge and skills concerning the core research problem may become the dominant frame for the study because that discipline has a gatekeeper status, controlling access to key information that persons with a particular disciplinary background are able to interpret correctly. In a project where the multilevel governance of natural resources is the core focus, one might expect that the dominant disciplines would be those that can be used to identify the potential irreversible losses of biological diversity (Heywood 1995) and the depletion of natural resources, including water. At this basic level the expertise is coming from the natural sciences: from disciplines such as conservation biology, and strands of hydrology and ecology. But for the assessment of the human impacts of biodiversity loss and resource depletion, and for interpreting their consequences for the human system, insights from economics might be considered core, and economics might be understood as a dominant discipline. For the study of the management of resources and design of policies for the abatement of biodiversity loss, political sciences could also be considered as a dominant discipline, at a meta-level, and conservation biology essential at the local level. In GoverNat the dominant disciplines are the social science disciplines of economics, political science and sociology, because the research focus is on the interlinkages between economic, political and social processes. However, there are additional roles for social science in this project. For example, Farrell *et al.* (2007) attribute to social science a special role in the design and implementation of interdisciplinary research projects, noting that as soon as we begin to formally consider how science should be related to policy, the social scientist becomes at the same time the observer and the observed, a target of external as well as internal inquiry. Similarly, Aram (2004) talks about exogenous (created by the 'real' problems of the community) and endogenous (concerned with the production of new knowledge) interdisciplinary knowledge, and a similar distinction between internal and external orientations is also discussed sometimes in terms of Mode 2 science knowledge (Gibbons *et al.* 1994). To our thinking, the whole GoverNat project can be described as an experiment in post-normal science (Funtowicz and Ravetz 1991) or a big, complex action research project (e.g. Hall 1985), depending upon which set of frames one chooses to use to describe it. Our aim here in this chapter is not to analyse GoverNat or to try to fit it into one of these descriptions, but to explore our own challenges as PhD students endeavouring to write dissertations that fit squarely within this domain of interdisciplinary sustainability science. In that respect, here in this chapter we are looking as much at ourselves as at our experiences and trying to learn from how we have responded to our situation.

Reflections on what we have encountered

In summing up the challenges we have so far encountered in this interdisciplinary project, we came up with the typology shown in Table 9.1, in which we identify core challenges and opportunities associated with what we find to be some of the key attributes of interdisciplinary research. Following our presentation of the typology, we then discuss our experience of each of these six attributes in a little more detail, before moving on to our conclusions.

The first challenge would seem to be the *definition of interdisciplinarity*. Is a project interdisciplinary when it just throws together people with different backgrounds and different interests, or should the interdisciplinarity be something more worked through? Aram (2004), for example, distinguishes between instrumental, conceptual and epistemological interdisciplinarity, and transdisciplinarity, depending on the depth of integration, but there are a wide variety of overlapping and sometimes contradicting definitions in use at the moment. What is clear is that the 'correct' definition, if indeed there is one, is not clear. And

Table 9.1 A typology of challenges and opportunities in interdisciplinary sustainability science work

Attribute	*Challenges*	*Opportunities*
Definition of interdisciplinarity	Various definitions; no single definition available and, with the GoverNat project, no common understanding of what is meant by the term	Careful clarification of a single definition or agreement to work from multiple definitions can provide a good starting point for collaboration
Different ontologies	Incommensurable ontologies, where differences are so great that the researchers cannot even understand each other, lead to disagreements and confusion about research objectives	Discussion about the inevitability of ontological diversity can provide an opportunity to reflect on one's own assumptions and on their implications for one's research
Normativity	Choices made in the course of sustainability science research come with normative baggage regardless of whether or not the researcher is aware of this	Mature reflection on one's own normative positions and their implications for the work can lead to better-quality research and reporting
Different epistemologies	In the GoverNat project, even though there is a lot of goodwill we have regularly encountered an inability to communicate across the disciplines, which seem to be linked to fundamentally different ideas how to construe the truth about a research topic	Recognizing the relationship between one's epistemology and one's observations opens up a whole new area for discussion regarding the presumptions that we make and the ethical and moral implications of our propositions
Different methodologies	Often there is no off-the-shelf method available for conducting the kind of empirical interdisciplinary research work that we are doing in the GoverNat project	Triangulation, the use of multiple methods, and taking the opportunity to build one's own methods by drawing from various disciplines can increase the robustness of the work
Lack of a disciplinary home	We have often had difficulty justifying our interdisciplinary research approaches to our more discipline-oriented peers	Not fitting into any one academic box brings a freedom to explore and to come up with something genuinely new

since PhD students are not in a position to decide which definition, if any, should eventually take the proverbial throne, we suggest that a careful clarification of the definition or definitions that one chooses to use, including a clear explanation for why one has chosen them, will need to be one of the first jobs in any interdisciplinary sustainability science PhD.

Second, it seems to us that all interdisciplinary researchers are working more or less in a sort of no man's land, between disciplines, where *a variety of different ontologies* are all more or less valid. Clear and valid assumptions regarding how the world behind the research topic works, regarding the nature of reality, are vitally important for conducting good research, and the ontological ambiguity that seems to accompany interdisciplinary research is a challenge that needs to be explicitly addressed. For example, over time we have discovered that there was a certain social science ontology behind the GoverNat framework, which was not made explicit and was not clear to many of the fellows at the start of the project. We have since learned that debates about ontology have been central to the so-called science wars (Latour 1999) and that our difficulties with the difference between social and natural science ideas of how the world works are not so unique. From this perspective it is no wonder that we, as PhD candidates, feel slightly lost when it comes to the task of defining our own interdisciplinary research ontologies. Few of us had any readily available answers to requisitve preceding epistoemological questions like: is there an observable reality independent of our perception? Or, do we need to cope with radical uncertainty about how we know things? The question of finding a shared ontology is solved perhaps more easily in narrow interdisciplinary projects, but as we have seen in the case of our GoverNat project, in research that bridges the study of the natural and social worlds the most fundamental of all ontological questions remains wide open to debate: to what extent, if at all, and in what respect, are we, humans, part of nature? Furthermore, it seems that the differences in ontology may not in the end be only between natural and social scientists; they may also be between different disciplines, within disciplines, between different schools of thought and between different individuals' perceptions of the world. That is to say, they may come all the way down to matters of individual style. We believe one way forward here could be to acknowledge the inevitable ontological diversity of interdisciplinary research and to try to appreciate the existence of a range of ontologies within the project. In our case, that means that we may need to accept that a single GoverNat ontology could not emerge during the project.

The challenge of coping with all these different ontologies brings us to the third attribute of interdisciplinarity included in our typology: *normativity*. Our appreciation for this attribute of interdisciplinary sustainability science research is related to the reflective pressure that our debates over ontology have brought upon us, making it necessary to ask ourselves 'why' questions in a new and more penetrating way. Any PhD student needs to ask themselves, why do I want to make a PhD? Why am I interested in this topic? Why did I set out on this quest? What do I want to achieve? Why have I made the decisions that I have made concerning my research approach? But for a sustainability science PhD student these questions take on an additional weight, in part because they are responsible for helping to justify one's ontological, epistemological and eventually also one's methodological choices. Even when working within a discipline, one still needs to have a clear ontology upon which to base a research design, but one is rarely required to give a clear argument defending the presumptions and giving justifications to support its appropriateness. However, in research contexts like the GoverNat project, it has been our experience that we are very often expected to justify our ontologies, and we have found that these justifications are fundamentally related to our choices regarding what question we are trying to answer with the research – that is to say, with our own normative agendas.

There are always values behind choices made in research, be they more or less explicit. However, our experience suggests that in interdisciplinary research generally, and especially when dealing with environmental governance problems, where the research aims to impact on policy, there is a great deal to be gained from being explicit about the normative choices that one makes. Researchers may not always be aware of the value choices they are making, since these might come pre-packed within disciplinary approaches or theories. But when debates about ontology take centre stage, these presumptions and prejudgements can be evaluated, adjusted or accepted, on the grounds that they serve the purpose of the research. This is not the same as being free from normativity. We view it rather as a mature way of handling the inevitability of normativity in sustainability science.

Closely linked to the challenges of different ontologies and normativity are the challenges of *different epistemologies*. By 'epistemology' we understand here the theory regarding how one can go about knowing a subject of observation. Do we assume that there is only one truth or several valid ways of knowing what is true, and how do we justify our methodological choices for revealing whatever kind of truth it is that we presume exists? The decision to use interviews in gathering data for the research may include an epistemological presumption that reliable answers to the research questions can be found by analysing oral testimonies of those involved. However, a good interview method also presumes that data content is partly controlled by the subjects (people being interviewed), so the epistemological presumption is that accuracy of the data depends not only on good data collection procedures but also on the goodwill of those being interviewed. Natural and social scientists often have different expectations regarding how to reveal 'what is really going on', and indeed regarding the extent to which that is possible.

Different methodologies result from the different ontologies and epistemologies. One needs to choose, for example, between inductive and deductive research designs and to decide on the roles that theory and method will play in the work. It seems to us that methodology in interdisciplinary work is not something off the shelf but needs to be carefully selected and also custom designed, according to the circumstances of each individual research setting and the investigative aims of the researcher(s). While this means that a lot of time and effort may need to be invested in the methods planning for an interdisciplinary sustainability science research project, combining various research methodologies offers students the possibility of exploring the issue from several different perspectives.

In our experience, all these challenges contribute towards making PhD candidates – at least, the ones writing this chapter – feel somewhat insecure and lost, with a feeling that they *lack a disciplinary home*. We find ourselves needing to work harder to legitimate our choices and we are regularly faced with the need to strike a balance between proving ourselves to our peers and teachers at the university and doing the issue-driven research on complex environmental governance phenomena, which is the ultimate aim of our sustainability science PhDs.

Conclusions

After working on our GoverNat PhDs, during which time we wrote the reflections reported above, and very many lengthy discussions about these challenges, we think we now know, in theory, where our main problems lie. The next challenge for us is to take charge of our research processes and to act out the successful interdisciplinary research process. Here one could easily start to get cold feet, since the agenda we have set for ourselves is quite ambitious. We imagine that many of the questions we have raised will not be solved during the course of our PhDs but will follow us throughout our research careers. Writing out all the troubles we have had in mind and being brave enough to expose our insecurities to you, our peers and our supervisors has proved to be a good strategy for us and has provided a great deal of fruitful exchange.

Looking back over our typology, among the various lessons we have learned, a golden piece of advice that we were offered along the way stands out: make sure you have your research question very clear. Of course, this is important for any PhD student, but from our experience we believe that for an interdisciplinary sustainability science PhD it is a matter of survival. It is not possible to know all the theories relating to any one discipline, but when one is doing an interdisciplinary PhD, the problem is compounded, since one is faced with a feeling that one should read all the available information from all the relevant disciplines before proceeding with the empirical work. One has to somehow be confident that for all its breadth, the research can still provide something valuable to science. E.O. Wilson's dream of a conscilience (Wilson 1998) – with an all-encompassing explanation of the world and a unity of knowledge – has to be quickly discarded as an aim of a PhD, even if it is still kept in mind as an ideal. Here we think that supervision is crucial: every PhD candidate needs to be able to trust the assessment of a more experienced supervisor to go on with their research questions. In the end, the final choice of the specific research question is always with the student writing the dissertation, and this is a choice that we recommend is considered very carefully.

Two main themes seem to emerge in our typology, and they are very much interrelated. One has to do with the *quality of interdisciplinary scientific work* and the other is about *dominance*: who gets to decide what is meant by interdisciplinarity, what ontological and epistemological assumptions are taken as a basis of a research project proposal, etc. What we think can be drawn out of the typology presented in Table 9.1 is that interdisciplinarity should not be used as a catchword but it is necessary to be clear about where everybody is standing in an interdisciplinary research project. We find it important to keep an open mind towards different ontologies and to be tolerant towards new ways of seeing things, keeping in mind that with a complex problem there is no one right way of conceptualizing it. Interdisciplinary PhD students should remain wary of different epistemologies and always remember to ask themselves how and why any data have been created, in order to see the underlying assumptions. Regarding methodology, it would seem wise not to put all the eggs in one basket but to examine the object of study with different lenses, using various methods. This is one of the upsides of lacking a disciplinary home: no one can tell you exactly how you should carry out your dissertation work. When you make sure you know why you are doing what you are doing, it is easier to justify your choices also to others. In a project as extensive as a PhD dissertation, one too often focuses on the challenges side of interdisciplinary work and thereby carries the weight of the world on one's narrow shoulders. Once in a while, one needs to be reminded that there is a lighter side to it all. Interdisciplinarity gives a lot of freedom to be creative and to be true to one's own motivations – or, to put it in more catchy words: it gives you the chance to follow your gut feelings.

Keys to happiness

Happily, some clarity has now started to appear for us amid the confusion, and we have begun to realize that we are not the only ones who are confused about the challenges we have discussed above. Debates on scientific methodology have been going on for as long as there has been scientific method, and there seems to be no one definition of what constitutes a discipline. Instead, there are a number of ways to approach interdisciplinary work (e.g. Aram 2004). Lyall *et al.* (2008) suggest that perhaps 'disciplines have survived for so long in the academic world in part because they serve the very useful function of constraining what the researcher has to think about'. The thought is disquieting for us and at the same time comforting. If it is the inherent and basic nature of interdisciplinary inquiries that makes things difficult, then at least we know we are in good company!

Three years seems like an awfully short time to tackle all the challenges mentioned here, and it would probably provide some peace of mind if we could forget about this time constraint and concentrate more on the quality and content of the work. However, in view of how PhDs are funded these days, that may not always be possible. Nonetheless, we believe that when doing an interdisciplinary PhD one needs time to read across the disciplines. This means that the preliminary research phase, in which one is to define the research questions, probably takes more time than in a disciplinary PhD. It is a great opportunity to learn and develop oneself towards the directions that seem meaningful for one's research work and career plans, but it is time-consuming if one wishes to do it well. Going through a painful period of self-reflection, as we four have, might save us some trouble in the future, since we will be less naive when we finish our studies, and, we hope, the lessons we have learned will help us to produce good-quality dissertations. Being exposed to many new things is exciting but we think it is wise to remember where one comes from and not to let the resources that one already holds go to waste: to have the aim, for example, to become an interdisciplinary biologist, as opposed to setting out to become, in the course of three years, something altogether new. One should be able to differentiate between the PhD and a lifetime research agenda; as the saying goes: a good PhD is a finished PhD.

Another word of advice is to look before you leap: taking on an interdisciplinary PhD may not be advisable for everybody. We find that it requires great enthusiasm for the topic being studied, a willingness to understand other perspectives and an ability to compromise on one's own views, where necessary. Interdisciplinary work would seem to attract people who are especially committed to making sense of the world, and, as was the case for us within GoverNat, shared green values may facilitate the initiation of interdisciplinary communication and a heightened goodwill in the face of confusions and misunderstanding. Tait and Lyall (2007) suggest that good qualities for an interdisciplinary researcher include flexibility and curiosity towards other disciplines, with communication and teamwork skills being of high value. To this, we would add the suggestion that a high tolerance for ambiguity can help ensure a good sleep at night for the interdisciplinary PhD student.

For the students and supervisors who might be reading this chapter, we would like to leave you with one parting thought that we bring with us, as we get back to the basic practical work of turning our research plans into PhDs: when it all seems to be too much, keep this in mind – your research question is your best friend. It does not have to be written in stone from the beginning. Part of its beauty and its value to you is that it is allowed to grow and change. Its imperfections are part of what make it lovable. If you're stuck and you don't know where to turn or what to do next, your research question will be there for you when everyone else seems to have left you on your own to navigate across the troubled waters of your interdisciplinary, intercultural dissertation voyage.

Acknowledgements

The main authors would like to thank Kate Farrell for the opportunity to work with the ideas raised in the GoverNat project and for her extremely helpful feedback. Also, we would like to acknowledge the support of Anna Wesselink, Sybille van den Hove and Felix Rauschmayer, and the comments of all the other fellows in the GoverNat project, which has functioned as a platform for our growth on the interdisciplinary research path. This research was financially supported by the European Union (European Commission, Marie Curie RTN GoverNat, Contract No. 0035536, www.governat.eu).

References

Aram, J.D. 2004. 'Concepts of interdisciplinarity: configurations of knowledge and action.' *Human Relations* 57(4): 379–412.

Balázs, B., Gy. Bela, B. Bodorkós, K. Milánkovics and Gy. Pataki. 2005. 'Preserving bio- and socio-diversity through Participatory Action Research.' *Living Knowledge: International Journal of Community Based Research* 5: 11–13.

Bromley, D.W. 2004. 'Reconsidering environmental policy: prescriptive consequentialism and volitional pragmatism.' *Environmental and Resource Economics* 28(1): 73–99.

Farrell, K.N. 2007. 'Living with living systems: the co-evolution of values and valuation.' *International Journal of Sustainable Development and World Ecology* 14(1): 14–26.

Farrell, K.N., R. Kemp, F. Hinterberger, C. Rammel and R. Ziegler. 2005. 'From * for * to governance for sustainable development in Europe: what is at stake for further research?' *International Journal of Sustainable Development* 8(1/2): 127–150.

Farrell, K.N., S. van den Hove and T. Luzzati. 2007. 'What lies beyond reductionism? Taking stock of interdisciplinarity research on ecological economics.' Paper given at European Society for Ecological Economics 2007 conference 'Integrating Natural and Social Sciences for Sustainability', Helmholtz Centre for Environmental Research, Leipzig, 5–8 June.

Funtowicz, S. 2001. 'Peer review and quality control.' In *International Encyclopedia of the Social and Behavioral Sciences*. Oxford: Elsevier Science.

Funtowicz, S.O. and Ravetz, J.R. 1991. 'A New scientific methodology for global environmental issues.' In *Ecological Economics: The Science and Management of Sustainability*, ed. R. Costanza. New York: Columbia University Press.

Gibbons, M., C. Limoges, H. Nowotny, S. Schwartzman, P. Scott and M. Trow. 1994. *The New Production of Knowledge: The Dynamics of Science and Research in Contemporary Societies*. London: Sage.

Gunderson, L.H. and C.S. Holling eds. 2002. *Panarchy: Understanding Transformations in Human and Natural Systems*. London: Island Press.

Hall, B. 1985. 'Research, commitment and action: the role of participatory research.' *International Review of Education* 30(3): 289–299.

Heywood, V.H. ed. 1995. United Nations Environment Programme, *Global Biodiversity Assessment*. Cambridge: Cambridge University Press.

Hiedanpää, J. 2005. 'The edges of conflict and consensus: a case for creativity in regional forest policy in southwest Finland.' *Ecological Economics* 55(4): 485–498.

Kates, R.W., W.C. Clark, R. Corell, J.M. Hall, C.C. Jaeger, I. Lowe, J.J. McCarthy, H.J. Schellnhuber, B. Bolin, N.M. Dickson, S. Faucheux, G.C. Gallopin, A. Grübler, B. Huntley, J. Jäger, N.S. Jodha, R.E. Kasperson, A. Mabogunje, P. Matson, H. Mooney, B. Moore III, T. O'Riordan and U. Svedin. 2001. 'Sustainability science.' *Science* 292(5517): 641–642.

Latour, B. 1999. *Pandora's Hope: Essays on the Reality of Science Studies*. Cambridge, MA: Harvard University Press.

Latour, B. 2004. *Politics of Nature: How to Bring the Sciences into Democracy*. Cambridge, MA: Harvard University Press.

Latour, B. 2005. *Reassembling the Social: An Introduction to Actor-Network-Theory*. Oxford: Oxford University Press.

Lyall, C., L. Meagher and J. Tait. 2008. 'A short guide to supervising interdisciplinary PhDs.' ISSTI Briefing Note no. 4, January. Institute for the Study of Science, Technology and Innovation, University of Edinburgh. Online, available at: www.issti.ed.ac.uk/publications/briefingnotes (accessed 2 February 2009).

Meadowcroft, J., K.N. Farrell and J. Spangenberg. 2005. 'Governance for sustainable development: developing a framework for sustainability governance in the European Union.' *International Journal of Sustainable Development* 8(1/2): 3–11.

Peltola, T. 2006. 'Harju poliittisena toimijana: toimijaverkot lämpölaitoksen sijoituspaikkakiistassa Kangasalla' (The esker as a political actor: actor-networks in debate over locating a heating plant in Kangasala). *Terra* 118(2): 67–80.

Reason, P. and H. Bradbury eds. 2006. *Handbook of Action Research*. London: Sage.
Rhoten, D. and A. Parker. 2004. 'Risks and rewards of an interdisciplinary research path.' *Science* 306(5704): 2046.
Tait, J. and C. Lyall. 2007. 'A short guide to developing interdisciplinary research proposals.' ISSTI Briefing Note no. 1, March. Institute for the Study of Science, Technology and Innovation, University of Edinburgh. Online, available at: www.issti.ed.ac.uk/publications/briefingnotes (accessed 2 February 2009).
Wilson, E.O. 1998. *Consilience: The Unity of Knowledge*. New York: Vintage.

10 Probing the boundaries of resilience science in practice

Brian H. Walker and C.S. Holling

Editors' note

The text of this chapter has been adapted from the two opening keynote speeches given by Brian Walker and C.S. (Buzz) Holling at the conference 'Resilience 2008: Resilience, Adaptation and Transformation in Turbulent Times – Preparing for Change in Social-Ecological Systems', which was held in April 2008 in Stockholm, Sweden.[1] Here, Brian Walker and Buzz Holling, two of the founders of the integrative ecological economics discourse on the resilience of social-ecological systems, take a look at the history and the future of this field of scholarly work, which has given rise to a new generation of individuals and institutes working on integrative, beyond reductionism, ecological economics.

The conference where these talks were given marked a new stage of development for the scientific discourse on resilience of social-ecological systems. Conducted mainly by a small community of scholars centred on the Resilience Alliance research network, this approach to producing 'beyond reductionism', interdisciplinary study of ecological economics has been one of the more widely recognized approaches within the mainstream of scientific research. The 2008 Stockholm conference marked an effort to open this discourse to a wider community of scholars and also marked its formal institutionalization in the form of the Stockholm Resilience Centre. The texts of Walker and Holling's speeches have been revised somewhat to fit more with the style of a book chapter, but their basic narrative, reflective tone has been retained. That is because the purpose of this chapter is to provide an illustration of how these two scholars have succeeded in developing and applying beyond reductionism interdisciplinary approaches to sustainable development and ecological economics research.

Introduction

It truly is a great pleasure for me [Brian Walker] to be able to introduce the science of the Resilience Alliance and the Resilience 2008 congress to you. I know that is a platitude – that people often say something like that at the beginning of a conference – but it really does mean a lot to me. Two years of intensive planning went into the preparations for Resilience 2008 and our aim was to hold a meeting on a much larger scale than we usually do, which we certainly achieved.

We wanted to do this because, over the years, many people have contacted the Resilience Alliance asking, 'how can we get in touch?' and saying, 'I'd like to work with you'. Since the success of our alliance depends on our remaining small, as opposed to a research centre or a university (a point that Buzz will talk about later in this chapter), it has not always been so clear how best to proceed with handling these kinds of requests. So, holding a conference, with a large international open call, has been our first effort to try to build up these new connections, to get in touch with people who are interested in our work and to explore how we can collaborate with you (if you're one of them).

While we are expecting a lot of surprises as we roll out this new phase of the Resilience Alliance's work, one thing we are pretty certain of is that we should start our conversations about collaboration by explaining a bit about what we are up to these days and where we see our work going in the coming years. As I have served as Science Director of the Alliance for the past eight years, that job falls to me.

The 2008 Stockholm Conference was put together, I think, because it was time to probe the boundaries of resilience science and practice. In the first instance that means establishing where we are at, which also means sharing information – not only among ourselves within the Alliance, but also, importantly, with interested people who have not been involved with us up to now. Collectively, among all of us here today there is a huge amount of understanding about ecological economics and social-ecological systems, but we each have only a little bit of that in our heads. If we can get all that understanding together, hopefully what we share will be a lot more than what each of us has going on independently. That also means that one of the aims of this conference was to advance the science, together, collaboratively.

After eight years of developments, we now need to consider where we want to go with the science that has been developed by the Resilience Alliance members. So that will be the main subject of my contribution to this chapter, but before going into that in greater detail, let me first take some time to review, in a little more detail just why around 250 people got together in April 2008 in Stockholm, Sweden, for this conference in the first place.

The Resilience Alliance, if we count the first few years when it was the Resilience Network that Buzz Holling set up, is now, in 2008, about twelve years old. We have published fourteen books, hundreds of different papers and currently have six books in preparation or in press.[2] As a body of work, these publications collectively reflect the development and state of the art of the Resilience Alliance work.

Our most current research activities are reflected in six forthcoming books:

- *Complexity Theory for a Sustainable Future* (Norberg and Cumming 2008);
- *Critical Transitions in Nature and Society* (Scheffer 2009);
- *Discontinuities in Ecological and Other Systems* (Allen and Holling 2008);

- *Foundations of Ecological Resilience* (Gunderson *et al.* 2009);
- *Governing Social-Ecological Transformations: Adapting to the Challenge of Global Environmental Change* (Boyd and Folke, forthcoming);
- *Principles of Resource Stewardship: Resilience-Based Resource Management in a Changing World* (Chapin *et al.* 2009).

Just these six most recent books cover a huge variety of empirical topics and types of investigation into the social-ecological systems of our planet, ranging from pure theory all the way through to concrete practice. The text *Principles of Resource Stewardship* (Chapin *et al.* 2009) will be the first real textbook on resilience and we are expecting that it will be finished in April 2009. There is a huge amount of information in the books and articles that have been published by Resilience Alliance (RA) members so far and it would be futile to try to summarize all of that work here. What I will do, rather, is present some of the current activities in the three broad areas of the RA's programme.

Three categories of activities

So, to start with where we are at, we divide the current Resilience Alliance programme of activity into three categories:

1 theory;
2 comparative case studies;
3 outreach, collaboration and communication.

The first of these, theory, is itself further divided up into three sections: work on critical transitions and backloops; non-computable uncertainty and resilience; and theory work concerning institutions, governance and resilience (Table 10.1).

The second major component of RA activities – comparative case studies – constitutes the core empirical foundation of the research. We have carried out studies in urban resilience, resilience in water systems and resilience in agricultural production landscapes, in marine resilience, and in resilience in indigenous societies (a new and developing area), in climate change and resilience, and a few overarching case studies on regional resilience (Anderies *et al.* 2006).

Our third area of activity is outreach, collaboration and communication. Up to now, the main activities here have been working directly with practitioners on the comparative case studies and developing a RA workbook.[3] So far, we have run some training courses based on the points that will go into the workbook we are developing, and we have worked a bit with the question of what it means to develop regional resilience programmes, for example in Australia, where I am based. We've also become involved in running participatory workshops, where we combine our understanding of resilience with the local knowledge of the people living and working with the resources and ecosystems that we are studying.

So those are the three main components of the Resilience Alliance work at the moment. Twelve years ago we began with the first two of these (theory and

Table 10.1 The three types of theory work on resilience

• Critical transitions and backloops Here we are working with very specific meanings for these terms, where 'critical transitions' comes from the work of Marten Scheffer (Scheffer and Westley 2007; Scheffer *et al.* 2008; Scheffer 2009) and what we call the 'backloop of the adaptive cycle' comes from Buzz Holling's original conceptual model of adaptation, resilience and collapse (Holling 1973, 2001; Gunderson and Holling 2002) – which is concerned with understanding and conceptualizing the dynamics of social-ecological change and evolution.
• Non-computable uncertainty and resilience This is related to the irreducible, significant uncertainty problem (the 'fat-tailed distribution' problem), and how to know when a system is approaching a threshold to an alternative system regime. It is being addressed by Steve Carpenter and other Resilience Alliance colleagues (e.g. Carpenter and Brock 2006). It is often quite tightly related to work on critical transitions and backloops, and so this strand has melded together quite a lot with the first one, particularly in the work of the groups led by Steve Carpenter and Marten Scheffer.
• Institutions, governance and resilience Here there is a lot of innovative theoretical work going on in Stockholm and in Arizona, at the Arizona State University's School of Sustainability, and fundamental work, empirical and theoretical, has been taking place now for many years now in Indiana, at Elinor Ostrom's Workshop in Political Theory and Policy Analysis.

cases). Basically, in the first instance, we had an interest in developing theory concerning social-ecological resilience, and we knew that we needed empirical information and case studies to evaluate and develop that theory. And eventually, as intended, the theory and cases came to inform each other. We found this to be a very important part of the Alliance's work because theory on its own can drift into a vacuum of abstractions, and case studies on their own become too particular and fail to identify generalizing principles.

But eventually we realized that we needed to incorporate the practice part of social-ecological systems within our assessments, since this is a fundamental component of how social-ecological problems are created and resolved. This led us to add the third main component of our work: close involvement with practitioners. However, we found that practitioners have very different concerns, and indeed a whole different language style, from scientists. So we needed to find a way to communicate effectively with them about the science behind the Alliance's research, in a style and language they can identify with, so they and we learn from each other. This is where the workbook I mentioned above, and the associated wiki website, come in, serving as a two-way communication tool for bridging our different ways of understanding. So now, in addition to the interplay between theory and cases, these communications and collaborations with practitioners are also feeding back into both theory development and the design and execution of our case studies.

Areas requiring attention in the future

The interactions between these three components (theory, cases and collaborations) has been one of the most important aspects of the Resilience Alliance's work over the past eight years, and this is something that I think needs to go forward with us into the next stage of our development; one could say that it is part of our transdisciplinary methodology. That being said, I view the question of how we go forward into this new stage as a very open one. So, rather than laying out a programme of research for the next years, what I would like to do here is offer a few suggestions for what I think might be fruitful lines of exploration for future work on the resilience of social-ecological systems.

Criticize and revise

First of all, it is time to criticize and revise the work that has been developed so far: to take a careful, critical look at what we think we know and where we are at. Recently, we published a book that also appears as a special issue of the journal *Ecology and Society* (Walker *et al.* 2006a) in which the concept of resilience in social-ecological systems is explored in great detail and the state of the art of research on this topic is reviewed. The first chapter of that book is titled 'A handful of heuristics and some propositions for understanding resilience in social-ecological systems' (Walker *et al.* 2006b). In that chapter there are five general heuristics and fourteen basic propositions about the characteristics of resilience, identified through review of the resilience case studies and case study comparisons that have been developed over the years. We now need to review that chapter carefully and to revise and delete and add to the propositions, so that we have an iterative, ongoing kind of state-of-the-science understanding. We can't call these propositions principles because they're not well enough grounded, but collectively they illustrate where we are at with the science. Significantly, I think we need a *different group of people from those who authored that chapter* to do this, in order to now criticize and revise that work and to take it into the next phase.

The last chapter of that book is titled 'Fifteen weddings and a funeral' (Anderies *et al.* 2006). The funeral is for the notion of maximum sustainable yield: to try finally, once and for all, to bury the notion that resources can be extracted from ecosystems at some defined maximum level without altering the feedbacks and therefore resilience of the ecosystem. The argument that maximum yield is a fool's errand is of course not new. Way back in 1977, Peter Larkin published the first major paper on this topic, titled 'Epitaph for the concept of maximum sustainable yield'. About fifteen years later, Buzz Holling and Gary Meffe wrote about it again, this time in terms of a pathology, in their paper 'Command and control and the pathology of natural resource management' (1996). And there were a number of articles following each of these major papers, where other authors picked up on and worked with this critique – that maximum sustainable yield is simply empirically naive – yet today it is *still* the dominant paradigm. My point here is that even though we need to revise and criticize our work, we still need to continue presenting critiques of these paradigmatic positions, where we find them to be problematic.

The more that people query the presumption of maximum sustainable yield, the more widely this notion will be questioned, but it is nonetheless frustrating to see so many unnecessary mistakes being made as a result of reliance upon an erroneous presumption. For example, in my own work in Australia with practitioners in river basin catchment planning, and elsewhere, it is still firmly ingrained in the minds of most people that you can get an ecosystem into some optimal state that will permanently deliver the maximum amounts of resources. The persistent ability of people to overlook the role that humans and human-based extractions play in the dynamics of an ecosystem, as *part of the system*, is astonishing. So, although it has been a task on our list for many years already, I think continuing, reiterating and improving the critique of maximum sustainable yield is something that needs to be included in the next phase of our work.

Looking forward, to how our own work on this point might be developed, there was in the 1970s an advance in the area of robust control, which took into account the inevitability that there would be shocks to the ecosystems and potentially also major shifts. Based on this, in place of policies intended to achieve optimization, in some circles at least, the idea of robust policies and readiness to respond to shocks was adopted. But robust control still assumes that you know all about the kinds of shocks the system has to cope with. It can't deal with complete surprise, and we need to move one step further, into a resilience approach that embraces real uncertainty, where shocks and shifts are no longer treated as exceptions but as the rule, and are handled as part of the fundamental governing dynamics of these systems.

The need for formal models

The fifteen weddings in the last chapter of that book (Anderies *et al.* 2006) are a collection of insights arising from the fifteen case studies that were compared in the book. One of the most important of those insights, as far as I'm concerned, is identification of the need for *formal models* of three fundamental aspects of resilience: (1) *multiple threshold-type behaviour*, instead of individual thresholds; (2) *backloop dynamics*, incorporating both *scale mismatches* and the kinds of *qualitative changes* that accompany phase shifts; and (3) *adaptive governance*, incorporating, for starters, the descriptive elements of leadership, trust and shadow networks and moving on from there.

Why do I emphasize the need for formal models? Because the rigour that goes with developing a formal model is what has been lacking up to now in some of our research on resilience. Buzz Holling's Lazy 8 (Holling 1986, 2001) is an incredibly powerful heuristic and we need to continue to use it as a heuristic, alongside whatever else we do. In that form it can continue to help us share explicitly and carefully, among ourselves and with others, what we think we understand about change in social-ecological systems. But formalizing this understanding, by incorporating these ideas into models, will push us to challenge the applicability of our ideas in particular systems.

At the moment, too much of our research is still descriptive, and moving forward to the stage of formal modelling is an important next step in advancing the science.

Scaling up and dealing with double whammies

Most of our investigations to date have been done at local and sometimes regional scales. Indeed, nearly all the resilience studies that we have are at the local scale. A few authors have dabbled in going further out but I think we need to ask ourselves, for the global resilience issues that we face today – and we really are confronting them at the global scale right now – how important are the scale-dependent global processes that simply do not operate at lower scales? And how far can we apply existing theory, developed through our case studies at local and regional scale, to global-scale processes? Do we need to develop entirely new propositions for global resilience issues? This an area that needs to be taken forward: what does it mean to talk about resilience with a focus at the global scale?

A more general area that also requires attention is the problem of double whammies. Up until now, we have mostly looked at the impacts of a single shock to a system and at whether that one system is resilient or not with respect to that one shock. But if we look around at our own case studies, we can see that understanding the dynamics associated with single shocks is simply not enough.

Really big transformative changes often seem to be triggered by at least two or more simultaneous or sequential shocks. For example, in my work on savannas (Walker 1993; Walker *et al.* 1981, 1986) I looked at ranches that had 'collapsed' – become ecologically degraded and economically not viable. Usually they could survive a drought, or a market downturn, but they couldn't survive the two occurring in combination. This is a very simple example but it points to an important gap in our current knowledge. It seems that the double whammies – that is to say, the multiple simultaneous shocks – are what really shift systems, and up to now we haven't done enough work on how to examine and look at these multiple shocks.

In order to develop this area of research we first need to consider what are the coupled or sequential shocks that are likely to occur and then we need to ask, how would we go about assessing them? For example, is the potential for the simultaneous occurrence of major climate change impacts and major oil shortages a looming double whammy at the global scale? If we think right now only about climate change impacts, we're close to a tipping point there, to seeing major changes in climate. Some people say we're already past the tipping point for major changes, but whether we are or not, what is happening is that there is a massive sudden global awareness of climate change. We're detecting climate impacts and this is changing what people are doing: the policies adopted by companies and governments and the daily activities of ordinary people throughout the world. At the same time – and this is really interesting, because it need not have been at the same time – we are close to, or again some say past, the peak oil point: where discovery of new reserves ceases to outstrip increased usage and we begin to run down the reserves (Hubbert 1949). When we do go past peak oil, or if we have, a very simple supply and demand relationship will kick in, where demand continues to rise and supply begins to fall. Since demand for oil is not so very elastic in the short term, when the peak oil tipping point is reached we are going to see an exponentially increasing price of energy and then perhaps a substantial drop in global economic activity. Either shock, on its own – passing the climate change tipping point, where fundamental changes in the global climate begin to occur, or passing the tipping point of peak oil, where energy prices begin to skyrocket – would be a great strain on global social-ecological systems. But what will happen if these two shocks come together, jointly escalating at the same time and developing in combination with each other, as two simultaneous major shocks, as opposed to individually: how will the world respond to that? Will world leaders, regional governments companies and individuals adopt an adaptation approach and try to remain resilient, leaving behind old patterns, maintaining ones that have been successful and changing in creative ways, as we would suggest needs to happen? Will they go for a planned, orchestrated transformation? Or will the world go through a variety of forced and very painful transformations, reacting to crisis situations as they emerge?

Perhaps this particular double whammy – major global climate change impacts presenting in conjunction with a peak oil energy supply crisis – will not play out, although it seems very plausible that we are already in the early stages of it right now. Still, this example gives an idea of the potential impacts that we are talking about here; we need to think more about the idea of double whammies (in terms of multiple shocks) and about how we might prepare for dealing with these situations.

Multiple thresholds

Related to the problem of double whammies is the issue of multiple thresholds. Where a social-ecological system as a whole is carefully examined, it is almost certain that more than one threshold will be discovered (e.g. Anderies *et al.* 2006): ecological, economic and social thresholds. And if one of these thresholds is crossed, it can lead to a cascading effect of crossing other thresholds.

Taken together, the existence of multiple thresholds and the propensity for double whammies make policy and management very difficult. But it's time we addressed this level of complexity.

Transformational change

We need to look into the question of transformational change versus increasing our efforts on adaptation and resilience of the current system regime (Walker *et al.* 2004; Olsson *et al.* 2006). This is a kind of segue from my previous point, because looking into the question of transformational change requires that we develop a better understanding of the conditions that are necessary for transformations, which probably include double whammies. I see this issue of transformations as important because, I would contend, much of what is needed in the world today is actually *not* to make existing system regimes more resilient; what is needed is to transform: to make the existing system states *less* resilient, so that we can change them and transform to some other kind of more desirable, resilient system. This applies right up to the scale of the global system – particularly the global economic system.

One of the practitioners I work with in the area of water catchment management always likes to quote the first rule of holes (which I'm told was coined by Warren Buffett): when you're in one, stop digging. I think this is the problem with many of the systems that we are looking at. The more people do to try to adapt their system to increasingly difficult conditions, the deeper the hole they're digging gets, and what they actually have to do is to get *out* of that hole. To get out of these holes we need to know how to *reduce* resilience, when that is what is required.

This then leads us to the question: could we develop rules for transformability? In some respects this is what they are working on in the Dutch discourse on transition management (Rotmans *et al.* 2001; Loorbach 2007; van der Brugge and van Raak 2007). Elinor Ostrom, in a paper with Thomas Dietz and Paul Stern, presents this set of eight generic rules for the persistence of common property systems (Dietz *et al.* 2003):

1 providing information;
2 dealing with conflict;
3 inducing rule compliance;
4 providing infrastructure;
5 being prepared for change;
6 analytic deliberation;
7 nesting;
8 institutional variety.

This kind of information is really useful, because it provides a kind of checklist for the necessary but not necessarily sufficient conditions for persistence. Using this list, we can say, if all eight of these rules for governing common property are in existence, then there is a good chance that the system will persist, but if some of them are not there, then it is a pretty sure bet that that system is not going to persist. Can we think about an equivalent set of criteria for what sort of things have to be in place for a system to be able to successfully transform itself into some other kind of system? And for steering that process in the directions that we think it should go?

Cost and value of resilience

Considering the question of where we think a system should go brings us to the issue of governance. To begin with, we need to consider how to identify and measure the benefits and costs of resilience – and I don't just mean in financial terms. This is a big challenge that has been put to us by managers and planners in our collaborative work. More often than not, when I talk to people about our work at the Resilience Alliance, they comment that it is all very well and good but they want to know how much enhancing resilience is going to cost, and what the real value of resilience is.

The cost of resilience may be in the form of forgone extra profits, or forgone extra yield, or direct expenditures – but there are going to be costs. How much yield or profit or income should be forgone today in the interest of being resilient? It depends, of course, on the consequences of not being resilient – the costs of crossing a threshold to an alternative system regime. And since we can only deal with this in probabilistic terms, it makes the task of presenting and comparing the two options difficult.

Identifying guidelines for what constitutes resilience is what we are doing with the RA workbook, and has been the heart of our efforts for the past eight years – where thresholds might be, and what sorts of changes and breakdowns in resilience might occur, etc. This work now needs to be complemented by a better understanding of the associated costs and values.

The first next step, then, is valuing specified resilience, and some of us within the Beijer Institute for Ecological Economics have been working on how to do that, taking the probability of crossing a known threshold times the consequences of crossing it, which we propose is one way of measuring the cost and the value of resilience (Walker *et al.* 2010). As long as the resilience is specified (meaning that we are talking about a single threshold, with respect to a single kind of pressure), and you can estimate a probability of the threshold existing, and the probability costs of crossing it, then you can come up with some realistic kind of idea of the costs and benefits of that resilience.

But what about general resilience? What is the cost of maintaining resilience in general, when you don't know what kind of shock might disrupt the system and what kind of threshold or thresholds might be most important? Can you assess the cost of not maintaining generalized resilience? This is important, because there is a danger associated with focusing too much on specified resilience. Basically, it is the same danger that we face with the principle of optimizing and with reductionism more generally, when the focus is on just one type of specified resilience. By making a system more resilient in one particular way, you may inadvertently be making it less resilient in other ways.

The question that really needs answering is: how much should we spend, or forgo, to increase resilience generally? Interestingly, reinsurance actuaries, who are basically concerned with predicting the expected future costs of running the global economic system, are very much preoccupied with this problem. They use a thing called 'ruin probability theory', which is a method for estimating the value that may be at risk at some point in the future if a firm happens to go bankrupt (Powers 1995; Gerber and Shiu 1998). They define this as the maximum loss, within a specified time horizon, not exceeded by a given probability. However, dealing with non-linear system dynamics and changing uncertainties – with what the actuaries call heavy-tailed, and what Steve Carpenter and his colleagues call fat-tailed, probability distributions (Carpenter and Brock 2006; Carpenter and Lathrop, 2008) – requires a completely different approach, and the conventional probability estimates from ruin probability theory could steer you in wrong directions. In the reinsurance industry at the moment there is a lot of interest in the likelihood of crossing thresholds and encountering non-linear shifts in global systems, because if and when this happens, it is going to be very costly.[4]

To see what I am getting at here, we can think about two global examples that are currently under discussion within the Resilience Alliance community. Let us consider, as my colleague Buz Brock suggested, that climate change is a slow driver, slowly increasing the (unknown) probability of 'bad' regime shifts. We don't know what these 'bad' shifts will be but it is a pretty fair guess that as global warming and related climate changes continue, the changes are bringing us closer and closer to some unpleasant thresholds in the earth system. If this is the case, how could we combine this understanding of tipping points and major changes in the global climate with estimates of the costs associated with crossing these thresholds, as compared with the costs of investing in the transformations that could lead to avoiding these tipping points?

Another example of how important it is to address these questions concerning costs and values from the perspective of global generalized resilience is the issue of connectedness. Charles Perrings recently raised this issue with me in an email exchange; with increasing global connectedness, there is now also an increasing correlation between what were previously basically regional risks. This problem of connectedness has been considered in other contexts (Tainter 1990; Fisk and Kerherve 2006), but I think we need to give it specific attention in the context of our work on resilience. That means that we need to be able not only to consider the risk and potential costs that would be associated with crossing one major threshold within one system, but also to anticipate when this might lead to cascades of radical change across systems and across regions (see Denman *et al.* 2007). And on top of this we can add the matter of double whammies, where heavily connected systems might meet multiple related thresholds simultaneously. The current globalized system of human interactions means that if something collapses in one part of the world, it is now much more strongly correlated with what is happening in other parts of world than was the case a few decades ago. We need to consider how the resilience of any single region is affected by the fact that it is now so much more strongly correlated with the resilience of other regions; but we also need to explore how this connectedness might work to our advantage, when we are trying to create transformations. These are areas that we haven't really thought about but that come, in my view, under the banner of general resilience, which could be very costly to lose.

To consider for a moment what those costs might be, I wonder, are we getting a bit of a taste of them with the sub-prime mortgage problem in the United States [and all that has since followed on from there]? Did economists predict this? If not, then why not? And, if they did, then why was this crisis not avoided? Did they, or the US government, foresee its global ramifications? Can the total expenditure on the salvaging of the world financial system be interpreted as the cost of losing generalized global economic resilience? Or does it even make sense to talk about costs and benefits in this way at this scale? I don't know, but these are the sorts of questions that I think we should explore much more deeply than we have up to now.

This leads us then to the somewhat contentious topic of economic valuation, which to me does not equal values, which I see as encompassing much more than just economic values and prices. The question of achieving 'desirable' system regimes always raises the question: 'desirable for whom?' Different segments of society value different things about an ecosystem and we can't take averages. Value is not just about the goods and services that an ecosystem delivers. It is also about the identity of the system. Interestingly, that very word – identity – was used by the participants associated with a catchment that we were studying in one of our participatory workshops. When we asked them what they really valued about the catchment that they live in and manage, they identified water, agricultural production and biodiversity; and then there was this thing they called their 'identity'. They couldn't really define it, but they knew what they meant and they didn't want it to change. Part of that feature that they called identity was actually the resilience of the system; it was about the whole system's ability (the ability of the catchment and its people) to maintain *its* identity. If you think about all that this feature 'identity' entails, it's very hard to do a straight economic analysis of it.

How do we understand and capture the value of a social-ecological system, and its resilience? Equations of motion, as beautiful as they may be to some, are just not sufficient for this purpose. We need a multi-perspective, multimedia representation of things; we need to be able to grasp the irreducible complexity of this thing that the people in our participatory workshops were calling 'identity'. I don't know how we do that but I can suggest that one of the directions that we need to head in is by talking about the art exhibition 'Changing Matters: The Resilience Art Exhibition' that was held in the Swedish Natural History Museum in conjunction with the Resilience 2008 conference, in Stockholm. The works of art at that exhibit were as much a part of the conference as any of the papers and lectures that were presented. They were selected by a committee that included some Resilience Alliance members, and that selection process was based not only on the artistic but also on the resilience science message of the submissions. Collectively, that exhibit – which included installations at, around and even using the main building where the conference was being held – starts telling us something about how we can talk about these irreducible aspects of resilience, about what those aspects of resilience that are not and cannot be captured within mathematical models.

At the Resilience 2008 congress the focus of the art exhibit was visual art and music, but at a future event it might be literary essays and poetry. This is about making a place for these more qualitative forms of sense-making within our work about resilience. The works selected for this first resilience science art exhibit are a wonderful, eclectic, multimedia mix that of course – and this is the point – cannot be described here just using words.[5] They represent the beginnings of a new area of work that needs to be developed if we are going to be able to represent things like the value of resilience – areas of work that contribute to us making a shift in our overall thinking, so that we are working not only to bring together social and natural science but also to include contributions from the humanities and the fine arts.

So this is the final challenge for the future that I would like to set out for us here: can science and the humanities, working together, provide the impetus for a transformational regime shift from the ruling command-and-control optimization and growth approaches of the global human system, to one based on resilience? I think that's the big challenge that faces us. The Resilience 2008 congress was able to give a forum where we could take some important first steps along that road but there remains a great deal more work yet to be done on this. I hope that those of you who have found yourself reading this book and this chapter will take up these challenges that I have outlined and will help with the work of developing the rich transdisciplinary collaborations that are needed for understanding and addressing the major social-ecological issues that stand before us.

Transition to Buzz Holling's lecture

But of course, if there is one thing we know from studying resilience, it is that looking forward only makes sense when you take into account where you have come from. For us at the Resilience Alliance, that means, first and foremost, the contributions and reflections of Buzz Holling, the father of Resilience. But before we turn to hear his thoughts on where our work on resilience might be headed in the coming years, I would like to take a moment to reflect on a few points from Buzz's own history.

C.S. 'Buzz' Holling did his primary degree studies Toronto, Canada, and his PhD in British Columbia, before beginning his research career working for the Canadian Department of Forestry in Sault Ste. Marie, Ontario, as a forest ecologist, which is where he started his famous entomological research (Holling 1959, 1965). Then he went on to the University of British Columbia, where he set up the Institute for Animal Resource Ecology. While there, he became director of IIASA (the International Institute of Applied Systems Analysis) in Vienna for a while, came back to British Columbia and then moved to Florida for a while, where he spent about ten or eleven years at the Department of Zoology at the University of Florida, and now he's come full circle and lives back at Nanaimo on Vancouver Island in British Columbia.

Most scientists, if they are lucky, have one truly big innovative idea in their lives. Buzz has had five, which is amazing. When he started off, working at

Sault Ste. Marie, he came up with the Holling Type I, II, III predator–prey responses (Holling 1959). That is a classic work and is still regularly quoted, so I think that was his first big idea. His idea about resilience came out in his famous paper about resilience and multiple stable states in ecosystems (Holling 1973). Then there is the idea of adaptive management, which has been developed a great deal within the Resilience Alliance but using fundamental ideas that originally came from work that Buzz got going with his book on the topic (Holling 1978), which has just been republished. He then came up with the notion of adaptive cycles and panarchy (adaptive cycles across scales), which has quickly become one of the most widely discussed concepts in environmental management and policy and is being applied in a great variety of settings (Gunderson *et al.* 1995; Holling 1986, 2001; Gunderson and Holling 2002; Holling *et al.* 2002a, b). And finally, there is his 'the world is lumpy' idea, which is about to come out in another book. It's quite remarkable when you think that someone leaves a legacy of five big ideas. I'm grappling to find one. It is wonderful for me to be able to introduce to you Buzz Holling, my mentor and friend, and the father of Resilience.

Some reflections on the resilience of resilience research [based on the content of Buzz Holling's keynote lecture at Resilience 2008]

Although this section has just been introduced by way of highlighting five big ideas that I've had and developed in the course of my scientific career, I'm not going to be talking about science in the following pages – at least, not the way that I usually do. Here I would like to take the opportunity to talk about some things that most scientists do not talk about very much, that we certainly don't write very much about, but which are every bit as important for making good science as the big ideas that we create, test and develop. In the following pages I'm going to talk about those things that provide our motivation to do research and about those things that keep us in a position where we can do the creative work that is so fundamental to doing good science. My aim here is to shed a little light on the conditions that give rise to those situations and to the moments that trigger some weird idea that eventually leads to a scientific discovery, the kind of weird ideas from which scientific insights are created!

I'm going to touch on points relating to the philosophy of science, science management and the design of good social-ecological research methodology, but basically, and mainly, what I am concerned with here is a topic on which I have a great deal of expertise and experience: being a scientist. As a practising scientist, I have had many opportunities to watch the amazing process through which scientific insights are created and I think it is a process that deserves more attention than it has gotten from us in recent years: the process where, from a cluster of weird ideas, as they begin to be tested in a puzzling way, slowly, more formative and coherent ideas begin to take shape; sometimes, after a period of probing and prodding, some of them turn out to be capable of living on, of continuing to have meaning even beyond their original conceptual setting, proving themselves to be persistent and relevant in other contexts; some die; and some never even make it into a cluster of weird ideas in the first place. While most good scientists are somehow vaguely aware of how important it is to be able to come up with weird ideas, this is not something that practising scientists tend to talk about in a formal sort of way. I want to talk about it here, in this chapter, because I think that our ability to solve the complex social-ecological problems of the future is going to depend upon our ability to continue creating important scientific insights in a changing environment of scientific practice. My aim here is not to provide any definitive answers on this topic but to raise a question for discussion and debate: what kind of conditions can make it possible for us to create the new scientific insights that we are going to need in order to move our research on social ecological resilience forward in the coming years?

Big ideas

As has been mentioned already above, it seems to me that I have had, in my career, five what I feel are wonderfully happy 'big ideas'. I see them as 'big ideas' because when they finally got to the point of being tested, an amazing thing happened: they took on a life of their own. I think that the experience I have had with these big ideas reflects an important part of the process of scientific discovery. As a scientist, once you have some weird but somehow plausible idea, you set about trying to find reasons why it is wrong; this is the process that Karl Popper (1963) described as falsification. We set up experiments to test whether our predictions match up with how things actually seem to be developing in the real world. If you've got a big idea, then, as you watch the results of the testing, perhaps over days, perhaps over years, something amazing happens. You begin to become convinced that your idea actually matches up with and helps to explain something that is happening in the real world. In that moment your understanding, both of your idea and of the real world, is expanded and changed. Immediately after that, you ask yourself: what are the consequences? What are the implications? Like an explorer encountering a radically new territory never seen or described before among his or her people, or when one first encounters new organisms, new types of relationships or new people, watching a big idea come to life is a bit like entering into a new world. Your eyes open up, your senses are all on full alert and your perception of the situation is enriched. In these situations even the language that we use changes, as we try to find appropriate words to describe the characteristics and content of this new world. That process, of choosing new words, is the creation of a nomenclature: some words one invents, some words one transforms – like resilience or lumps. With them, whole new ways of thinking about the world are created: whole new perspectives are opened up and one suddenly sees new things that one didn't, or couldn't, notice before, because we didn't have the words or the ideas required to describe them.[6]

It is through this creative process that the big ideas that move science forward come into being. So, if we need more new big ideas, then we need to understand the processes and conditions that make this kind of creative insight possible within science in the first place. How can we design research projects and institutions where there is room to create these important novel ideas that may eventually turn out to pass the test of scientific puzzling, proving themselves to be usefully consistent with demonstrable empirical reality? Where do these ideas come from? And what is it about the organizations within which they come about that has made it possible for them to appear and to avoid being smothered? The material informing my exploration of these questions here is my own personal experience of having worked for sixty years as a practising scientist, and so this text is, in that respect, very personal. It is not a formal scholarly synthesis concerning the question of institutional design and social-ecological change, like the ones that Elinor Ostrom has developed with her analysis of common property systems (1990, 2005). It is not even a formal assessment of the social-ecological and practical issues concerning the institutions of academic research, as is presented in some of the other chapters in this collection. It is just a single, personal reflection on my own singular experience, which comes from a long career of working on systems ecology and ecological economics. Although it is certainly no basis for establishing any new nomenclatures, perhaps this reflection can provide a few promising, or even weird, ideas worth puzzling over and exploring.

Novelty-friendly institutions

Much of what I have discovered and written about institutions over the years, concerning, for example, adaptive management (Holling 1978) or panarchy (Gunderson and Holling 2002), came, at least in some respects, from my own practitioner-based assessments of the structures and processes that I saw operating within the various organizations for which I have worked. For example, I think that friendliness towards novelty, whether it is intentional or accidental, is a context that is favourable for encountering, clustering and exploring the new, sometimes awkward, ideas that are the building blocks of scientific innovation. Interestingly, whatever the reason may be, it happens to be the case that at every organization where I've worked, I have entered at a point when it was undergoing some burst of novelty.

When I began working with the Canadian Department of Forestry, it was right after World War II, in 1948. Although that probably sounds as if it was a very unintellectual environment, in reality it was a time of great intellectual freedom for scientists. After the war and in the looming shadow of the astounding scientific achievements that accompanied its end – not least among them being the creation of the atomic bomb – the leaders of the most powerful countries around the world saw that there was a very real chance that they would be dominated, in the future, from within their own countries, by novel kinds of new science. Remember, it was during World War II that optimization and many of the various mathematical techniques that we use today in modelling were first developed. Whether we like to think about it or not, they were developed in a war setting and were used to gain the upper hand in political struggles for power.

Competing to have stronger science than the countries one opposed actually became part of a sort of generally applied post-war security strategy for most industrialized countries. Canada, being of the opinion that it was too small to dominate in the competition, either with force or with numbers, decided to establish novel research centres – what we would today call 'centres of excellence' – across the country, in order to strike out ahead of the pack. Centres were set up for agriculture, including provision for the study of genetics, for forestry, because that is such a dominant resource aspect in Canada, and for fisheries.

Interestingly, some of the exceptional names that have put their imprint on ecology come from a small group of people who all worked at these centres: for example, Bill Ricker in fisheries was noted for his classic modelling work; Bill Wellington, one of the founders of bioclimatology, published thoroughly innovative work on insect behaviour; and Frank Morris led the world in insect population dynamics and modern statistics. These men were really the giants of their day, each coming up with 'big ideas' and each working, like me, at this time, within organizations that were exceptionally novelty-friendly, where we were actually encouraged to scan the horizons of our understanding.

When rigidity starts setting in ...

During that period, at the end of World War II, there were perhaps three real 'centres of excellence' in ecological science in the whole world and one of them was this community of researchers that came from these Canadian government laboratories. It was a wonderfully exciting experience to work for the forest research centre at that time. We were encouraged not only to study practical problems but also to explore innovative topics and to study problems that we thought might be important. We were exploring the horizons of the scientific knowledge of our day, and when we developed an idea that looked as though it was going to have what it takes to live a life of its own – that is to say, a 'big idea' – it was instantly grabbed and endorsed by just about anyone and everyone within the community and became a new part of the horizon of knowledge that we were working to extend.

Eventually it got to the point where the institutional organizers who were responsible for directing our work could no longer understand the work that was being created within their own organizations. They literally could not follow what we were doing. As a result, they could not judge whether it was what they thought we should be doing. This was not a good situation. Gradually, more and more operational problems began to pile up. The administration attempted, somewhat in vain, to keep abreast of the scientific creations coming from their own staff. At the same time, the Canadian academic system discovered that they could not hire anybody who knew the state of the art in ecological science, on the one hand because the Canadian government had put all of the country's resources and best people into these government labs and on the other because, partly as a result of this allocation of resources towards the research centres, the state of the art was constantly and rapidly shifting. The universities were even facing staffing shortages, because the people who were capable of teaching ecological science were all being employed in the specialized, research-only government labs. And finally, this overall problem then had the knock-on effect that, owing to a staffing shortage in the education system, there were an inadequate number of ecological science students coming up out of the universities to reinforce the government's environment research at the labs over the medium and the long term.

Watching this process from the inside, I began to see a pattern in this setting that I have come to see in more and more different social situations over the years: it seems to me that there is, in some scientific organizations, a natural life cycle, much like the one that we can see operating in many of the ecological organizations that we call ecosystems. That is to say, at least in the scientific organizations where I have worked, there seem to be some very fundamental similarities between the social organization of our research institutes and those of the ecological systems that we study. Both start off in life with a great flood of innovation. In the beginning, at a new research institute, there is the excitement, a pioneering spirit, and the kind of almost automatic mutual support that occurs when a group is coming together to deal with a common problem, in this case the problem of identifying new scientific objects and developing new theories, to generate new ideas and to explore their consequences and implications. Within this first phase there is a slow build-up of capability. For lack of a better word, we may call this social or organizational capital, which is accompanied by an accumulation of special knowledge specific to the organization's research topic. If all goes well, then this social capital (the institutional and organizational products arising from the work of the various people conducting research at the institute) is combined with the new knowledge they are creating, and the specific results of that work become more and more evident, not only to people working within the institute but also to those outside it. Eventually, these results and new understanding are slowly transferred to larger and larger arenas, taking on a life of their own beyond the research context within which they were created. As this process of creation takes hold within a research organization, the work of managing it eventually starts to require more and more rules and regulations, and more and more bureaucracy. This accumulation of organizational structure leads the research institute to become more and more rigid, less and less flexible, and less and less able provide the novelty-friendly spaces that seem to be so important for generating new ideas and extending, testing and consolidating them into the big ideas that move science forward. So, we can see a progression: after having started out with a wonderful novelty-friendly environment of exploration and innovation, successful achievement of innovations – manifest in the creation of new knowledge that can be used productively by other scientists – seems to lead, as a *consequent result of that success*, to the gradual emergence of ever more rigid, novelty-crushing organizational structures.

At some point, as I watched this process occur over and again within the various organizations where I was working, I became convinced that this simultaneous gaining of structure and losing capacity to support novelty creation was the same kind of process as what I had observed in the forests of Canada.[7] The forests that I studied usually started off with seedlings, growing and maturing over time, becoming, as it were, established. It seemed to me that, eventually, once the primary species of a forest had become established, various different additional tree species would then begin to appear. Slowly, the energy demands impinging on the freedom of that forest system would increase, as all these different species of trees, and their animal companions, would begin to become established. Gradually the forest makes possible more and more accumulation of materials, in the form of living and dead plants and animals, and various forms of foods and wastes, and for the associated stored-up energy that they embody. So far so good. However, it seems that as this accumulation process goes on and on, the forest also slowly becomes less and less able to maintain the diversity that had originally helped it to become so well established in the first place. Its development dynamics become more and more dominated by the big battle competitions taking place between a few lead species, and energy is invested more and more in maintaining the status quo.

A fully mature boreal forest is actually a very rigid thing: rich, interesting and varied but also rigid. At this mature stage, the richness of materials, resources and organizational structure that have been accumulated in the course of its progression towards maturation have now been captured by a few climax species (see Clements 1916), preventing other novelty from appearing. Once we open up our thinking to the possibility that similar dynamics are at play in the maturation of human social organizations, we can consider whether perhaps the rigidities to be observed in mature scientific organizations don't have a similar origin.

The organization where I started my scientific career after World War II, the Canadian Forestry Service, was in many respects like a young forest on its way to maturing. During the time I was working there, it went through the stages of this process: innovation, change, with increasing variety and diversity, then increasing productivity and accumulation of social and organizational capital, eventually then reaching a point of substantially increased rigidity. In a forest, that rigidity creates what I would call an accident waiting to happen. At this stage the energy moving through the system, which had previously been invested in novelty creation and the development of new structures, is now all being directed towards maintaining the status quo, to maintaining the newly achieved complexity of the system. Whether it turns out to be a forest fire, an insect outbreak or just an inability to bounce back after a very damaging storm, one way or another eventually this rigid system will break. And when it does, the stocks and flows of energy that had been dedicated to maintaining this mature organizational capital which had been invested in the structure of the forest – in the complexity of the system, or what we might call 'the environment' – are released.

Suddenly, with that release, bearing in mind that some of it leaks away, of course, this energy, which had previously been invested in maintaining the old rigid structure of the forest, is now, in the disorganized state that follows a collapse, once again available for creative purposes, and the resources of the system can once again be combined in novel ways.

Climax and collapse in research institutes: creating conditions conducive to novelty creation

Without wishing to underplay their differences, to my thinking the forests I studied at the beginning of my career and the organizations I have worked within throughout it can be seen to move through very similar cycles of change. At the beginning they look very simple, and as time progresses, their path of development is also very predictable, moving through an initial period of plentiful creativity, perhaps gaining ground and becoming established, perhaps disappearing, eventually, if they survive, moving on through a stage of establishment and towards an inevitable moment when they begin to become less and less relevant, more and more rigid, less and less able to propagate novelty. It is, of course, possible to invent ways to get around this progression, and this is indeed part of how forest management works. But I think we are still learning about how to do this for a research institute, about what is possible and what works. There is a lot known about how to foster creativity in places like the product development teams of a company, but very little is known about how or whether that can translate into systems and practices that can support creativity in our research institutions, or indeed, whether those kinds of practices should be used there at all. Perhaps there are fundamental differences between the kind of team and organizational creativity that is appropriate for product development and the kind that is appropriate for supporting creativity in science.

In this past year the government of Sweden has made an exceptional effort to take up this challenge by inventing the Stockholm Resilience Centre at Stockholm University, which aims to create a fundamentally novelty-friendly institution.[8] It is basically intended to be like a Skunks Works® for socio-ecological systems science, where a select group of highly skilled individuals is given total freedom to work on an important but poorly understood problem.[9] It is the only entity in the history of that university that transcends the institution's disciplinary management structures, with the unit heads speaking not to a dean but directly to the vice-chancellor. In its structures and its style the Stockholm Resilience Centre takes up the challenge of exploring how we can develop ways for getting around this accumulation of rigidity in our research organizations. As I write, they are still in that turbulent early phase of pioneering exploration. The question is: what will become of the organization over time? Will it grow rigid and brittle, losing its resilience and stifling creativity, or will it be able to develop science management strategies that can keep it vital and relevant? How can we manage such a dynamic research organization, if we can do this at all, in a way that avoids the organization becoming more and more rigid and less and less relevant over time?

Research management and ecosystems of ideas

If it is indeed the case that this kind of change process – of innovation, rigorous exploration and testing, consolidation, leading eventually to increasing rigidity and reduced resilience – is played out in the maturation of our research organizations, then, in our effort to design novelty-friendly environments for research, we are once again looking at the question of how to cope with what we call, in resilience science, the adaptive cycle (Gunderson and Holling 2002). Recognizing that all systems have special attributes, perhaps the very same adaptive cycle that we have seen in ecosystem after ecosystem is also at play here; but this time we are talking about the resilience of the ecosystems of our ideas.

If we think the comparison through, we can recall that, while the 'standard' adaptive cycle is certainly to be observed in many ecosystems, we also see instances where ecosystems actually pause within that adaptive cycle, perhaps because only a very small amount of resources are available to fuel the expansion phase, as with the semi-arid savannah systems in Australia. These systems seem to be able to maintain their structure without going through the full boom and bust type of adaptive cycle. A 'capital'-intensive system, like a boreal forest in Canada, which has a great amount of resources available to fuel its take-off phase, can continue with good momentum all the way through to the peak system structure of a climax forest, until it ends up, finally, with a full collapse. By contrast, in these semi-arid savannah systems we see a more stochastic change process dominating the system dynamics. With lots of very little mini-flips taking place, the system is characterized by an almost constant preparedness to create novelty. If this observation, about the relationship between resource availability and rigidity, does translate to research organizations, which I think it could, then perhaps part of what we are looking for in the organizational design of our research institutes is to mimic the more stochastic change that dominates in these semi-arid savannah systems, where lots of very little mini-flips keep the system from becoming too rigid or too top-heavy.

Of course, there are a lot of other factors to consider here, regarding everything from the psychological impact that this dynamic might have on the scientists all the way across to the question of how suitable such a setting would be for carrying out rigorous scientific investigations. But it is important to recall that my aim here is not to prove a proposition, or even to test a claim, but to introduce an idea that might be worthy of further investigation; we are at the first stage of innovative thinking here, where weird ideas that might be valid are tolerated even when they cannot be rigorously substantiated. With that in mind, we can take a closer look at how different organizational dynamics might play out in the daily life of a practising scientist, drawing examples, once again, from my own experiences.

Funnily enough, I always seemed to follow that big boreal cycle around, arriving at the creative phase and leaving at the point where the organization began to start getting rigid. Perhaps that is just a characteristic of my own personality. I think we all somehow, being living systems, also have these kinds of cycles inherent within our beings. Perhaps some of us let these cycles determine what we do, letting them serve as signals for when it is time to go or when it is time to get started with the work of generating novelty, whereas others invest their time and energy into creating and driving the cycles within and around them, working to maintain and extend the organizations in which they are working, while accepting that phases of creativity and rigidity are just part of life.

In my own career one might say that I followed the first of these two patterns, taking signals from, instead of investing in, these cycles of change, and in some ways I see that as a great loss on my part. For example, although I have worked with a lot of really wonderful research groups over the years, although I am a widely respected scientist and now also an old man, I have no one single organizational home. This is because every time an organization where I was working started to settle down and get firmly established, we seemed to be reaching a point where things were starting to become more rigid, and so I would leave. Upon reflection, it seems to me now that I left because the organizations were starting to reach a stage where the work that had originally attracted me – work that was taking place within a climate of innovation – had now gone through the first stages of its adaptive cycle. Having established some really interesting new ideas, as we did for example at the Canadian Department of Forestry in the 1950s, we then moved on to the work of developing and using these new insights. At this stage a lot of new work would be spawned and, just at this stage, time and again, in organization after organization, I would always start to feel grumpy. And it was literally just that: I would get irritated with the administration. I would start to blame everybody but myself for the new rigidity that was emerging within what I had previously experienced as a wonderfully creative, novelty-friendly environment. At times I would get so irritated that I would even invent ways to test whether the organization was still flexible, which sometimes had very interesting results. That's how I ended up taking a sabbatical in Hawaii, for example, to study fish systems while I was working at the Canadian Department of Forestry. Here I was, in the Canadian Forestry Department, and they supported me on a fully paid sabbatical to study fish in Hawaii! Basically, I proposed the project as a kind of a test, to see whether the system was still flexible enough to let me do something so off the wall. It was; so of course then we had to go to Hawaii. That itself was a wonderful experience in its own right, but it also triggered the creation of a completely new research organization: the Institute of Resource Ecology, at the University of British Columbia. Once again I found myself in that exciting early stage of scientific work, where the development of new ideas and scientific innovation is the focus and an interest in novelty creation is regarded as a good thing.

Although that institute was officially known as the Institute of Animal Resource Ecology (IARE), I mention it here using the original name, because this tells something about the challenges that we faced then and still face today when setting out to develop work on integrative subjects, like study of the resilience of social-ecological systems. Although it didn't really change anything as far as the content of the work was concerned, the word 'animal' had to be put into the name because of the response of the botanists at the university, who said: how could you possibly say you're studying ecology unless you have the word botany in the name? And for a variety of reasons we couldn't see that working, so Pete Larkin (1977), one of my close colleagues at the time, suggested that we could get around this problem if we just stuck the word 'animal' into the name. That is important to note here because setting up an Institute of Resource Ecology was an important first step on the long road that we have travelled with the Resilience Alliance and are now travelling with the Stockholm Resilience Centre, making room for the innovative kind of integrative social-ecological systems thinking that puts together economic and social and ecological ideas and understanding.

Setting up and working at the Institute of Resource Ecology was a wonderful experience. The institute was awarded a generous grant by the Ford Foundation, the university agreed to cover the salaries of the staff that were hired as faculty and the institute was designed to become a part of the university. In the first five years it was just amazing; magical things happened. There were all kinds of exciting people coming in – some sticking around; some being hired to remain as faculty; some failures but some successes. It was like an experiment; a centre of excellence on this subject was being formed and we were generating fundamentally new understanding (Birnbaum-More *et al.* 1990). Again, as I had after World War II at the Department of Forestry, I found myself in an exciting, innovative, pioneering time. This research community of faculty, established scientists and students (undergraduate and graduate students and postdocs) began to form fundamental new ideas in a fruitful environment and began to test them both in practice and in theory. And then, once again, I got grumpy. After all this was developed, the institute was becoming part of the university system, just as we had originally hoped that it would. I was becoming established and I got caught up in the institutional dynamics of that process of establishment. The university vice-president, who had been backing us very strongly – just as the vice-chancellor of the University of Stockholm is now doing for the Stockholm Resilience Centre – retired. I didn't think his replacement knew what to do with us and I was watching this exciting, novelty-friendly organization that we had created become part of the establishment. And there I was, up to my old tricks again, responding negatively to the increasing institutional and intellectual rigidity growing up around me.

So I started looking around again for a new place, a place that was more able to handle the novelty-creation work that I so prefer, one that was, so to speak, at the start of its innovation stage of development. And I discovered another quasi-governmental organization where I thought I could get back into the innovative phase of the cycle: IIASA (the International Institute of Applied Systems Analysis). IIASA is a committee name. It is based just outside of Vienna and was formed during the Cold War to bring together scientists from both sides of the so-called Iron Curtain, mainly from the world's two great powers at that time – the Soviet Union and the alliance of the United States of America and Great

Britain – along with a number of other nations. Its scientific focus was to address problems of a universal or global character: the kinds of problems that every country in the east and in the west would be facing – that is to say, problems of 'advanced industrial societies'.[10] The Russians wanted it to be called the Cybernetics Institute and the Americans wanted 'Common Problems' in the name, so IIASA was the compromise.

The idea was to draw upon the history of a vital global community – science – which has its own international culture and economy, in order to help bridge the seemingly insurmountable divide that was developing at that time between the superpowers. IIASA was established to try to take advantage of the international character of science, which transcends international boundaries – for example, where we do peer reviews without being paid, even though this takes up a lot of our time, because it is part of how our community works, in order to maintain our community. And where, although we may have substantial communication barriers of language and culture, when we talk about the science, at least we can all be equally comfortable talking with a Russian (or Soviet) colleague or an American one, or a Japanese, Colombian, African, Indian or German one, for that matter. So the idea was basically to set scientists to work on developing a kind of integrative science that would play a role in helping to resolve complex problems encountered in all 'advanced industrial societies' and in the process to help bridge the East–West divide by setting scientists from both sides of that divide to work on the collective task of solving problems that would affect everyone on the globe.

Howard Raiffa, who was a noted decision theorist from Harvard, was the first director at IIASA. He was brilliant, and also a complete maverick in his management style, which meant that under his supervision IIASA was fundamentally novelty-friendly. He would have an intuition about someone and say yeah, come and join us. Of course, he would double-check their abilities too, but in its early years IIASA was built up with this maverick style of Raiffa's. One interesting characteristic problem of running this organization was the need to provide social support for a team of scientists made up of about eighty to a hundred people from all over the world who needed to live and work in this international, interdisciplinary community. That meant that one of the major tasks of the organization turned out to be just keeping the people involved, the scientists and their families, happy. I mention this because in this chapter I am trying to point out the importance of keeping in mind the basic human aspects associated with setting up a productive research organization. Big ideas, scientific innovations that can fundamentally change the world, are discovered by people who feel free to explore new weird ideas and the way in which a research organization is managed, including its practices for supporting its personnel, can have a big impact on how at ease and how adventurous these personnel feel: good science is fun!

When I first joined IIASA I was in charge of one of the institute's two major projects. The first one, Energy Systems, was run by Wolf Haefele, a wonderful man with whom I never agreed – regarding the science, that is. Wolf was the head of the fast breeder reactor programme in Germany and he had a very Teutonic management style – top-down, with people working for him – whereas I had a totally different approach. I was in charge of the Ecology and Environment project and had set up a sort of parallel processing organization, with lots of external workshops and lots of external people bound together around some general questions that were basically all about stability.

That Wolf Haefele and I could set up these two completely different structures within the same organization illustrates just how much freedom we had there. We were able to get some really talented people involved on the Environment and Ecology project. The team included contributions from Howard Raiffa, himself a leader in decision theory; George Danzig, who invented optimization theory and linear programming; Mike Ferring, who was developing new approaches to hydrological engineering modelling; and Bill Clark, whose energy and organization were central in implementing our work. He is now very well known for his work on multinational decisions for big environmental policy and is a major bridge joining resilience and vulnerability concepts. We learned things on that project that we had never even thought of, that we didn't even recognize. Out of all that creative work came a synthesis of tested methods, which began to bear more and more on our understanding of ecological problems. For example, some of the things that we learned from optimization, which we got from the economics and decision theory people with whom we were working, turned out to be immensely valuable. However, other things that we picked up from them turned out to be useless, at least when we applied and tested them for use in our own research, and probably, we came to believe, for anyone.

During the time when I was working at IIASA, we came up with a menu of formal, systematic approaches, of tested and proven value, that could be used for examining a great variety of ecological processes ranging from the spruce bud worm outbreaks in the forests of eastern Canada and of Bavaria, to the dynamics of the savannah systems in Australia, the shallow lake systems in the Netherlands and the deep lake ones in the US Midwest. And as we proceeded in carrying out this standardized approach, to study these various different systems, suddenly the elements of a bigger picture came together, which we could then, in turn, begin to examine systematically. It was an exciting time! And then the process of becoming established began once again.

I stayed at IIASA for two years and then went back to the University of British Columbia. But when I got back to Canada I walked right back into that rigid situation I had left behind me and was right back to getting irritated with the administration and with the university structures. I thought that they didn't really understand what we were doing and I had that same unease as before, that feeling that I had had at the Forestry Department in the 1960s. So when IIASA approached me again a few years later, in the early 1980s, to ask if I would serve as director, my reaction was twofold: on the one hand, I was thinking, this 'new' institute was no longer really all that new, so I figured it was probably getting rigid too, but on the other hand, since it had gone through nine years of innovative exploration, perhaps what it really needed now was a new thrust of innovation. I was not at all sure what to do. The situation at the university was complex and there was also a complex political situation at that time at IIASA.

In any case, I was getting fidgety again, so I decided to accept the offer and head back to Vienna. And things certainly got interesting, although not in the way that I had expected. Two months after I got to Vienna, in 1980, Ronald Reagan came into office in the United States and many of the multilateral agreements that had been established around the world were ended, including support for the international work of the US national academies of science. Suddenly, millions of dollars were removed from the IIASA budget and the whole situation changed. But the money wasn't even the most important factor. This shift in the politics also revealed the careful balance in the power games being played out between the Russians and the Americans who were working within IIASA. With so much US money and, perhaps more importantly, US political support for the project being pulled out, the Russians no longer had – I'm not going to say enemy – a sparring partner against whom they could compete, and the mischief that this generated was amazing. It was not anything like plotting or espionage, just sheer ordinary human mischief, as the balance that had been helping to keep rivalries in check simply disappeared.

I tried to address the problem by pretending that new power was coming in, which I did by hiring a man named Chester Cooper, a wonderful guy, deeply knowledgeable about global change issues, who also happened to have a background with the CIA. I knew the Russians would find out about his history and he was a person whom I could work with, intellectually, which was the main reason for hiring him. For a while, getting him in there as assistant director allowed the whole system to stabilize, which turned out to be what the institution really needed at that time, and after about three or four years in Vienna I went back to the University of British Columbia again: no great fireworks this time around, no new big ideas. But I had learned a lot about research management and organization while working as director of IIASA.

As I began to learn more about these rhythms of innovation, growth, collapse and reorganization in our own research organizations, I began to observe some additional patterns. In some organizations the process could occur in a natural way. Certainly this was still disturbing for the people caught up in the middle of the changes, but it was exciting and inspiring too. However, in other organizations, movement through this cycle seemed to be an extremely difficult process that could even lead to a total collapse of the creative environment. While I am convinced that there are similarities between an ecological system and a human social system – deep similarities, I think – there also seem to be some very interesting differences that humans add to the dynamics, mainly because we have *expectations and a special ability to control the world around us*.

At the end of the first part of my career, which sort of started about thirty-five years ago with the resilience paper (Holling 1973), this is where I had got to with my thinking on the problem of how to organize good social-ecological systems research. The insights that were develop in that resilience paper (ibid.) had forced me to shift my focus away from the idea that control of a given ecosystem was hovering around a single variable, to thinking about variability as a form of stability, operating within boundaries. This led, of course, to the work of testing whether those stability boundaries do actually exist and operate in this way, and the results of that work completely changed the way that we were thinking about stability. So, at that time, in the early 1970s, I encountered a sort of tipping point in my own thinking about how living systems maintain their stability. Although I had not thought formally about what that implied for the stability of the organizations that we work in, as research scientists, I can see today that I brought these ideas with me when I took over as director of IIASA. This opened my eyes to a lot of possibilities but also to the challenges that stand in the way of setting up genuinely novelty-friendly research organizations designed to support the kind of creative study of complex social-ecological problems that is needed today.

The Resilience Network, the Resilience Alliance: good on small islands

After IIASA I continued with my own research, based in Florida, working with a number of colleagues to follow up and continue to test the ideas that had sprung up in the 1970s and 1980s. This eventually led, in the mid-1990s, to the organization of a workshop bringing together in person a collaborative international network of people all working on problems of resilience, which in turn eventually led to us setting up the Resilience Alliance, and then the Stockholm Resilience Centre and the first Resilience 2008 conference, where Brian Walker and I gave the opening speeches that have been transformed into this book chapter. At that time, back in the 1990s, we called it the Resilience Network and I will describe here in some detail how it all got started, because the decisions that we took about how to set up that network reflected the application of the ideas about research organization that I have outlined here. So, this process that we went through in setting up the Resilience Alliance was also an experiment to test the validity of some of my weird ideas about how perhaps research organizations, innovation and cycles of change are related to each other in a kind of ecology of ideas.

It all started off with a workshop that we held on a small island off the coast of Georgia in the United States, where we got a group of people together to write a proposal to develop a research project that linked up analysis of the human, social, ecological and mathematical (there was not a lot of economics, but more mathematical analysis) aspects of the earth's environmental systems. The place where we met was called Little St Simons Island – a wonderful place owned by a single family, and we had the whole island to ourselves. We did a lot of thinking and walking on the beach and came up with the basic ideas for the research proposal, which a few of us then wrote up and submitted to the MacArthur Foundation. Of course, we had done a lot of preparation work with the foundation before we submitted the proposal, but all it basically said in the end was: although economics and ecology have had a lot of conflicts, in social reality and in scholarly study, perhaps the reason is not because one or the other is wrong in some fundamental way but because each is correct in some fundamentally *different* way. So we proposed the following solution: if we combine these two partial representations of social-ecological reality into an integrative whole, within a single Theory [meaning here a formal theory of science, like the Theory of Relativity, with a big T], then perhaps we could make a great leap forward in understanding the environmental problems of late industrial societies. That was the basic scientific argument underlying the project that eventually led to the Resilience Alliance, but there was more to the project than just that. There was also the beginnings of a vision for how we might create an organization with enough room for all the different ideas that needed to be put together to do this work, enough structure to help us produce rigorous scientific results and enough flexibility to make sure there was room for those wonderful weird ideas that we were going to need in order to move all this forward.

We had a lot of freedom to make these choices about how to organize the research, since our proposal was very broad and very basic, but it is worth noting that it would never be enough to get support today, which I see as a real problem. Today, the big funding groups, the private foundations, which are not exclusively but dominantly in the United States, have moved on from their own phase of flexible innovation, which benefited us in the 1990s, to a more and more business management-oriented kind of organized control of research. Only a few foundations have not, and they have explicitly chosen to remain open to funding work in the innovation phase. This is a problem because it is this innovative phase that is so important for creating new understanding: where the expected outcomes are still unclear, where there are real risks that you end up down a blind alley. This is where foundation support is really needed. Back in the early 1990s we could still get this kind of support from the MacArthur Foundation, but I remember one of the people on the board giving a first hint of the way that foundations were heading, saying, 'Well, what are the measures of your success that we can use to judge you when you're finished?' My answer was 'I have no idea: this is new, this is novelty, I'm not going predict what we're going to discover, I simply don't know.' Now of course I was saying that for effect. What she wanted was the number of papers, and the number of conferences and so forth, which are things that we do, of course, because they part of carrying out the work, but these aren't really the outcomes, at least as far as we're concerned; as scientists, the real outcomes that we were looking for were the scientific insights. This MacArthur grant gave us freedom to embark on a new phase of innovative engagement with the topics that we had started to address at IIASA back in 1973, and we started out with as little structure as we could achieve, organizing a series of workshops around the world, all on the topic of resilience in social-ecological systems, and mostly on small islands.

Since the whole thing had started with such a wonderfully creative experience on Little St Simons Island, we decided that, as much as possible, we'd have all the meetings on islands. Interestingly, we began to observe a pattern in the kinds of people and processes that were effective at the workshops. This gave us a sort of formula that we could use that was both enormously productive, with respect to idea generation and idea testing, and also, importantly, fun! We found that the workshops had to be flexibly organized, so that there was a lot of opportunity for pairs of people to wander on the beach talking in great detail about something that had come up in a more general discussion, getting deep into the roots of a topic, while other groups of people might be relaxing and digesting the thoughts of the day, playing music, singing, or writing limericks (that was an invention of Brian Walker's). And it was that mix of organized discussions and creative activities that formed the basis for the science that has led to where we are now with the concept of resilience, which Brian has outlined in detail earlier in the chapter. We made a lot of effort to create opportunities for flexible fun, for people to unexpectedly encounter each other and to end up leaving the workshop saying, 'Boy, that was fun!' In the midst of our efforts to solve difficult problems, it seems that we can forget that good science depends on *creativity*. When we are trying to foster innovation in science, we need to make space for the creative people and the creative processes that are the key drivers leading us towards new understanding.

Using this formula of small-island workshops, we had an extremely productive first five years of work, developing the fundamental integrative concepts regarding resilience of social-ecological systems, which eventually led to the panarchy book (Gunderson and Holling 2002) and three other key texts on resilience: one in economics (Janssen 2003), one on the characteristics of large-scale ecosystems (Gunderson and Pritchard 2002) and one that was essentially about what has now come to be called adaptive governance (Berkes *et al.* 2002). The common aim of all these works was the linking of social, ecological and economic systems, and the panarchy book was basically the attempt at fundamental integration, where I poured out everything that I thought I knew. To be fair, it should be said that the panarchy book is, at times, very dense, but it is the first comprehensive effort to bring this integrative thinking together within a single text and it marks a real step forward in our thinking on the topic.

Along the way, as we prepared these first major texts, we began to notice a sub-set of scholars in our midst who were 'good on islands' and who turned out to be really important for the work. To be sure, there were other people who made outstanding intellectual contributions, but this sub-group of people who were 'good on islands' were the ones moving the work forward. They would work like the dickens and contribute unique ideas that they enjoyed connecting with other people's ideas. They had a real interest in the joys of mutual discovery. Somehow these people seemed to be really important to the creative process of developing this fundamentally new understanding of complex social-ecological systems that we were able to present in the first set of Resilience Alliance books, produced in the early 2000s. One might go so far as to say that islands and poetry are part of our methodology for doing resilience science, bringing art and science back together as part of the process of going beyond reductionism, as in the art exhibition that was held as part of the Resilience 2008 conference. Intensifying our collaborations with people who were 'good on islands' and adopting a meeting format that made space not only for good science but also for other kinds of creativity was absolutely central to our success with this early work on social-ecological resilience.

Now of the estimated 300 international scholars who were part of these series of workshops funded by the MacArthur Foundation, about 10 per cent of them were ... well, certainly they were good on islands, but they were also people who had some singular quality that made them become a centre point or node for our activities. This raised the question of how to proceed, of how to maintain the possibility for those folks to continue working together. So we decided to invent another experiment, a new organization – a kind of meta-organization, and that was the Resilience Alliance. And we adopted certain rules in an effort to keep the organization flexible. For example, we decided not to own anything. Once you own something, you get trapped into material conditions that we figured would lead into an adaptive cycle, making the organization eventually become irrelevant. We aimed to have the minimum possible amount of organization: just two to four people as staff, people known internationally for the outstanding excellence of their scholarship, who would provide quality work and lend an image of prestige and authority to the organization.

After a couple of years we ended up with fifteen groups around the world (mostly at universities), each providing a modest membership fee (about $7,000) to cover the operating costs of the Alliance. Although it was small, the fee was often difficult to get. While a university might give money easily enough for travel, membership in another organization was very tough. Nevertheless, people managed to get the money, and that provided the core support that we needed to create and operate this flexible organization. Our aim, recalling the observations above about the constant mini-flips encountered in savannahs, was to operate in a sort of state of 'permanent transience'. People came in and out, going back to their home institution and drawing on the strengths of the various institutions within the Alliance. It was all very flexible in format and enormously stimulating for the creation of new ideas.

Eventually this led to a second round of books and the consolidation of new ideas that Brian Walker has already summarized in the first half of this chapter. So, the Resilience Alliance was sort of the third step in bringing forward and working through these ideas that began in the 1970s, about organization and dynamic stability. But it was also an experiment, which seems to have turned out pretty well, putting that understanding into practice in the design of research organizations. Now that it has gone through its first eight years, I had supposed that if it was a boreal forest-type system, it should be just about beginning to collapse by now. Actually, I went along very sceptically to the meeting of the Resilience Alliance governing board just before the Resilience 2008 conference, asking myself, 'Is it finally at that stage of stagnated irrelevance?' Much to my surprise, I found that it wasn't. Brian had brought in some new groups of scholars, the climate change group at the Tyndall Centre (with Neil Adgers and Kate Brown) and Terry Hughes' Resilience Institute, studying the coral reefs of the world, and then there was a new group taking shape at Arizona State University, with their growing ability to integrate economic, anthropological and ecological knowledge. We seem to have been able to continue adding new thinkers and groups to the Alliance, so that the same vitality, the same climate of innovation, is, quite remarkably, still there. And by choosing in 2008 to step down as director, Brian Walker has now provided the conditions for the Resilience Alliance to go through a new stage of reorganization and renewal, which we are right in the midst of now, which is going to be completely different from what happened when we set up the Alliance in the first place.

So why, at this phase in its progression through the organizational cycle, where I expected that that the Resilience Alliance should be collapsing, or at least becoming less and less relevant, is this not the case? Have we achieved our goal of having a kind of permanent transience? Were we right to think that this kind of permanent transience could foster continuing creativity? Or are we missing something, because we are too close to the problem? Perhaps we have pushed the cycle to develop in new ways? At just the time when I was expecting increased rigidity within the Alliance, a new, more formalized offshoot institute was created, in the form of the Stockholm Resilience Centre (SRC). One explanation is that the SRC has been able to take up some of structuring pressure that would otherwise be playing out within the Alliance. So we have these two events coming together: the Resilience Alliance, which is going to begin going through its next cycle of development, and still can only be judged on the basis of its ability to retain and generate innovation and collaboration; and the founding of the Stockholm Resilience Centre, with its formal institutional leadership in the form of Carl Folke and Johan Rockström, with strong institutional support from the Stockholm University, and an exciting group of staff and students from all over the world. Both organizations are setting out to carve new research territory at this critical time in human history, and both have taken part of their structure from the ideas I have presented here regarding the similarities between cycles of change in ecosystems and cycles of change in research organizations.

Conclusions

When we started the social-ecological systems analysis work of the Resilience Alliance, back in the 1990s, part of what we imagined was going to emerge – although we didn't know when – was precisely complex ecological economic events like the joining up of the food and energy markets that we are seeing now with biofuels, which has suddenly become very clearly a big problem. Actually, the whole topic of biofuels is a very good final example of how a lack of abilities to develop integrative policies has led to reduction of diversity and resilience in the world's ecosystems. In this case, not only in the energy production system but also in our crop production systems we have seen a dramatic loss of resilience, which is now being compounded by this new pressure to turn an already failing global agricultural system into a system to produce fuel for a failing energy system that is serving a failing economic system. Strangely enough, this is precisely what we predicted back twelve years ago when we began our first discussions of social-ecological resilience back on Little St Simons Island, where we identified the need to develop research that could link up analysis of the human, social, ecological and economic parts of the earth's environmental system.

We have come a long way in the past twelve years with our efforts to create novelty-friendly intellectual environments that can help us develop this resilience science. We have been able to establish two very different organizations: first the Resilience Alliance and more recently the Stockholm Resilience Centre – two institutions and hundreds of scholars. It is a lot more than we had twenty years ago, but we should not forget that these two institutions are still exceptional and that the academic context within which most research is carried out still remains strictly divided into disciplinary domains and keeps moving through big, sweeping iterations of the adaptive cycle without taking these dynamics into account. The Resilience Alliance and the Stockholm Resilience Centre are two places where we can come together as scholars interested in studying the pressing social-ecological questions of our time, to create and innovate, to explore and discover the new ideas that may help us to find our collective way through the global crises of the coming decades. If we are lucky and manage them well, perhaps these organizations will continue to offer us beacons of light and forums for creativity for many years to come.

Notes

1 For more information and proceedings of the Resilience 2008 conference, see http://resilience2008.org.

2 For a complete list of publications arising from the Resilience Alliance collaborations, see the bibliography of Alliance-related publications at www.resalliance.org.

3 At a special session during the Stockholm Resilience 2008 conference, Alison Quinlan, Communications Director for the Alliance, presented the workbook and a new version of the associated wiki website – http://wiki.resalliance.org – that presents a sort of 'how to do a resilience assessment of your region'. One of our aims with the wiki website is to expand this area of activity in new directions: to make it possible for the whole international community of people interested in resilience to collectively contribute to this resilience workbook. I think it's a very exciting development.

4 The lecture upon which this chapter text is based was given in April 2008, before the September 2008 state takeover of the mortgage holding companies Fannie Mae and Freddie Mac and the collapse of the investment bank Lehman Brothers, which marked the onset of the 2008 global financial crisis.

5 For more information on the Resilience 2008 Art Exhibit, see http://resilience2008.org.

6 Editors' note: This topic is discussed extensively in the academic literature on science studies and even by some authors contributing chapters to this book. The comments made here in this chapter are reflections from the perspective of a practising scientist, based on his own understanding of his own work, and are not intended to engage directly with the content or critiques developed in that discourse.

7 I tend to think in terms of forests because I worked on forests in the early years of my scientific career.

8 See www.stockholmresilience.org.

9 Skunk Works® is a term coined in 1943 by Lockheed Martin and now copyrighted by the firm to describe a special team of scientists and engineers, in their case of military aircraft, who are given substantial intellectual and administrative autonomy to meet an applied development specification that requires state-of-the-art science. See www.lockheedmartin.com/aeronautics/skunkworks/ for more on the history of the Skunk Works®.

10 Here it is important to recall that at the time when I joined IIASA, in the early 1970s, these words – East and West and Iron Curtain – triggered a whole set of very specific reactions. Basically, IIASA was an effort to say that even in the midst of the huge tensions of the Cold War, at least science and scholarship could collaborate across these seemingly impenetrable national boundaries.

References

Allen, C.R. and C.S. Holling eds. 2008. *Discontinuities in Ecological and Other Systems*. New York: Columbia University Press.

Anderies, J.M., B.H. Walker and A.P. Kinzig. 2006. 'Fifteen weddings and a funeral: case studies and resilience-based management.' *Ecology and Society* 11(1): 21. Online, available at: www.ecologyandsociety.org/vol11/iss1/art21/.

Berkes, F., J. Colding and C. Folke eds. 2002. *Navigating Social-Ecological Systems: Building Resilience for Complexity and Change*. Cambridge: Cambridge University Press.

Birnbaum-More, P.H., F.A. Rossini and D.R. Baldwin eds. 1990. *International Research Management: Studies in Interdisciplinary Methods from Business, Government, and Academia*. New York: Oxford University Press.

Boyd, E. and C. Folke eds. Forthcoming. *Governing Social-Ecological Transformations: Adapting to the Challenge of Global Environmental Change*. Cambridge: Cambridge University Press.

Carpenter, S. and W. Brock. 2006. 'Rising variance: a leading indicator of ecological transition.' *Ecology Letters* 9: 311–318.

Carpenter, S. and R. Lathrop. 2008. 'Probabilistic estimate of a threshold for eutrophication.' *Ecosystems* 11(4): 601–613.

Chapin, F.S. III, G.P. Kofinas and C. Folke eds. 2009. *Principles of Resource Stewardship: Resilience-Based Resource Management in a Changing World*. Frankfurt am Main: Springer.

Clements, F.E. 1916. *Plant Succession*. Washington, DC: Carnegie Institute.

Denman, K.L., G. Brasseur, A. Chidthaisong, P. Ciais, P.M. Cox, R.E. Dickinson, D. Hauglustaine, C. Heinze, E. Holland, D. Jacob, U. Lohmann, S. Ramachandran, P.L. da Silva Dias, S.C. Wofsy and X. Zhang. 2007. 'Couplings between changes in the climate system and biogeochemistry.' In *Climate Change 2007: The Physical Science Basis: Contribution of Working Group I to the Fourth Assessment Report of the Intergovernmental Panel on Climate Change*, eds. S. Solomon, D. Qin, M. Manning, Z. Chen, M. Marquis, K.B. Averyt, M. Tignor and H.L. Miller. Cambridge: Cambridge University Press.

Dietz, T., E. Ostrom and P.C. Stern. 2003. 'The struggle to govern the commons.' Science 302(52): 1907–1912.

Fisk, D.J. and J. Kerherve. 2006. 'Complexity as a cause of unsustainability.' *Ecological Complexity* 3(4): 336–343.

Gerber, H.U and E.S.W. Shiu. 1998. 'On the time value of ruin.' *North American Actuarial Journal* 2(1): 48–78.

Gunderson, L.H. and C.S. Holling eds. 2002. *Panarchy: Understanding Transformations in Human and Natural Systems*. London: Island Press.

Gunderson, L.H. and L. Pritchard eds. 2002. *Resilience and the Behavior of Large-Scale Systems*. Washington, DC: Island Press.

Gunderson, L.H., Holling C.S. and S.S. Light. 1995. *Barriers and Bridges to the Renewal of Ecosystems and Institutions*. New York: Columbia University Press.

Gunderson, L.H., C.R. Allen and C.S. Holling eds. 2009. *Foundations of Ecological Resilience*. Washington, DC: Island Press.

Holling, C.S. 1959. 'Some characteristics of simple types of predation and parasitism.' *Canadian Entomologist* 91: 385–398.

Holling, C.S. 1965. 'The functional response of predators to prey density and its role in mimicry and population regulation.' *Memoirs of the Entomological Society of Canada* 45: 3–60.

Holling, C.S. 1973. 'Resilience and stability of ecological systems.' *Annual Review of Ecology and Systematics* 4: 1–23.

Holling, C.S. ed. 1978. *Adaptive Environmental Assessment and Management*. Chichester, UK: John Wiley.

Holling, C.S. 1986. 'Resilience of ecosystems; local surprise and global change.' In *Sustainable Development of the Biosphere*, ed. W.C. Clark and R.E. Munn. Cambridge: Cambridge University Press.

Holling, C.S. 2001. 'Understanding the complexity of economic, ecological and social systems.' *Ecosystems* 4(5): 390–405.

Holling, C.S. and G.K. Meffe. 1996. 'Command and control and the pathology of natural resource management.' *Conservation Biology* 10(2): 328–337.

Holling, C.S., L. Gunderson and D. Ludwig. 2002a. 'In quest of a theory of adaptive change.' In *Panarchy: Understanding Transformations in Human and Natural Systems*, ed. L.H. Gunderson and C.S. Holling. Washington, DC: Island Press.

Holling, C.S., L. Gunderson and G. Peterson. 2002b. 'Sustainability and panarchies.' In *Panarchy: Understanding Transformations in Human and Natural Systems*, eds L.H. Gunderson and C.S. Holling. Washington, DC: Island Press.

Hubbert, M.K. 1949. 'Energy from fossil fuels.' *Science* 109(2823): 103–109.

Janssen, M. ed. 2003. *Complexity and Ecosystem Management*. Cheltenham, UK: Edward Elgar.

Larkin, P.A. 1977. 'An epitaph for the concept of maximum sustainable yield.' *Transactions of the American Fisheries Society* 106(1): 1–11.

Loorbach, D. 2007. *Transition Management: New Mode of Governance for Sustainable Development*. Utrecht: International Books.

Norberg, J. and G. Cumming eds. 2008. *Complexity Theory for a Sustainable Future*. New York: Columbia University Press.

Olsson, P., L.H. Gunderson, S.R. Carpenter, P. Ryan, L. Lebel, C. Folke and C.S. Holling. 2006. 'Shooting the rapids: navigating transitions to adaptive governance of social-ecological systems.' *Ecology and Society* 11(1): 18. Online, available at: www.ecologyandsociety.org/vol11/iss1/art18/.

Ostrom, E. 1990. *Governing the Commons: The Evolution of Institutions for Collective Action*. New York: Cambridge University Press.

Ostrom, E. 2005. *Understanding Institutional Diversity*. Princeton, NJ: Princeton University Press.

Popper, K. 1963. *Conjectures and Refutations*. London: Routledge & Kegan Paul.

Powers, M.R. 1995. 'A theory of risk, return, and solvency.' *Insurance: Mathematics and Economics* 17(2): 101–118.

Rotmans, J., R. Kemp and M. van Asselt. 2001. 'More evolution than revolution: transition management in public policy.' *Foresight* 3(1): 15–31.

Scheffer, M. 2009. *Critical Transitions in Nature and Society*. Princeton, NJ: Princeton University Press.

Scheffer, M. and F.R. Westley. 2007. 'The evolutionary basis of rigidity: locks in cells, minds, and society.' *Ecology and Society* 12(2): 36. Online, available at: www.ecologyandsociety.org/vol12/iss2/art36/.

Scheffer, M., E.H. van Nes, M. Holmgren and T. Hughes. 2008. 'Pulse-driven loss of top-down control: the critical-rate hypothesis.' *Ecosystems* 11(2): 226–237.

Tainter, J.A. 1990. *The Collapse of Complex Societies*. Cambridge: Cambridge University Press.

van der Brugge, R. and R. van Raak. 2007. 'Facing the adaptive management challenge: insights from transition management.' *Ecology and Society* 12(2): 33. Online, available at: www.ecologyandsociety.org/vol12/iss2/art33/.

Walker, B.H. 1993. 'Rangeland ecology: understanding and managing change.' *Ambio* 22(2–3): 80–87.

Walker, B.H., D. Ludwig, C.S. Holling and R.M. Peterman. 1981. 'Stability of semi-arid savanna grazing systems.' *Journal of Ecology* 69(2): 473–498.

Walker, B.H., D.A. Matthews and P.J. Dye. 1986. 'Management of grazing systems: existing versus an event-orientated approach.' *South African Journal of Science* 82: 172.

Walker, B.H., C.S. Holling, S.R. Carpenter and A. Kinzig. 2004. 'Resilience, adaptability and transformability in social–ecological systems.' *Ecology and Society* 9(2): 5. Online, available at: www.ecologyandsociety.org/vol9/iss2/art5/.

Walker, B.H., J.M. Anderies, A.P. Kinzig and P. Ryan. 2006a. 'Exploring resilience in social-ecological systems through comparative studies and theory development: introduction to the special issue.' *Ecology and Society* 11(1): 12. Online, available at: www.ecologyandsociety.org/vol11/iss1/art12/.

Walker, B.H., L.H. Gunderson, A.P. Kinzig, C. Folke, S.R. Carpenter and L. Schultz. 2006b. 'A handful of heuristics and some propositions for understanding resilience in social-ecological systems.' *Ecology and Society* 11(1): 13. Online, available at: www.ecologyandsociety.org/vol11/iss1/art13/.

Walker, B.H., L. Pearson, M. Harris, K.-G. Maler, C.-Z. Li, R. Biggs and T. Baynes. 2010. 'Incorporating resilience in the assessment of inclusive wealth: an example from South East Australia.' *Environment and Resource Economics* 45(2): 183–202.

11 Beyond reductionism

Issues for future research on sustainability

Arild Vatn

Introduction

The 'complexity vision' of nature and society is changing our research agenda. It has first of all challenged the dominant reductionist approaches. It has resulted in the formulation of a series of new concepts and perspectives. We are, however, still grappling with what complexity means and implies for both natural and social science research.

Within the natural sciences, reductionism has been the leading vision. It has very much been the test of being scientific. However, fields like ecology and bioinformatics have been arenas facilitating some change in this perspective. As an example, the genome project – dominantly built on a reductionist perspective – came to illustrate some of the restrictiveness of reductionist methodology itself. Sequencing the gene structure gave few answers to questions raised about the dynamics of biological systems, be it a cell or a full body. Rather, it raised a series of new issues that are now pointing towards the need to study more carefully the *relationships* between genes, cells and their environments.

The complexity vision also has importance for the social sciences. In this case, the history is a bit different, however. Here, what we observe is foremost a holist perspective that has, for a long time, been competing with an individualist ontology. Not least in classic sociology – for example in the traditions formed by Durkheim, Parsons, etc. – the focus has been mainly on social structures and the functioning of these as constituting social wholes. The individualist perspective, on the other hand, has found its most elaborate forms within economics. Its focus is on the autonomous individual agent, a perspective that has gained substantial influence across the whole of the social sciences, splitting it more or less in two. The sociologist Anthony Giddens has emphasized the problems involved in this polarization, and his engagement in developing an understanding of the dynamics between agents and structures has been among the more recent developments bringing an increased focus on complexity into the social sciences. Now we observe that some economists – for example, Arthur *et al.* (1997) and Colander (2000) – have also put this kind of complexity on the agenda.

Ecological economics has the ambition to span both social and natural sciences. Its focus is on the dynamics across nature–society boundaries. While itself quite a heterodox tradition, it may be generally described as anti-reductionist and characterized by a concentration on complex systems. The main focus seems to be on the complexity of economy–ecology interrelations (e.g. Mayumi and Giampietro 2006; Ramos-Martin 2003) and on human values (e.g. Martinez-Alier *et al.* 1998; Spash 2000, 2006; Munda 2004). Until recently, there has been less emphasis given to questions of human action, exceptions being found in Gintis (2000) and Reisch and Røpke (2004).

In the world of academic inquiry, complexity science is still in its infancy, tracing its roots basically back to the end of World War II. The aim of this chapter is to elaborate on two interlinked sets of issues in ecological economics related to the complexity vision. The first is its implications for the understanding of the nature–society interfaces. The second concerns the understanding of cooperative human action. Both foci are chosen on the basis of a specific normative orientation: what complexity implies for our research towards fostering sustainable development. More specifically, the motivation is to develop some ideas concerning the future direction of sustainability research, emphasizing the increased need for more engagement with the issue of human perception and human action in a complex world where actions and perceptions are, by necessity, interlinked.

Complexity in the natural and social sciences

The literature on complexity could itself easily be described as complex. Lloyd (2006) offers thirty-two different definitions of the word, and many more are found in the literature at large. Despite this variation, the concept of complexity tends to be linked to the idea of systems. Moreover, complexity seems to depend on a certain type of interaction between parts that can be identified to form some sort of a whole. A standard phrase in this field is the observation that 'the whole is more than the sum of its parts'. While this clearly departs from reductionism, it begs the question of what this 'more' might mean. The present section is an attempt to make an inquiry into this issue.

Complexity in the natural sciences

The reductionist vision of the natural sciences implies that, for example, ecological features can be reduced to biological, which in turn can be reduced to chemical and finally physical characteristics. The idea has been that understanding the parts makes it possible for us to understand the whole. While this vision has certainly brought about great advances in human understanding of the world around us, the promise never really materialized in the sense that it has made us able to fully understand the dynamics of systems of parts. It has, however, facilitated the division of the natural sciences, resulting in a lot of instrumental knowledge, which has proved quite useful for 'engineering' natural systems.

The problems inherent in reductionism have appeared at two levels. First, side effects of instrumental interventions have become increasingly visible and have turned out to be very difficult to handle. Second, trying to combine these separate knowledges based on reductionist principles has, as already indicated, turned out to be very difficult. While the first experience illustrates the complexity or non-linearity of natural systems in practical terms, the second takes us beyond simple empirical observations to the level of ontology. For example, in complex systems the dynamics of higher-level systems do not necessarily follow the rules that regulate the dynamics of lower-level parts. As appreciation for these complex dynamics and side effects has increased, it has created interest in describing and understanding complexity, with scholars emphasizing that there are distinct characteristics for each level, which are, nonetheless, related to each other. Recent experiences from the human genome project can be used to illustrate the point.

The gene is a biochemical structure – a sequence of nucleotides. The idea behind the Genome Project was to establish a full overview of the number and structure of genes. A prevalent idea was that each gene coded for a specific protein, demanding about 70,000 genes to accomplish the approximately 70,000 proteins found in the human body. Instead, the project[1] was only able to identify about 30,000 protein-encoding genes, which is less than the double the number found in the, by comparison, extremely simple *Caenorhabditis* worm and just 20 per cent more than the number found in a plant. As Baltimore (2001: 816) emphasizes, '[U]nless the human genome contains a lot of genes that are opaque to our computers, it is clear that we do not get our undoubted complexity over worms and plants by using more genes.'

Certainly one should not be surprised by this finding. Biologists have long emphasized the importance of interactions between biological entities at different levels and with their environments. As an example, the working of cells is observed to be dependent upon signals from the environment within which they operate. Their membranes recognize environmental signals through the activity of receptor proteins. Environmental signals activate receptor proteins, causing them to bind with complementary effector proteins (see, for example, Beavo and Brunton 2002). These proteins are understood as switches that control, for example, the cell's own production and reproduction activities.

Two important elements for understanding the dynamics of complex systems could be emphasized on the basis of the following short story. First, the interrelation between the element – the cell – and its environment – other cells; liquids, etc. – is critical for the working of the cell itself. This seems not only to relate to the obvious – the needs for exchanges following from cell metabolisms – but also to the working of processes within the cell. Second, the environment influences the working of the cell through the way the cell 'perceives' its environment – that is, through the operation of the receptor proteins. Without asking the more fundamental question about what 'life is', we can nevertheless see how 'more than the parts' here is about how the parts interact dynamically.

The ideas of Robert Rosen (e.g. 1991, 1998) are interesting to revisit in this context. Basing his work on the ideas of Nicholas Rashevsky, Rosen developed the concept of 'relational biology' in opposition to the standard reductionist vision and what he denoted the 'machine metaphor' of contemporary biology. While Rosen's thinking is far too involved to be reasonably covered in this short chapter, I would like to emphasize a couple of his ideas. First of all, Rosen understands organisms as wholes, where components exist as parts of an underlying organization. While reductionism dispenses with organization as the first step of analysis, in order to get down to the parts – for example, down to the molecular structure of the gene – relational biology emphasizes how parts acquire their function and identity from the overall structure within which they are embedded. So while the reductionist approach, in the words of Rosen, implies 'throw[ing] away the organization and keep[ing] the underlying matter', the relational alternative implies 'throw[ing] away the matter and keep[ing] the underlying organization' (1991: 119). While this must not be understood as implying that matter is of no importance, it shifts the focus and represents an intriguing answer to how wholes are more than the sum of parts. The 'more' is embedded in the relations between the parts, and, most radically, a part taken alone is a *different entity* from when it is operating within the system where it has a functional role.

Another feature of Rosen's thinking relates to the qualitative aspect of these relations. Referring to the structure of languages or communication – that is, syntax and semantics – Rosen describes the reductionist programme as reducing all semantic expressions to syntax. This means that all information inherent in a system is assumed to be reducible to structures without meaning. While the concept of meaning must here certainly be understood in a more general way than what is the standard 'meaning' in the human language – more like function or 'purpose' – Rosen's interpretation emphasizes how a description of the matter of DNA, on its own, will not capture all relevant information about the complex system – that is, the human genome.

In his work, Rosen emphasizes the self-organizing capacity of natural living systems. This links up with another literature that highlights complex systems as evolving systems, namely resilience theory. Like Rosen, Holling (2001) and Gunderson and Holling (2002) conceptualize living systems as complex wholes, rather than trying to explain them by breaking their attributes down into component parts. Here the focus is on what makes a living system resilient and on what triggers change. Living systems may endure long periods of stability, but they can also experience periods of rapid change, as described by the concept of attractor shifts. Hence, they can be understood to go through different phases or cycles of exploitation, conservation, release and reorganization. Gunderson and Holling (2002) describe the dynamics of such complex systems along three dimensions: the potential for change, internal controllability and the adaptive capacity or resilience of a system. Understanding systems as self-organizing, they focus on the capacity of the system to adapt to unexpected shocks and, when necessary, to reorganize.

The issue of change is something different when seen from the perspective of a single entity – be it a cell, a body or a species – as opposed to when it is observed from the level of a system, for which each of these constituent entities are understood as parts. While changes across the biota may result in increased diversity, enhanced adaptability, etc. of the system as a whole, these changes may cause problems for certain parts; for example, certain life forms may go extinct. Even more important, interventions that intentionally transform certain relations or remove certain parts of the system – for example, those brought about by human engineering – may result in abrupt attractor shifts, harbouring the capacity to establish very different and often more demanding environments, as seen from the perspective of the human species itself. Anthropogenic climate change is perhaps the most obvious example, but many others are easily found: desertification due to deforestation, salination of soils due to irrigation, population collapses in fisheries, etc.

Complexity in the social sciences

Moving to the social sciences, the object of study is the human and its institutions. While the human is a biological entity and hence must follow laws or dynamics as described by natural science, added to this is the capacity for self-consciousness, intentionality and the capability to communicate and to coordinate action through the establishment of social arrangements like institutions.

While it is impossible to draw a strict distinction between the human and other species along these dimensions, there is little disagreement about the fact that humans have capacities to reflect, communicate and intentionally coordinate their collective activities at a level far beyond that of any other species. This has fostered a great capacity to accommodate change which represents both a tremendous wealth of possibility and an enormous challenge for humanity.

Institutions – that is, the conventions, norms and legal rules of a society – are a form of communication device with different capacities and dynamics as compared with the kind of 'communication' that takes place between cells and their environment, for example in the form of receptor proteins. While I have already emphasized that the transmission of information between cells can be described by using the language of semiotics – that is, syntax and semantics – this communication is somewhat different from the communication between bodies that are characterized by self-awareness, and hence have the capacity to deliberately design such communication devices.

Authors like Boyd and Richerson have explained the development of this capacity as a form of co-evolution between genes and culture or, we could say, between genes and institutions as the concept is used here (see Richerson *et al.* 2002; Richerson and Boyd 2005). Their argument is that the question of genes versus culture is not an either–or issue. Rather, genetic capacities can be understood to have facilitated cultural developments that next have influenced the further evolution of human genetic traits. As an example, the ability to form symbols, which is thought to have materialized through human use of a variety of sounds (the ability to vocalize being a genetically dependent capacity), made it possible for humans to develop rudimentary spoken language. Increasing reliance upon this ability then favoured those who had a relatively good capacity for developing, understanding and using symbols – for utilizing spoken language as a coordination device. Over time, such abilities can be understood to have worked back on the evolution of the human brain, as the capacity to use common language has changed the selection environment for both individuals and groups, so that further development of the human brain's capacity to operate symbolically is supported. Hence, Richerson *et al.* (2002: 414) emphasize that they 'believe that the human capacity to live in tribes evolved by the co-evolution of genes and culture. Rudimentary cooperative institutions created by cultural group selection would have favored genotypes that were better able to live in more cooperative groups'.

Cultural variation is a core part of the way that Boyd and Richerson explain co-evolution between humans and their social environments, arguing that cultural variation is more susceptible to group selection than is genetic variation. They strengthen this argument by emphasizing that their model only requires social and not physical survival or extinction of groups of humans and collections of human practices. Sober and Wilson (1998) adopt a similar approach, emphasizing that, while social norms and cultural evolution are not required for group selection, they vastly increase its potential. Also arguing along these lines, Lotka (1945) pointed to the profound difference between the great speed with which cultural evolution can take place and the slow, plodding process of physical evolution, distinguishing between the two by coining the terms *exo-* (outside the body) and *endo-* (within the body) somatic evolution.

Looking specifically at institutions, we can observe that these structures both simplify and add complexity to human life. They simplify in the sense that humanly constructed concepts or conventions offer classifications of items and processes in the natural world, bringing perceptive order to the tremendous variation and enormous amount of information that the natural systems around us present. This makes it possible for us humans to develop common understandings of our observations and gives us the capacity to communicate about them. Making use of our capacity to build social institutions, we can share information and develop explanations, making sense of the world around us.

In contrast to the world of a cell or a chain of proteins, our perceptions of ourselves and of those around us can change not only as a result of changes in genetics – for example, a better receptor protein, ear or eye – but also through the collective creation of new concepts or conventions. This implies that the concept of a relation acquires additional meaning at the level of systems with conscious parts, taking into account the fundamental qualitative changes that are associated with conscious relations. So, institutions also add complexity. They construct a whole new separate sphere of activity – a sphere of concepts and social relations, which must be comprehended and navigated. This concerns the conventions of a society: language, measurement scales, practices, etc. It also concerns the norms and formal rules defining proper, obligated or forbidden behaviours.

Over thousands of years, these systems of human social institutions have grown tremendously, in both coverage and sophistication. Their duality – the fact that they both reduce and increase complexity – can be understood as an inherent aspect of institutions themselves. Their role in providing simplification is very important for enhancing our capacity to use institutions to create new relations, and hence new complexities.

Understandings of what the social is and implies vary substantially across the different social sciences. Basically, we can divide this variety into two sets of ontological and epistemological programmes – most easily characterized by the difference between methodological individualism and methodological holism. Methodological individualism is a type of reductionism claiming that all explanations, both of specific acts and of the social phenomena that follow from these acts, should be explained exclusively on the basis of the individuals involved. Individual purpose is the source of all action, and social phenomena are a pure summary product of individual action. In addition, these social phenomena (or structures) do not have any influence on the behaviour of the individuals except that they may operate as *external constraints* on their ability to fulfil their intention. Given this understanding, institutions are seen as constraints on the behaviour of completely autonomous individuals who each maximize their individual utility. Methodological individualism is a fundamental characteristic of mainstream economics and of game theory. It also characterizes the so-called new institutional economics (e.g. North 1990), broad strands of political science, and 'rational choice sociology' (e.g. Coleman 1990).

According to methodological holism, social phenomena can only be explained by reference to other social phenomena. This has been a dominant understanding in parts of sociology and social anthropology. Behaviour is explained by the institutional structures of a society – by the roles within which people act. Durkheim was one of the first scholars to emphasize the idea that 'social facts' should be explained only by reference to other 'social facts'. Later, holism gained a strong position in American sociology, especially in the 1950s and 1960s, with Talcott Parsons' structural-functionalism. He and his followers saw societies as internally related and self-sustaining systems of roles, operating within an environment. Hence, he worked not least on identifying functional prerequisites that a society must achieve in order to sustain itself. For Parsons, society was a 'whole', with different 'parts' performing certain tasks of crucial importance for keeping the whole system working. These tasks were the functions. In Parsons' view, the system of roles is the structural core of the social system. From a methodological holist perspective, it is the role that forms an individual's motivations and 'makes the act'.

While methodological individualism reduces everything to the agent, it can be argued that methodological holism is also a type of reductionist programme – reducing everything to the structures of society. While it is systems oriented, and hence fulfils a potential criterion of a non-reductionist programme, the individual intentional agents are rather invisible in the holist paradigm, as it is normally characterized.

The agent–structure divide has long split the social sciences into two quite distinct camps, not least kept alive by the strong position of the agent-oriented discipline of economics. However, several attempts to bridge this gap are noticeable over the years. While the basis for the integration varies, I would include the work of Berger and Luckmann (1991 [1967]), Bourdieu (1977, 1990), Bhaskar (1989, 1998 [1979]) and Giddens (1984, 1987) as parts of this effort. As an example, in his structuration theory Giddens (1984) accounts for a certain autonomy of both agents and structures. Although structures (institutions) are seen as enduring creations, they are still understood to be produced, reproduced and changed by human agents. They are both constructs that make humans able to act and structures upon which humans are acting.

Following on from this intellectual development, we can observe in more recent times an increased focus on how the relations between agents and structures work. This goes all the way from asking how such relations define the identity of individuals to understanding how social systems work and change. In this debate, different social scientists still seem to put somewhat different emphasis on the individual or the structural side of the coin. The main issue here, however, is not to dwell upon those differences and the associated debates, but to observe that the attempt to get beyond reductionism results in the development of models in which relational aspects play a fundamental role. As we have seen, this was also the case for non-reductionist natural science approaches. Hence, there is similarity involved despite the fact that how relations develop, how they are maintained and changed, is different in purely physical and in intentional social systems.

Complexities in the interface between nature and society

The interface between nature and society – between natural processes and human action – is characterized by some specific types of complexities. Facilitating sustainable development depends upon our understanding of these complexities. This relates both to our capacity to avoid challenging the fundamental integrity of natural systems and to our capacity to adapt to inevitable changes. The latter of the two follows from three basic observations about human environment relations. First, many important natural environmental systems are evolving, self-organizing systems. They change. Second, human use impacts the dynamics of these systems in ways that are hard to foresee. So, while an important element in policies for sustainable development is to better understand the working of natural systems and the potential impacts of human interventions, our knowledge will always be heavily restricted and is constantly becoming outdated. The third element follows from the observation that complex systems are non-reducible. Since any description that we as humans are able to produce must somehow slice away part of the complexity, a multiplicity of non-equivalent descriptions exist for each environmental system. This implies that even the definition of what sustainability is will have to be a contentious issue involving choices regarding the dimensions and categories of description. Formulating a useful definition of sustainability would seem to require a continuous and collective social self-reflection over which dynamics or values to prioritize.

As I have emphasized, humans have the capacity to intentionally change their patterns of interaction, not least through making changes in the institutional structures that shape and are shaped by their society. As I see it, the core dynamics for moving towards sustainability lie here – that is, in how we are able to develop institutions that make sustainable futures possible.

To illustrate some of the core elements in this for research concerning the nature–society interface, let us consider Figure 11.1. Each part of the structure described in the framework is itself a complex whole. A typical feature of natural environments (I) is that they are characterized by a tremendous number of interlinked processes working over different scales in time and space. As agents in different positions (III)[2] act in these environments, their decisions get, by necessity, interlinked too, resulting in patterns of interactions (V) that represent, not least, patterns of resource use, which have the capacity to change the state of the resource (VI) and even the attributes of the natural environment (I) – that is, changed attractors; attractor shifts. In trying to master their environments, human agents have developed technologies (II) and institutions (IV). Technologies influence how humans interact with natural resources (burning coal in an open fire, as against in a smelter or a steam engine). Institutions – on the other hand – define who has access to natural resources and facilitate coordination of interacting (and sometimes conflicting) choices.

The basic capacity to produce technology and to form institutions has facilitated tremendous growth in human capabilities. Since, however, human societies are dependent on the overall functioning of their environments, this expansion of our power for resource appropriations is now seriously challenging the capacities of environmental systems to sustain well our form of living.

The complexities involved in this are many. First of all, natural systems are also evolving and may themselves feature abrupt changes despite our observations that they have been macroscopically quite stable over at least the medium-range temporal scales of 10^3–10^4 years – that is, since the last Ice Age.[3]

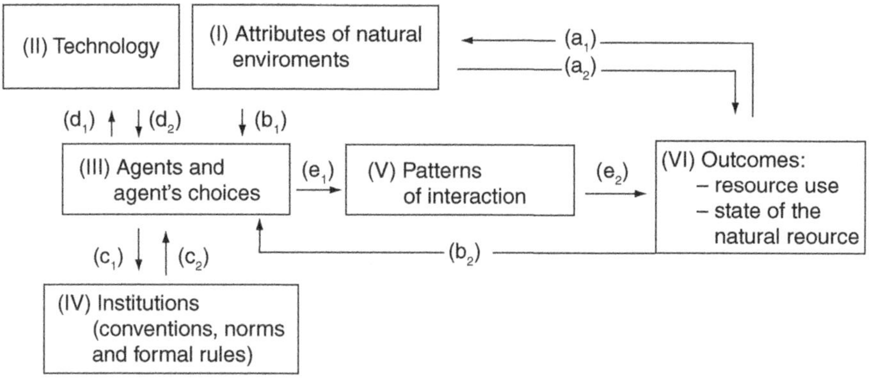

Figure 11.1 A framework for studying nature–society interactions (source: developed from Vatn 2005).

The arrows a_1 and a_2 in Figure 11.1 relate to the working of natural systems. They concern how the changes humans make in reorganizing natural processes exert influence back onto the characteristics of the natural environment and how natural environments influence – often in unanticipated and profound ways – the state of resources whose dynamics we have intentionally transformed. The dynamics of a_1 and a_2 may work over tremendous scales of time and space, and their effects are – owing to complexity – often difficult to relate to specific actions when they first appear. Typical examples of a_1 are the effects of human transformation and release of matter on biodiversity and global climate change. Typical examples of a_2 are the shifting of forests into agricultural land, changing next the hydrological and nutrient dynamics of the very same area, which has an influence back on the productivity of the cleared land.

Humans have the capacity to perceive the dynamics of nature, including changes caused by their actions – cf. arrows b_1 and b_2. Given that the systems involved in these relations are complex, these human perceptions are not unitary or definitive and will result in the creation of various non-equivalent descriptions (Giampietro 2003; Mayumi and Giampietro 2006). Moreover, these issues are linked, as ignorance also concerns lack of insights into which non-equivalent descriptions could be produced – a form of closed ignorance, in the wording of Faber *et al.* (1996). Such closed ignorance can be understood as a special type of uncertainty that is a fundamental feature of complex problems. It is not so much something that can be reduced or eliminated, but more something with which we must coexist and cope.

Concerning uncertainty more generally, Knight (1921) distinguished between four different sources: perception uncertainty, anticipation uncertainty, effect uncertainty and implementation uncertainty. Effect uncertainty concerns lack of knowledge about consequences of our actions and is related not least to a_1 and a_2. Perception and anticipation uncertainty concern the descriptive domain and relate to the concept of non-equivalent descriptions as already emphasized. The former concerns the inability to completely perceive and represent the present as it is. The latter relates to the compounded problem of inferring the future from our incomplete perception of the present. Both these types of uncertainties are linked to the b-arrows in Figure 11.1 and imply that ignorance will always be non-zero.

While the emergent properties of complex systems, by necessity, imply some level of irreducible ignorance (Faber *et al.* 1996; Giampietro 2003; Mayumi and Giampietro 2006), we can still expand our insights into the dynamics even of complex systems. Doing so demands, however, that science accepts the challenges of complexity and engages in developing concepts and models that take its study beyond the present disciplinary boundaries, creating new ways of supporting the cooperation that is needed to develop what Giampietro (2003) calls 'mosaic' interdisciplinary descriptions and associated complex models.

In this endeavour the validity of various non-equivalent descriptions of the complex world must be respected. The consequence of this is both to accept pluralism in the building of descriptions and to accept that this pluralism implies an inescapable normative element to be inherent in any scientific undertaking (e.g. Norgaard 1994; Stirling 2006). These insights have formed the basis for the idea of post-normal science (Funtowicz and Ravetz 1993), which emphasizes the emergence of a changed relation between facts and value judgements, and hence between science and policy. This leads to an increased focus on the challenges associated with decision-making under conditions of conflicting perspectives and/or irresolvable ignorance.

This takes us back to Figure 11.1, reminding us that knowledge has always had a collective dimension. Concepts and models that are common to a group of people are a type of convention. Hence, they can be classified as institutions (Vatn 2005). Looking first at the scientists as a subgroup of agents, we have already seen how the reductionist science ideal has implicated the separation of scientific inquiry into disciplines – an institutionalization of specialties based on a set of conventions, norms and rules (c_1). These are next influencing scientists' work and agendas (c_2). This works well for simple systems and has fuelled technological development (d_2) of unprecedented force, offering new opportunities for human choice in general (d_1). In turn, these opportunities have made it possible for us to become involved in processes of expanded and changed resource uses (e_1 and e_2). It is here (VI), however, that the assumption of simple systems underlying technological development – for example, combustion technologies, synthetic fertilizers and pesticides, polychlorinated biphenyls, GMOs – reaches its limitations, as the natural systems react to the use of these simple technologies with all their complex dynamics.

The problems observed here have created a demand for a reinstitutionalization of science to facilitate stronger interdisciplinary engagement. This call is, to a large extent, a response to the need to understand the consequences of new technologies and of the new ways in which humans are using and impacting on environmental resources. The issues are, however, wider. Coming to grips with the complexity of our environmental contexts and with the complexity of our own ability to understand them also has implications for how we structure economic activity. Two aspects seem to stand out, and they are both related to the reductionism that we still consistently find in science.

First, given the existence of non-trivial closed ignorances and interdependencies 'forced' upon us by the natural environment, the question of responsibility becomes both crucial and demanding. This is about who carries the burden of proof for determining whether an institution or practice should be changed. In technical terms, we may say that it is about whether we should avoid Type 1 or Type 2 errors: whether we should focus on avoiding taking something as true when it is in fact false (leading for example to the shutdown of a factory when the contamination was actually due to another pollution source), or whether we should, under certain circumstances, risk such mistakes, in the hope that doing so might help reduce the chance that we take as false something that eventually turns out to true (such as the proposition that human activity is impacting the global climate system). While again this is fundamentally a normative question, the choices we make, which are ultimately about how we institutionalize our treatment of uncertainty and ignorance, can have very large consequences for how technological change and human–environment interactions are managed.

Second, coming to terms with the complexity and interlinkages of natural systems raises serious questions about how we organize economic decisions. Today's dominating economic system is based on *separating* decision-making into individual responsibilities of legal entities that 'communicate' in a *one-dimensional* way – via market prices. In this way we divide up decisions and responsibilities, letting one value dimension – exchange value – guide our usage. This approach has been very productive for facilitating economic growth. However, it is a system that fits very poorly with the dynamics of the natural environment upon which the economy rests. This was a minor problem when the volume of economic activity was small compared to the volume of environmental processes. That is no longer the case, and we find ourselves faced with a situation where the 'engine of growth' may even ruin its own future material basis.

Coping with this complexity and the related interdependencies may demand the development of new institutional structures to guide economic life – that is, the institutions that govern choices made by agents when they act in capacities such as producers, consumers and politicians. In order to support the establishment of sustainable human–environment relations, such institutional structures should be capable of capturing the multidimensionality of economic choices and facilitate integration of knowledge and judgements across decisions. A core aspect here is the question of how we understand the motivation of human beings. Reductionist social science – taken to its greatest sophistication in neoclassical economics – emphasizes the autonomy of human agents. From this flows the logic of separated choice domains, where it is presumed that each agent makes choices based only on their own preferences. As already emphasized, the alternative understanding sees humans as products of social circumstances. Institutions are not only constraints on individuals who are maximizing personal utility. They offer meaning and can facilitate cooperation as well as competition. Collaborative institutions may facilitate the development of common interests, just as the institutionalization of separated interests may itself create separated interests. Hence, the core issue here concerns the arrows c_1 and c_2 in Figure 11.1: how institutional change may facilitate agents' choices and foster patterns of interaction that include appreciation for human interdependencies and for the dynamics of natural systems. Studying this question demands a broad perspective on human interaction.

Human cooperation in a complex natural world

As I have already emphasized, two types of reductionism are very visible in social sciences: the reduction of values to one dimension and the reduction of the relations between institutions and agents to mere external constraints on autonomous behaviour. Understanding human action in a more relational way opens up room for a very different manner of thinking about how to facilitate sustainability. I will argue here that an institutional model – more specifically, a model seeing institutions as rationality contexts – has the potential to better capture the complexities of these relations.

Different models of human action

To develop this argument I will start with a brief recollection of the standard economic model: the rationality-as-maximizing-individual-utility (RMIU) model. It presumes that human beings are acting on the basis of a given set of preferences. They are also assumed to be maximizing entities, aiming for the highest possible level of individual utility dictated by these preferences. Maximizing utility implies two things. First, it requires commensurability; all values must be transformable into a single dimension – individual utility. Second, individual utility is presumed to be the only motivation for the agent's behaviour.

Concerning value commensurability – that is, assuming that values can be represented using a single unit of measure – this has been questioned on both philosophical and empirical grounds. The literature on lexicographic preferences and value incommensurabilities is voluminous: for example, Georgescu-Roegen (1954), Lancaster (1971), O'Neill (1993), Spash and Hanley (1995), Fiske and Tetlock (1997), Holland (1997), Beckerman and Pasek (2001) and Spash (2006). This literature essentially builds upon the general argument that there is a plurality of non-reducible value dimensions. The philosophically based critique emphasizes, for example, that the existence of ethical dimensions to human choice is fundamentally incommensurate with, say, exchange values. The empirically based documentations relate both to observations regarding blocked exchanges and to motivations behind protest bids and lexicographical preferences in contingent valuation studies.

Concerning motivation, the RMIU model reduces the focus to the consequences associated with choices made on the basis of the utility of separated individuals. The implication is that people act instrumentally – in the case of independent choices – or strategically – in the case of interdependent choices. Moreover, it demands a certain type of consistency in human behaviour – for example, transitive ranking. As with value commensurability, we have observed a substantial debate concerning the validity of this perspective. Testing the model has proved difficult. The utility function is unobservable, and basing tests on people's expressions about what they prefer has been met with hostility among most economists. The problem is not new, and Samuelson's (1948) remedy – to infer preferences from observed behaviour – does not solve it. As an example, consider if we witness what seems to be inconsistent choice – intransitive rankings, for instance. This cannot be used as definitive proof against the model, because it can be claimed that we have just misinterpreted the agent's utility function, and the inconsistency vanishes by reinterpreting what the agent 'is after' (Boland 1981).

Certainly the maximization model is hard to falsify as long as the motivation is presumed to be unobservable. There are then ample opportunities to reformulate the utility function in order to make the data fit. Hence, the model lends itself to testing only in situations where a reformulation of the utility function cannot explain what happens. The phenomenon of preference reversals, documented especially in the psychological literature on choice (e.g. Lichtenstein and Slovic 1971; Slovic and Lichtenstein 1983; Tversky and Kahneman 1986), is one of very few instances where a reformulation is irrelevant. In these experiments it is observed that people do not choose what they state as the preferred. These kinds of observations raise serious doubts about the human *ability to rank alternatives* consistently even when all relevant information is available.

Nevertheless, there have also been many studies appearing over the years showing that people can act in ways that come quite close to what the model of individual rationality suggests, for example Holt *et al.* (1986), Smith (1991, 2000) and Davis and Holt (1993). These choice situations are, however, quite simple, and this observation has spurred development of newer studies where institutional framings are being used to help people act 'rationally' in the face of complex choice situations. Shogren (2006) points out that putting a sufficiently large cost on what he terms irrational behaviour makes people act more in line with the model of maximizing behaviour. He offers a series of examples showing that through intelligent institutional design, people can be made to behave in ways that are more consistent with the expectations of the RMIU model. Then, however, a more complex understanding of behaviour is actually being introduced: that of interactions between institutions and agents. So, one may reasonably pose the question as to whether the basic individualistic model is really still intact in Shogren's examples.

An alternative to the above would be a model that conceptualizes choice as being based on a *plurality of motivations or rationalities*. As values are plural, motivations may also be so. As institutions may help people choose what is individually rational, they may similarly support social rationality. Hence, people may in some situations choose on the basis of what offers the largest individual gain, while in other situations the interest of the group that one belongs to or concern for the care of others may be what is important.

A variety of literatures support this hypothesis. As an example, people's ability and willingness to cooperate, despite the losses that doing so may imply for the individual, have been documented across a wide variety of disciplines. We see this in many anthropological studies, not least in those emphasizing the role of reciprocity (e.g. Sahlins 1965). Cooperative behaviour or social rationality also takes on a core position within some branches of sociology (e.g. Etzioni 1988). Finally, the will to cooperate is documented in much of the research on common pool resource management (e.g. Ostrom 1990, 2005). Certainly this literature does not say that cooperation or social rationality is the only capacity in the human repertoire. What it does, however, is emphasize that this capacity exists and is evidenced in many situations.

A large number of supplementary insights are also now available from the experimental literature in economics and psychology. This concerns experiments like ultimatum and dictator games, public goods games and various trust games – see, for example, Gintis (2000), Ostrom (1998, 2000), Fehr and Falk (2002), Gintis *et al.* (2005), Bowles (2004) and Vatn (2005, 2008, 2009). These experiments show that people are often willing to share, despite the fact that doing so offers no personal gains. Similarly, people are often willing to bear costs to make others cooperate in spite of the fact that doing so incurs an extra cost for them. These analyses have helped to spur a renewed and growing interest in the concept of reciprocity.

Similarly, specific studies on various forms of altruism, such as those of Batson (1990) and Batson and Shaw (1991), have added important insights concerning plural motivation. However, one should also be careful to remember the limitations of experiments of this kind. They are, in some sense, themselves reductionist, being set up to control for many important variables in a way that is not possible for real-life observations. Despite its reductionist methodology, this body of research supports a complex understanding of human motivation in contrast to the simplistic understanding of the individualistic models. Grounds for trusting these findings are strongly enhanced by the fact that the experimental results seem to support conclusions obtained in the field, as emphasized for example by Gintis *et al.* (2005) and Ostrom (1998).

The agent–institution interfaces

The institutions-as-rationality-context (IRC) hypothesis is an alternative to the RMIU model. It is based on the idea that institutions have the capacity to 'penetrate' or change individuals' motivations. Because of this, behaviour changes as the institutional context changes. This is a kind of relational understanding of human action, which takes the relationship between agents and institutions to be operationally important and which thereby offers an explanation for how and why, in the social sphere too, 'wholes are more than the sum of their parts'.

Exploring this agent–institution interface, we first observe that the literature discussed above documents both individual and institutional variation. Hence, in public goods games the degree of cooperation varies between agents within the same game. However, the way the game is structured also influences the level of cooperation. Here factors like established trust, possibilities to punish non-cooperators, the norms invoked, etc. seem to be influential. For more detailed documentation and discussion of this, see Vatn (2005, 2008, 2009).

The variation between different formulations of a game – such as the various external rules set – indicates the direct role that institutions have in shaping agent behaviour. However, institutions also have indirect influences, affecting the spirit of the 'game' and the way individuals perceive themselves and each other. Hence, the difference in the behaviour of the same person when acting as teacher as opposed to playing hockey in a team cannot be explained just by different external control mechanisms; it also requires a different perception of what constitutes the logic of the two roles and situations

When Shogren (2006) argued – as we have seen – that institutions may help people act 'rationally', he was implicitly endorsing an institutions-as-rationality-contexts interpretation of the role of institutions in decision-making. However, while in his description there is only one type of rationality – that of maximizing individual utility – the alternative hypothesis of plural rationality and institutions-as-rationality-contexts offers a very different understanding of the role of institutions. It encompasses the idea that people can act both on the basis of individual rationality – as with maximizing individual utility – and on the basis of social rationality – including the will to cooperate, to act in solidarity, to act altruistically, etc. Under this model the institutional context can be understood to help people sort out which logic is expected in the specific situation.

It would seem that a capacity to act on the basis of plural motivations including forms of 'other-oriented' rationality would make human coordination simpler. Some degree of self-care is obviously necessary for an individual to survive. However, the capacity to form groups and to cooperate has been found to be of similar importance – cf. Sober and Wilson (1998) and Richerson and Boyd (2005). There are a vast number of situations where we, as individuals, intervene in each other's lives, intentionally or otherwise. This is not least an effect arising from the fact that we operate within the same environments. Having the capacity to take the interests of other people into account when making choices would in such situations make life easier and could help avoid potential conflicts. Taken together, these various elements of interpretation offer potential explanations for the development of plural motivations.

Presuming that we can now take the existence of a plurality of motivations (or rationalities) as given, we immediately encounter the difficult question of how individuals choose between these motivations. One way of understanding this is to think of institutions foremost as signalling which logic – individual or social – is expected. Hence, in one choice situation the institutional context signals to the agent that they only need to consider what is best for themselves. In another, the emphasis is on what is best for the group to which one belongs. In yet a third it may be about duties of care for the other. Returning to our framework in Figure 11.1, this implies that arrow c_2 carries messages to the agent about which logic or rationality pertains. This in turn influences next agents' choices, and finally different patterns of interaction appear across different institutional settings. Hence, by just including an appreciation for the role of institutions and presuming them to have the capacities outlined above, a great deal of the complexity of human behaviour can be explained. Institutions can be seen as a form of communication device that makes it possible for people to solve various kinds of coordination problems.

In some sense this conclusion seems self-evident. We 'all know' that the same person can at one moment be a tough business leader pursuing the goal of maximizing the firm's net revenues and in the next instant be a caring mother coming home and taking on the fundamentally different, but equally institutionalized, role of motherhood. Examples of this plurality of personal motivations and rationalities are plentiful in everyday life.

In another sense, however, this conclusion is not self-evident at all. The interplay between institutions and individuals is complex and we are far from understanding how it works. Contrasting the standard rationality-as-maximizing-individual-utility (RMIU) model with the institutions-as-rationality-context (IRC) hypothesis is illuminating. Let us assume that we observe an altruistic act: a person helps another person who is in some kind of trouble. The latter is a stranger and the former does not expect to meet the latter again. Hence, it is clear that helping is not in any way 'paying off' later. The standard RMIU model has problems with explaining this observation. Expanding the RMIU models to include a 'warm glow' (e.g. Andreoni 1990) or 'guilt feeling' (e.g. Ostrom 1998), etc. offers an alternative solution to the IRC-based explanation. When people seem to act altruistically, this behaviour can still be portrayed as a form of individual utility maximization by just including internal rewards and punishments.

An institutionalist response to this explanation would first of all note that if internal rewards etc. are at all involved, these are themselves socially constructed (Etzioni 1988). It is the very existence of social norms about good and bad behaviour that causes a feeling of, for example, pride or guilt. Ostrom also emphasizes this. Hence, the implied interpretation is that institutions 'push' individuals to shift between different socially constructed utility functions. For example, if the institutional setting is that of making a business contract, one would not feel bad about taking advantage of information that the other party does not have. However, if the same is done when helping a friend, this may seem very different and cause guilt feelings. So while the standard RMIU model can explain 'altruism' only by referring to avoidance of external sanctions, the above solution accepts internalization of socially constructed norms resulting in changed utility functions. It renounces the autonomy of the individual. It accepts, however, that choice is about utility maximization. So while institutions influence what offers utility – serving as rationality contexts – action is still based on calculation. Let us call this understanding $\text{IRC}_{\text{singular}}$. It is a richer picture than the RMIU, but continues nevertheless to assume a one-dimensional motivation structure.

There are two distinct reasons for taking the IRC hypothesis beyond $\text{IRC}_{\text{singular}}$. First, as I have already emphasized, maximizing is difficult. People tend not to be able to handle the complex informational challenges in a way that results in a single best option. Let us call this the *cognitive aspect*. Second, motivations may – as has already been emphasized – be truly plural. Helping somebody, restraining one's own interests to facilitate the better solution for the group, etc., may not be based on a calculation of benefits and costs. It may follow the logic of *appropriateness*. In one situation it is appropriate to think about oneself only, while in other situations it is expected that we do what is in the interest of the group. By bringing the cognitive and social aspects of motivational complexity onto the scene, we have moved to $\text{IRC}_{\text{plural}}$.

The cognitive aspect relates to conventions or 'rules of thumb'. Here, complex chains of cause and effect may be individually hard to disentangle. Collective learning takes place, resulting in the establishment of various rules about what is wise to do (e.g. Screpanti 1995). This helps the individual to solve insurmountable information and modelling problems, since they can draw on the collective body of knowledge and experience, making them literally wise beyond their years. Studying how farmers make decisions is very revealing in this sense. They act in a complex environment where collected knowledge about experience, from parents, extension services, neighbours, etc., has resulted in a long list of 'rules of thumb' – if so, do this. These rules make it possible to do farming, and any attempt to reduce them to a set of consistent trade-off algorithms would require, at the very least, a great deal of calculation and would in the end still fail to capture important subtleties of this body of information.

The issue of appropriateness relates to the functioning of norms. Norms may actually do two things for a community. They signal whether the issue at hand is about individual or social rationality – for example, the norm of competitiveness versus the norm of care. They may also offer direct descriptions concerning what to do in specific situations – for example, the norm of not littering, the norm of not taking more than one's share, the norm of bringing a gift when visiting. In such situations the content of the choice is 'made by the institution'. What the individual does is to interpret which is the right norm to follow, not whether following the norm maximizes that individual's utility.

Both $IRC_{singular}$ and IRC_{plural} point towards a richer, more complex understanding of human behaviour than the RMIU model. The interplay between agents and institutions is shifted from that of constraints being put on isolated individuals to that of advanced forms of coordination and communication taking place between individuals in different social settings and over time. It is these complex forms of interaction, which the IRC hypotheses allow for, that make different forms of cooperation possible.

Institutions are a kind of collective experience in a settled form that makes a great variety of interactions possible. Certainly, institutions create stickiness to any situation. Otherwise, they could not structure interactions in the way that they do. Nevertheless, they are also continuously changing as far as a community is able to agree and implement what now seems to serve them better as a group – that is, arrow c_1 in Figure 11.1.

Certainly institutions are not neutral. They protect certain interests and values, producing and reproducing these same interests and values. They give power to certain groups and ostracize others, and so on. This is a straightforward effect arising from the relational interdependence between institutions and agents. Inasmuch as we accept an IRC model, we cannot avoid this dynamic. The social and political questions then become which interdependencies to emphasize and which interests and values to protect.

Expanding the research agenda for sustainable development

So what does the above mean for sustainability research? First of all, it implies that doing such research demands interdisciplinarity, as has also been emphasized in many of the other chapters of this volume. It also implies that there is a need for research groups to be able to form analyses and communicate across disciplines, ideally in a way that enables us to discuss the full range of connections illustrated by the framework of Figure 11.1.

Certainly, not all research can operate at this level. More focused work is also needed – both within disciplines and across disciplines – operating within frames that are much narrower than what is implied in Figure 11.1. A core issue is then: how can we let experiences from broader interdisciplinary analyses help frame the more specific analyses? Doing so implies a call to take seriously not least the incompatibilities appearing in different analyses and to focus our research towards considering how the research in 'my field' is capable of bridging with other research to overcome these incompatibilities. Such an attitude would compel us to spell out the various 'pre-analytical visions' upon which we base our analyses and would push us to create more common ground between and across disciplines, which should gradually make it easier to do interdisciplinary research.

Sustainability is foremost about what humans do. It is hence a little surprising to observe that very little sustainability-oriented research has been focused on human action. This is not least the case for ecological economics, even though there are exceptions. Concerning human action, what sustainable development demands is, first and foremost, increased cooperation and cooperative capacity. In this field I see three interlinked research agendas as being most important:

1 understanding social complexity;
2 understanding how to foster cooperative human behaviour;
3 understanding how to expand or transpose the human capacity to cooperate in local and homogeneous small-group situations to global and heterogeneous settings.

In a sense, point 1 is to take the issue of value complexity one step further into the realm of institutional analysis, looking at the relations between institutional structures and the question of which logic or meaning social complexities offer in specific situations or contexts. Basically, the challenge here is to penetrate deeper into the issue of *how* 'the whole becomes more than the sum of its parts'. The present chapter has, I hope, offered some direction for how this kind of research might be developed further. In relation to sustainability issues, its importance is mainly to establish a good basis for subsequent research within areas 1 and 2 above. It has, however, the capacity to offer inputs regarding fundamental ontological and epistemological questions that have made so many of us give up reductionist science.

The idea of points 2 and 3 is to take the knowledge established under 1 into the realm of social practice: asking how we can establish institutions that foster cooperation – and, more specifically, the kind of cooperation that is needed for humans to live sustainably. Certainly, at the level of local communities a good deal of research exists supporting the idea that cooperation may flourish under favourable conditions. It is what establishes communities. From the previous section one should take home the point that humans have the capacity to cooperate and that this capacity is at least as characteristic a human feature human as is selfishness. The question is not whether we can collaborate; the problem seems rather to lie elsewhere. It relates to the challenge of sustaining cooperation, given the individual variations involved. There seems to be a crucial asymmetry here that is of utmost importance. A cooperative outcome demands participation from almost all to be sustained, as a few free-riders have the capacity to blow it all up. It is therefore clear that establishing and sustaining cooperative conditions is not a simple task. Moreover, it would appear to be against present trends in much of modern institutional development. The trends of reductionist science, as exemplified by the RMIU and the institutionalization of the primacy of the individual, are companions and they remain today the dominant way of thinking about human organization. Hence, in this field of research we face not only theoretical and vast empirical challenges, but also great ideological counter-forces that are supported by those believing in reductionist models.

If establishing cooperation is challenging, even at the local level, how can it be possible to expand the idea to the global stage? We live in an era of enormous global change. This is evident along all three of the standard sustainability dimensions: environmental, social and economic. The lives and futures of all humans on the planet are interlinked via these dimensions in ways that we have never experienced before. What this seems to demand is expanding the kinds of effective cooperation that we see in local communities to the global level. It seems unlikely, however, that a simple scaling up would work. Instead, the complexity of the relations that make cooperation work at the local level may tell us something about how it could work at the global stage. What seems clear is that single analytics and one-dimensional approaches are not going to provide us with the information and analyses that are required to take up the challenge of developing these new forms of cooperation.

The reductionist model would demand that the problems of physical, social and economic interdependencies that we envision would need to be split up into separate forms of independences in order to make clear assessments, and in the end could be put back together through some kind of summation. I find this literally impossible when concerned with environmental interconnections and utterly unacceptable when concerned with social consequences. It may turn out to be the case that we are unable to develop cooperative institutions (quickly enough) to handle the increasing number of coordination problems human society is facing in the twenty-first century. However, if we cannot yet even begin to conceptualize what kinds of institutions we will need in order to advance our coordination capacities, then this is where we must start to expand our insights. This process must not be sidelined into a debate about whether a reductionist or a relationist model is the better one to use. We should by now be able to get past that.

Notes

1 Actually, there were two projects, the one undertaken by the International Human Genome Sequencing Consortium and the one by Celera Genomics. While the first was a public project, Celera Genomics was a private company.
2 The model is general, and may hence describe situations where agents are individuals or organizations. Moreover, individuals may act in different roles, for example as consumers, producers, scientists, citizens, as defined by the institutions.
3 In this respect the past 10,000–12,000 years seem different from earlier interglacial periods, which seem to have experienced substantial variations in, for example, temperatures within much shorter periods (Solomon *et al.* 2007).

References

Andreoni, J. 1990. 'Impure altruism and the donations to public goods: a theory of warm-glow giving.' *Economic Journal* 100: 467–477.

Arthur, W.B., S.N. Durlauf and D.A. Lane eds. 1997. *The Economy as an Evolving Complex System II*. Reading, MA: Addison-Wesley.

Baltimore, D. 2001. 'Our genome unveiled.' *Nature* 409: 814–816.

Batson, C.D. 1990. *The Altruism Question: Toward a Social Psychological Answer*. Hilldale, NJ: Lawrence Erlbaum.

Batson, C.D. and L.L. Shaw. 1991. 'Evidence for altruism: toward a pluralism of prosocial motives.' *Psychological Inquiry* 2(2): 107–122.

Beavo, J.A. and L.L. Brunton. 2002. 'Cyclic nucleotide research – still expanding after half a century.' *Nature Reviews Molecular Cell Biology* 3(9): 710–718.

Beckerman, W. and J. Pasek. 2001. *Justice, Posterity, and the Environment*. Oxford Oxford University Press.

Berger, P.L. and T. Luckmann. 1991 [1967]. *The Social Construction of Reality: A Treatise in the Sociology of Knowledge*. London: Penguin.

Bhaskar, R. 1989. *Reclaiming Reality*. London: Verso.

Bhaskar, R. 1998 [1979]. *The Possibility of Naturalism*, 3rd ed. Hemel Hampstead, UK: Harvester Wheatsheaf.

Boland, L.A. 1981. 'On the futility of criticizing the neoclassical maximization hypothesis.' *American Economic Review* 71(5): 1031–1036.

Bourdieu, P. 1977. *Outline of a Theory of Practice*. Cambridge: Cambridge University Press.

Bourdieu, P. 1990. *The Logic of Practice*. Cambridge: Polity Press.

Bowles, S. 2004. *Microeconomics: Behavior, Institutions, and Evolution*. Princeton, NJ: Princeton University Press.

Colander, D. ed. 2000. *The Complexity Vision and the Teaching of Economics*. Cheltenham, UK: Edward Elgar.

Coleman, J.S. 1990. *Foundations of Social Theory*. Cambridge, MA: Harvard University Press.

Davis, D.D. and C.A. Holt. 1993. *Experimental Economics*. Princeton, NJ: Princeton University Press.

Etzioni, A. 1988. *The Moral Dimension: Toward a New Economics*. New York: The Free Press.

Faber, M., R. Manstetten and J. Proops. 1996. *Ecological Economics: Concepts and Methods*. Cheltenham, UK: Edward Elgar.

Fehr, E. and A. Falk. 2002. 'Psychological foundations of incentives.' Joseph Schumpeter Lecture. *European Economic Review* 46(4–5): 687–724.

Fiske, A.P. and P.E. Tetlock. 1997. 'Taboo trade-offs: reactions to transactions that transgress the spheres of justice.' *Political Psychology* 18(2): 255–297.

Funtowicz, S.O. and J.R. Ravetz. 1993. 'Science for the post-normal age.' *Futures* 25(7): 739–755.

Georgescu-Roegen, N. 1954. 'Choice, expectations and measurability.' *Quarterly Journal of Economics* 48(4): 503–534.

Giampietro, M. 2003. *Multi-scale Integrated Analysis of Agroecosystems*. Boca Raton, FL: CRC Press.

Giddens, A. 1984. *The Constitution of Society: Outline of the Theory of Structuration*. Berkeley: University of California Press.

Giddens, A. 1987. *Social Theory and Modern Sociology*. Stanford, CA: Stanford University Press.

Gintis, H. 2000. 'Beyond *Homo economicus*: evidence from experimental economics.' *Ecological Economics* 35(3): 311–322.

Gintis, H., S. Bowles, R. Boyd and E. Fehr. 2005. *Moral Sentiments and Material Interests: The Foundations of Cooperation in Economic Life*. Cambridge, MA: MIT Press.

Gunderson, L.H. and C.S. Holling eds. 2002. *Panarchy: Understanding Transformations in Human and Natural Systems*. London: Island Press.

Holland, A. 1997. 'Substitutability, or why strong sustainability is weak and absurdly strong sustainability is not absurd.' In *Valuing Nature? Economics, Ethics and Environment*, ed. J. Foster. London: Routledge.

Holling, C.S. 2001. 'Understanding the complexity of economic, ecological and social systems.' *Ecosystems* 4(5): 390–405.

Holt, C.A., L. Langan and A.P. Villamil. 1986. 'Market power in oral double auctions.' *Economic Inquiry* 24(1): 107–123.

Knight, F.H. 1921. *Risk, Uncertainty and Profit*. Boston: Houghton Mifflin.

Lancaster, K. 1971. *Consumer Demand: A New Approach*. New York: Columbia University Press.

Lichtenstein, S. and P. Slovic. 1971. 'Reversals of preference between bids and choices in gambling decisions.' *Journal of Experimental Psychology* 89(1): 46–55.

Lloyd, S. 2006. *Programming the Universe: A Quantum Computer Scientist Takes On the Cosmos*. New York: Alfred A. Knopf.

Lotka, A.J. 1945. 'The law of evolution as a maximal principle.' *Human Biology* 17(3): 167–194.

Martinez-Alier, J., G. Munda and J. O'Neill. 1998. 'Weak comparability of values as a foundation for ecological economics.' *Ecological Economics* 26(3): 277–286.

Mayumi, K. and M. Giampietro. 2006. 'The epistemological challenge of self-modifying systems: governance and sustainability in the post-normal science era.' *Ecological Economics* 57(3): 382–399.

Munda, G. 2004. 'Social multi-criteria evaluation: methodological foundations and operational consequences.' *European Journal of Operational Research* 158(3): 662–677.

Norgaard, R.B. 1994. *Development Betrayed: The End of Progress and a Coevolutionary Revisioning of the Future*. London: Routledge.

North, D.C. 1990. *Institutions, Institutional Change and Economic Performance*. Cambridge: Cambridge University Press.

O'Neill, J. 1993. *Ecology, Policy and Politics: Human Well-Being and the Natural World*. London: Routledge.

Ostrom, E. 1990. *Governing the Commons: The Evolution of Institutions for Collective Action*. Cambridge: Cambridge University Press.

Ostrom, E. 1998. 'A behavioral approach to the rational choice theory of collective action.' Presidential address, American Political Science Association, 1997. *American Political Science Review* 92(1): 1–22.

Ostrom, E. 2000. 'Collective action and the evolution of social norms.' *Journal of Economic Perspectives* 14(3): 137–158.

Ostrom, E. 2005. *Understanding Institutional Diversity*. Princeton, NJ: Princeton University Press.

Ramos-Martin, J. 2003. 'Empiricism in ecological economics: a perspective from complex systems theory.' *Ecological Economics* 46(3): 387–398.

Reisch, L. and I. Røpke eds. 2004. *Consumption Perspectives from Ecological Economics*. Cheltenham, UK: Edward Elgar.

Richerson, P.J. and R. Boyd. 2005. *Not by the Genes Alone: How Culture Transformed Human Evolution*. Chicago: University of Chicago Press.

Richerson, P.J., R. Boyd and B. Paciotti. 2002. 'An evolutionary theory of commons management.' In *The Drama of the Commons*, ed. National Research Council: Committee on the Human Dimensions of Global Change: Division of Behavioral and Social Sciences and Education, E. Ostrom, T. Dietz, N. Dolsak, P.C. Stern, S. Stovich and E.U. Walker. Washington, DC: National Academy Press.

Rosen, R. 1991. *Life Itself: A Comprehensive Inquiry into the Nature, Origin and Fabrication of Life*. New York: Columbia University Press.

Rosen, R. 1998. *Essays on Life Itself*. New York: Columbia University Press.

Sahlins, M. 1965. 'On the sociology of primitive exchange.' In *The Relevance of Models for Social Anthropology*, ed. M. Banton. London: Tavistock.

Samuelson, P.A. 1948. 'Consumption theory in terms of revealed preferences.' *Economica* 15(60): 243–253.

Screpanti, E. 1995. 'Relative rationality, institutions and precautionary behaviour.' In *On Economic Institutions: Theory and Applications*, ed. J. Groenewegen, C. Pitelis and S.-E. Sjöstrand. Cheltenham, UK: Edward Elgar.

Shogren, J. 2006. 'A rule of one.' *American Journal of Agricultural Economics* 88(4): 1147–1159.

Slovic, P. and S. Lichtenstein. 1983. 'Preference reversals: a broader perspective.' *American Economic Review* 73(4): 596–605.

Smith, V.L. 1991. *Papers in Experimental Economics*. Cambridge: Cambridge University Press.

Smith, V.L. 2000. *Bargaining and Market Behavior: Essays in Experimental Economics*. Cambridge: Cambridge University Press.

Sober, E. and D.S. Wilson. 1998. *Unto Others: The Evolution and Psychology of Unselfish Behavior*. Cambridge, MA: Harvard University Press.

Solomon, S., D. Qin, M. Manning, Z. Chen, M. Marquis, K.B. Averyt, M. Tignor and H.L. Miller eds. 2007. *Climate Change 2007: The Physical Science Basis. Working Group I Contribution to the Fourth Assessment Report of the Intergovernmental Panel on Climate Change*. Cambridge: Cambridge University Press.

Spash, C.L. 2000. 'Multiple value expression in contingent valuation: economics and ethics.' *Environmental Science and Technology* 34(8): 1433–1438.

Spash, C.L. 2006. 'Non-economic motivation for contingent values: rights and attitudinal beliefs in the willingness to pay for environmental improvements.' *Land Economics* 82(4): 602–622.

Spash, C.L. and N. Hanley. 1995. 'Preferences, information and biodiversity preservation.' *Ecological Economics* 12(3): 191–208.

Stirling, A. 2006. 'Analysis, participation and power: justification and closure in participatory multi-criteria analysis.' *Land Use Policy* 23(1): 95–107.

Tversky, A. and D. Kahneman. 1986. 'Rational choice and the framing of decisions.' In *Rational Choice: The Contrast between Economics and Psychology*, ed. R.M. Hogarth and M.W. Reder. Chicago: University of Chicago Press.

Vatn, A. 2005. *Institutions and the Environment*. Cheltenham, UK: Edward Elgar.

Vatn, A. 2008. 'Institutions and rationality.' In *Assessing the Evolution and Impact of Alternative Institutional Structures*, ed. S. Batie and N. Mercuro. London: Routledge.

Vatn, A. 2009. 'Cooperative behaviour and institutions.' *Journal of Socio-Economics* 38(1): 188–196.

Index

Page numbers in *italics* denote tables, those in **bold** denote figures.